Born This Day

To my wife, my love, my partner, my friend

To Wendy

Born This Day

*A Book of Birthdays and
Quotations of Prominent People
Through the Centuries*

by ROBERT A. NOWLAN

McFarland & Company, Inc., Publishers
Jefferson, North Carolina, and London

Acknowledgments: I thank all those whose suggestions, encouragement, friendship, love and understanding made the completion of this project a joy. These include Claire Bennett, Tom Clarie, Robert Cymbala, Don Duman, Saeed Fakhriravari, John Hill, Marty and Steve Johnson, Grace Kelly, Eve Kyburg, Rod and Sarah Lane, Annabel Lee, Jack Maselli, Diane McLeese, Danny and Lynne Nowlan, Mary Nowlan, Michael and Kitty Nowlan, Steve Nowlan, Rocco and Rae Orlando, Daniel and Sharon Ort, Walter Petroskey, Ed Schoonmaker, Bob Washburn and Eric Witkowski.

As ever my work is dedicated to the memory of my beloved mother Marian Shields Nowlan. I am grateful for the love and encouragement of my father Robert A. Nowlan, Sr., my children Robert, Philip and Edward; Edward's wife Amy and their daughter and son, my grandchildren Alexandra, Tommy and John; Jennifer and her husband Peter Golanski; and Evan and Andrew Wright.

British Library Cataloguing-in-Publication data are available

Library of Congress Cataloguing-in-Publication Data

Nowlan, Robert A.
    Born this day : a book of birthdays and quotations of prominent people through the centuries / by Robert A. Nowlan.
      p. cm.
    Includes index.
    ISBN 0-7864-0166-4 (library binding: 50# alk. paper) ∞
    1. Quotations, English.   2. Birthday books.   3. Literary calendars. I. Title.
PN6084.B5N69   1996
082—dc20   96-4189
                                          CIP

Manufactured in the United States of America

McFarland & Company, Inc., Publishers
  Box 611, Jefferson, North Carolina 28640

Contents

Acknowledgments   iv

Preface   1

Birthdays   3

Index of People   229

Preface

I pray you
you (if any open this writing)
Make in your mouths the words that were our names.
Epistle to Be Left in the Earth
—Archibald MacLeish

It is interesting to learn which prominent people in history and in the news today share one's birthday, and to read some of the wit or wisdom of such individuals. This book serves both interests. For each day of the year, seven individuals, famous or infamous, dead or alive, together representing nearly every profession and place on the earth, are chosen from among those born on that particular date. Capsule descriptions of the individuals and their claims to fame are provided. One quotation is chosen to represent each individual's unique ideas, outlook, or sense of humor.

The choice of the individuals and the quotations to be featured is largely a function of the particular day of the year. Some days abound with such a number of prominent persons who had many interesting things to say that it was quite difficult to narrow the field to seven. On other days, however, there is a comparative scarcity of well-known people who have generated highly quotable words. For such days the choices are relatively simple.

The decision of whom to include was made first on the basis of the quality of the quotation, second on the prominence of the individual and third in the interest of preserving a rough balance in the periods of time represented. As for the quotations themselves, there could be no precise formula for selecting one quotation over another. How for instance to choose the perfect quotation from a William Shakespeare? I confess to picking one from among the many that mean something special to me, and I hope others will find my selections worthy.

The most familiar quotation associated with a prominent individual is not always chosen, particularly if a slightly less familiar one seems to have more enduring relevance. On the other hand familiar quotations whose authors are not readily known are included, because it seemed possible that others might share my delight in finally discovering who said some long familiar words.

The persons whose words appear in this volume are neither all good nor

1

all bad. Their influences on the world range from great to minor. Generally, their pronouncements seem to have some universal and timeless wisdom; in other cases, individuals explain themselves or make an interesting observation about their times or some other prominent person whom they have known. The speakers and authors include philosophers, artists, composers, musicians, politicians, businessmen, labor leaders, actors, generals, admirals, soldiers, scientists, explorers, clergymen and religious leaders, athletes, poets, sculptors, historians, sociologists, inventors, revolutionaries, feminists, dictators, murderers, criminals, jurists, educators, engineers, technicians, journalists, civil rights activists, monarchs, popes, directors, reformers, anarchists, tyrants, physicians, lawyers, theologians, dancers, naturalists, diplomats, celebrities, aviators, prodigies, columnists, models, astronauts, comedians, psychologists, economists, fashion designers, playwrights, critics, statesmen, editors, cartoonists and even clowns.

Each of them has something to say worth hearing. Some quotations strike a universal chord, some shock, some may even outrage, some contradict the quotes of others, some are funny, some are very serious, some are prophecies, some remember, some warn, some express regret. Some speak of the fundamental questions that have always engaged the interest of humans: love, death, loyalty, eternity, freedom, sexuality, duty, right and wrong, proof, miracles, marriage, children, regrets, revenge, past, present, future, violence, war, sorrow, cause and effect, ambition, insanity, habit, fate, means and ends, human nature, guilt, work, searches, illness, talent, genius, winning and losing, weather, people, perfection, patriotism, magic, luck, kindness, men and women, hatred, fears, honesty, democracy, creation, apologies, beauty, choices, rights, romance, pleasures, optimism and pessimism, liberals and conservatives, prejudices, peace, religion, souls, worries and so many others.

I hope that readers will enjoy the quotations and the description of the prominent individuals who have made them as much as I have enjoyed choosing them.

ROBERT A. NOWLAN

Birthdays

January 1

1767 **Maria Edgeworth:** English children's writer of Irish life and moral tales. Author of the familiar saying: "Jack of all trades and master of none." Novels: *Castle Rackrent, Belinda* and *The Absentee.*
Some people talk of morality, and some of religion, but give me a little smug propriety.

1819 **Arthur Hugh Clough:** English poet who wrote pastoral works. Espoused progressive social views and disliked class distinctions. His "long vacation" poem "The Bothie," was received with both delight and outrage. "Amours de Voyage," an ironic narrative was published posthumously.
What we all love is good touched up with evil / Religion's self must have a spice of devil.

1863 **Baron Pierre de Coubertin:** French educator who revived the Olympic games in Greece in 1896. His creed has become that of the Games.
The most important thing in the Olympic Games is not winning, but taking part; the essential thing in life is not conquering, but fighting well.

1879 **E.M. [Edward Morgan] Forster:** English novelist. Member of the Bloomsbury Group. Works include *A Passage to India, A Room with a View* and *Howards End.* Also wrote volumes of essays, short stories and collaborated on the libretto of Benjamin Britten's opera *Billy Budd.*

Death destroys a man: the idea of Death saves him.

1909 **Barry Goldwater:** Conservative U.S. senator from Arizona (1952–64, 1969–87). Unsuccessful Republican presidential candidate (1964). An architect of the conservative revival in the Republican Party. Author of *The Conscience of a Conservative.*
A government that is big enough to give you all you want is big enough to take it all away.

1919 **J.D. [Jerome David] Salinger:** U.S. novelist and short-story writer. His novel *The Catcher in the Rye,* the story of precocious Holden Caulfield, still sells some 250,000 copies annually. Other works: *Franny and Zooey* and *Raise High the Roof Beam, Carpenters.*
I keep picturing all these little kids in this big field of rye. ... If they're running and they don't look where they're going I have to come out from somewhere and catch them.

1942 **"Country Joe" McDonald:** U.S. singer, songwriter and musician. Leader of a political rock group of the sixties, Country Joe & the Fish. Played at the Monterey Pop Festival (1967) and Woodstock (1969). Anti–Vietnam War protester.
The most revolutionary thing you can do in this country is change your mind.

January 2

1752 **Philip Morin Freneau:** American sailor, poet, journalist, rebel. Commanded a privateer in the Revolutionary War. Captured by the British. He wrote *The British Prison Ship*, while a prisoner. Edited the *National Gazette*. Often called the first American professional journalist.

Tobacco surely was designed / To poison and destroy mankind.

1857 Martha Carey Thomas: American educator and author. Organizer of Bryn Mawr College in 1884. Dean and professor of English (1885–94). President (1894–1922). Author of *The Higher Education of Women.*

Women are one-half of the world but until a century ago ... it was a man's world. ... The man's world must become a man's and woman's world.

1865 W. Lyon Phelps: American educator and author. Taught 41 years at Yale and was instrumental in popularizing the teaching of contemporary literature. Introduced Russian novelists to American readers. Wrote *Essays on Modern Novelists* and *Some Makers of American Literature.*

The fear of life is the favorite disease of the twentieth century.

1903 Sally Rand: American fan- and belly-dancer. Gained notoriety when arrested for giving an "obscene performance" at Chicago's World Fair (1933). Plied her trade on stage and in clubs into her seventies.

The Rand is quicker than the eye.

1915 John Hope Franklin: American historian, educator and author. First African-American president of the American Historical Association (1978–79). Wrote: *From Slavery to Freedom: A History of American Negroes* and *Land of the Free.*

One feels the excitement of hearing an untold story.

1920 Isaac Asimov: Prolific Russian-born U.S. writer of over 300 books. He was also a biochemist. Coined the term "robotics." Novels include *Foundation, The Caves of Steel, The Naked Sun* and *I, Robot.*

Violence is the last refuge of the incompetent.

1928 Daniel Rostenkowski: Former U.S. congressman from Illinois. Longtime powerful chairman of Ways and Means Committee. He was forced to resign his chairmanship because of questions of unethical behavior. The same questions cost him reelection in 1994.

I'm a feller who works in the vineyard of compromise.

January 3

106 B.C. Cicero [Marcus Tullius]: Roman statesman, orator and philosopher. Sought a political career, attaining the consulship in 63 B.C. Delivered famous speeches, known as "Philippics," against Mark Antony. Murdered by Antony's soldiers.

Wise men are instructed by reason; men of low understanding, by experience; the most ignorant, by necessity; the beasts, by nature.

1793 Lucretia Coffin Mott: U.S. abolitionist, feminist, reformer and Quaker minister. Made her home a sanctuary for runaway slaves. With Elizabeth Stanton organized the first women's rights convention (1848).

We too often bind ourselves by authorities rather than by the truth.

1803 Douglas William Jerrold: English wit, dramatist and journalist. An original contributor to *Punch*, using the pseudonym "Q." Editor of several magazines and newspapers. Novels: *The Story of a Feather* and *Mrs. Caudle's Curtain Lectures.*

Honest bread is very well—it's the butter that makes the temptation.

1883 Earl Clement Attlee: English political leader. As labor prime minister, he led England into welfare state (1945-51), introducing the National Health Service.

Democracy means government by discussion, but it is only effective if you can stop people talking.

1892 J.R.R. [John Ronald Reuel] Tolkien: English author and philologist. Professor of language and literature at Oxford. Scholarly works include studies

of Chaucer and an edition of *Beowulf*. Best known for his fantasy stories *The Hobbit, The Lord of the Rings* and *The Silmarillion*.
It's the job that's never started as takes longest to finish.

1900   **Dorothy Arzner:** Former American film editor who became Hollywood's only woman director of the thirties. Films: *Merrily We Go to Hell, Nana, Craig's Wife* and *Dance Girl Dance*.
It is my theory that if you have authority, know your business and know you have authority, you have the authority.

1909   **Victor Borge:** Witty Danish-born pianist, comedian and musical satirist. Became an American favorite through television appearances on "The Ed Sullivan Show." Made numerous one-man television specials and concert appearances with leading symphonic orchestras.
Laughter is the shortest distance between two people.

January 4

1785   **Jacob Grimm:** German philologist and lexicographer. With brother Wilhelm, they are best known for *Grimm's Fairy Tales*. Jacob did most of the work on the definitive *German Dictionary*.
When we consider the richness, good sense and strict economy of English none of the other living languages can be put beside it.

1858   **Carter Glass:** American politician and government official. U.S. representative from Virginia (1902–19). U.S. secretary of the treasury (1918–20). U.S. senator (1920–46). Helped draft the Federal Reserve Bank Act of 1913. Determined opponent of New Deal legislation.
A liberal is a man who is willing to spend somebody else's money.

1883   **Max Eastman:** American editor, poet, critic and social analyst. Founder of the Marxist magazine, *Masses*. Best known for *The Enjoyment of Poetry*.
A poet in history is divine, but a poet in the next room is a joke.

1896   **Everett Dirksen:** U.S. politician. Representative from Illinois (1933–51), senator (1951–69). Republican minority leader (1959–69). Supported New Deal domestic programs while championing an isolationist foreign policy. Delivered key Republican support for Civil Rights Acts.
A billion here, a billion there—pretty soon it adds up to real money.

1914   **Jane Wyman:** U.S. film actress who appeared in B movies as a wisecracking dame before studios discovered she had acting ability. Won an Academy Award for *Johnny Belinda*. Other films: *The Yearling* and *Magnificent Obsession*. Former wife of Ronald Reagan.
If you asked Ronnie the time, he'd tell you how to make a watch.

1935   **Floyd Patterson:** U.S. boxer. Middleweight gold medal winner at 1952 Olympics. World heavyweight champion (1956), defeating Archie Moore. Lost title to Ingemar Johannson (1960). First to regain crown by beating Johannson (1961).
The fighter loses more than his pride in the fight, he loses part of his future. He's a step closer to the slums he came from.

1937   **Grace Bumbry:** American mezzo-soprano. Studied voice with Lotte Lehmann. Appearing in Wagner's *Tannhaüser*, she became the first African American to be featured in the role of a goddess. Invited by Jacqueline Kennedy to sing at the White House. Has sung at most of the great opera houses of the world.
I've gone from reluctance to acceptance to gung-ho.

January 5

1767   **Jean Baptiste Say:** French economist best known for his law of markets. A disciple of Adam Smith, Say expounded the Scottish economist's views in *La Decade*, which he edited.
It is the aim of good government to stimulate production, of bad government to encourage consumption.

1779   **Stephen Decatur:** U.S. Naval commodore in the War of 1812. Served against the French and the war with Tripoli. Forced Algerian pirates to declare the American flag inviolable. Famous toast:

Our country! In her intercourse with foreign nations, may she always be in the right; but our country, right or wrong.

1876 Konrad Adenauer: First chancellor of the Federal Republic of Germany (1949–63). Led West Germany's amazing economic recovery after WWII. An official in the Weimar government, he was dismissed from all offices by the Nazis and imprisoned.

We all live under the same sky, but we don't have the same horizon.

1882 Herbert Bayard Swope: American journalist and war correspondent for *New York World*. Awarded a Pulitzer Prize in 1917. Executive editor (1920–29). Noted crusader. Originated op-ed page.

I cannot give you the formula for success, but I can give you the formula for failure— which is: Try to please everybody.

1918 Jeanne Dixon: American astrologer, clairvoyant, psychic and writer. Proponent of extra sensory perception (ESP). Makes yearly predictions. Claims her visions are messages from God.

Respect is what we owe; love is what we give.

1931 Alvin Ailey: U.S. dancer and choreographer. Trained with Martha Graham. Formed the Alvin Ailey American Dance Theatre (1958), a popular multiracial modern dance ensemble. Most famous dance: "Revelations."

I think the people come to the theater to look at themselves. I try to hold up the mirror.

1932 Umberto Eco: Italian novelist and semiotician. Has a "taste and passion for the Middle Ages." Best known work: *The Name of the Rose*, the story of an English Franciscan who solves a murder mystery in a medieval monastery.

The real hero is always a hero by mistake, he dreams of being an honest coward like everybody else.

January 6

1412 Joan of Arc: French saint and national heroine. "Maid of Orleans." Heard voices exhorting her to make the dauphin king and drive the English from France. Had several victories before being captured, tried for heresy and witchcraft by the French clergy and burned at the stake.

The Lord will open a way for me through the midst of them.... For that was I born.

1878 Carl Sandburg: U.S. journalist, poet and biographer. Pulitzer Prize in history for biography of Abraham Lincoln. Poetry: "Chicago Poems" and "Good Morning, America." Awarded a Pulitzer for his *Collected Poems* (1950). Published *The American Songbook*.

A baby is God's opinion that the world should go on.

1882 Sam Rayburn: "Mr. Democrat." U.S. congressman from Texas (1913–61). Speaker of the House (1940–46, 1949–53, 1955–61). Southern populist who sponsored New Deal legislation and supported Roosevelt and Truman's foreign power.

A jackass can kick a barn down, but it takes a carpenter to build one.

1900 Kathryn Cavarly Hulme: American author. Wrote *The Wild Place*, *The Nun's Story* and *Undiscovered Country*.

Never forget that God tests his real friends more severely than the lukewarm ones.

1920 Early Wynn: Hall of Fame baseball pitcher with Washington Senators, Cleveland Indians and Chicago White Sox. Won more than 300 games. Cy Young winner (1959).

That space between the white lines— that's my office. That's where I conduct my business.

1931 E.L. [Edward Lawrence] Doctorow: American novelist. Editor of the *New American Library* (1960-64). His best-known work *Ragtime* combines historical figures with fiction. Also wrote *The Book of Daniel*, based on the story of the

Rosenbergs who were executed for spying.

Writing is an exploration. You start from nothing and learn as you go.

1937   **Lou Holtz:** U.S. football coach with New York Giants, University of Arkansas, University of Minnesota and the University of Notre Dame, with whom he won a national title (1988). Known for lesson-filled one-liners.

The man who complains about the way the ball bounces is likely the one who dropped it.

January 7

1718   **Israel Putnam:** American Revolutionary soldier. Fought in the French and Indian War, rescued at the last minute from being burned at a stake by Indians. Given command of Connecticut forces, he planned the fortifications at the Battle of Bunker Hill.

Men, you are all marksmen—don't one of you fire until you see the whites of their eyes.

1768   **Joseph Bonaparte:** Corsican-born king of Naples and Sicily and of Spain. Eldest surviving brother of Napoleon I. His army was defeated by Wellington at Victoria. Spent much of his life in exile in New Jersey.

Gold is, in the last analysis, the sweat of the poor, and the blood of the brave.

1873   **Charles Pierre Peguy:** French nationalist, poet, philosopher and Christian socialist. In 1900, he founded *Cahiers de la quinzaine* in which he published his own work and that of other writers. Works: *Le Mystère de la charité de Jeanne d'Arc* and *L'Argent*.

Freedom is a system based on courage.

1873   **Adolph Zukor:** Hungarian-born film pioneer and executive. Formed Famous Players to bring popular plays to the screen. Merged his company with Jesse Lasky's productions, changing its name to Paramount. The centenarian autobiography is *The Public Is Never Wrong*.

Fish stinks from the head.

1901   **Zora Neale Hurston:** U.S. dramatist, novelist, folklorist and cultural anthropologist. Wrote of rural black life. Prominent in the Harlem renaissance. Novels: *Jonah's Gourd Wine, Their Eyes Were Watching God* and *Seraph on the Suwanee*.

Research is formalized curiosity. It is poking and prying with a purpose.

1912   **Charles Addams:** U.S. cartoonist. Best known as creator of the macabre, gruesome, but strangely loveable *Addams Family* which appeared regularly in the *New Yorker* magazine. The strip is the basis for a television series and two films.

I suppose I was trying to scare myself, but all in all, I had a normal healthy childhood.

1929   **Terry Moore:** Hollywood sex-pot actress in films such as *Mighty Joe Young, Bernardine* and *Peyton Place*. Claimed to have been married to Howard Hughes.

Hollywood, where an intrigue and a victim are born every time two people meet.

January 8

1572   **Thomas Dekker:** English dramatist and writer of prose pamphlets. Memorable for lively depictions of London life. Best known and most popular play, *The Shoemaker's Holiday*.

Were there no women, men might live like gods.

1601   **Baltasar Gracian:** Spanish Jesuit prose writer. Published collection of 300 maxims, offering a distillation of wisdom. Best known for allegorical novel *The Critic*, in which civilization and society are seen through the eyes of a savage.

Truth always lags behind, limping along on the arm of Time.

1881   **William Thomas Piper:** American aircraft manufacturer of the first successful mass-produced inexpensive planes.

A speech is like an airplane engine. It may sound like hell but you've got to go on.

1908   **Pamela Frankau:** English author. Novels: *The Willow Cabin* and *A Wreath of the Enemy*. Wrote *The Offshore Light* using the pseudonym Eliot Naylor. Daughter of novelist Gilbert Frankau.

The English find ill-health not only interesting but respectable and often experience death in the effort to avoid a fuss.

1914   Thomas Watson, Jr.: U.S. business executive. President of IBM. U.S. ambassador to U.S.S.R. (1979–82).

In the next 40 years we will accomplish so much more than in the past 40 years that people will wonder why we didn't do more in the first 40.

1935   Elvis Presley: "The King." U.S. singer and actor. Most popular rock 'n' roll singer of 1950s and 1960s. Hits: "Don't Be Cruel," "Hound Dog," "Love Me Tender" and "Are You Lonesome Tonight?" Made more than thirty films.

I don't know anything about music. In my line you don't have to.

1942   Stephen Hawking: British physicist and mathematician. Most brilliant theoretical physicist since Einstein. Established link between black holes and thermodynamics. His body, but not his mind, is afflicted with amyotrophic lateral sclerosis. He communicates with the aid of a computer. Wrote the popular *A Brief History of Time.*

The goal is simple. It is complete understanding of the universe.

January 9

1859   Carrie Chapman Catt: U.S. leader of women's rights movement. Reorganized National Woman Suffrage Association, transforming it into the League of Women Voters. Spent the latter years of her life campaigning for world peace.

When a just cause reaches its flood-tide, as ours has done ... whatever stands in the way must fall before its overwhelming power.

1890   Karel Čapek: Czech writer, playwright, novelist and essayist. Best remembered for play *R.U.R.* (Rossum's Universal Robots), first use of the word "robot."

A short life is better for mankind, for a long life would deprive man of his optimism.

1902   Sir Rudolph Bing: Anglo-Austrian impresario. Cofounder and director of the Edinburgh Festival (1935–49). General manager of Metropolitan Opera (1950–72).

We are similar to a museum. My function is to present old masterpieces in modern frames.

1904   George Balanchine: Russian-born choreographer. Named ballet-master and choreographer for the Russian Ballet in Paris (1925). Founded School of American Ballet (1934). Cofounder Ballet Society which emerged as the New York City Ballet in 1948. Artistic director (1948–83).

Old people don't get tired—it's only the young who tire. Confusion exhausts them.

1908   Simone De Beauvoir: French novelist, essayist, and influential feminist. Articulate exponent of Sartre's philosophy of existentialism. Wrote *The Second Sex*, a pioneering feminist text. Other works: *Memoirs of a Dutiful Daughter* and *A Very Easy Death.*

One is not born a woman, one becomes one.

1913   Richard M. Nixon: Thirty-seventh president of the United States. Red-baiting California congressman and senator. Dwight Eisenhower's running-mate, serving two terms as vice-president. Lost close election for president to John F. Kennedy (1960). Elected president (1968). Resigned 1974 under threat of impeachment because of the Watergate scandal.

When the President does it, that means that it is not illegal.

1941   Joan Baez: U.S. folksinger, songwriter and civil rights activist. Her voice is of remarkable purity and clarity. Imprisoned briefly for refusing to pay taxes to protest Vietnam War.

Non-violence is a flop. The only bigger flop is violence.

January 10

1592 Henry King: English bishop and poet. Wrote the solemn and moving *Exequy* for his young wife, one of the greatest English elegies. Published *Poems, Elegies, Paradoxes, and Sonnets.*
Nature's true-born child, who sums his years / (Like me) with no arithmetic but tears.

1750 Thomas Erskine: Lord Chancellor of England. Defended personal liberties. Author of pamphlets "Observations on the Prevailing Abuses in the British Army" and "The Unconditional Freeness of the Gospel in Three Essays."
I maintain that opinion is free and that conduct alone is amenable to the law.

1834 Lord Acton [John E.E. Dalberg]: English historian, Christian liberal. Editor of *The Rambler*, a Roman Catholic monthly. Founder-editor of the *Cambridge Modern History.*
The danger is not that a particular class is unfit to govern, every class is unfit to govern.

1887 Robinson Jeffers: American poet. Works include: "Roan Stallion," "The Woman at Point Sur" and "At the Fall of an Age."
Lend me the stone strength of the past and I will lend you / The wings of the future, for I have them.

1903 Barbara Hepworth: English abstract sculptor. One of the foremost nonfigurative sculptors of her time. Made Dame of the British Empire. Works: "Reclining Figure," "Winged Figure" and "Four-Square."
I rarely draw what I see. I draw what I feel in my body.

1945 Rod Stewart: British singer and guitarist. Hits: "Maggie May," "Tonight's the Night" and "Do Ya Think I'm Sexy?"
Half the battle is selling music, not singing. It's the image, not what you sing.

1949 George Foreman: U.S. boxer. World heavyweight champ (1973–74). Lost title to Muhammad Ali. Regained it at 46 in 1994. Oldest champion of all time.
The question isn't at what age I want to retire, it's at what income.

January 11

1757 Alexander Hamilton: U.S. statesman, lawyer and author. Federalist Party leader. First U.S. secretary of treasury. Killed in duel with Aaron Burr.
A national debt, if it is not excessive, will be to us a national blessing.

1842 William James: U.S. philosopher, physiologist and teacher. Brother of Henry James. Works include: *Pragmatism*, and *Principles of Psychology*. Helped found the American Society for Psychical Research.
Thinking is what a great many people think they are doing, when they are merely rearranging their prejudices.

1864 H. George Selfridge: British merchant. Founded Selfridge and Co., Ltd., a major British department store. Claimed "the customer is always right."
Remember always that the recollection of quality remains long after the price is forgotten.

1870 Alice Hegan Rice: U.S. humorist and children's writer. Wrote: *Mrs. Wiggs of the Cabbage Patch, A Romance of Billy Goat Hill* and *The Lark Legacy*. Active civic worker.
It ain't no use putting up your umbrella till it rains.

1873 Dwight Morrow: U.S. lawyer, financier and statesman. Father of Anne Morrow Lindbergh. Ambassador to Mexico, where his work set a strong precedent for the Good Neighbor policy.
We judge ourselves by our motives and others by their actions.

1897 Bernard De Voto: U.S. editor, critic, historian and novelist. Wrote "Easy Chair" column for *Harpers*. Editor of *The Saturday Review of Literature* (1936–38). Wrote *Mark Twain's America* and produced an edition of the journals of Lewis and Clark.

Pessimism is only the name that men of weak nerves give to wisdom.

1903   Alan Paton: South African novelist, humanitarian. A founder of Liberal Association of South Africa. Wrote *Cry, the Beloved Country, Too Late the Phalarope* and *Ah, But Your Land Is Beautiful.*

To give up the task of reforming society is to give up one's responsibility as a free man.

January 12

1729   Edmund Burke: British politician, writer, statesman. Worked for a more conciliatory policy towards American colonies. Author of *Reflections on the French Revolution.*

The only thing necessary for the triumph of evil is for good men to do nothing.

1746   Johann Heinrich Pestalozzi: Swiss educational reformer. Pioneer in providing mass education for poor children. His method of education consisted of a gradual unfolding, prompted by observation, of children's innate facilities.

Education is nothing more than the polishing of each simple link in the great chain that binds humanity together and gives it unity.

1878   Ferenc Molnár: Hungarian playwright, novelist, short-story writer. His play *Liliom* is the basis for the musical *Carousel.* Also wrote: *The Devil* and *The Good Fairy.*

The dead have nothing except the memory they've left.

1893   Hermann Goering: German Nazi leader. WWI flying ace. Built Germany's air force. Founded the Gestapo (secret police). Committed suicide before he was to be hung for war crimes.

In the struggle for life and death there is no legality.

1908   José Limón: Mexican-born dancer, choreographer and teacher. Ranks with Martha Graham as a creator of modern dance. His José Limón Company became the first American modern dance company to tour Europe.

Dancers aren't pompous; they're too tired.

1920   James Farmer: U.S. civil rights activist. Helped found Congress of Racial Equality (1942). Served as its first director. Leader of 1961 freedom rides.

Equality cannot be seized any more than it can be given. It must be a shared experience.

1944   Joe Frazier: "Smokin' Joe." American boxer. 1964 Olympic heavyweight champ. World heavyweight champ (1970–73). Fought Muhammad Ali three times, winning once. Career record, 32-4-1 with 27 KOs.

Kill the body and the head will die.

January 13

1785   Samuel Woodworth: American journalist and verse writer. Pen name "Selim." Best known as the author of "The Old Oaken Bucket." Editor of the *New York Mirror.*

How dear to this heart are the scenes of my childhood, / When fond reflection recalls them to view.

1808   Samuel P. Chase: U.S. jurist, lawyer, teacher. U.S. Treasury secretary (1861–64). Originated national banking system. Chief justice of Supreme Court (1864–73).

I would rather that people should wonder why I wasn't president than why I was.

1832   Horatio Alger, Jr.: American author of popular boys' books such as *Ragged Dick* and *Tattered Tom.* They pointed out a moral and their heroes triumphed over adversity.

I wrote my name upon the sand, / And trusted it would stand for age; / But, soon, alas! the refluent sea / Had washed my feeble lines away.

1884   Sophie Tucker: "The Last of the Red Hot Mamas." U.S. singer, comedienne, vaudeville star. Appeared on stage, in films, on television, and in nightclubs. Signature song: "Some of These Days."

I have been poor, and I have been rich. Rich is better.

1890   **Elmer Davis:** Broadcast newsman. Director of Office of War Information during WWII. Joined ABC after the war, conducting a nightly newscast until 1953.

This will remain the land of the free only so long as it is the home of the brave.

1919   **Robert Stack:** U.S. actor who gave Deanna Durbin her first screen kiss in *First Love*. Best known as Eliot Ness in televisions's "The Untouchables."

If you're a star you go through the front door carrying roses instead of the back door carrying garbage.

1925   **Gwen Verdon:** U.S. dancer, Tony-winning actress on Broadway, star in films and television. Best known for her role of Lola in *Damn Yankees*, both on Broadway and film.

I imagine the reason I don't feel any different as a star is that I never expected to be a star.

January 14

1730   **William Whipple:** American Revolutionary leader, legislator and soldier. Signer of the Declaration of Independence. Member of Continental Congress (1776–79). Brigadier general in the Revolutionary Army.

Human passion is the hallucination of a distempered mind.

1875   **Dr. Albert Schweitzer:** French theologian, musician, medical missionary. Set up a native hospital in French Equatorial Africa in 1913. A renowned organist, he wrote a biography of Johann S. Bach.

Example is not the main thing in life— it is the only thing.

1882   **Hendrik Willem Van Loon:** American journalist and historian. Editor,

with Grace Castagnetta of *The Songs America Sings*. Books: *The Story of Mankind, The Story of the Bible* and *The Story of the Pacific.*

The history of the world is the record of a man in quest of his daily bread and butter.

1896   **John Dos Passos:** U.S. novelist and war correspondent. Wrote the antiwar novel, *Three Soldiers*. Best known work is the experimental trilogy *U.S.A.* (*The 49th Parallel, 1919* and *The Big Money*) as a vast portrait of American society.

People don't choose their careers. They are engulfed by them.

1904   **Sir Cecil Beaton:** Noted photographer of British royalty and entertainment celebrities. Designed sets for stage, opera and ballet productions.

Perhaps the world's second worst crime is boredom. The first is being a bore.

1919   **Andy Rooney:** American humorist, author and television personality. Shares his varied and sometimes controversial views on television's "60 Minutes."

Death is a distant rumor to the young.

1925   **Yukio Mishima:** Japanese novelist, playwright, essayist. Works: *Confession of a Mask, The Temple of the Golden Pavilion* and *Sea of Fertility*. Committed ritual suicide in traditional Samurai manner as a protest of the Westernization of Japan.

The period of childhood is a stage on which time and space become entangled.

January 15

1622   **Molière:** Stage name of Jean Baptiste Poquelin. French comic dramatist. Attacked hypocrisy and vice in French society. Among his most famous comic masterpieces are *Le Misanthrope* and *Le Tartuffe.*

The true touchstone of wit is the impromptu.

1897   **Stringfellow Barr:** U.S. educator. As president of St. John's College,

Annapolis, Maryland, he required students to know 120 classics of world literature. His 1958 warning:

Today, colleges have come to think of students as customers, and as long as they do, we'll have the higher illiterates we see on campuses today.

1906   Aristotle Onassis: Greek shipping executive. Started oil tanker business (1935) that grew to become a large fleet of cargo and passenger ships. Dumped mistress Maria Callas to marry Jackie Kennedy.

The secret of business is to know something that nobody else knows.

1908   Edward Teller: Hungarian-born U.S. physicist. "Father of the H-bomb." As a scientist, repudiated any moral implications of his work.

We would be unfaithful to the tradition of Western civilization if we were to shy away from exploring the limits of human achievement.

1914   H.R. [Hugh Redwald] Trevor-Roper: English historian, author, Cambridge University professor. Won international fame for *The Last Days of Hitler*. An amusing and abrasive lecturer and essayist.

The function of genius is not to give new answers, but to pose new questions which time and mediocrity can solve.

1918   Gamal Abdul Nasser: Egyptian leader. Led the coup d'état against King Farouk. First president of Egypt and of United Arab Republic. Unsuccessful in his ambition to build an Arab empire stretching across North Africa.

People do not want words—they want the sound of battle ... the battle of destiny.

1929   Martin Luther King, Jr.: U.S. clergyman. Led black boycott against segregated buses in Montgomery, Alabama (1955). Advocated non-violent resistance. Organized massive civil rights march on Washington, D.C. (1963). Awarded Nobel Peace Prize (1964). Assassinated (1968).

Nothing in all the world is more dangerous than sincere ignorance and conscientious stupidity.

January 16

1749   Vittorio Alfieri: Greatest Italian tragic poet. Spent his early life in extensive travel and dissipation. Turned his attention to literature; made a methodical study of the classics. Wrote: *Cleopatra*, *L'America libera* and *Parigi sbastigliata*.

Often the test of courage is not to die but to live.

1872   Edward G. Craig: English actor and stage designer. Son of Ellen Terry and William Godwin. His aim was to simplify scenes and emphasize actors in his stage designs. Published the quarterly, *The Mask* (1908–29).

That is what the title of artist means: one who perceives more than his fellows, and who records more than he has seen.

1874   Robert W. Service: English-born Canadian poet and journalist. Wrote popular ballads about frontier life. Best known for "Rhymes of a Rolling Stone" and "The Shooting of Dangerous Dan McGrew."

Ah! The clock is always slow; / It is later than you think.

1901   Fulgenico Batista y Zaldivar: Cuban dictator who led an army coup against President Machado. President (1940–44) and later overthrew President Pio (1952). Ruled as dictator until overthrown by the forces of Fidel Castro (1959).

A government needs one hundred soldiers for every guerrilla it faces.

1909   Ethel Merman: U.S. singer, actress. "Queen of Broadway." Her booming powerful voice brought down the house in musicals such as *Girl Crazy*, *Annie Get Your Gun*, *Call Me Madam*, and *Gypsy*.

Always give them the old fire, even when you feel like a squashed cake of ice.

1911   Jay Hanna "Dizzy" Dean: Colorful, bragging hall-of-fame right-handed baseball pitcher with Cardinals and Cubs. Last NL pitcher to win 30 games in a season, 30-7 (1934). As a baseball announcer, he was criticized for his grammar.

It ain't braggin' if you kin do it.

1935   **A.J. [Anthony Joseph] Foyt:** U.S. auto racer. seven-time USAC / CART national champion. Four-time Indy 500 winner. Only driver to win Indy 500, Daytona 500 and 24 hours of Le Mans.

Every car has a lot of speed in it. The trick is getting the speed out of it.

January 17

1706   **Benjamin Franklin:** U.S. statesman, diplomat, inventor, scientist and printer. Published *Poor Richard's Almanack* (1732–57). Helped draft and signed the Declaration of Independence. Minister to France. Proved the existence of electricity. Invented Franklin stove, bifocal spectacles and lightning rod.

Experience keeps a dear school, but fools will learn in no other.

1860   **Anton Chekhov:** Russian playwright and master short-story writer. Plays include: *The Seagull, Uncle Vanya, Three Sisters* and *The Cherry Orchard.* Married actress Olga Knipper who appeared as the female lead in many of his plays.

There is nothing new in art except talent.

1863   **Konstantin Stanislavsky:** Russian actor, director, producer and acting teacher. Developed the theory of acting he called the "method," most successful in the works of Chekhov, Gorky and Andreyev. Cofounder and director of Moscow Art Theatre.

Remember, there are no small parts, only small actors.

1899   **Al Capone:** U.S. mobster. "Scarface Al." Most powerful crime boss of his day. Ran most of Chicago and the surrounding area (1925–31). Imprisoned for federal income tax evasion.

You can get much further with a kind word and a gun than you can with a kind word alone.

1899   **Robert Maynard Hutchins:** U.S. educational reformer. President of University of Chicago at 30. Chancellor (1945–51). Critic of overspecialization and failure of American universities to maintain and enlarge intellectual traditions of the Western world.

The death of a democracy is not likely to be an assassination by outburst. It will be a slow extinction from apathy, indifference and undernourishment.

1927   **Tom Dooley:** U.S. author, lecturer. "Jungle doctor." Made a career of providing medical aid in underdeveloped countries.

I have spent six years of my life among different men, and always I find that the similarities outweigh the differences. Each life is infinitely precious as a life, everywhere.

1942   **Muhammad Ali [Cassius Clay]:** U.S. boxer. Only three-time heavyweight champion (1964–67), 1974–78, 1978–79). Career record, 56-5, 37 KOs, 19 successful title defenses.

Service to others is the rent I pay for my room here on earth.

January 18

1689   **Charles-Louis de Secondat Montesquieu:** French lawyer, philosopher and man of letters. Wrote *Lettres persanes,* a series of 160 fictional letters satirizing religious intolerance, individuals, institutions and royal power.

We should weep for men at their birth, not at their death.

1782   **Daniel Webster:** U.S. lawyer, politician and orator. Congressman from New Hampshire (1813–17 and 1823–27). Massachusetts senator (1827–41 and 1845–50). Secretary of state (1841–43 and 1850–52). A Whig, he refused his party's nomination for president (1844).

There is nothing so powerful as truth— and often nothing so strange.

1840   **Henry Austin Dobson:** English writer of light verse. Published monographs of Fielding, Steele, Hogarth, Goldsmith and others. Poetry: "Vignettes in Rhyme" and "Proverbs in Porcelain."

Time goes, you say? Ah no! / Alas, Time stays, we go.

1882   A.A. [Alan Alexander] Milne: English dramatist, novelist and humorous journalist. Wrote light essays and comedies. Best known for his children's books, written for his own son, Christopher Robin, particularly: *Winnie the Pooh* and *The House at Pooh Corner.*
I am a Bear of Very Little Brain, and long words Bother me.

1904   Cary Grant: Handsome, debonair English-born actor, equally at home in adventure, romantic or comedy films such as: *The Awful Truth, The Philadelphia Story* and *To Catch a Thief.*
When people tell you how young you look, they are also telling you how old you are.

1908   Jacob Bronowski: English scientist, philosopher, poet, literary critic, dramatist, physicist and mathematician. Wrote *The Common Sense of Science* and *The Origins of Knowledge and Imagination.*
That is the essence of science: ask an impertinent question and you are on the way to a pertinent answer.

1913   Danny Kaye: U.S. actor, comedian and humanitarian. Special Oscar (1954) for service to industry and American people. Well known for fund-raising activities in behalf of UNICEF. Films: *Up in Arms, The Secret Life of Walter Mitty* and *Wonder Man.*
Life is a great big canvas; throw all the paint on it you can.

January 19

1798   Auguste Comte: French philosopher and founder of positivism. Applied methods of observation and experimentation used in sciences to philosophy, social science and religion.
Love, our principle; order, our foundation; progress, our goal.

1807   Robert E. Lee: American military leader. Resigned U.S. commission to become commander-in-chief of Confederate forces. Victorious at Fredericksburg and Chancellorsville. Defeated at Gettysburg. Surrendered at Appomattox Courthouse.
It is well that war is so terrible, or we should grow too fond of it.

1809   Edgar Allan Poe: U.S. Poet, short-story writer. Invented modern detective story with "The Murders in the Rue Morgue." Other stories: "Tales of the Grotesque, Arabesque" and "The Fall of the House of Usher." Poems: "The Raven," and "Annabel Lee."
All that we see or seem / Is but a dream within a dream.

1839   Paul Cézanne: French post-Impressionist painter. Considered by many as the greatest figure in modern French painting. His style dynamically assembles simple masses of color and shapes in contrasting planes of still lifes, landscapes and figure studies. Paintings: *Card Players, Mont Sainte-Victoire with Large Pine Trees* and *L'Oeuvre.*
Nature must be treated through the cylinder, the sphere, the cone.

1887   Alexander Woolcott: American journalist, writer and drama critic. Hosted radio show, "The Town Crier" (1929–42). Wrote for *New Yorker* magazine. Leading member of the Algonquin Round Table of writers, musicians and artists.
Writing is the art of putting black words on white paper in succession until the impression is created that something has been said.

1904   Roger Blough: American corporation lawyer, steel executive and philanthropist. Chairman of the board and CEO of U.S. Steel (1955–69). Member of corporation's executive committee (1956-76).
Steel prices cause inflation like wet sidewalks cause rain.

1943   Janis Joplin: "Pearl." Hard-drinking, hard-living U.S. white blues-rock singer. Died of heroin overdose (1970). Biggest hit: "Me and Bobby McGee."
Don't compromise yourself. You are all you've got.

January 20

1732   **Richard Henry Lee:** American Revolutionary patriot. Signer of the Declaration of Independence. U.S. senator from Virginia (1789–92). Made the motion in the Continental Congress, June 1776:
That these United Colonies are, and of right ought to be, free and independent states.

1806   **Nathaniel Parker Willis:** U.S. poet, editor, journalist and playwright. Founded *The American Monthly Magazine* and *The New York Mirror*. Works: *Inklings of Adventure* and *Letters from Under a Bridge*.
He who binds / His soul to knowledge, steals the key to heaven.

1889   **Huddie "Leadbelly" Ledbetter:** American folk and blues musician. Imprisoned for murder in 1918, pardoned in six years, then imprisoned again in 1930 for attempted murder. Released in 1934 through the efforts of folklorists John and Alan Lomax. Songs highlight the plight of blacks during the Great Depression.
My guitar is half my life and my wife is the other half.

1896   **George Burns:** U.S. vaudeville comedian. Married partner Gracie Allen. Then had successful radio and television shows until Gracies death. At eighty, he found a new career in movies, clubs and television. Academy Award for *The Sunshine Boys*.
Acting is all about honesty. If you can fake that, you've got it made.

1910   **Joy Adamson:** Austrian-born British author, naturalist. Lived in Kenya. Won international fame by writing *Born Free*, the story of lioness Elsa.
How could she know that it needed all the strength of my love for me to leave her now and give her back to nature—to let her learn to live alone until she might find her pride— her real pride.

1920   **Federico Fellini:** Italian director, actor and screenwriter of films such as *La Strada, La Dolce Vita, Eight and a Half* and *Satyricon 69*.
The artist is simply the medium between his fantasies and the rest of the world.

1926   **Patricia Neal:** American actress. Oscar winner for *Hud*. Other films: *The Fountainhead, The Hasty Heart* and *A Face in the Crowd*.
Happy? Who's really happy? Let's say it is enough not to be unhappy and let it go at that.

January 21

1737   **Ethan Allen:** American Revolutionary commander of the "Green Mountain Boys," who captured Ft. Ticonderoga, 1775. Taken prisoner by the British. Held in captivity (1775–78).
Virtue and vice are the only things in this world, which with our soul, are capable of surviving death.

1829   **Oscar II:** King of Sweden (1872–1907) and of Norway (1872–1905). An outstanding orator who loved music and literature. Published books of verse and wrote on historical subjects. A domestic conservative who sought Scandinavian cooperation.
I would rather have my people laugh at my economics than weep for my extravagance.

1864   **Israel Zangwill:** English novelist and playwright. A leading Zionist. Widely known for his novels on Jewish themes including *Children of the Ghetto* and his play *The Melting Pot*.
America is God's Crucible, the great Melting Pot where all the races of Europe are melting and re-forming.

1905   **Christian Dior:** French fashion designer. After WWII, introduced "new look" of long hemlines and full skirts.
There is no such thing as an ugly woman—there are only the ones who do not know how to make themselves attractive.

1925   **Benny Hill:** English comedian. Worked his way up through men's clubs, revues and end-of-pier shows to become television personality of the year (1954). Best known for his bawdy and slapstick-filled television comedy show.

That's what show business is—sincere insincerity.

1940 **Jack Nicklaus:** U.S. golfer. All-time leader in major tournament wins, 20; including 6 Masters, 5 PGAs, 4 U.S. Opens, 3 British Opens. Named Golfer of Century by PGA (1988).

In golf you're always breaking a barrier. When you bust it, you set yourself a little higher barrier and try to break that one.

1941 **Placido Domingo:** Spanish opera tenor. Among the world's leading lyric-dramatic tenors. Among his many successes are roles in *Tosca, Otello, Carmen* and *Tales of Hoffman*.

Longevity is both physical and mental. How fast you develop depends on the individual voice, but if you sing with an uneasy technique at 22, then at 40 your career has troubles.

January 22

1561 **Sir Francis Bacon:** English philosopher, statesman, essayist. Lord Chancellor of England (1618). Published works on philosophy of science. He was the practical creator of scientific induction. Works: *The Advancement of Learning, Novum Organum* and *New Atlantis*.

Knowledge and human power are synonymous.

1729 **Gotthold Ephram Lessing:** German critic, dramatist, writer on aesthetics, physician and epigrammatist. Defender of independent thinkers. Works: *Miss Sara Sampson, Emilia Galotti* and his novel plea for tolerance, *Nathan der Weise*.

A heretic is a man who sees with his own eyes.

1788 **George Gordon, Lord Byron:** English poet. Profligate life-style. Created the "Byronic hero"—a defiant, melancholy young man, brooding on some past, mysterious sin. Works: "Childe Harold's Pil-

grimage," "Lara," "Siege of Cornith" and "Don Juan."

And, after all, what is a lie? 'Tis but / The truth in masquerade.

1849 **August Strindberg:** Swedish playwright, novelist, short-story writer. Later works are the first example of Swedish realism. His plays *The Father, Miss Julie* and *The Creditors* make him a forerunner of expressionism and a major influence on modern theater.

All the blessings of civilization are either curses or superfluous.

1874 **D.W. [David Wark] Griffith:** U.S. director. Most influential figure in early history of American film. A founder of United Artists. Films: *The Birth of a Nation, Intolerance,* and *Orphans of the Storm*.

Taken as drama, war is, in some ways unsatisfactory.

1890 **Frederick M. Vinson:** U.S. politician, jurist. Chief justice of the Supreme Court (1946–53). Upheld powers of federal government versus individual rights.

Wars are not "acts of God." They are caused by man, by man-made institutions, by the way in which man has organized his society. What man has made, man can change.

1909 **U Thant:** Burmese teacher, journalist, independence agitator. Secretary General of United Nations General Assembly (1962–72). Played a major diplomatic role during the Cuban crisis.

In modern war there is no such thing as victor and vanquished ... there is only a loser, and that loser is mankind.

January 23

1783 **Stendahl:** Pseudonym of Marie Henri Beyle. French novelist and critic, he wrote biographies and critical works on art, literature and music. Best known for novels: *The Red and the Black* and *The Charterhouse of Parma*.

A novel is a mirror that strolls along a

highway. Now it reflects the blue of the skies, now the mud puddles under foot.

1832 Édouard Manet: French painter. Forerunner of impressionists. Paintings: *Luncheon on the Grass* and *Bar at the Folies-Bergère.* His genius was only recognized after his death.
The country only has charms for those not obliged to stay there.

1862 David Hilbert: German mathematician worked on the theory of algebraic invariants, the foundations of geometry and axiomatics.
The infinite! No other question has ever moved so profoundly the spirit of man.

1899 Humphrey Bogart: U.S. actor with cult status. Best in roles as average guys reluctantly thrust into demanding situations, who somehow rise to the occasion. Oscar winner for *The African Queen.* Nominated for *Casablanca* and *The Caine Mutiny.* Memorable in *The Petrified Forest, The Maltese Falcon* and *The Big Sleep.*
The whole world is three drinks behind.

1915 Potter Stewart: U.S. jurist, lawyer. Judge of U.S. Court of Appeals, Sixth Circuit (1954–58). Independent and moderate associate justice of the Supreme Court, appointed 1959.
Fairness is what justice really is.

1919 Ernie Kovacs: Brilliant creative U.S. comedian. Offbeat humor best featured in his irreverent and imaginative TV show "The Ernie Kovacs Show" (1955-56). Killed in a car crash (1962).
Television, a medium. So called because it is neither rare nor well done.

1928 Jeanne Moreau: French actress of the Comédie-Française and Théâtre National Populaire. Respected film star in *The Lovers, Jules and Jim,* and more recently, *The Summer House.*
There are never ten ways to do something. Only one. That is a question of morality. You have to be true to yourself and to others.

January 24

1670 William Congreve: English dramatist. Considered master of Restoration comedies. Wrote *The Old Bachelor, Love for Love* and *The Way of the World.*
Courtship is to marriage, as a very witty prologue to a very dull play.

1712 Frederick the Great: Prussian king, military leader (1740–86). Noted for social reforms. Led Prussia in the Seven Years' War. A writer and composer as well as a great military commander. Under his rule Prussia became a major European power.
God is always with the strongest battalions.

1732 Pierre de Beaumarchais: French author, courtier and dramatist. Best know for his satirical plays *Barber of Seville* and *Marriage of Figaro.*
It is not necessary to understand things in order to argue about them.

1832 Joseph H. Choate: U.S. lawyer, diplomat, orator. Distinguished for over 50 years of public service. Works: *American Addresses* and *Arguments and Addresses.*
Do not make long prayers; always remember that the Lord knows something.

1862 Edith Wharton: U.S. novelist, short-story writer. Wrote of life among the middle-class and aristocratic New York society of the 19th and early 20th centuries. Works: *Ethan Frome, The Age of Innocence* and *The Old Maid.*
There are two ways of spreading light; to be the candle or the mirror that reflects it.

1915 Robert Motherwell: American artist. One of the founders of Abstract Expressionism in New York City in the 1940. Interest in Freud and psychoanalysis led to spontaneous paintings and huge images.
Art is much less important than life, but what a poor life without it.

1928 Desmond Morris: British zoologist and writer. Wrote best-selling *The Naked Ape,* a study of human behavior. Hosted many television programs on animal and social behavior.

There are one hundred and ninety-three living species of monkeys and apes. One hundred and ninety-two of them are covered with hair. The exception is a naked ape self-named Homo-sapiens.

January 25

1627   **Robert Boyle:** Anglo-Irish physicist and chemist. Major founder of modern science. Advocated careful experimentation, thorough description and publication of results. Discovered Boyle's Law: volume of gas changes in simple proportion to pressure.
I am not ambitious to appear a man of letters; I could be content the world should think I had scarce looked upon any other book than nature.

1736   **J.L. Lagrange:** French mathematician. Called "The Lofty Pyramid of the Mathematical Sciences" by Napoleon, who made him a Count of the Empire. A great analyst, his attack on mechanics marked the first complete break with Greek tradition.
When we ask advice, we are usually looking for an accomplice.

1759   **Robert Burns:** Scotland's greatest poet. Best known for his lyrics written in the Scottish venacular, praising lowland life. Songs include: "Auld Lang Syne" and "Comin' Thru the Rye."
The best laid schemes o' mice and men / Gang aft a-gley.

1874   **W. Somerset Maugham:** English novelist, playwright and short-story writer. Works include: *Of Human Bondage, The Moon and Sixpence* and *The Razor's Edge*. Best known for short stories including "Rain."
It is bad enough to know the past; it would be intolerable to know the future.

1882   **Virginia Woolf:** English novelist, critic, essayist. Used techniques of interior monologue and stream of consciousness. Committed suicide by drowning. Novels: *Mrs. Dalloway* and *Orlando*.

If you do not tell the truth about yourself you cannot tell it about other people.

1919   **Edwin Newman:** American news commentator, author. Defender of clear use of English language. Books: *Strictly Speaking* and *A Civil Tongue*.
The prevalence of "Y'know" is one of the most far-reaching and depressing developments of our time.

1933   **Corazon C. Aquino:** Filipino political leader. Widow of assassinated Benigno Aquino. Defeated Ferdinand Marcos in 1986 for presidency by leading nonviolent "people's power" campaign.
One must be frank to be relevant.

January 26

1715   **Claude-Adrien Helvétius:** French philosopher. His controversial "De l'ésprit" advanced the view that sensation is the source of all intellectual activity and self-interest is the motivating force of all human action.
By annihilating desires you annihilate the mind.

1871   **Samuel Hopkins Adams:** U.S. journalist and editor. Exposed quack patent medicine in "The Great American Fraud," which spurred the passage of the Pure Food and Drug Act of 1906.
It is better that a marriage end by a clear severance than be slowly stifled to death through years of intolerable contact.

1880   **Douglas MacArthur:** U.S. military adviser to the Philippines prior to WWII. Ordered to withdraw from Corregidor (1941) pledging "I shall return." Liberated Philippines (1944-45). Commander of occupation forces Japan (1945-50). Commander-in-chief U.N. forces Korea (1950-51). Dismissed by Truman.
There is no security on this earth, there is only opportunity.

1925   **Paul Newman:** U.S. actor, director. Famous for his piercing blue eyes and anti-heroic roles. Nominated for Oscars for *Cat on a Hot Tin Roof, The Hutler, Hud,*

Cool Hand Luke, Absence of Malice, The Verdict and *Nobody's Fool*. Received Oscar for *The Color of Money*.

Acting is a question of absorbing other people's personalities and adding some of your own experience.

1929 Jules Feiffer: U.S. cartoonist, screenwriter. Satirist for *The Village Voice*, *Playboy*, *London Observer*. Awarded Pulitzer Prize (1986). Screenplay for *Carnal Knowledge*.

Who would have guessed that maturity is only a short break in adolescence?

1944 Angela Davis: American revolutionary, black militant, communist activist, author. Acquitted of charges of kidnapping, murder and conspiracy in connection with shootout at Marin County courthouse.

This culture is one of resistance, but a resistance of desperation.

1961 Wayne Gretzky: "The Great One." Hockey player with Edmonton, Los Angeles and St. Louis. All-time scoring champion with more than 800 goals. Leads in career points and assists.

Skate to where the puck is going and not to where it's been.

January 27

1756 Wolfgang Amadeus Mozart: Austrian musical genius, composer. Child prodigy. Composed over 600 works in every genre, unsurpassed in lyric beauty, rhythmic variety and melodic invention. Works: *The Marriage of Figaro, Don Giovanni* and *The Magic Flute*.

Neither a lofty degree of intelligence nor imagination nor both together go to the making of genius. Love, love, love, that is the soul of genius.

1775 Friedrich von Schelling: German writer, critic and philosopher. Works: *Thoughts on Poetry, Of the World-Soul*, and *System of Transcendental Idealism*.

Architecture in general is frozen music.

1832 Lewis Carroll: Pseudonym of Charles Dodgson, English minister, mathematician and author. Best known for classic fantasies *Alice in Wonderland* and *Through the Looking Glass*, written for Alice Liddell, daughter of the head of Oxford college. Also did work in symbolic logic.

When I use a word it means just what I choose it to mean—neither more nor less.

1850 Samuel Gompers: English-born U.S. labor leader. A cigar maker by trade, in 1886 he helped found the American Federation of Labor (AFL). Served as its first president (1886–1924).

The worst crime against working people is a company which fails to operate at a profit.

1872 [Billings] Learned Hand: American jurist whose more than 2000 opinions ranged through all fields of law. Chief justice of the federal court of appeals, serving on the court for 52 years. His opinions so influenced the U.S. Supreme Court that he was known as its "10th man."

In the end it is worse to suppress disrest than to run the risk of heresy.

1900 Hyman Rickover: Russian-born American admiral and educator. Known as "Father of the Atomic Submarine." Supervised construction of the first nuclear submarine, U.S.S. *Nautilus* (1947-54).

If you're going to sin, sin against God, not the bureaucracy. God will forgive you, but the bureaucracy won't.

1948 Mikhail Baryshnikov: Russian-born American dancer, choreographer, director, actor. Defected from the Soviet Union (1974). He has a gravity-defying style. Has worked with the American Theater Ballet and New York City Ballet as well as appearing in films such as *The Turning Point*.

The essence of all art is to have pleasure in giving pleasure.

January 28

1807 Robert McClure: Irish Arctic explorer. Commanded a ship in a John

Ross Franklin Arctic expedition. Given credit for being the first to complete the Northwest Passage, although Franklin is given credit for discovering the passage.

A = r + p (Adventure equals risk plus purpose.)

1851   **Jose Marti:** Cuban poet, patriot. Leader of Cuban struggle for independence. Deported for political activities. Died leading an invasion of Cuba (1895).

Man needs to suffer. When he does not have real griefs he creates them. Griefs purify and prepare him.

1873   **[Sidonie-Gabrielle] Colette:** French novelist. Music-hall dancer and mime. Her early books were written in collaboration with her first husband Henri Gauthier-Villars. Her best known later works include the *Claudine* series and *Gigi*.

Pessimists have good appetites.

1887   **Artur Rubinstein:** Polish-born American concert pianist. Child prodigy. Became U.S. citizen in 1946. Made over 200 recordings. Famed for interpretations of Chopin.

The seasons ... are authentic, there is no mistake about them, they are what a symphony ought to be: four perfect movements in intimate harmony with one another.

1892   **Ernst Lubitsch:** German-born actor, director. Moved to Hollywood. Focused attention on two main themes— sex and money. Examples of films with the "Lubitsch Touch": *The Love Parade*, *Ninotchka* and *To Be or Not to Be*.

Nobody should try to play comedy unless he has a circus going on inside.

1912   **Jackson Pollock:** U.S. painter. Leader of abstract expressionist movement in the U.S. Initiated the Op art movement of fifties and sixties. His "drip" painting *One* is 17 feet long. Other works: *No. 32* and *Echo and Blue Poles*.

Painting is self-discovery.

1933   **Susan Sontag:** American essayist, philosopher, novelist, short-story writer and filmmaker. Best known for essays on avant-garde culture. Books: *The*

Style of Radical Will, On Photography and *Illness as a Metaphor.* Coined word "camp."

Depression is melancholy minus its charms.

January 29

1737   **Thomas Paine:** American colonial political philosopher. Wrote *Common Sense*, which advocated immediate independence from England. Other works: *The Rights of Man*, in support of the French Revolution and *The Age of Reason*, favoring deism.

Government, even in its best state, is but a necessary evil; in its worst state, an intolerable one.

1843   **William McKinley:** Twenty-fifth U.S. president (1897–1901). Governor and congressman from Ohio. Advocated protectionism. In his first term, U.S. went to war with Spain. Assassinated by anarchist Leon Czolgosz at beginning of second term.

Our differences are politics. Our agreements, principles.

1866   **Romain Rolland:** French essayist, novelist, biographer and polemical writer. Author of ten-volume epic *Jean Christophe*. Took an active role in the Dreyfuss affair. Nobel prize winner (1915).

A hero is a man who does what he can.

1874   **John D. Rockefeller, Jr.:** U.S. philanthropist. Used vast family fortune to fund Rockefeller Institute for Medical Research, and Rockefeller Center in New York City. Major supporter of Admiral Byrd's polar expeditions, restoration of Colonial Williamsburg and Lincoln Center for the Performing Arts.

Our responsibility, every opportunity an obligation, every possession a duty.

1880   **W.C. Fields:** U.S. vaudeville, stage, radio and screen performer. Eccentric comedian and master juggler. Noted for large red nose, gravel voice and dislike of children. Films: *David Copperfield, My Little Chickadee,* and *The Bank Dick.*

If at first you don't succeed, try, try again. Then quit. No use being a damn fool about it.

1939 **Germaine Greer:** Australian author, educator and lecturer. Author of *The Female Eunuch*, one of the most successful feminist books. It portrayed marriage as a legalized form of slavery for women.
Loneliness is never more cruel than when it is felt in close propinquity with someone who has ceased to communicate.

1954 **Oprah Winfrey:** American television personality, actress. Highest paid entertainer on television. Hosts a nationally syndicated talk show. Oscar nomination for *The Color Purple.*
You can have it all. You just can't have it all at one time.

January 30

1775 **Walter Savage Landor:** English poet, literary critic and essayist. Outstanding classicist. Best known work: the prose dialogue "Imaginary Conversations."
Absence quickens our love and elevates our affections. Absence is the invisible and corporeal mother of ideal beauty.

1846 **Francis H. Bradley:** British philosopher. Most important person in the Absolute Idealist movement of his period. Works: *Ethical Studies, Principles of Logic* and *Appearance and Reality.*
Metaphysics is the finding of bad reasons for what we believe upon instinct.

1862 **Walter Damrosch:** German-born U.S. conductor, composer and educator. Became music adviser to NBC radio (1927). Pioneered weekly music appreciation broadcasts.
Various composers have been walking around jazz like a cat around a plate of hot soup, waiting for it to cool off, so that they could enjoy it without burning their tongues.

1882 **Franklin Delano Roosevelt:** Thirty-second U.S. president. Served three full terms and part of a fourth (1933–45). Led the United States out of the Depression by initiating many reforms. Expanded government power through New Deal programs. Played a major role in the Allied alliance in WWII with Great Britain and the U.S.S.R. Stricken with polio (1921).
The only limit to our realization of tomorrow will be our doubts of today.

1909 **Saul Alinsky:** U.S. social activist. Self-proclaimed "professional radical." Taught the use of picketing, sit-downs, strikes and boycotts to exert pressure on businesses and governments.
In any fight with the Establishment, you can count on it for at least one glorious gaffe that will bring renewed life to your languishing cause.

1912 **Barbara Tuchman:** U.S. historian. Pulitzers for her best-selling historical books *The Guns of August* and *Stilwell and the American Experience in China.*
Every successful revolution puts on in time the robe of the tyrant it has deposed.

1937 **Vanessa Redgrave:** Strong-willed, outspoken British actress of a prominent acting family. Militant supporter of Worker's Revolutionary Party. Oscar nominated for *Morgan!, Isadora, Mary, Queen of Scots* and *The Bostonians.* Won for *Julia.*
Integrity is so perishable in the summer months of success.

January 31

1797 **Franz Schubert:** Austrian composer. Combined classical and romantic styles. Major works: *Trout Piano Quintet, C Major Symphony* and *B minor Symphony*, known as the *Unfinished Symphony.* Greatest exponent of German Leider. Wrote "Ave Maria."
No one really understands the grief or joy of another.

1903 **Tallulah Bankhead:** Legendary U.S. actress. Lauded equally for her stage performances and tempestuous, quick-witted personality and uninhibited behavior. Known for a deep, raspy voice and explosive laugh. Starred in *The Little Foxes* and *Private Lives.*
We're all paid off in the end, and the fools first.

1915   **Thomas Merton:** French-born U.S. clergyman and author. Joined the Trappist order. Wrote the best-selling autobiography *The Seven Storey Mountain,* prompting many to become monks. He maintained voluminous correspondences. Wrote on poetry and social criticism.
The biggest human temptation is ... to settle for too little.

1919   **Jackie Robinson:** First black of the modern era to play major league baseball with Brooklyn (1947). Rookie-of-the-year (1947), MVP (1949), hall of fame (1962), four-sport athlete at UCLA. Civil rights activist.
Fear is a two-edged sword that sometimes cuts the wielder.

1923   **Carol Channing:** Comic actress. Saucer-eyed entertainer of U.S. stage, nightclubs, television and movies. Smash hit as "Lorelei Lee" in Broadway's *Gentlemen Prefer Blondes.* Also starred in *Hello, Dolly.*
Laughter is much more important than applause. Applause is almost a duty. Laughter is a reward. Laughter means they trust you.

1923   **Norman Mailer:** U.S. novelist and journalist. Known for iconoclast writings: *The Naked and the Dead, Armies of the Night* (Pulitzer) and *The Executioner's Song* (Pulitzer).
Sentimentality is the emotional promiscuity of those who have no sentiment.

1931   **Ernie Banks:** "Mr. Cub." Hall of fame shortstop–first baseman for Cubs (1953–71). Hit 514 HRs. MVP (1958, 1959). Voted "Greatest Cub Ever" (1969).
You must try to generate happiness within yourself. If you aren't happy in one place, chances are you won't be happy any place.

February 1

1552   **Sir Edward Coke:** English jurist and legal writer. His defense of the supremacy of the common law against claims of royal prerogative were a profound influence on the development of English law and the constitution.
No restraint, be it ever so little, but is imprisonment.

1787   **Richard Whatley:** English scholar, logician, theological writer. Anglican archbishop of Dublin. Supported Catholic emancipation and worked for unsectarian religious instruction. Unpopular because of his caustic wit and outspokenness.
To know your ruling passion, examine your castles in the air.

1901   **Clark Gable:** U.S. movie star. "The King." His charmingly naughty smile and self-confidence represented the ultimate in masculinity for millions. Nominated for Oscars for *Mutiny on the Bounty* and *Gone with the Wind,* won for *It Happened One Night.* Others: *Red Dust, San Franciso* and *The Misfits.*
It's an extra dividend when you like the girl you're in love with.

1902   **Langston Hughes:** U.S. poet, author, journalist. Expressed black view of America with *Shakespeare in Harlem* (1942). Wrote in dialect, using blues and jazz rhythms. Other works: *Famous Negro Heroes of America* and *First Book of Africa.*
Humor is laughing at what you haven't got when you ought to have it.

1904   **S.J. [Sidney Joseph] Perlman:** U.S. author. Noted for humorous short stories and screenplays for the Marx brothers. Oscar for screenplay of *Around the World in Eighty Days.* Books: *Strictly from Hunger, One Touch of Venus* and *Acres and Pain.*
There is such a thing as too much couth.

1918   **Muriel Spark:** Scottish novelist, satirist. Editor of *Poetry Review* (1947-49). Published critical biographies on Wordsworth, Mary Shelley and Emily Brontë. Best known for her novel, *The Prime of Miss Jean Brodie.*
It is impossible to persuade a man who does not disagree, but smiles.

1931   **Boris Yeltsin:** President of the Republic of Russia and prime minister of the Russian Federation since 1990. Trying to institute economic reform in the largest country of the former U.S.S.R. he has employed both parliamentary and military means to push his programs.

You can build a throne out of bayonets, but you can't sit on them long.

February 2

1745 Hannah More: English playwright and religious writer. Best known for her philanthropic works written for the benefit of the poor. Publications: "Sacred Dramas," "Estimate on the Religion of the Fashionable World" and "Cheap Repository Tracts."

We do not so much want books for good people, as books which will make bad ones better.

1754 Charles Maurice de Tallyrand-Perigord: French statesman and diplomat. Leading politician of his time. Minister of Foreign Affairs for Napoleon I. Helped restore the Bourbons. Negotiated Treaty of Paris. Brilliantly represented France at the Congress of Vienna. Had a brilliant knack for surviving many changes in government.

Mistrust first impulses, they are always good.

1859 Henry Havelock Ellis: English scientist. Pioneer author on psychology of sex. Conducted first study of homosexuality. Advocated sex education. Author of *Studies in the Psychology of Sex*, the first detached treatment of the subject free of guilt feelings.

What we call progress is the exchange of one nuisance for another nuisance.

1882 James Joyce: Irish novelist, poet. Wrote *Ulysses* (1922). Noted for complex design and combination of realism and stream of consciousness. *Ulysses* was banned in the United States as obscene until 1933. Other writings: *Portrait of the Artist as a Young Man* and *Finnegans Wake*.

The now, the here, through which all future plunges to the past.

1901 Jascha Heifetz: American violinist. Child prodigy. Noted for silken tone, careful regard for composer's markings. Settled in the United States after the Russian Revolution.

No matter what side of an argument you're on, you always find some people on your side that you wish were on the other side.

1905 Ayn Rand: U.S. novelist and philosopher. Began her career as a playwright and screenwriter. Created superior characters to illustrate philosophy of rational self-interest, which she called objectivism, best illustrated in her novels *The Fountainhead* and *Atlas Shrugged*.

Wealth is the product of man's capacity to think.

1915 Abba Eban: Israeli diplomat. U.N. representative (1949–59). Ambassador to U.S. (1950–59). Author of *Israel in the World*.

History teaches us that men and nations behave wisely once they have exhausted all other alternatives.

February 3

1811 Horace Greeley: American newspaper editor. Founder and editor of *New York Tribune* (1841–72). Crusader against slavery. Liberal Republican presidential candidate (1872).

Wisdom is never dear, provided the article is genuine.

1821 Elizabeth Blackwell: English-U.S. physician. First American woman to earn a M.D. degree (1849). Founded New York Infirmary (1849) and London School of Medicine for Women (1875).

For what is done or learned by one class of women becomes, by virtue of their common womanhood, the property of all women.

1826 Walter Bagehot: English economist and literary critic. Editor of *Economist* (1860–77). Applied concept of evolution to political societies. Wrote *English Constitution, Physics and Politics* and *Literary Studies*.

Stupidity is nature's favorite resource for preserving steadiness of conduct and consistency of opinion.

1874 Gertrude Stein: U.S. writer, patron of the arts (1920s). Conducted a celebrated salon for writers in her Paris home between the two world wars. Named the members "The Lost Generation." Wrote *Three Lives, Tender Buttons* and *The Autobiography of Alice B. Toklas.*

What is the answer? ...In that case, what is the question?

1894 Norman Rockwell: American illustrator. Using oils, he developed a realistic style, idealizing small-town America. His works appeared in magazines including *St. Nicholas, Colliers, Look* and most especially *The Saturday Evening Post.*

I say that if you can tell a story in a picture, and if a reasonable number of people like your work, it is art.

1909 Simone Weil: French mystic and social philosopher. Served with Republican forces in the Spanish Civil War. Worked for Free French in London during WWII. Died of voluntary starvation in an attempt to identify with the Resistance fighters in France. Posthumously published books: *Waiting for God* and *Gravity and Grace.*

Evil being the root of mystery, pain is the root of knowledge.

1940 Fran [Francis] Tarkington: Football quarterback, 18 seasons for Vikings and Giants. Player of the year (1975). NFL records: threw for 47,003 yards and 342 TDs.

It's a lonesome walk to the sidelines, especially when thousands of people are cheering your replacement.

February 4

1802 Mark Hopkins: U.S. educator, theologian. President, Williams College (1836–72). Famous for his ability to arouse students to express their thoughts and natures. U.S. president James A. Garfield saluted him with "A pine bench, with Mark Hopkins at one end of it and me at the other, is a good enough college for me!"

Language is the picture and counterpart of thought.

1842 Georg Brandes: Danish critic and scholar. Believed it was his mission to bring Denmark out of cultural isolation. Best known for his monumental *Main Currents in 19th Century Literature* (6 volumes, 1871–87).

The stream of time sweeps away errors and leaves the truth for the inheritance of humanity.

1876 Sarah N. Cleghorn: American author, poet, suffragist, civil rights worker, pacifist and antivivisectionist. Published *A Turnpike Lady, The Spinster* and *Portraits and Protests.*

The golf links lie so near the mill / That almost any day / The laboring children can look out / And see the men at play.

1897 Ludwig Erhard: German statesman, economist. Economics minister, West Germany (1949–63). Chief architect of the nation's post WWII economic recovery. Chancellor (1963–66).

A compromise is the art of dividing a cake in such a way that everyone believes he has the biggest piece.

1902 Charles Lindbergh: "The Lone Eagle." U.S. aviator. Made first nonstop solo trans–Atlantic flight from New York to Paris (1927). Championed isolationism (1939–41). Flew Pacific combat missions, WWII.

In wilderness I sense the miracle of life, and behind it our scientific accomplishments fade to trivia.

1906 Dietrich Bonhoeffer: German Lutheran pastor. Protested against anti–Jewish legislation. Part of German Resistance movement which planned Hitler's overthrow. Arrested and hanged (1945).

Action springs not from thought, but from a readiness for responsibility.

1921 Betty Friedan: U.S. feminist, author. Wrote *The Feminine Mystique* (1963). Founded National Organization of

Women (NOW) in 1966. President until 1970.

Man is not the enemy here, but the fellow victim. The real enemy is women's denigration of themselves.

February 5

1626   **Marquise Marie de Sevigne:** Member of French court society. Over a period of 25 years wrote more than 1500 letters which provide a portrait of her age.

In love affairs it is only the beginnings that are amusing. Therefore, you should start over again as soon as possible.

1788   **Sir Robert Peel:** English political leader. Major founder of the Conservative Party. As home secretary founded the London Police Force (1829), whose constables are known as "bobbies." Prime minister (1834–35, 1841–46).

Agitation is the marshaling of the conscience of a nation to mold its laws.

1838   **Abram Joseph Ryan:** American Roman Catholic priest, poet. Poet of the Confederacy. Poems: "The Conquered Banner," "The Lost Cause," "The Sword of Robert E. Lee" and "The March of the Deathless Dead."

Some reckon their age by years, / Some measure their life by art; / But some tell their days by the flow of their tears, / And their lives by the moans of their hearts.

1900   **Adlai E. Stevenson II:** U.S. politician, diplomat. Participant at the foundation of U.N., San Francisco (1946). Illinois governor (1948–52). Twice Democratic candidate for presidency. Defeated each time by Eisenhower. U.S. delegate to U.N. (1961–65).

Nothing so dates a man as to decry the younger generation.

1914   **William S. Burroughs:** American author. Chief speaker for "Beat movement." His novel *Naked Lunch* graphically deals with the surreal world of the drug addict. Also wrote *The Soft Machine* and *Nova Express.*

Modern man has lost the option of silence.

1934   **Henry Aaron:** Hall of fame outfielder with the Braves and Brewers. All-time leader in HRs (755) and RBIs (2297); MVP (1957).

Making the majors is not as hard as staying there, staying interested day after day. It's like being married. The hardest part is staying married.

1939   **Jane Bryant Quinn:** U.S. writer and television correspondent. Financial business columnist for *Newsweek*. Wrote *Everyone's Money Book.*

Lawyers are operators of the toll bridge across which anyone in search of justice has to pass.

February 6

1878   **Walter B. Pitkin:** American psychologist, journalist, editor. Wrote the pop psychology book *Life Begins at Forty.*

[Politicians] are the semi-failures in business and the professions, men of mediocre mentality, dubious morals, and magnificent commonplaceness.

1895   **George Herman "Babe" Ruth:** Baseball's most dominant player. A successful pitcher-outfielder with the Red Sox. Became home run king when traded to Yankees. Had 714 career HRs; 60 in 1927.

Never let the fear of striking out get in your way.

1902   **Louis Nizer:** Celebrated U.S. lawyer, author. Specialized in cases in the entertainment field. Books: *My Life in Court* and *The Jury Returns.*

A speaker who does not strike oil in ten minutes should stop boring.

1911   **Ronald Reagan:** Fortieth president of the United States. Known for conservative policies and appointments. Oldest and the first divorced president. Governor of California. Film and television actor.

Politics is just like show business. You have a hell of an opening, coast for a while, and then have a hell of a close.

1913   **Mary Leakey:** English anthropologist whose discoveries of fossils in East Africa helped push back the dates of the first true man to almost four million years ago.
In archaeology you almost never find what you set out to find.

1919   **Zsa Zsa Gabor:** Hungarian actress and celebrity. She and her sisters made marrying wealthy men an art form. A congressman called her "the most expensive courtesan since Madame de Pompadour."
Macho does not prove mucho.

1940   **Tom Brokaw:** U.S. newscaster. NBC's White House correspondent. Host of the morning "Today Show" (1976). NBC anchorman since 1981.
It's easy to make a buck. It's a lot tougher to make a difference.

February 7

1477   **Sir Thomas More:** English statesman, lawyer, poet and author. Wrote *Utopia,* 1516, of an ideal state based on reason. Appointed Lord Chancellor, 1529. Executed 1535 for refusing to accept Henry VIII as head of the Church. Canonized 1935.
If evils come not, then our fears are vain; / And if they do, fear but augments the pain.

1812   **Charles Dickens:** Pseudonym, Boz. English novelist. Novels include *Oliver Twist, A Christmas Carol, David Copperfield, A Tale of Two Cities* and *Great Expectations.* Made public readings, private theatricals, speeches, wrote innumerable letters, pamphlets, and plays and ran a successful magazine.
In the little world in which children have their existence ... there is nothing so finely perceived and as finely felt, as injustice.

1863   **Anthony Hope:** Pseudonym of Anthony Hope Hawkins. English novelist and lawyer. Chiefly remembered for his "Ruritanian" romances *The Prisoner of Zenda* and the sequel *Rupert of Hentzau.*

Boys will be boys. And even that wouldn't matter if only we could prevent girls from being girls.

1863   **Laura Ingalls Wilder:** U.S. author of *Little House in the Big Woods,* basis of television's "Little House on the Prairie."
Once you begin being naughty, it is easier to go on and on, and sooner or later something dreadful happens.

1877   **Godfrey Harold Hardy:** English mathematician. Introduced work of self-taught Indian genius Srinivasa Ramanujan to mathematical world. Wrote his mathematical philosophy in laymen's terms in *A Mathematician's Apology.*
A mathematician, like a painter or a poet, is a maker of patterns. If his patterns are more permanent than theirs, it is because they are made with ideas.

1883   **Eubie Blake:** U.S. jazz pianist, composer. Son of former slaves. Played piano in a "sporting house." Appeared in vaudeville with Noble Sissle. Wrote: "I'm Just Wild About Harry" (1927). The ragtime revival brought him out of retirement in his eighties. Received Presidential Medal of Honor (1982).
The world goes on no matter what you do.

1885   **Sinclair Lewis:** U.S. novelist. His best works are characterized by satire and realism: *Main Street, Babbitt, Arrowsmith* (Pulitzer), *Elmer Gantry* and *Dodsworth.*
Intellectually I know that America is no better than any other country; emotionally I know she is better than every other country.

February 8

1577   **Robert Burton:** English philosopher and humorist. His great work was *The Anatomy of Melancholy,* a learned miscellany on the ideas of his time.
A blow with a word strikes deeper than any blow with a sword.

1819   **John Ruskin:** English writer and art critic. Believed faith, morality, education and good social conditions were prerequisites of creating good art. Works: *Modern Painters, The Seven Lamps of Architecture* and *The Stones of Venice.*

Let us reform our schools, and we shall find little reform needed in our prisons.

1820 William Tecumseh Sherman: Union army general. Led the "March to the Sea," and the burning of Atlanta. Ended Republican Party's attempts to draft him as their presidential candidate by saying:

I will not accept if nominated and will not serve if elected.

1825 Harriet J.H. Robinson: American suffragist, mill worker, writer. Best known for *Massachusetts in the Woman Suffrage Movement.* Other books: *The New Pandora* and *Loom and Spindle, or, Life Among the Early Mill Girls.*

Skilled labor teaches something not to be found in books or colleges.

1851 Kate Chopin: American author of novels of Cajun and Creole life, including *Bayou Folk, A Night in Acadie* and *Désirée's Baby.*

There are some people who leave impressions not so lasting as the imprint of an oar upon the water.

1878 Martin Buber: Jewish philosopher, theologian, Zionist thinker. Saw Israel an ideal place for fulfillment of nationalist and humanist aspirations. Author of *Tales of Rabbi Nachman* and *Kingship of God.*

Play is the exultation of the possible.

1931 James Dean: Charismatic U.S. actor, died in a car crash at age 24 before his last film was released. Personified "cool" for young people of fifties. Films: *Rebel Without a Cause, East of Eden* and *Giant.*

Death is the only thing left to respect. Everything else can be questioned. But death is true. In it lies the only nobility for man and beyond it the only hope.

February 9

1865 Mrs. Patrick [Beatrice] Campbell: Leading English actress of turn of the century London stage. Shaw wrote Eliza Doolittle role in *Pygmalion* especially for her.

It doesn't matter what you do in the bedroom as long as you don't do it in the street and frighten the horses.

1866 George Ade: American humorist, playwright. Wrote popular column for Chicago *Record*, and the plays, *The Country Chairman* and *The College Widow.*

Anybody can win, unless there happens to be a second entry.

1874 Amy Lowell: American poet, critic, biographer. Leader of imagist movement. Wrote numerous poems in free verse and polyphonic prose. Works: *A Dome of Many-colored Glass* and *Sword Blades and Poppy Seeds.*

All books are either dreams or swords; / You can cut, or you can drug, with words.

1909 Dean Rusk: American statesman. President of the Rockefeller Foundation (1952–61). Secretary of state (1961–69). Played a major role in the Cuban crisis of 1962. Defended U.S. involvement in Vietnam.

The United States is not just an old cow that gives more milk the more it's kicked in the flanks.

1914 Bill Veeck: Zany American baseball owner of Browns, Indians and White Sox. Enlivened games with a midget batter, exploding scoreboards and giveaways.

It isn't the high price of stars that is so expensive, it's the high price of mediocrity.

1923 Brendan Behan: Irish playwright. His three years in an English reform school for the possession of explosives for the IRA led him to write the autobiographical *Borstal Boy.* His plays, *The Quare Fellow* and *The Hostage* are based on two more prison terms.

An author's first duty is to let down his country.

1944   **Alice Walker:** American novelist and poet. Best known for her third and most popular novel *The Color Purple*, winner of the 1983 Pulitzer Prize for fiction. Other works: *In Search of Our Mothers' Gardens* and *Living by the Word*.
Womanism is to feminism as purple is to lavender...

February 10

1609   **Sir John Suckling:** English poet, dramatist and courtier. Best known for his lyrics. His masterpiece is "Ballad Upon a Wedding." Also wrote "A Session of Poets" and "The Goblins."
'Tis expectation makes a blessing dear, / Heaven were not heaven, if we knew what it were.

1868   **William Allen White:** "The Sage of Emporia." U.S. journalist, editor and owner of *The Emporia* [Kansas] *Gazette* (1895–1944). Pulitzer, editorial writing (1923). Pulitzer Prize, for his autobiography (1947).
Consistency is a paste jewel that only cheap men cherish.

1890   **Boris Pasternak:** Russian lyric poet, novelist. His novel *Doctor Zhivago* was rejected for publication in the U.S.S.R., but an Italian edition appeared, earning the author a Nobel Prize he was forced to reject.
In every generation there has to be some fool who will speak the truth as he sees it.

1894   **Harold MacMillan:** English statesman. Conservative prime minister (1957–63). Gained a nuclear test–ban treaty (1963). Hurt by the Profumo Scandal.
A Foreign Secretary is forever poised between a cliche and an indiscretion.

1898   **Bertolt Brecht:** German poet and dramatist. Collaborated with Kurt Weill on his major work *The Three Penny Opera*. Other plays: *The Life of Galileo, Mother Courage and Her Children* and *The Good Woman of Setzuan*.
Poverty makes you sad as well as wise.

1927   **Leontyne Price:** American operatic soprano. Known for her role as Aïda. Has won more than twenty Grammy awards. Received Presidential Medal of Freedom award (1964).
All token blacks have the same experience. I have been pointed at as a solution to things that have not been solved.

1946   **Donovan [Leitch]:** Scottish singer. A pied piper–like figure of the "flower power" rock movement of the sixties. Songs: "Mellow Yellow" and "Jennifer Juniper."
The softer you sing the louder you're heard.

February 11

1657   **Bernard De Fonteunelle:** French scientist and man of letters. Wrote conversations between historical figures in order to circulate new philosophical ideas.
It isn't very intelligent to find answers to questions which are unanswerable.

1802   **Lydia M. Child:** American abolitionist, suffragist, writer, journalist and editor. Founded and edited first U.S. children's monthly, *Juvenile Miscellany* (1826-34).
We first crush people to the earth, and then claim the right of trampling on them forever because they are prostrate.

1847   **Thomas Alva Edison:** "Wizard of Menlo Park." U.S. inventor of first electric bulb and nearly 1300 other items. Pioneer in motion picture industry. Discovered "Edison effect," basis of modern electronics. Named to Hall of Fame of Great Americans (1960).
We do not know one millionth of one percent about anything.

1900   **Tommy Hitchcock:** American-born polo player. Generally regarded as the world's greatest during the two decades just prior to WWII. Received his ten-goal rating (1922).
Lose as if you like it; win as if you were used to it.

1907   **William J. Levitt:** U.S. businessman, community planner. Leader of the postwar housing revolution in the U.S. built Levittown.
Any fool can build homes—what counts is how many you can sell for how little.

1925   **Virginia E. Johnson:** U.S. sexologist. With William H. Masters did work in sex therapy and wrote *Human Sexual Response.*
Your sexuality is a dimension of your personality, and whenever you are sexually active, you are expressing yourself—the self that you are at that moment, the mood that you're in, the needs that you have.

1934   **Mary Quant:** English fashion designer. Developed "Chelsea Look," sixties. High priestess of the Mod cult and mother of the mini-skirt. First fashion designer named officer of the Order of the British Empire. Her description of a fashionable woman:
She is sexy, witty and dry-cleaned.

February 12

1663   **Cotton Mather:** Colonial clergyman. Pastor, Second Church of Boston. Helped establish Boston as a culture center. Advocated use of scientific evidence in witchcraft trials.
Charity ... is kind, it is not easily provok'd, it thinks no evil, it believes all things, hopes all things.

1791   **Peter Cooper:** U.S. inventor, manufacturer, philanthropist. Designed and constructed first U.S. steam locomotive, the "Tom Thumb."
The Dealers in money have always, since the days of Moses, been the dangerous class.

1809   **Charles Darwin:** English naturalist. Developed a theory of evolution through natural selection after five-year voyage on the H.M.S. *Beagle* to South America and the Galapagos Islands. Books: *Origin of Species* and *The Descent of Man.*
A man who dares to waste one hour of time has not discovered the value of life.

1809   **Abraham Lincoln:** Sixteenth U.S. president. Led Union during Civil War. Published the Emancipation Proclamation, freeing slaves. Delivered famous address at dedication of Gettysburg memorial cemetery. Assassinated by actor John Wilkes Booth.
As I would not be a slave, so I would not be a master. This expresses my idea of democracy. Whatever differs from this, to the extent of the difference, is no democracy.

1880   **John L. Lewis:** U.S. labor leader. President of United Mine Workers of America (1920–60), most powerful union in country at the time. Broke with the CIO to form the AFL.
He that tooteth not his own horn, the same shall not be tooted.

1893   **Omar Bradley:** U.S. army general. Led U.S. ground troops at the Normandy invasion. First permanent chairman of the U.S. joint Chiefs of Staff (1949–53). Promoted to five-star general (1950).
We have grasped the mystery of the atom and rejected the sermon of the Mount. ... Ours is a world of nuclear giants and ethical infants.

1938   **Judy Blume:** U.S. author of frank books for adolescents. *Are You There God? It's Me Margaret* (1970) is her candid approach to the onset of puberty.
My own adolescent rebellion came late. Somewhat around the age of 35. I don't recommend waiting till then. Better to drag your parents through it than your kids.

February 13

1825   **Julia Ripley Dorr:** American poet, novelist and essayist. Poems: "Afternoon Songs," "November," "A Red Rose," "A Cathedral Pilgrimage," "Silence," "Darkness" and "Grass-Grown."
Grass grows at last above all graves.

1877   **Sidney Smith:** American cartoonist with *Chicago Tribune* (1911–35). Created "The Gumps" comic strip (1917).
One evil in old age is that, as your time

is come, you think every little illness the beginning of the end. When a man expects to be arrested, every knock at the door is an alarm.

1892   **Robert H. Jackson:** U.S. jurist, lawyer. Associate justice of the Supreme Court. Opposed monopolies. Supported civil liberties. Believed in judicial restraint. Chief counsel at the Nuremberg war crimes trials (1945–46).
The validity of a doctrine does not depend on whose ox it gores.

1903   **Georges Simenon:** Belgian-born French novelist. Created Inspector Maigret. Wrote over three hundred books, including autobiographical works and diaries.
Writing is not a profession but a vocation of unhappiness.

1910   **Margaret Halsey:** U.S. author, wrote travel memoirs *With Malice Towards Some, Some of My Best Friends Are Soldiers* and *Folks at Home.*
Every time I think I've touched bottom as far as boredom is concerned, new vistas of ennui open up.

1918   **Patty Berg:** U.S. Hall of fame golfer. Helped form LPGA. Served as its first president. Won more than eighty pro tournaments.
If I were a man I wouldn't have a half dozen Tom Collinses before going out to play golf, then let profanity substitute for proficiency on the golf course.

1923   **Charles "Chuck" Yeager:** American test pilot. Trained as a fighter pilot, flying many European missions in WWII. First to break the sound barrier in 1953, flying the Bell X-1A two and a half times the speed of sound.
If you want to grow old as a pilot, you've got to know when to push it, and when to back off.

February 14

1401   **Leon Battista Alberti:** Italian architect, poet, art theorist, moral philoso-

pher and mathematician. His architectural works are among the best examples of the pure Classical style. One of the most brilliant figures of the Renaissance.
Men can do all things if they will.

1612   **Samuel Butler:** English poet and satirist. His great mock epic *Hudibras* ridiculed the Puritans. It brought him immense popularity, especially with King Charles II.
A definition is the enclosing of a wilderness of ideas within a wall of words.

1766   **Thomas R. Malthus:** English political economist and clergyman. Pioneer in modern population theory. Anonymously published his "Essay on the Principle of Population."
Population, when unchecked, increases in a geometric ratio. Subsistence only increases in an arithmetical ratio.

1817   **Frederick Douglass:** U.S. abolitionist, orator, journalist. Son of a slave and white father. Bought his freedom. Founded *The North Star,* a newspaper he published for 17 years.
No man can put a chain about the ankle of his fellowman, without at least finding the other end of it about his own neck.

1882   **George Jean Nathan:** American essayist and critic. Founded *The American Mercury* and *American Spectator.*
The artist and censor differ in this wise: that the first is a decent mind in an indecent body and that the second is an indecent mind in a decent body.

1894   **Jack Benny:** U.S. comedian, violinist in vaudeville, films, radio and television. Played a wisecracking miser, but was actually generous and modest. Master of timing. Eternally 39.
I don't deserve this award, but I have arthritis and I don't deserve that either.

1913   **Jimmy Hoffa:** U.S. union leader. President, International Teamster Union (1957–71). Imprisoned for jury-tampering and fraud (1967–71). Pardoned by President Nixon. Disappeared 1975, presumed dead.
I do unto others what they do unto me, only worse.

February 15

1564 **Galileo Galilei:** Italian astronomer, physicist, philosopher. Ran afoul of the Catholic Church for defending the Copernican system, which maintains the earth revolves around the sun and not the other way around. Tried by the Inquisition, he was forced to recant.

You cannot teach a man anything, you can only help him to find it within himself.

1748 **Jeremy Bentham:** English philosopher, jurist, economist and social reformer. Founder of utilitarianism, first systematic effort to describe and evaluate all human acts. Pioneering works: *A Fragment of Government* and *Introduction to the Principles of Morals and Legislation.*

Lawyers are the only persons in whom ignorance of the law is not punished.

1820 **Susan B. Anthony:** U.S. social reformer. Crusader for women's suffrage. Organized International Council of Women (1888) and International Woman Suffrage Alliance (1904) with Elizabeth Stanton.

I always distrust people who know so much about what God wants them to do to their fellows.

1861 **Alfred North Whitehead:** English mathematician, philosopher. Made major contributions to mathematics, logic, philosophy of science and meta-mathematics. Coauthored *Principia Mathematica* with Bertrand Russell.

Civilization advances by extending the number of important operations which we can perform without thinking about them.

1882 **John Barrymore:** "The Great Profile." U.S. stage matinee idol and movie star. Films: *Dr. Jekyll and Mr. Hyde, Don Juan, Grand Hotel* and *Dinner at Eight.*

The trouble with life is that there are so many beautiful women and so little time.

1883 **Sax Rohmer:** Pseudonym of Arthur Sarsfield Ward. English mystery writer. Creator of the sinister Chinese criminal genius Dr. Fu Manchu, featured in many spine-chilling tales.

There is no incidental music to the dramas of real life.

1935 **Susan Brownmiller:** American author, feminist. Wrote best-selling *Against Our Will*, about women and rape.

My purpose in this book has been to give rape its history. Now we must deny it a future.

February 16

1497 **Philip Schwarzerd Melanchton:** German religious leader. *Loci Communes* is the first great Protestant work on dogmatic theology. Succeeded to the leadership of the German Reformation after Luther's death. Wrote guidelines leading to first modern school system in Saxony.

In necessary things, unity; in doubtful things, liberty; in all things, charity.

1822 **Sir Francis Galton:** English anthropologist. Founded modern technique of weather mapping. Devised the system of fingerprint identification. Coined word "eugenics." Studied heredity and color-blindness.

Well-washed and well-combed domestic pets grow dull; they need the stimulus of fleas.

1838 **Henry Adams:** American historian. Son and grandson of presidents, he choose scholarship over politics. Editor and journalist for the *North American Review.* Harvard history professor. Wrote *The Education of Henry Adams.*

A teacher affects eternity; he can never tell where his influence stops.

1876 **George M. Trevelyan:** English historian. Works include *Garibaldi and the Thousand, British History of the Nineteenth Century English Social History.*

Education has provided a vast population able to read but unable to distinguish what is worth reading.

1886 **Van Wyck Brooks:** American critic, biographer. Associated with magazine *The Seven Arts.* Wrote *The Flowering of New England: 1815-1865* (Pulitzer).

Earnest people are often people who habitually look on the serious side of things that have no serious side.

1904   **George Kennan:** U.S. diplomat, historian. Proposed policy of "Containment" in dealing with the Soviet Union after WWII. Pulitzer prizes for *Russia Leaves the War* (1956) and *Memoirs 1925-50* (1967).

A war regarded as inevitable or even probable and therefore much prepared for, has a very good chance of eventually being fought.

1959   **John McEnroe:** Four times number one tennis player in world (1981–84). Nine grand slam titles. Noted for his displays of temper on the court.

The important thing is to learn a lesson every time you lose.

February 17

1864   **Andrew Barton "Banjo" Paterson:** Australian journalist, poet. Wrote words of "Waltzing Matilda," adapted from a traditional ditty which became Australia's national song.

Once a jolly swagman camped by a billabong, / Under the shade of a coolibar tree, / And he sang as he sat and waited for his billy-boil, / You'll come a-waltzing, Matilda, with me.

1874   **Thomas J. Watson:** U.S. industrialist. Converted a financially ailing manufacturer of business machines into the international giant IBM. President and director (1914–49). CEO and chairman of the board (1949–56).

Think ... Think about Appearance, Association, Action, Ambition, Accomplishment.

1879   **Dorothy Canfield Fisher:** American novelist of stories of Vermont life. Wrote *The Montessori Mother, The Brimming Cup* and *Something Old, Something New.* Member of the Book-of-the-Month Club selection committee (1926–51).

A mother is not a person to lean on, but a person to make leaning unnecessary.

1889   **H.L. [Haroldson Lafayette] Hunt:** U.S. oilman. In his lifetime, one of the richest men in the world. Financed "Life Line," an anti-communist radio program.

I didn't go to high school, and I didn't go to grade school either. Education, I think, is for refinement and is probably a liability.

1902   **Marian Anderson:** American contralto, concert artist. First African American to perform a major Met role (1955). U.S. delegate to U.N. (1955). U.S. Congressional Medal (1977). Speaking of racial prejudice:

Sometimes, it's like a hair across your cheek. You can't see it, you can't find it with your fingers, but you keep brushing at it because the feel of it is irritating.

1942   **Huey P. Newton:** U.S. political activist, civil rights leader. Co-founder of Black Panther Party with Bobby Seale. Reason for adopting the name:

The panther is a fierce animal, but he will not attack until he is backed into a corner, then he will strike out.

1963   **Michael Jordan:** Basketball superstar. Led North Carolina to NCAA title (1984). Has two Olympic gold medals (1984, 1992). Led Chicago Bulls to three consecutive NBA titles (1991–93). Left the game to try baseball, then returned to basketball in 1995. Arguably the best basketball player ever.

When I'm on my game, I don't think there's anybody that can stop me.

February 18

1838   **Ernst Mach:** Austrian physicist. His study of airflows revealed a sudden change of airflow over an object moving close to the speed of sound. Unit for speed of sound is named after him.

Physics is experience, arranged in economical order.

1862   **Charles M. Schwab:** U.S. manufacturer. "Boy Wonder" of the steel industry. President of U.S. Steel (1901–3). President of Bethlehem Steel (1903–13). Chairman of the Board (1913-39).

Personality is to a man what perfume is to a flower.

1894   Andrés Segovia: Spanish classical guitarist, teacher. In 1985, awarded the Gold Medal of the Royal Philharmonic Society of London. Reinstated the guitar as a concert instrument. Made many transcriptions for the guitar. Explaining why he maintained such a heavy concert schedule at so an advanced an age:
I will have eternity to rest.

1898   Luis Munroz Marin: Puerto Rican politician, poet. Founder of the Commonwealth of Puerto Rico. First elected governor of Puerto Rico (1948–64).
There is an old saying on the island, that a man must do three thing during his lifetime: plant trees, write books and have sons. I wish, they would plant more trees and write more books.

1922   Helen Gurley Brown: U.S. author, magazine editor. Wrote best-selling *Sex and the Single Girl* (1962). Editor *Cosmopolitan* (1965–).
Never fail to know that if you are doing all the talking, you are boring somebody.

1928   Len Deighton: Leading English author of spy novels. Best sellers: *The Ipcress File, Funeral in Berlin* and *The Billion Dollar Brain.*
In Mexico an air conditioner is called a politician, because it makes a lot of noise but doesn't work very well.

1931   Toni Morrison: American author. Taught at Howard University before becoming a senior editor at Random House. Explores the stories of rural African Americans in novels *Song of Solomon, Tar Baby* and *Beloved,* for which she won a Pulitzer prize in 1988. Nobel Prize winner (1993).
Definition belongs to the definer—not to the defined.

February 19

1473   Nicolaus Copernicus: Polish astronomer. Laid the foundation for modern astronomy by asserting that the earth and the other planets revolved around the sun in individual orbits while spinning on their axes. His findings were met with hostility, as they challenged ancient teachings of Earth as the center of the universe.
Finally we shall place the Sun himself at the center of the Universe.

1717   David Garrick: English actor and theater manager. Dominated the English stage for 30 years in the 18th century. Joint manager of Drury Lane (1747–76). Actors' Garrick Club established in his honor (1831).
Lee others hail the rising sun: / I bow to that whose course is run.

1893   Sir Cedric Hardwicke: English stage and screen actor. Made his name in Shaw's plays and *The Barretts Of Wimpole Street.* Films: *Stanley and Livingstone, Tom Brown's School Days* and *The Winslow Boy.*
Good actors are good because of the things they tell you without talking. When they are talking they are slaves of the dramatist. It is what they can show the audience when they are not talking that reveals the fine actor.

1896   André Breton: French artist, poet, novelist and essayist. Founded Surrealist movement. Wrote three manifestos that made the most important statements of the movement. Editor of *La Révolution surrealiste.* Major novel, *Najda.*
Words make love with each other.

1912   Stan Kenton: American bandleader, arranger, composer. Bands featured precise reed sections and cutting brass sound. Success was enhanced by vocalists Anita O'Day and June Christy. Hits: "Artistry in Rhythm," "Eager Beaver" and "And Her Tears Flowed Like Wine."
Rock 'n' Roll is the kindergarten of jazz.

1917   Carson McCullers: American novelist, short-story writer. Works reflect the sadness of lonely people. Wrote "The Heart Is a Lonely Hunter," "The Member of the Wedding," and "The Ballad of the Sad Cafe."
Once you have lived with another it is a great torture to live alone.

1940   **Smokey Robinson:** U.S. singer, songwriter. Formed "The Miracles," which he left 1972 to do a solo act. Hits: "Tears of a Clown," "The Tracks of My Tears" and "Being with You."
Weed does nothing but cloud your mind and make you think you are something you are not.

February 20

1794   **William Carleton:** Irish novelist. Outstanding observer of peasant life. Most famous work was two series, both entitled, *Traits and Stories of Irish Peasantry* (1830 and 1833).
We arg'ed the thing at breakfast, we arg'ed the thing at tea, / And the more we arg'ed the question the more we didn't agree.

1829   **Joseph Jefferson:** American stage actor, identified with the role of Rip Van Winkle. Appeared on the stage for 72 years.
We are but tenants, and ... shortly the great Landlord will give notice that our lease has expired.

1874   **Mary Garden:** Scottish-born U.S. opera soprano. Considered the greatest singing actress in history. Created the role of Mélisande in Debussy's *Pelléas et Mélisande* at the composer's request. Associated with the Chicago Grand Opera (1910–30). Asked the secret of her youthfulness:
I have never been married.

1887   **Vincent Massey:** Canadian statesman, diplomat. University chancellor. High Commissioner of Canada. Governor-General of Canada. Minister to the United States. Brother of actor Raymond Massey.
What we should have is a Canadian character. Nobody looks his best in somebody else's clothes.

1901   **René Dubos:** French-born U.S. bacteriologist. Discovered tyrothricin, the first commercially produced antibiotic. Had a great concern for the need to protect the environment.

The most important pathological effects of pollution are extremely delayed and indirect.

1902   **Ansel Adams:** American landscape photographer, notable for his technical and artistic innovations in depicting Western wilderness and mountain panoramas, especially the Yosemite in the 1930s.
A picture is usually looked at, seldom looked into.

1924   **Sidney Poitier:** U.S. actor, director. Generally acknowledged as Hollywood's first black movie superstar. Nominated for Oscar for: *The Defiant Ones*; Oscar winner for *Lilies of the Field*.
We all suffer from the preoccupation that their exists ... in the loved one, perfection.

1941   **Buffy Sainte-Marie:** Canadian-born Cree Indian folksinger and writer of songs about her heritage and the cause of peace. Co-wrote "Up Where We Belong." Also wrote "Universal Soldier" and "Until It's Time for You to Go."
The white man wants everyone who isn't white to think white.

February 21

1801   **John Henry Cardinal Newman:** English churchman. Leader of the Oxford Movement. Resigned as Protestant vicar of St. Mary's. Converted to Catholicism. Became a cardinal (1879). Wrote *Catholicism in England* and *The Idea of a University*.
To live is to change, and to be perfect is to have changed often.

1821   **Charles Scribner, Jr.:** U.S. publisher. Founder with Isaac Baker (1846) the New York publishing firm which became Charles Scribner's Sons in 1878. Founder and publisher of *Scribner's* magazine.
Reading is a means of thinking with another person's mind; it forces you to stretch your own.

1895   **Joseph Fields:** U.S. playwright and screenwriter. Collaborated with Jerome Chodorov on successful Broadway musicals,

My Sister Eileen, Junior Miss and *Anniversary Waltz* and with Anita Loos on *Gentlemen Prefer Blondes.*

My advice to writers who are trying to write comedy is to try to have the comedy come from the characters and the situation and not try to work their jokes in.

1903   **Anaïs Nin:** French-born U.S. novelist, diarist. Best known for *The Diary of Anaïs Nin,* journals spanning the years 1931–74, detailing the avant-garde life of Paris and New York and coming to terms with her feminine identity. Novels: *House of Incest* and *A Spy in the House of Love.*

The only abnormality is the incapacity to love.

1907   **W.H. [Wystan Hugh] Auden:** Anglo-American poet, dramatist. Regarded one of the major poets of the 20th century. Called the "Poet of the Thirties" for his prodigious production of poems and literary criticism. Works: *The Age of Anxiety* (Pulitzer), *The Dance of Death* and *Look, Stranger!*

Death is the sound of distant thunder at a picnic.

1927   **Erma Bombeck:** U.S. columnist, author. Syndicated column "At Wit's End" humorously dealt with life of a suburban housewife and mother.

It seemed rather incongruous that in a society of supersophisticated communication, we often suffer from a shortage of listeners.

1936   **Barbara Jordan:** U.S. politician, lawyer. First black woman to serve in Texas legislature in 20th century. U.S. representative (1972–78). Ignited 1976 Democratic National Convention with her keynote speech.

If you're going to play the game properly, you'd better know every rule.

February 22

1732   **George Washington:** First U.S. president. Commander-in-chief of Continental forces during American Revolution. As president he attempted to enlist the ablest men in the country to serve in the government. Warned against the dangers of party politics and foreign entanglements.

There can be no greater error than to expect or calculate upon real favors from nation to nation.

1778   **Rembrandt Peale:** American painter and lithographer. Painted a strong but idealized likeness of George Washington which enjoyed great popularity. His masterpiece is a painting of Thomas Jefferson.

O don't be so sorrowful, darling! / And don't be sorrowful, pray; / Taking the year together, my dear, / There isn't more night than day.

1788   **Arthur Schopenhauer:** German philosopher and author. His chief work *The World as Will and Idea* emphasizes the central role of human will as the creative, primary factor in understanding. His views influenced existentialism and scores of writers and artists, including Wagner, Tolstoy, Proust and Mann.

The two foes of human happiness are pain and boredom.

1810   **Frédéric Chopin:** Polish composer. Creator of a unique romantic style. Moved to Paris where he lived with novelist George Sand (Madame Dudevant) and wrote concertos, sonatas, nocturnes, etudes, mazurkas, polonaises, waltzes and a funeral march.

Every difficulty slurred over will be a ghost to disturb your repose later on.

1819   **James Russell Lowell:** American poet, editor, critic, diplomat. Long poem: "The Vision of Sir Launfal." Chairman of modern languages at Harvard and first editor of *The Atlantic Monthly.*

A compromise is a good umbrella but a poor roof.

1892   **Edna Vincent Millay:** American poet. After Vassar she lived in Greenwich Village. Poetry volumes: *A Few Figs from Thistles* and the Pulitzer Prize–winning *The Harp Weaver and Other Poems.*

My candle burns at both ends, / It will not last the night, / But ah, my foes and oh my friends— / It gives a lovely light.

1900 Luis Buñuel: Spanish-born director. With Salvador Dali scripted surrealistic film, *An Andalusian Dog*. His surrealistic masterpiece *The Golden Age* assaulted Church, Establishment and middle-class morality.
Mystery is the essential element in every work of art.

February 23

1633 Samuel Pepys: English politician, best know for his *Diary*. He met the outstanding personalities of his day. Diary written in shorthand between 1660 and 1669, was deciphered and published in 1825.
A man that cannot sit still ... and cannot say no ... is not fit for business.

1685 George Frideric Handel: German-English composer. Gained a reputation as a keyboard virtuoso and as an operatic composer. Wrote "Water Music." Experimented with oratorios. Best known for the *Messiah*. He believed the "Hallelujah" chorus was divinely inspired.
I did think I did see all Heaven before me—and the great God Himself.

1743 Meyer Rothschild: German moneylender whose business would be expanded by his five sons into the House of Rothschild financial dynasty, first among banking houses of the world.
It requires a great deal of boldness and a great deal of caution to make a great fortune, and when you have got it, it requires ten times as much wit to keep it.

1868 W.E.B. [William Edward Burghardt] Du Bois: U.S. historian, sociologist and civil rights leader. Founder of National Negro Committee which became National Association for the Advancement of Colored People (1909). Joined Communist Party (1961), moved to Ghana, renouncing U.S. citizenship.
Men must not only know, they must act.

1883 Karl Theodor Jaspers: German psychologist, philosopher. A founder of modern existentialism. Stripped of teaching position at Heidelberg by the Nazis, who banned his works. He stayed in Germany. Awarded Goethe Prize (1947) for his uncompromising stand. Wrote *The Great Philosophers* and *The Future of Mankind*.
The beginning of modern science is also the beginning of calamity.

1904 William L. Shirer: American author, journalist. CBS broadcaster of momentous events in Europe (1937–40). Wrote a column for *New York Herald*. Blacklisted during the McCarthy era. Wrote *The Rise and Fall of the Third Reich*.
Perhaps America will one day go fascist democratically by popular vote.

1929 Leslie Halliwell: British journalist, cinema manager, television program buyer, author of much admired and highly opinionated *Halliwell's Filmgoers Companion* and *Halliwell's Movie Guide*.
Cynics have claimed there are only six basic plots. **Frankenstein** *and* **My Fair Lady** *are really the same story.*

February 24

1500 Charles V: King of Spain (1516-50). Holy Roman emperor (1519–56). Last emperor to pursue the medieval ideal of universal empire and the last to be crowned by the pope.
To God I speak Spanish, to women Italian, to men French and to my horse—German.

1824 George William Curtis: U.S. essayist, orator and editor. Began the "Editor's Easy Chair" papers in *Harper's Monthly*. Principal lead writer for *Harper's Weekly*.
My advice to a young man seeking deathless fame would be to espouse an unpopular cause and devote his life to it.

1836 Winslow Homer: American painter. Began his career as lithographer and an illustrator for magazines such as *Harper's Weekly*. Moved to Protus Neck, an isolated fishing village on the U.S. eastern seaboard where he painted maritime scenes for the rest of his life.

Never put more than two waves in a picture, it's fussy.

1852   George Moore: Irish novelist, playwright, poet and critic. Introduced naturalism to the Victorian novel. Wrote *Esther Waters* and his autobiographical trilogy *Hail and Farewell.*
A man travels the world in search of what he needs and returns home to find it.

1885   Chester W. Nimitz: U.S. admiral. Commanded U.S. naval forces in Pacific, WWII. Directed battles of Coral Sea and Midway. Directed landings on the Solomons, Gilberts, Marshalls, Marianas, Philippines, Iwo Jima and Okinawa. Speaking of the marines at Iwo Jima:
Uncommon valor was a common virtue.

1927   Mark Lane: Controversial U.S. lawyer and author. Wrote *Rush to Judgement,* about the Warren Commission findings on the assassination of Kennedy. Anti–Vietnam War activist.
Do not weep for them, America. Your children, far braver than you, were a moment in the conscience of man.

1928   Michael Harrington: American social scientist, author. Best known for landmark study, *The Other America,* in which he showed that growing affluence creates a growing subculture of poverty.
Poverty is expensive to maintain.

February 25

1841   Pierre Auguste Renoir: French painter. Leader and founder of the French Impressionist movement. Used reds, orange and gold to portray nudes in sunlight.
You've got to be a fool to want to stop the march of time.

1866   Benedetto Croce: Italian philosopher, statesman, critic and historian. Made major contributions to idealistic aesthetics. Minister of education (1920–21). Opposed the totalitarianism of Mussolini. Forced to resign his professorship at Naples.
Philosophy removes from religion all reason for existing.

1873   Enrico Caruso: Italian operatic lyric tenor. For dramatic effect, he often resorted to the "coup de glotte," which became known as the "Caruso sob." Excelled in realistic Italian operas such as *Tosca* and *Pagliacci.*
[A great singer should have] a big chest, a big mouth, ninety per cent memory, ten per cent intelligence, lot of hard work and something in the heart.

1888   John Foster Dulles: U.S. government official, diplomat. U.S. delegate to U.N. (1946–50). U.S. Secretary of state (1953–59). Prime architect of U.S.'s containment policy of communism.
If you are scared to go to the brink you are lost.

1904   Adelle Davis: American nutritionist expert, author. Crusader for the use of natural foods. Wrote *Let's Cook It Right* and *Let's Eat to Keep Fit.*
We are indeed much more than what we eat, but what we eat can nevertheless help us to be more than what we are.

1917   Anthony Burgess: Pen name of John Anthony Burgess Wilson. English novelist, critic and composer. Major characters are often comic victims. He has a violent view of the future. Novels: *The Long Day Wanes, A Clockwork Orange* and *Earthly Powers.*
The possession of a book becomes a substitute for reading it.

1925   Lisa Kirk: U.S. supper club and Broadway stage actress and singer. Famed for rendition "I'm Always True to You, Darling, in My Fashion" from *Kiss Me Kate.*
A gossip is one who talks to you about others; a bore is one who talks to you about himself; and a brilliant conversationalist is one who talks to you about yourself.

February 26

1564   Christopher Marlowe: English dramatist, poet. Established blank verse in drama. Wrote *Tamburlaine the Great, The Tragical History of Dr. Faustus* and

The Famous Tragedy of the Rich Jew of Malta.

There is no sin but ignorance.

1802 **Victor Hugo:** French poet, novelist, dramatist. Leader of Romantic movement in France. Elected to the Constituent Assembly (1848). Exiled by Napoleon III. Works: *Les Contemplations, The Hunchback of Notre Dame* and his greatest novel *Les Misérables.*

There is always more misery among the lower classes than there is humanity in the higher.

1852 **J. H. [John Harvey] Kellogg:** U.S. surgeon. Founder of the health food industry with his industrialist brother W.K. (Will Keith) Kellogg. Developed a process of making a nourishing breakfast of corn flakes.

The tobacco business is a conspiracy against womanhood and manhood. It owes its origin to that scoundrel, Sir Walter Raleigh, who was likewise the founder of American slavery.

1857 **Émile Coué:** French pharmacist and psychotherapist. Pioneer of "auto-suggestion." His system became world famous as "Couéism," expressed in his famous formula:

Every day, in every way, I'm getting better and better.

1916 **Jackie Gleason:** U.S. actor, comedian. Found his niche in television's "The Honeymooners" and "The Jackie Gleason Show." Tony Award for Broadway's *Take Me Along.* Oscar nominated for *The Hustler.* Other films: *Requiem for a Heavyweight* and *Soldier in the Rain.*

Thin people are beautiful but fat people are adorable.

1921 **Betty Hutton:** "The Blonde Bombshell." U.S. actress and singer. Song hits: "Murder, He Said" and "Doctor, Lawyer, Indian Chief." Got her film break as a replacement for ailing Judy Garland in *Annie Get Your Gun.* Other films: *The Miracle of Morgan's Creek* and *The Greatest Show on Earth.*

Nobody loved me unless I bought them, so I bought everybody.

1928 **Fats Domino:** Rhythm and blues piano-playing singer, influenced by Fats Waller. Hits: "Ain't That a Shame" and "Blueberry Hill." Rock and Roll Hall of Fame (1986). Grammy's Lifetime Achievement Award (1987).

A lot of fellows nowadays have a B.A., M.A. or Ph.D. Unfortunately they don't have a J.O.B.

February 27

1807 **Henry Wadsworth Longfellow:** American poet, translator, college professor at Harvard. Poems: "The Wreck of the Hesperus," "The Village Blacksmith," "The Children's Hour," "Evangeline," "Hiawatha" and "The Courtship of Miles Standish."

All things must change to something new, to something strange.

1886 **Hugo L. Black:** U.S. senator from Alabama (1927–37). Supreme Court associate justice (1937–71). Wrote opinion forbidding prayers in schools.

The layman's constitutional view is that what he likes is constitutional and that which he doesn't like is unconstitutional.

1896 **Arthur William Radford:** American admiral. Engaged in the Gilbert and Marshall Islands campaigns during WWII. Chairman, Joint Chiefs of Staff (1953–57).

A decision is the action an executive must take when he has information so incomplete that the answer does not suggest itself.

1902 **John Steinbeck:** U.S. novelist, short-story writer. Pulitzer Prize (1940), Nobel Prize (1962). His major work, *The Grapes of Wrath,* made an eloquent plea for human values and common justice. Also wrote *Tortilla Flat, Of Mice and Men, East of Eden* and *The Wayward Bus.*

It is the nature of man as he grows older ... to protest against change, particularly change for the better.

1912 **Lawrence Durrell:** Anglo-Irish novelist, poet, playwright. His reputation was made with the publication of *Justine,* the first novel of *The Alexandra*

Quartet, which also included: *Balthazar*, *Mountolive* and *Clea*.

History is the endless repetition of the wrong way of living.

1932 Elizabeth Taylor: Beautiful English-born actress. Nominated for Oscars for *Raintree County*, *Cat on a Hot Tin Roof* and *Suddenly Last Summer*. Won for *Butterfield 8* and *Who's Afraid of Virginia Woolf?* Married eight times, including twice to actor Richard Burton.

You find out who your real friends are when you're involved in a scandal.

1934 Ralph Nader: American political activist, writer. Founder of consumer rights movement in the United States. Wrote *Unsafe at Any Speed*, about GM cars (1965).

The speed of exit of a civil servant is directly proportional to the quality of his service.

February 28

1533 Michel de Montaigne: French moralist. Creator of the personal essay. Wrote three volumes of essays, 1580, 1588, 1595. Advocated humanistic morality.

The greatest thing in the world is to know how to be one's own.

1797 Mary Lyon: U.S. educator. Founded Mt. Holyoke College, first women's college in the United States (1837).

Trust in God—and do something.

1823 Joseph Ernest Renan: French skeptical writer, philosopher and historian. Abandoned traditional Catholic faith after studying Greek and Hebrew biblical criticism. Author of controversial *The Life of Jesus*.

The agnostic's prayer: O Lord, if there is a Lord, save my soul, if I have a soul.

1895 Marcel Pagnol: French playwright, screenwriter, film director. Widely known for his witty trilogy about life in Marseilles—*Marius*, *Fanny* and *César*.

The most difficult secret for a man to keep is his own opinion of himself.

1901 Linus Pauling: U.S. chemist. Awarded Nobel Prize for chemistry (1954). Major advocate of nuclear disarmament and end to nuclear testing. Nobel Peace Prize (1962). Advocated major doses of vitamin C to maintain health.

Science is the search for truth—it is not a game in which one tries to beat his opponent, to do harm to others.

1915 P.B. [Peter Brian] Medawar: British biologist. Co-winner of the 1960 Nobel Prize for medicine with Sir Mac-Farlane Burnet for the discovery of acquired immunological tolerance.

The human mind treats a new idea the way the body treats a strange protein; it rejects it.

1941 Alice May Brock: U.S. writer, restaurateur. Owner of "Alice's Restaurant," made famous in a song by Arlo Guthrie and a movie of the same name.

Tomatoes and oregano make it Italian, wine and tarragon make it French. Sour cream makes it Russian; lemon and cinnamon make it Greek. Soy sauce makes it Chinese; garlic makes it good.

February 29

1468 Pope Paul III: Pope from 1534 to 1549. Member of the circle of Lorenzo de Medici. Summoned the Council of Trent to reform the Church. Guilty of lax personal morality and gross nepotism. Threatened an uncooperative Michelangelo:

There is no redemption from hell!

1731 Charles Churchill: English poet, wit and satirist. Noted for his savage onslaughts of his critics. Wrote lampoons and polemical satires in heroic couplets, "The Rosciad," "The Apology," "The Ghost" and "The Prophecy of Famine."

Few have reason, most have eyes.

1736 Ann Lee: Known as "Mother Lee." English-born mystic and religious leader. Founder of American sect of Shakers at Niskayuna, near Albany, New York.

It is not I that speak, it is Christ who dwells in me.

1792 Gioacchino Rossini: Italian opera composer. Wrote 39 operas, including: *The Barber of Seville* and *William Tell.* A superb craftsman who created atmospheres of excitement for his audiences.
Give me a laundry list and I will set it to music.

1896 William Wellman: U.S. director. Used his experience as an Ace pilot in WWI with Lafayette Escadrille to direct first Oscar winning film, *Wings.*
Epitaph for the directors who fell at the crossroads of the world: date, long ago; Leaving It to Posterity to Know the Truth.

1904 John "Pepper" Martin: U.S. baseball player. One of the leaders of the *Gas House Gang* of St. Louis Cardinals in the thirties.
You can take an ol' mule and run him and feed him and train him and get him in the best shape of his life, but you ain't going to win the Kentucky Derby.

1908 Balthus [Comte Balthazar Klossowski De Rola]: French artist of Polish descent. Self-taught painter, noted for doll-like portraits and interiors with adolescent girls.
Some say my paintings are sinister and abnormal. But I have had the same vision since I was four. Perhaps that is abnormal.

March 1

1837 William Dean Howells: American novelist, editor, critic and poet. His association with *Harper's* magazine (1886-91) made him king of critics in America, writing an "Easy Chair" column (1900-20). Author of *Criticism and Fiction, Years of My Youth* and *My Mark Twain.*
Some people can stay longer in an hour than others can in a week.

1848 Augustus Saint-Gaudens: Irish-born American sculptor. Influenced by the Italian Renaissance. Foremost sculptor of his time. Major works: *Lincoln* in Lincoln Park, Chicago, and the equestrian statue of General Sherman in New York's Central Park.
What garlic is to salad, insanity is to art.

1858 George Simmel: German philosopher and sociologist. Wrote essays on sociological methodology, metaphysics and aesthetics. He is instrumental in establishing sociology as a social science. Books: *Philosophy of Money* and *On Women, Sexuality and Love.*
He is educated who knows how to find out what he doesn't know.

1880 Lytton Strachey: English biographer. Began writing career as a critic with *Landmarks in French Literature.* Member of the Bloomsbury Group. Biographies: *Eminent Victorians, Queen Victoria* and *Elizabeth and Essex: A Tragic History.*
Statistics are mendacious truths.

1914 Ralph Waldo Ellison: American writer. Inspired by Richard Wright to turn to writing. Works show a major concern with identity. His literary reputation rests on first, and only, novel, *Invisible Man,* which won National Book Award (1953); Presidential Medal of Freedom (1969).
When a child has no sense of how he should fit into society around him, he is culturally deprived.

1917 Dinah Shore: U.S. singer and actress. Films include: *Thank Your Lucky Stars* and *Up in Arms.* Hit songs: "I'll Walk Alone" and "Buttons and Bows." Television's "Dinah Shore Show" won five Emmys in fifties.
Trouble is a part of your life, and if you don't share it, you don't give the person who loves you a chance to love you enough.

1935 Judith Rossner: American novelist. Best known for her best-selling novel *Looking for Mr. Goodbar,* based on the murder of a young New York woman. Also wrote *Attachments.*
A lie was something that hadn't happened but might just as well have.

March 2

1793 Sam Houston: U.S. politician, soldier, lawyer. Leader of fight with Mexico for control of Texas. President of Republic of Texas (1836-38, 1841-44).

Democrat Texas senator (1846–59), governor (1959–61).
There is not an American on earth but what loves land.

1829 **Carl Schurz:** German-born U.S. statesman, journalist and orator. Political reformer who led the Liberal Republicans and the Mugwumps. U.S. senator from Missouri (1869–75). U.S. secretary of the Interior (1877–81). Editor, *New York Evening Post* (1881–84).
Our country, right or wrong! When right to be kept right; when wrong, to be put right.

1876 **Pope Pius XII:** Italian Roman Catholic pope (1939–58). Remained neutral during WWII. Vigorously opposed communism.
Labor is not merely the fatigue of the body without sense or value: nor is it merely a humiliating servitude. It is a service of God, the vigor and fullness of human life, the gauge of eternal rest.

1880 **Ivar Kreuger:** Swedish industrialist and financier. Cornered world's match trade through irregular practices. Committed suicide 1932.
But what certainty is there about money, which after all, holds all the world together? It depends on the good will of a few capitalists to keep to the agreement that one metal is worth more than another.

1904 **Theodor Seuss Geisel:** Dr. Seuss. American author and illustrator of immensely popular humorous children's books including *The Cat in the Hat, Green Eggs and Ham* and *The Grinch Who Stole Christmas.* He became synonymous with learning to read.
Adults are obsolete children and the hell with them.

1931 **Mikhail Gorbachev:** U.S.S.R. political leader. Secretary general of U.S.S.R. from 1985 until December 25, 1991, when it was dismantled. Initiated policies of perestroika (restructuring Soviet economy) and glasnost (openness of information). Awarded Nobel Peace Prize (1990).
What the 21st century will be like

depends on whether we learn the lessons of the 20th century and avoid repeating its worst mistakes.

1931 **Tom Wolfe:** Popular name of journalist, pop-critic and novelist Thomas Kennerley Wolfe. Proponent of the New Journalism. Much of his work first appeared in *Rolling Stone* magazine. Coined phrase "radical chic." Wrote *The Electric Kool-Aid Acid Test* and *The Bonfire of the Vanities.*
A cult is a religion with no political power.

March 3

1652 **Thomas Otway:** English dramatist and poet. After failing as an actor he turned to writing. Translated Racine and Molière. Wrote Restoration comedies. His masterpiece is *Venice Preserved.*
Ambition is a lust that is never quenched, but grows more inflamed and madder by enjoyment.

1756 **William Godwin:** English novelist, political theorist. Leading radical of 18th century. Husband of Mary Wollstonecraft and father of Mary Shelley. His masterpiece, *The Adventures of Caleb Williams.*
The ... source of crime is ... one man's possessing in abundance that of which another man is destitute.

1847 **Alexander Graham Bell:** Scottish born–U.S. / Canadian inventor. First to patent and commercially exploit the telephone. Founded *Science* journal. Also invented the photophone and the graphophone. Pioneer in aeronautics.
Great discoveries and improvements invariably involve the cooperation of many minds. I may be given credit for having blazed the trail but when I look at the subsequent developments I feel the credit is due to others rather than myself.

1868 **Alain:** Pen name of Émile Chartier. French philosopher, essayist and teacher. Like Socrates, he tried to provoke thought by stimulating and shocking men's minds. His writings were mostly in the form of "propos," short aphoristic essays like fables or parables.

Nothing is more dangerous than an idea, when you have only one idea.

1895 **Matthew Ridgeway:** U.S. army general. Directed airborne assaults on Europe (1943–45). Commander of U.N. forces in Korea (1951–52). Supreme commander Allied Forces in Europe (1952-53).

The more you sweat in peace, the less you bleed in war.

1911 **Jean Harlow:** U.S. actress. The platinum blonde beauty proved to be a deft comedienne in *Red-Headed Woman* and *Dinner at Eight.* The original blonde bombshell died at 26.

Men like me because I don't wear a brassiere. Women like me because I don't look like a girl who would steal a husband. At least not for long.

1962 **Jackie Joyner-Kersee:** Track and field two-time world champion in both long jump (1987, 1991) and heptathlon (1987, 1993). Won Olympic gold in 1988 and 1992. Sullivan Award winner (1986). Only woman to be named *Sporting News* "Man" of the Year.

I always had something to shoot for each year; to jump one inch further.

March 4

1745 **Charles Dibdin:** British composer, actor, theatrical manager. Appeared in a popular series of one-man musical entertainments. Wrote over 1,000 songs, including "Snug Little Island."

Then trust me there's nothing like drinking / So pleasant on this side of the grave; / It keeps the unhappy from thinking, / And makes e'en the valiant more brave.

1880 **Channing Pollock:** American drama critic and dramatist. Wrote 30 plays, including *Such a Little Queen, Roads to Destiny* and *Mr. Moneypenny.* Also wrote the song, "My Man," made famous by Fanny Brice.

A critic is a legless man who teaches running.

1888 **Knute Rockne:** U.S. football player and coach. Career record at Notre Dame, 105-12-5 in 13 years. His teams won three consensus national championships (1924, 1929, 1930). Killed in plane crash (1931).

Show me a good and gracious loser and I'll show you a failure.

1913 **John Garfield:** Intense U.S. stage and film actor. Forerunner of James Dean, Marlon Brando and Paul Newman. Oscar nominated for *Four Daughters* and *Body and Soul.*

Hollywood dangles a fortune at you, and you get softened. Money seeps through. You begin to step up the pace for more money. Before you know it, you're rich and a failure.

1932 **Miriam Makeba:** South African singer. Leading singer of African-jazz music. Hit: "Pata Pata." Among her five husbands were Hugh Masekela and Stokely Carmichael.

There are three things I was born with in this world, and there are three things I will have until the day I die: hope, determination and song.

1934 **Jane Goodall:** British anthropologist. Known for her years of work with and study of African chimpanzees.

The male [chimp] has no part in family life, but the bond between a mother and her offspring is strong until the young are mature. If the mother is killed, an older sister will often "babysit" with her orphaned younger siblings.

1936 **Jim Clark:** Scottish auto racer. Two-time Formula One world champion. Won Indy 500 (1965). Killed in a car crash (1968).

When you are a racer, there isn't time to worry about the dangers.

March 5

1133 **Henry II:** King of England (1154–89). One of the most powerful and respected monarchs. Had a falling out with his friend Thomas à Becket whom he had appointed his chancellor archbishop. They clashed over clerical privileges. In a rage Henry uttered the words that four knights used as a pretext to murder Becket in his cathedral.

Who will free me from this turbulent priest?

1639   **Charles Sedley:** English poet, dramatist, courtier and member of parliament. Prominent member of the group of court wits called "the merry gang." Best known works: "Bellamira," "The Grumbler" and "The Mulberry Garden."

She deceiving, I believing; what need lovers wish for more?

1870   **Frank Norris:** American novelist and journalist. On the staff of "The Wave," San Francisco, *McClure's Magazine* and Doubleday, Page. Wrote *McTeague, The Octopus* and *The Pit.*

The People have a right to the Truth as they have a right to life, liberty and the pursuit of happiness.

1887   **Heitor Villa-Lobos:** Brazilian composer, music educator. Proponent of Brazilian folk music. Wrote more than 1400 works including: "Bachianas Brasileiras" and "Choros."

Happy is one who lives in this holy land with no chosen race nor preferred creed.

1891   **Chic Johnson:** U.S. comic. Former ragtime pianist. In 1914 teamed with Ole Olson in a popular vaudeville comedy act. Their biggest success was *Hellzapoppin'*, a mad, nearly surrealistic film version of their Broadway hit.

And may you laugh as long as you live.

1908   **Rex Harrison:** English stage and film actor. An adroit master of "black-tie" comedy. Marvelous both on stage and screen as Prof. Henry Higgins in *My Fair Lady*, for which he won an Oscar. Other films: *Blithe Spirit, The Rake's Progress* and *The Ghost and Mrs. Muir.*

Tomorrow is just a fiction of today.

1922   **Pier Paolo Pasolini:** Italian director, screenwriter, novelist. Films: *Teroma, The Gospel According to St. Matthew* and *Accatone!*

The power of consumer goods ... has been

engendered by the so-called liberal and progressive demands of freedom, and, by appropriating them, has emptied them of their meaning, and changed their nature.

March 6

1475   **Michelangelo (Buonarroti):** Italian sculptor, painter, architect and poet of the Renaissance. One of greatest and most influential artists of all time. Sculpting: *Pietà, David* and *Moses.* Painted his masterpiece on ceiling of Sistine Chapel (1508–12), and *Last Judgment* on end wall (1542).

The more the marble wastes, the more the statue grows.

1483   **Francesco Guicciardii:** Italian historian and diplomat. Wrote *Storia d'Italia*, a dispassionate monument of Italian historiography

Advice is less necessary to the wise than to fools; but the wise derive most advantage from it.

1806   **Elizabeth Barrett Browning:** English poet. Wife of Robert Browning. Works: *Sonnets from the Portuguese, The Seraphim and Other Poems* and *Poems Before Congress.*

God answers sharp and sudden on some prayers, / And thrusts the thing we have prayed for in our face, / A gauntlet with a gift in it.

1831   **General Philip Sheridan:** Union army general. Commanded Army of the Shenandoah (1864–65). Cut off Robert E. Lee's line of retreat at Appomattox. His assessment of his assignment as a young officer:

If I owned Texas and Hell, I would rent out Texas and live in Hell.

1885   **Ring Lardner:** American humorist, short-story writer of satirical tales of American life in early 20th century. Had an infallible ear for vernacular. Collection of stories: *You Know Me, Al* and *Guillible's Travels.*

"Are you lost, daddy?" I asked tenderly. "Shut up," he explained.

1920 **Roger Price:** American publisher and comedian. Creator of "Doodles." Founder of Price-Stern-Sloan Publishers.
Democracy demands that all of its citizens begin the race even. Egalitarianism insists that they all finish first.

1926 **Alan Greenspan:** U.S. government official. Chairman Federal Reserve System. Controller of the nation's money. Sees it as his obligation to control inflation.
If I seem unduly clear to you, you must have misunderstood what I said.

March 7

1849 **Luther Burbank:** U.S. botanist. Pioneer in improving food plants through grafting and hybridization. Developed new potato, new varieties of plums and berries, new flowers.
Men should stop fighting among themselves and start fighting insects.

1850 **Tomáš Masaryk:** Czech statesman, philosopher, patriot. Chief founder and first president of Czechoslovak Republic (1918–35). Instituted extensive land reform and tried to reconcile church and state.
Dictators always look good until the last minute.

1875 **Maurice Ravel:** French composer. Known for Impressionist style. Composed scintillating and dynamic music. Made masterful use of wind instruments and unusual percussion effects. Works include "Daphnis et Chloe," "La Valse" and "Bolero."
Music, I feel must be emotional first and intellectual second.

1888 **William L. Laurence:** Russian-born journalist. Science writer for *New York Times*. Books: *Dawn Over Zero: The Story of the Atomic Bomb* and *New Frontiers of Science*. Pulitzer Prize for reporting (1937, 1946).
And just at that instance there rose from the bowels of the earth a light not of this world, the light of many suns in one.

1909 **Anna Magnani:** Earthy Italian actress of international films. Oscar for *The Rose Tattoo*. Nominated for *Wild Is the Wind*. Others: *Open City* and *Ways of Love*.
Great passions don't exist; they are liar's fantasies. What do exist are little loves that may last for a short or longer while.

1930 **Antony Armstrong-Jones:** Earl of Snowden. English photographer, known for his celebrity photographs. Ex-husband of Britain's Princess Margaret.
I have learned only two things are necessary to keep one's wife happy. First, let her think she is having her own way. Second, let her have it.

1938 **Janet Guthrie:** Auto racer. First woman to qualify and race at the Indianapolis 500 (1977). Placed ninth at Indy (1978). When her strength for the sport was questioned, she observed:
You drive the car, you don't carry it.

March 8

1788 **William Hamilton:** Scottish metaphysician and teacher. Exerted a remarkable influence over the thought of the younger generation in Scotland. Main work, *Lectures on Metaphysics and Logic*, was published posthumously.
On earth there is nothing great but man; in man there is nothing great but mind.

1799 **Simon Cameron:** U.S. newspaper owner, editor, political boss. U.S. senator from Pennsylvania. Lincoln's secretary of war (1861–62). Minister plenipotentiary to Russia (1862–63).
An honest politician is one who, when he is bought, stays bought.

1841 **Oliver Wendell Holmes, Jr.:** American jurist, son of the celebrated author of the same name. Appointed to U.S. Supreme Court (1902). Known as "The Great Dissenter" because of his eloquent dissents on First and Fourth Amendment cases.
Life is an end in itself, and the only question as to whether it is worth living is whether you have enough of it.

1859 **Kenneth Grahame:** Scottish essayist, author. Fame rests on the children's classic *The Wind in the Willow*, with its quaint riverside characters, Rat, Mole, Badger and Toad.
As a rule, indeed, grown-up people are fairly correct on matters of fact; it is in the higher gift of imagination that they are so sadly to seek.

1888 **Stuart Chase:** American author and economist. Wrote *The Tragedy of Waste, A New Deal, The Tyranny of Words* and *The Proper Study of Mankind*.
Democracy ... is a condition where people believe that other people are as good as they are.

1890 **George M. Humphrey:** U.S. secretary of the treasury (1953–57). Board chairman of the National Steel Corporation. Believed in the trickle-down theory of economics.
It's a terribly hard job to spend a billion dollars and get your money's worth.

1909 **Claire Trevor:** U.S. stage and screen actress. Often played cynical, tough girls with hearts-of-gold. Oscar nominated for *Dead End*, won the award for *Key Largo*.
What a holler would ensue if people had to pay the minister as much to marry them as they have to pay a lawyer to get them a divorce.

March 9

1606 **Edmund Waller:** English poet and politician. Noted for contribution to the development of the heroic couplet. Poems: "Sacharissa" and "Go, Lovely Rose." Barely escaped execution plotting in behalf of Charles I against parliament.
To man, that was in th' evening made, / Stars gave the first delight; / Admiring, in the gloomy shade, / Those little drops of light.

1763 **William Cobbett:** English essayist, journalist, radical politician and agriculturist. Champion of the poor. His writings embody the history of the common people between the 18th century revolutions and the dawn of the Victorian era. Works: "Rural Rides" and "History of the Reformation."
To be poor and independent is very nearly an impossibility.

1824 **A. Leland Stanford:** U.S. financier, philanthropist. President and director, Central Pacific railroad (1863–93). California governor (1861–63). U.S. senator (1885–93). Founded Stanford University (1885).
The advantages of wealth are greatly exaggerated.

1881 **Ernest Bevin:** English union leader, politician. As minister of labor (1940–45), mobilized manpower for WWII. Foreign minister (1945–51). Helped lay the basis for NATO.
There has never been a war yet which if the facts had been put calmly before the ordinary folks, could not have been prevented. The common man is the great protection against war.

1892 **Victoria Sackville-West:** English poet and novelist. Maintained her marriage to diplomat Harold Nicolson despite both their homosexual affairs. Wrote *The Land, The Edwardians* and *No Signposts in the Sea*.
I have come to the conclusion, after many years of sometimes sad experience, that you cannot come to any conclusion at all.

1918 **Mickey Spillane:** U.S. writer. His Mike Hammer, private-eye novels *I, the Jury* and *My Gun Is Quick*, emphasized sex and violence.
A writer is someone who always sells. An author is one who writes a book that makes a big splash.

1943 **Bobby Fischer:** U.S. chess master. First American to hold world chess title, defeating Boris Spassky, 1972. Temperamental, controversial and immodest.
Once you think that your own mind is not your friend anymore ... you are on your way to insanity.

March 10

1503 **Ferdinand I:** Holy Roman Emperor from 1558. Faced the threat of the encroachment of the Ottoman Empire led by Syleyman II, the Magnificent, into Europe. He also sought to revive Catholicism in Eastern Europe.
Let justice be done, though the world perish.

1772 **Friedrich Von Schlegel:** German romantic poet, critic. Defined romantic poetry as "progressive universal poetry." Advocated free love in novel *Lucinde*. Published pioneering work on Sanskrit and Indo-Germanic linguistics. Books: *Philosophy of History* and *History of Literature.*
The historian is a prophet in reverse.

1858 **Henry Watson Fowler:** English lexicographer. With brother F.G. Fowler wrote *The King's English*, 1906. Compiled dictionaries based on the *Oxford English Dictionary.* Wrote: *A Dictionary of Modern English Usage*, 1926.
Prefer geniality to grammar.

1892 **Arthur Honegger:** French-born Swiss composer. Member of Les Six, a group of Parisian composers. Best Known works: *Pacific 231, King David* and *Joan of Arc at the Stake.*
There is no doubt that the first requirement for a composer is to be dead.

1918 **Heywood Hale Broun:** American sportswriter and actor. Son of U.S. journalist Heywood Broun.
Sports do not build character. They reveal it.

1940 **David Rabe:** American playwright. Made his reputation with *Sticks and Bones* and *The Basic Training of Pavlo Hummel.*
Nothing, not even writing, is as completely fulfilling as being successful in athletics. ... Like a writer, an athlete knows what real pain is.

1958 **Sharon Stone:** Sexy blonde film actress. Her fame primarily rests on her role in *Basic Instinct* as a underwearless writer and ice-pick murderer.
Women are taught to manipulate with femininity. I've learned to get what I want by being direct and fearless.

March 11

1544 **Torquasto Tasso:** Italian poet. Wrote romantic epic "Rinaldo" at 18. His masterpiece, "Gerusalemme Liberta," is the epic tale of the capture of Jerusalem during the first crusade.
Any time that is not spent on love is wasted.

1890 **Vannevar Bush:** U.S. electrical engineer. Built first analog computer (1925). Instrumental in founding Manhattan Project, which developed fission bomb.
It is a man's mission to learn to understand.

1903 **Dorothy Schiff:** U.S. publisher. Director *New York Post* (1939–42). Owner, president and publisher from 1943.
Taxes seem to me to be far less demoralizing than private charities. I am glad to be taxed because it is the least devastating way to meet social needs both for the underprivileged and the overprivileged.

1916 **Harold Wilson:** English Labor politician, statesman and economist. Prime minister (1964–70 and 1974–76). His government's economic plans were undermined by the balance-of-payments crisis. Abroad he was unsuccessful in an attempt to impose sanctions against supremacist Rhodesia.
A week is a long time in politics.

1926 **Ralph Abernathy:** U.S. civil rights leader, clergyman. Succeeded Martin Luther King as president of the Southern Christian Leadership Conference.
I'm sick and tired of black and white people of good intent giving aspirin to a society that is dying of a cancerous disease.

1931 **Rupert Murdoch:** Controversial Australian publisher. Owned British and American newspapers, including *The Times of London, New York Post* and *Boston Herald.*

Newspapers don't change tastes. They reflect taste.

1934   Sam Donaldson: ABC news correspondent. Appears on "Prime Time Live." Famous for shouting questions to passing presidents.
The questions don't do the damage. Only the answers do.

March 12

1554   Richard Hooker: English theologian. Author of the *Laws of Ecclesiastical Polity* (1593–97), which anticipates the common consent grounds for government of Locke and Rousseau.
Change is not made without inconvenience, even from worse to better.

1672   Sir Richard Steele: Irish-born British essayist, dramatist and politician. Known for his writings in the periodicals *The Tatler* and *The Spectator*. His works are the beginning of the domestic novel.
Reading is to the mind what exercise is to the body.

1890   Vaslav Nijinsky: Russian dancer. One of the world's greatest ballet dancers. Created roles in *Les Sylphides, Le Spectre de la Rose* and *Scheherazade*. Choreographed *The Afternoon of a Faun,* and *The Rite of Spring.*
God does not want men to overtax themselves. He wants men to be happy.

1922   Jack Kerouac: American novelist, poet. His works *On the Road* and *The Subterraneans* epitomized what he named the "Beat Generation," a label he later regretted and repudiated.
I don't know. I don't care. And it doesn't make any difference.

1928   Edward Albee: American playwright. Leading exponent of the "Theater of the Absurd." Best known for *The Zoo Story, The American Dream* and *Who's Afraid of Virginia Woolf?*
Sometimes it's necessary to go a long distance out of the way in order to come back a short distance correctly.

1932   Andrew Young: American political leader. Ambassador to U.N. (1977–79). Mayor of Atlanta (1982–92). Awarded French Legion of Honor (1982).
Influence is like a savings account. The less you use it, the more you've got.

1946   Liza Minnelli: U.S. singer, dancer, actress. Multi-talented daughter of Judy Garland and director Vincente Minnelli. Won Oscar for *Cabaret* (1972).
Reality is something you rise above.

March 13

1733   Joseph Priestley: English chemist, clergyman. Study of gases resulted in discovery of ammonia, sulphur dioxide and oxygen.
In completing one discovery we never fail to get an imperfect knowledge of others of which we could have no idea before, so that we cannot solve one doubt without creating several new ones.

1872   Willie Keeler: "Wee Willie." Baltimore, Brooklyn and New York National League outfielder. Career batting average of .341. Led National League in batting (1894–98). Member of the Hall of Fame (1939). His hitting advice:
Keep your eye on the ball and hit 'em where they ain't.

1884   Sir Hugh Walpole: New Zealand–born English novelist. Wrote short stories, criticisms, essays, travel books and plays. Novels: *The Secret City, The Cathedral* and *The Herries Chronicle.*
The whole secret of life is to be interested in one thing profoundly and in a thousand other things well.

1886   Jean Starr Untermeyer: U.S. poet. Author of "Growing Pains," "Dreams Out of Darkness" and "Job's Daughter."
In bad times poets prophesy. They are dedicated to courage and their function, for one thing, is to relate the material world and the moral world, interpreted in no narrow sense.

1892   Janet Flanner: American journalist. *New Yorker* correspondent for 50 years. Wrote "Letter from Paris." Her first political profile was of Hitler.

The stench of human wreckage in which the Nazi regime finally sank down to defeat has been the most shocking fact of modern times.

1900 George Seferiades: Pseudonym Seferis: Greek poet and diplomat. Ambassador to Lebanon (1953–57) and the United Kingdom (1957–62). Wrote lyrical poetry, collected in *The Turning Point* and *Mythistorema.* First of his country to win the Nobel Prize in literature.

They were lovely, your eyes, but you didn't know where to look.

1911 L. Ron Hubbard: U.S. religious leader and science fiction writer. In 1950, formulated dianetics, a method of achieving mental and physical health, the basis of his religion Scientology.

A society in which women are taught anything but the management of a family, and the creation of the future generation is a society which is on the way out.

March 14

1854 Paul Ehrlich: German bacteriologist. Pioneer in haematology and chemotherapy. Developed a treatment for syphilis. Discovered "silver bullets," chemicals that act primarily on disease-causing organisms without harming healthy cells. Shared Nobel Prize (1908) with Ilya Mechnikov.

The first rule of intelligent tinkering is to save all the parts.

1868 Maxim Gorky [Aleksey Maksimovich Peshkov]: Russian writer. First great Russian proletarian author. Depicted wretched lives of the lowest levels of Russian society. Wrote *Chelkash, Foma Gordeyev* and *The Lower Depths.*

Lies—there you have the religion of slaves and taskmasters.

1877 Edna Woolman Chase: American editor-in-chief of *Vogue* magazine (1914–55). Organized first U.S. fashion show (1944).

Fashion can be bought. Style one must possess.

1879 Albert Einstein: German-born U.S. physicist formulated the general theory of relativity (1916). Awarded Nobel Prize (1921). Although a Pacifist, he was one of a group of scientists to suggest that energy of split atoms could be used in bombs. Spent the latter part of his life trying to establish a unified field theory that comprised quantum theory and his general theory of relativity.

The pursuit of truth and beauty is a sphere of activity in which we are permitted to remain children all of our lives.

1923 Diane Arbus: American photographer who rebelled against her work in conventional fashion photography. Sought to portray people "without masks." Achieved fame in the sixties with her studies of "freaks."

A photograph is a secret about a secret. The more it tells you the less you know.

1925 John Barrington Wain: English author and critic. His first four novels debunk the virtues of the postwar British. Works include: *Living in the Present, Weep Before God* and *The Pardoner's Tale.*

Poetry is to prose as dancing is to walking.

1928 Frank Borman: U.S. astronaut on *Gemini 7* flight (1965), and *Apollo 8* flight, the first manned flight around moon (1968). President and CEO of Eastern Airlines (1975–76). Elected chairman of board (1976).

Exploration is really the essence of the human spirit.

March 15

1767 Andrew Jackson: "Old Hickory." Soldier, lawyer, planter. Seventh U.S. president (1829–37). First to be elected by a mass base of voters. Rewarded supporters by establishing the "Spoils System." Military hero at the Battle of New Orleans (1815).

One man with courage makes a majority.

1779 William Lamb Melbourne: Second Viscount. English statesman and prime minister (1834–41). Queen Victoria's friend and political advisor during the early years of her reign. Husband of novelist Lady Caroline Lamb.

Never disregard a book because the author of it is a foolish fellow.

1782 Thomas Hart Benton: American statesman, orator and author. U.S. senator from Missouri (1821–51). Wrote two-volume *Thirty Years' View* and fifteen-volume *An Abridgement of the Debates of Congress.*

This new page opened in the book of our public expenditures, and this new departure taken, which leads into the bottomless gulf of civil pensions and family gratuities.

1915 David Schoenbrun: U.S. journalist. Foreign correspondent France (1946–62). Chief of CBS Washington bureau (1962–63). ABC news (1963–79). Books: *The Three Lives of Charles de Gaulle* and *Vietnam: How We Got In, How to Get Out.*

Being a great power is no longer much fun.

1916 Harry James: American trumpet player and bandleader. Hits: "You Made Me Love You," "I Don't Want to Walk Without You" and "I've Heard That Song Before." Was married to Betty Grable.

…When you're worried and upset, you don't feel like playing and you certainly can't relax enough to play anything like good jazz.

1926 Norm Van Brocklin: "The Dutchman." U.S. football quarterback and coach. Led NFL in passing three times, punting twice. Led L.A. Rams and Eagles to NFL titles. MVP (1960).

If you don't discipline them [his players], they won't know you love them. There's no love on third down and one. You need discipline then.

1933 Ruth Bader Ginsberg: Associate justice of the U.S. Supreme Court, appointed by Bill Clinton (1993).

The emphasis must be not on the right to abortion but on the right to privacy and reproductive control.

March 16

1751 James Madison: Political theorist and fourth president of the U.S. (1809–17). Contributed to the Federalist Papers. Sponsored the first ten amendments (Bill of Rights) to Constitution.

The truth is that all men having power ought to be mistrusted.

1903 Mike Mansfield: U.S. politician, diplomat, engineer. Montana U.S representative (1943–53) and senator (1953–76). Senate majority leader (1961–76). Ambassador to Japan (1977–88).

After all, even a politician is human.

1912 Patricia Nixon: Wife of Richard M. Nixon, thirty-seventh U.S. president. Sacrificed her life in order to advance the career of her husband.

Being first lady is the hardest unpaid job in the world.

1926 Jerry Lewis: Zany U.S. comedian. Once teamed with Dean Martin on television, in nightclubs and films. After the split, he became a cult hero, crowned by serious French critics as "Le Roi du Crazy." Hosts annual telethon for muscular dystrophy, raising over $300 million.

Comedy is a man in trouble.

1927 Daniel Patrick Moynihan: U.S. politician. Professor of Education and Urban Politics, Harvard (1966–72 and 1975–). U.S. Ambassador to India (1973–74) and U.N. (1975–76). U.S. senator from New York (1977–).

To strip our past of glory is no great loss, but to deny it honor is devastating.

1940 Bernardo Bertolucci: Italian director, screenwriter of films: *Once Upon a Time in the West, The Conformist, Last Tango in Paris* and *The Last Emperor* for which he received an Oscar for directing and screenwriting.

Pornography is not in the hands of the child who discovers his sexuality by masturbating, but in the hands of the adult who slaps him.

1955 **Isabelle Huppert:** Versatile French actress. Cannes Film Award for Best Actress (1977). Films: *César and Rosalie, Violette, Entre Nous,* and *Madame Bovary. Acting is a way of living out one's insanity.*

March 17

1781 **Ebenezer Elliott:** English industrialist and poet. Active Chartist. Denounced social evils, especially the "bread tax" in his "Corn Law Rhymes."
What is a communist? One who hath yearnings / For equal division of unequal earnings.

1820 **Jean Ingelow:** English poet and novelist, she wrote devotional poetry, lyrics and ballads. Remembered for her narrative poem "High Tide on the Coast of Lincolnshire" (1571).
I have lived to thank God that all my prayers have not been answered.

1899 **Arthur E. Summerfield:** U.S. businessman and government official. G.O.P. strategist and money-raiser. Postmaster General in the Eisenhower administration. On his banning of D.H. Lawrence's *Lady Chatterley's Lover* in 1959:
I make no claim of being a literary critic ... but I feel I have some sense for what is decent and what is filthy ... and filth is filth.

1902 **Bobby Jones:** U.S. golfer. Won U.S. Open and British Open plus U.S. and British Amateurs (1930), becoming the only Grand Slam winner. Founded Masters Tournament (1934).
Competitive golf is played mainly on a five-and-a-half inch course, the space between your ears.

1915 **Gale McGee:** American historian, politician and statesman. U.S. senator from Wyoming (1959–77). Chairman Senate Post Office and Civil Service Committee (1969–77). On learning that Arthur E. Summerfield was banning books:

I'm going to introduce a resolution to have the Postmaster General stop reading dirty books and deliver the mail.

1920 **Sheikh Mujibur Rahman:** Liberator of Bangladesh. President and prime minister. Killed in a military coup.
In the war between falsehood and truth, falsehood wins the first battle and truth the last.

1938 **Rudolph Nureyev:** Soviet-British ballet dancer. Defected from U.S.S.R. and the Leningrad Kirov Ballet. Became permanent guest artist at Royal Ballet, London. Partner of Margot Fonteyn (1962–79). Noted for suspended leaps and fast turns. Roles: *Swan Lake, Don Quixote* and *Romeo and Juliet.*
A pas de deux is a dialogue of love. How can there be conversation if one partner is dumb?

March 18

1782 **John C. Calhoun:** U.S. South Carolinian politician. Champion of states rights. Opposed prohibition of slavery in newly admitted states. U.S. secretary of war (1817–25), vice president (1824–32).
Irresponsible power is inconsistent with liberty, and must corrupt those who exercise it.

1837 **Grover Cleveland:** U.S. politician. Twenty-second and twenty-fourth U.S. president (1885–89 and 1893–97). Attempted to lower the tariff. Supported creation of Civil Service Commission.
He mocks the people who proposes that the Government shall protect the rich and that they in turn will care for the laboring poor.

1844 **Nikolai A. Rimsky-Korsakov:** Russian composer of Romantic music. Operas: *The Snow Maiden, Le Coq d'or* and *Scheherazade.* Known for brilliant instrumentation.
God does not bless the tears of sorrow, / God blesses the tears of celestial joy.

1869 **Neville Chamberlain:** English prime minister (1937–40). Ever associated with appeasement for signing the Munich Pact, which granted most of Hitler's demands, leaving Czechoslovakia defenseless.

In war, whichever side may call itself the victor, there are no winners, but all are losers.

1915   Richard Condon: American author of best-sellers *The Manchurian Candidate* and *Prizzi's Honor.*

It is the rule, not the exception, that otherwise unemployable public figures inevitably take to writing for publication.

1921   Edgar Z. Friedenberg: U.S. educator and author. Professor of education, Dalhouse University, Canada. Books: *The Vanishing Adolescent, Coming of Age in America* and *The Dignity of Youth and Other Atavisms.*

Part of the American dream is to live long and die young.

1932   John Updike: American novelist, short-story writer and poet. Explores human relationships in contemporary society. Books: *The Witches of Eastwick, The Centaur* and *Rabbit, Run.*

Creativity is merely a plus name for regular activity ... any activity becomes creative when the doer cares about doing it right, or better.

March 19

1721   Tobias George Smollett: Scottish novelist. Wrote realistic satires on the folly, selfishness and cruelty of mankind. Spent several years in journal editing, translating and writing historical and travel works. Books: *The Adventures of Roderick Random* and *Humphrey Clinker.*

Facts are stubborn things.

1813   Dr. David Livingstone: Scottish-born British medical missionary, African explorer. Discovered Lake Ngami, the Zambesi River, the Victoria Falls and Lake Nyasa. Found in Ujiji by journalist Henry Stanley, who was sent to look for him by the *New York Herald.*

Men are immortal until their work is done.

1821   Sir Richard Burton: English explorer, author. Discovered Lake Tanganyika. Traveled in West Africa, Brazil, Damascus and Trieste. Made a literal translation of the *Arabian Nights.*

Indeed he knows not how to know who knows not also how to unknow.

1860   William Jennings Bryan: "The Great Commoner." Three-time unsuccessful presidential candidate. Prosecutor in the "monkey trial," a test case on the banning of teaching evolution in Tennessee schools. Made the famous "Cross of Gold" speech.

The humblest citizen of all the land, when clad in the armor of a righteous cause is stronger than all the hosts of Error.

1891   Earl Warren: Chief justice, Supreme Court (1953–69). Presided over period of rapid change in civil rights. Wrote decision in school desegregation case, *Brown vs. Board of Education.* Headed official investigation of assassination of John F. Kennedy.

The only thing we learn from history is that we do not learn.

1930   Ornette Coleman: American jazz saxophonist, trumpeter, violinist and composer. Toured Europe as part of a trio. Composed "Skies in America." A musician who stirs equal amounts of interest and controversy.

Jazz is the only music in which the same note can be played night after night but differently each time.

1933   Phillip Roth: American novelist, short-story writer. Concentrates mostly on Jewish-American life and modern society. Won National Book award for *Goodbye, Columbus.* Also wrote *Portnoy's Complaint* and *Zuckerman Unbound.*

Satire is moral rage transformed into comic art.

March 20

43 B.C.   Ovid [Publius Ovidius Naso]: Latin poet. First major writer of the Roman Empire. In Middle Ages, Ovid's poetry

was one of the major sources of Western man's knowledge of antiquity. Works: *Medea, Heriodes, Ars amatoria* and *Metamorphoses.*
Time is the best medicine.

1828 **Henrik Ibsen:** Norwegian dramatist. Father of modern drama. Wrote realistic plays emphasizing social problems and psychological conflicts: *Peer Gynt, A Doll's House, Ghosts, The Wild Duck* and *Hedda Gabler.*
The thing is, you see, that the strongest man in the world is the man who stands most alone.

1856 **Frederick Taylor:** American engineer. Chief engineer of Midvale steelworks in Pennsylvania. Introduced time-and-motion study as an aid to efficient management. Wrote *The Principles of Scientific Management.*
It's easier to make a reporter into an economist than an economist into a reporter.

1882 **René Coty:** French statesman. Last president of the French Fourth Republic. After the constitutional crisis precipitated by generals in Algeria, he assisted the return to power of Charles de Gaulle.
It's taken me all my life to understand that it is not necessary to understand everything.

1883 **Wilfred Funk:** American publisher and author. President of Funk and Wagalls (1925–40). Books: *30 Days to a More Powerful Vocabulary* (with N. Lewis) and *Word Origins and Their Romantic Stories.*
I wish the reader might be encouraged to walk among words as I do, like Alice in Wonderland, amazed at the marvels they hold.

1904 **B.F. [Burrhus Frederic] Skinner:** American psychologist. A leading proponent of behaviorism, of the belief that man is controlled by external factors and free will does not exist. Invented "Skinner's Box" for observing animals' stimulus-response behavior.
Education is what survives when what has been learnt has been forgotten.

1957 **Spike Lee:** American director. His films have won praise for presentations of black themes and stories. Condemned by some as racist, by others as advocating violence. Films: *Do the Right Thing, Mo' Better Blues* and *Malcolm X.*
We can't rely on anyone but ourselves to define our existence, to shape the image of ourselves.

March 21

1685 **Johann Sebastian Bach:** German composer of the late Baroque Period. Noted organist. Wrote vast numbers of cantatas, sonatas, preludes, fugues and chorale preludes for organ. Works: "Brandenburg Concertos," "Well-Tempered Clavier" and "Goldberg Variations."
I was made to work; if you are equally industrious, you will be equally successful.

1763 **Johann Paul Friedrich Richter:** German novelist and humorist. Combined idealism with "Sturm und Drang." Works: *Extract's from the Devil's Papers, Hesperus* and *Leyana.*
Criticism is a practice which strips the tree of both caterpillars and blossoms.

1806 **Benito Juarez:** Mexican leader and revolutionary hero. Born of Zapotec Indian parents. As president of the Mexican republic, fought the French and their puppet emperor Maximilian.
By what right do the Great Powers of Europe invade the lands of simple people ... kill all who do not make them welcome ... destroy their fields ... and take the fruit of their toil from those who survive? ... The world must know the fate of any usurper who sets his foot upon this soil.

1839 **Modest Moussorgsky:** Russian composer. Founder of realistic national music. Works: *Pictures from an Exhibition, Night on Bald Mountain* and his masterpiece, the opera *Boris Godunov.*
Art is not an end in itself, but a means of addressing humanity.

1905 **Phyllis McGinley:** Canadian-born Pulitzer Prize–winning U.S. poet and author of children's books. Also wrote prose essays. Works: *Pocketful of Wry, The Horse Who Lived Upstairs, Selected Verses from Three Decades* and *A Little Girl's Room.*

Sticks and stones are hard on bones. / Aimed with angry art, / Words can sting like anything, / But silence breaks the heart.

1922 **Julius K. Nyerere:** Prime minister and president of Tanganika (1962-64). Negotiated the union of Tanganika and Zanzibar as Tanzania (1964). As president led the new nation on a path of Socialism. When his policies failed, he resigned in 1985.

Small nations are like indecently dressed women. They tempt the evil minded.

1930 **John Malcolm Fraser:** Australian statesman. Liberal prime minister (1975-83). A member of the Commonwealth Group of Eminent Persons which worked to replace apartheid in South Africa.

Self-criticism is luxury all politicians should indulge in, but it is best done in private.

March 22

1808 **Caroline Norton:** English poet and novelist. Charges of adultery by her husband made her a notorious figure. Her countersuit greatly influenced the Marriage and Divorce Act of 1857, abolishing some injustices against women. Wrote *The Sorrows of Rosalie.*

They serve God well / Who serve his creatures.

1868 **Robert A. Millikan:** U.S. physicist. Proved that electricity consists of particles. Determined the charge on the electron, for which he was awarded the Nobel Prize (1923). Invented term cosmic rays which he showed came from space.

Civilization consists in the multiplication and refinement of human wants.

1884 **Arthur H. Vandenberg:** U.S. public official. Editor of the Grand Rapids *Herald*, from 1906 to 1928. Republican senator from Michigan (1928-51). Played

an important role in the formation of the U.N.

It is less important to redistribute wealth than it is to redistribute opportunity.

1907 **James M. Gavin:** U.S. Army general, diplomat. Served at the Battle of the Bulge and Normandy, WWII. U.S. ambassador to France (1960-62). Critic of U.S. military strategy in Vietnam.

If you want a decision, go to the point of danger.

1908 **Louis L'Amour:** American writer of over 100 books, mostly Western novels, of which *Hondo* is his best known. Awarded the Presidential Medal of Freedom in 1984.

A man ought to do what he thinks is right.

1923 **Marcel Marceau:** French pantomimist. World famous mime; created the character "Bip" in 1947. Devised the mime-drama *Don Juan*, the ballet *Candide* and about 100 pantomimes, including *The Creation of the World.*

Do not the most moving moments of our lives find us without words?

1930 **Stephen Sondheim:** American composer, lyricist. Lyric-writer for Leonard Bernstein's *West Side Story*. Shows as lyricist and composer: *Company, Follies, A Little Night Music* and *Into the Woods.*

I prefer neurotic people. I like to hear rumbling beneath the surface.

March 23

1749 **Pierre-Simon Laplace:** French mathematician and astronomer. Applied his mathematical knowledge to the study of the stability of orbits in the solar system. Modernized theory of probability.

All the effects of nature are only the mathematical consequences of a small number of immutable laws.

1857 **Fannie Farmer:** "Mother of Level Measurements." American cookery expert. Established cooking school (1902). One of the first to stress importance of following

recipes. Author of *The Boston Cooking School Cook Book.*
Progress in civilization has been accompanied by progress in cooking.

1887 **Sidney Hillman:** Lithuanian-born American labor leader. First president of the Amalgamated Clothing Workers of America (1914–46). A founder of the Congress of Industrial Organizations.
Politics is the science of who gets what, when and why.

1900 **Erich Fromm:** German-born psychologist, philosopher. Developed a humanist psychology. Sought to identify the sources of man's estrangement from himself in an industrial society. Books: *Escape from Freedom* and *The Sane Society.*
Love is the only sane and satisfactory answer to the problem of human existence.

1908 **Joan Crawford:** U.S. actress in films for over five decades. Played leading ladies well into her fifties. Best as a bitch-goddess. Oscar nominated for *Possessed* and *Sudden Fear.* Won for *Mildred Pierce.*
A star will last always, as in the heavens. A personality will go down just as quick as it appears.

1912 **Wernher Von Braun:** German-born U.S. engineer. Early rocketry pioneer. Developed Germany's V-2 missiles, WWII and U.S. rocket engine program, culminating in manned moon flight.
Basic research is when I'm doing what I don't know I'm doing.

1929 **Sir Roger Bannister:** British athlete, physician. First to run a mile race in under four minutes (3:59.4, May 6, 1954).
If a man coaches himself, then he has only himself to blame when he is beaten.

March 24

1834 **William Morris:** English poet, artist, manufacturer and socialist. His firm revolutionized the art of house decoration and furniture in England. Founded a Society for the Protection of Ancient Buildings in 1877.

Have nothing in your house that you do not know to be useful or believe to be beautiful.

1855 **Andrew Mellon:** U.S. financier, philanthropist. Developed extensive interests in coal, railroads, steel and water power. Secretary of treasury (1921–32), ambassador to Great Britain (1932–33). Donated his art collection and building to house National Gallery of Art (1937).
A nation is not in danger of financial disaster merely because it owes itself money.

1855 **Sir Arthur Wing Pinero:** English playwright, actor, essayist. Most successful playwright of his day. Wrote some fifty plays, including *The Second Mrs. Tanqueray* and *Trelawney of the Wells.*
From forty till fifty a man is at heart either a stoic or a satyr.

1855 **Olive Schreiner:** South African novelist, feminist, social critic. Worker for human rights. Pseudonym, Ralph Iron. Her novel *The Story of an African Farm* was the first imaginative work to come from her country.
The barb in the arrow of childhood suffering is this; its intense loneliness; its intense ignorance.

1890 **John Rock:** American physician and scientist. Roman Catholic developer of the birth control pill.
A society which practices death control must at the same time practice birth control.

1902 **Thomas E. Dewey:** U.S. politician. "Racket-busting" prosecuting attorney for New York City (1935–37). New York governor (1943–55). Twice unsuccessful Republican candidate for president (1944, 1948).
Things that are bad for business are bad for the people who work for business.

1951 **Pat Bradley:** U.S. golfer. Member of the LPGA Hall-of-Fame. Has earned more than $4 million in prizes.
When I would play badly, Mom would give me a shoulder to cry on, but Daddy would tell me to pick myself up and dig in.

March 25

1862   **George Sutherland:** English-born American politician and jurist. Congressman from Utah (1901–3). U.S. senator (1905–17). Pushed passage of the 19th (woman suffrage) Amendment to the U.S. Constitution. Justice of the Supreme Court (1922–37).

For the saddest epitaph which can be carved in memory of a vanished liberty is that it was lost because its possessors failed to stretch forth a saving hand while yet there was time.

1881   **Béla Bartók:** Hungarian composer, pianist. Employed Hungarian folk themes in his opera, *Bluebeard's Castle*, ballets, *The Wooden Prince* and *The Wonderful Mandarin* and piano collection, *Mikrokosmos*.

Competition is for horses, not artists.

1881   **Mary Webb:** English novelist and poet. In her novels including *The Golden Arrow* and *Precious Bone* she conveyed rich and intense impressions of the Shropshire countryside and its people, doing for her home what Thomas Hardy did for Dorset.

If you stop to be kind, you must swerve often from your path.

1908   **Sir David Lean:** British director. Oscar winner for *The Bridge on the River Kwai* and *Lawrence of Arabia*. Others: *Blithe Spirit, Brief Encounter, Great Expectations, Doctor Zhivago, Ryan's Daughter* and *A Passage to India*.

Always cast against the part and it won't be boring.

1921   **Simone Signoret:** German-born French actress. An intelligent, sensuous woman, who projected strength and vulnerability at the same time. Oscar winner for *Room at the Top*. Nominated for *Ship of Fools*.

Chains do not hold a marriage together. It is threads, hundreds of threads, which sew people together through the years.

1925   **Flannery O'Connor:** American short-story writer, novelist. Most of her fiction is set in the South. Stories blend a strong religious faith with the grotesque. Novels, *Wise Blood* and *The Violent Bear It Away*.

Knowing who you are is good for one generation only.

1934   **Gloria Steinem:** U.S. feminist, journalist. Activist for women's rights. Cofounded *Ms.* magazine (1971). Founded Coalition of Labor Union Women and Women USA.

Some of us are becoming the men we wanted to marry.

March 26

1850   **Edward Bellamy:** U.S. author and journalist. Achieved immense popularity with his Utopian romance, *Looking Backward*, which predicted a new social order. It influenced economic thinking both in the U.S. and Europe.

Looking Backward *was written in the belief that the Golden Age lies before us and not behind us.*

1874   **Robert Frost:** American poet. Best known for his verse dealing with New England life written in traditional verse forms. Poems: "The Road Not Taken," "Birches," "Stopping by Woods on a Snowy Evening" and "The Gift Outright." Pulitzer prizes for *New Hampshire* (1923), *Collected Poems* (1930) and *A Further Range* (1936).

In three words I can sum up everything I've learned about life. It goes on.

1893   **James Bryant Conant:** U.S. chemist, educator and diplomat. President of Harvard (1933–53). Chaired Defense Research Committee (1941–46), which developed atomic bomb. Ambassador to West Germany (1955–57). Headed a Carnegie Corporation study of U.S. high schools.

There is only one proved way of assisting the advancement of pure science—that of picking men of genius, backing them heavily, and leaving them to direct themselves.

1911   **Tennessee Williams:** American playwright. Often considered the foremost dramatist of the post–WWII era. Plays:

New York. Drama Critics' Circle Award winner *The Glass Menagerie*, Pulitzer Prize winners *A Streetcar Named Desire*, and *Cat on a Hot Tin Roof*, *Sweet Bird of Youth* and *The Night of the Iguana*.

Life is an unanswered question, but let's still believe in the dignity and importance of the question.

1913 **Cyril O. Houle:** U.S. educator and author. Leading U.S. authority in the field of adult education.

Adults can learn most things better than children, though it may take them longer.

1930 **Sandra Day O'Connor:** U.S. lawyer, jurist. First woman appointed to the U.S. Supreme Court where she is considered a moderate.

It is difficult to discern a serious threat to religious liberty from a room of silent, thoughtful schoolchildren.

1942 **Erica Jong:** American writer. Her first novel, *Fear of Flying*, detailed the sexual misadventures of a young woman. It became a runaway best-seller.

Everyone has a talent. What is rare is the courage to follow the talent to the dark places where it leads.

March 27

1797 **Alfred de Vigny:** French poet, dramatist and novelist. Wrote of his experiences as a captain in the Royal Guards, in *Servitude et grandeur militaires*. His masterpiece is the romantic drama *Chatterton*, written for his love, actress Marie Dorval.

The existence of the soldier, next to capital punishment, is the most grievous vestige of barbarism which survives among men.

1879 **Edward Steichen:** Luxembourg-born American photographer. Noted for pioneering efforts to establish photography as a fine art and his studies of nudes. Organized the world-famous exhibition "The Family of Man" (1955).

Photography records the gamut of feeling written on the human face, the beauty of the earth and skies that man has inherited, and the wealth and confusion man has created.

1886 **Ludwig Mies van der Rohe:** German-born American architect. Leading practitioner of 20th century functionalist architecture. A pioneer of glass skyscrapers. Buildings: Seagram Building, New York City, and the Public Library, Washington, D.C.

Less is more.

1899 **Gloria Swanson:** U.S. silent screen actress in films such as *Male and Female*, *The Great Moment*, *Queen Kelly*. Oscar nominated for *The Trespasser*, *Sadie Thompson* and *Sunset Boulevard*.

I've given my memoirs far more thought than any of my marriages. You can't divorce a book.

1912 **James Callaghan:** Leader of Britain's Labor Party. Chancellor of the Exchequer in the Harold Wilson government, introducing some of the most controversial taxation measures in British history. Prime Minister (1976–79).

A lie can be half way around the world before the truth has got its boots on.

1914 **Budd Schulberg:** U.S. novelist, screenwriter. Wrote *What Makes Sammy Run?* a best-selling novel about film industry people, Oscar winner for the screenplay of *On the Waterfront*.

All fiction is fact, fact deepened and reorganized. All that any author has to work with is his own experience.

1924 **Sarah Vaughan:** "Sassy." American singer and pianist. Noted for her pure yet sophisticated styling. One of the great jazz singers, ranking alongside Billie Holliday and Ella Fitzgerald.

I like horns. When I was singing with bands, I always wanted to imitate the horns. Parker and Gillespie, they were my teachers.

March 28

1515 **Saint Teresa of Avila:** Spanish religious reformer, author. Returned Carmelite order to its original austerity of total withdrawal. Wrote beautiful mystical literature.

Spirit is the life of God within us.

1592 **Johann Amos Comenius:** Czech educational reformer and author of the first illustrated textbook. It was used for 200 years. Pioneer of new language teaching methods.

Let us have an end in view, the welfare of humanity; and let us put aside all selfishness in consideration of language, nationality or religion.

1862 **Aristide Briand:** French statesman. Eleven times French premier. Foreign minister (1925–32). Worked for the renunciation of war. Shared the Nobel Peace Prize with Gustav Stresemann, advocating a United States of Europe.

People think too historically. They are always living half in a cemetery.

1891 **Paul Whiteman:** "The King of Jazz." American musician, bandleader. Pioneer of "sweet style." Regarded by many as the inventor of jazz. Responsible for George Gershwin's experimentations with symphonic jazz. Introduced the composer's *Rhapsody in Blue* in concert.

Jazz came to America 300 years ago in chains.

1909 **Nelson Algren:** American author. Wrote brutally realistic novels about life in Chicago slums: *The Man with the Golden Arm* and *A Walk on the Wild Side.*

Never eat at a place called Mom's. Never play cards with a man called Doc. And never lie down with a woman who's got more trouble than you.

1914 **Edmund Muskie:** U.S. politician, lawyer. Governor of Maine. U.S. senator. Secretary of state during Carter administration.

In Maine we have a saying that there's no point in speaking unless you can improve on silence.

1928 **Zbigniew Brzezinski:** U.S. government official, political scientist. Assistant to President Carter for national security affairs (1977–81).

A Geneva settlement is like a tall mountain, full of crevices and sharp rocks. ... You don't go to it in a straight line. You go through zigs and zags.

March 29

1790 **John Tyler:** Tenth U.S. president. First vice president to attain presidency upon the death of a president, William Henry Harrison. He wrote this verse at age 65 for his wife Julia:

The seaman on the wave, love, / When storm and tempest rave, love, / Look to one star to save, love, / Thou art that star to me!

1819 **Isaac Mayer Wise:** American religious leader. Founded Reformed Judaism in the United States. Worked to establish Palestine as a home for the Jews.

It is much easier to write a long book than a short one.

1889 **Howard Lindsay:** American dramatist, producer, actor. Co-wrote with Russel Crouse, *Life with Father*, which he starred in on Broadway (1939–46).

An optimist in the atomic age is a person who thinks the future is uncertain.

1892 **Joseph Cardinal Mindszenty:** Hungarian religious leader. Became internationally known in 1948 when he was arrested by the Communist government, charged of treason and sentenced to life imprisonment. He wrote the following note just before his arrest.

I have taken no part in any conspiracy of any kind ... any confession ... even if authenticated by my signature ... will have been only the result of human frailty. In advance, I declare all such action null and void.

1916 **Eugene McCarthy:** "Clean Gene." U.S. politician. Minnesota congressman (1949–59), Senator (1959–70). Democratic presidential peace candidate (1968 and 1972).

The only thing that saves us from the bureaucracy is its inefficiency.

1918 **Pearl Bailey:** American singer. Starred in Broadway productions *St. Louis Woman* and all-black cast of *Hello, Dolly*. Films: *Carmen Jones* and *Porgy and Bess*.

Hungry people cannot be good at learning or producing anything except perhaps violence.

1925   **Emlen Tunnell:** "Offense on Defense." One of best defensive backs ever. New York Giants and Green Bay Packers (1948–61). Had 79 career interceptions. Football Hall of Fame (1967).
Tackling is football. Running is track.

March 30

1135   **Moses Maimonides:** Jewish philosopher, jurist, physician. Organized and clarified Torah, the Jewish oral law. Attempted to reconcile the Bible, Jewish tradition and Aristotle. Wrote *Guide of the Perplexed.*
Intelligence is the link that joins us to God.

1568   **Sir Henry Wotton:** English poet, connoisseur and diplomat. Wrote poems "You meaner beauties of the night" and "Character of a Happy Life." Also wrote *The Elements of Architecture.* Ambassador to Venice.
An ambassador is an honest man sent to lie abroad for the good of his country.

1746   **Francisco de Goya y Lucientes:** Spanish painter, etcher. The three phases of his career: portraits and genre works, powerful romantic depictions of heroes of war, and macabre renderings of nightmare subjects. Became famous for his portraits.
The sleep of reason produces monsters.

1820   **Anna Sewell:** English novelist. An invalid most of her life, she wrote *Black Beauty,* the story of a horse, as a plea for the more humane treatment of animals.
We call them dumb animals, and so they are, for they cannot tell us how they feel, but they do not suffer less because they have no words.

1844   **Paul Verlaine:** French poet. Among the first symbolists. Prominent in the bohemian literary life of Paris. Wrote *Songs Without Words* and *The Accursed Poets.*
What have you done, you there / Weeping without cease, / Tell me, yes you, what have you done / With all your youth?

1853   **Vincent Van Gogh:** Dutch post–Impressionist painter. Noted for brilliant colors and swirling brush strokes. Committed suicide (1890). His paintings became popular 50 years after his death. Paintings: *The Potato Eaters, Sunflowers* and *Cornfields with Flight of Birds.*
One may have a blazing hearth in one's soul, and yet no one ever comes to sit by it.

1880   **Sean O'Casey:** Irish dramatist. Works were noted for his rigid social conscience and his vitality of language. Plays: *Juno and the Paycock* and *The Plough and the Stars,* an anti-war drama which provoked a full-scale riot, and caused him to leave Ireland for good.
Life is a song in one ear, and a lament in the other.

1937   **Warren Beatty:** U.S. actor, producer, director and writer. Brother of Shirley MacLaine. Nominated for Oscars for *Bonnie and Clyde, Heaven Can Wait, Reds* (also nominated for writing, won for directing) and *Bugsy.*
Even the promiscuous feel pain.

March 31

1596   **René Descartes:** French mathematician, philosopher. Originated analytic geometry, the marriage of algebra and geometry. His philosophical theories formed the basis for 17th century rationalism. Originated modern scientific method.
In order to reach the Truth, it is necessary, once in one's life, to put everything in doubt—so far as possible.

1621   **Andrew Marvell:** English poet, satirist and public official. Poems: "The Garden," "To His Coy Mistress," and "A Dialogue Between the Soul and Body."
My love is a birth as rare / As 'tis for object strange and high; / It was begotten by despair / Upon impossibility.

1809   **Edward Fitzgerald:** English translator, man of letters. His most famous work, the translation of the *Rubaiyat of Omar Khayyam.*

*The Moving Finger writes; and having
writ / Moves on; nor all your Piety nor Wit
/ Shall lure it back to cancel half a Line /
Nor all your Tears wash out a Word of it.*

1914   **Octavio Paz:** Mexican poet, essayist, social philosopher and critic. Poetry is lyrical, expressing the deep loneliness of man which can be transcended through sexual love, compassion and faith.
Reality is a staircase going neither up nor down. We don't move, today is today, always is today.

1924   **Leo Buscaglia:** American educator, lecturer on interpersonal relationships.
Never idealize others. They will never live up to your expectations. Don't overanalyze your relationships. Stop playing games. A growing relationship can only be nurtured by genuineness.

1927   **Cesar Chavez:** U.S. labor-union organizer. Founder and first president of United Farm Workers, AFL-CIO. Employed nonviolent tactics, including fasts, marches, strikes and boycotts.
In some cases non-violence requires more militancy than violence.

1948   **Al Gore, Jr.:** American political leader. Democratic senator from Tennessee (1958–92). Vice president of the U.S. (1993–).
When you have the facts on your side, argue the facts. When you have the law on your side, argue the law. When you have neither, holler.

April 1

1578   **William Harvey:** English physician, physiologist, anatomist. The discoverer of circulation of blood (1628). Also did work on animal reproduction.
All we know is still infinitely less than all that still remains unknown.

1815   **Prince Otto Von Bismarck:** "The Iron Chancellor." German statesman. Founder and first chancellor of Unified German states into one empire under Prussian leadership (1871). Deliberately provoked the Franco-Prussian War (1870–71). Presided over the Congress of Berlin (1878).
Laws are like sausages. It's better not to see them being made.

1858   **Agnes Repplier:** U.S. essayist and biographer. Wrote *Books and Men, Counter-Currents* and *In Pursuit of Laughter.* Biographer of Père Marquette, Junipero Serra and Agnes Irwin.
People who cannot recognize a palpable absurdity are very much in the way of civilization.

1868   **Edmond Rostand:** French playwright of poetic, romantic drama. Achieved international and enduring fame with his play *Cyrano de Bergerac.* Other verse-plays: *The Eaglet* and *Chantecler.*
A great nose indicates a great man—Genial, courteous, intellectual, virile, courageous.

1897   **Alberta Hunter:** American blues singer who wrote her own songs. Sang with bands of King Oliver and Louis Armstrong. Made several successful international tours. Made a remarkable comeback at age 82.
I'm not living the blues, I'm just singing for the women who think they can't speak out. Can't a man alive mistreat me, 'cause I know who I am.

1922   **William Manchester:** U.S. novelist, biographer. Commissioned by Jacqueline Kennedy to write *Death of a President.* She changed her mind, unsuccessfully suing to prevent its publication. Other works: *The Arms of Krupp* and *American Caesar.*
Men do not fight for flag or country, for the Marine corps or any other abstraction. They fight for one another.

1931   **Rolf Hochhuth:** German playwright. Known for the controversial subject of his plays. *The Representative* accuses Pope Pius XII of not intervening to stop Nazi persecution of Jews. *Soldiers* accused Winston Churchill of being involved in the assassination of a Polish wartime leader.
Truth is with the victor—who, as you know, also controls the historians.

April 2

742   Charlemagne: French ruler. King of the Franks. Conqueror of almost all Christian lands in Europe (768–814). His goal was to consolidate order and Christian culture among the nations under his control, but his empire didn't survive long after his death.
To have another language is to possess a second soul.

1725   Giovanni Jacopo Casanova: Italian clergyman, soldier, violinist, author and adventurer. Wandered throughout Europe for 20 years, meeting all the greatest men and women of the day. His memoir, *History of My Life*, was a bawdy account of his loves.
Doubt begins only at the last frontiers of what is possible.

1805   Hans Christian Andersen: Danish writer of fairy tales, poet, novelist, dramatist. Wrote 168 fairy tales that mix mature wisdom and gay whimsy. Stories: "The Red Shoes," "The Ugly Duckling" and "The Emperor's Clothes."
Every man's life is a fairy tale, written by God's fingers.

1840   Émile Zola: French writer, critic. Leader of the naturalist school. His passion for social reform was translated into action in his famous *J'Accuse* letter, in defense of Captain Alfred Dreyfus. Novels: *Nana, Earth* and *The Beast in Man*.
A work of art is a corner of creation seen through a temperament.

1862   Nicholas Murray Butler: U.S. educator. President Columbia (1901–45). Helped found Teacher's College at Columbia and establish Carnegie Endowment for International Peace (1925–45). Nobel Peace Prize (1931).
An expert is one who knows more and more about less and less.

1891   Max Ernst: French painter, sculptor. Worked in expressionistic mode of surrealism, later a convert to dadaism. Works: *Oedipus Rex* and *Polish Rider*.
I have never seen a beautiful painting of a beautiful woman. But you can take an ugly woman and make a beautiful painting of her. It is the paint itself that should be beautiful.

1927   Kenneth Tynan: English drama critic. Supported the raw new drama of the *Angry Young Men*. Literary manager of National Theatre in sixties. Cowrote musical *Oh! Calcutta*.
Show me a congenital eavesdropper with the instincts of a Peeping Tom and I will show you the makings of a dramatist.

April 3

1593   George Herbert: English clergyman and devotional poet of the metaphysical school of John Donne. Wrote "A Priest in the Temple," published in *Remains*.
Every mile is two in Winter.

1783   Washington Irving: American essayist, biographer, historian. Wrote humorous and satirical pieces using the name of Diedrich Knickerbocker, a quaint and humorous Dutchman. Works: *Rip Van Winkle* and *The Legend of Sleepy Hollow*.
Great minds have purposes, others have wishes.

1822   Edward Everett Hale: American clergyman, author. Helped found Unitarian Church of America. Wrote novel *Man Without a Country*.
To look up and not down / To look forward and not back / To look out and not in, and / To lend a hand.

1823   William Marcy Tweed: "Boss Tweed." U.S. corrupt politician and criminal. Notorious "boss" of the Tammany Society. As commissioner of public works for New York City he controlled the city's finances. Gigantic frauds were exposed by the *New York Times* (1871). Died in a New York jail.
As long as I count the votes, what are you going to do about it?

1837   John Burroughs: U.S. naturalist and nature writer. Wrote *Wake-Robin, Birds and Poets* and *The Breath of Life*.—
The John Burroughs Memorial Association

was established in his memory to encourage writing in natural history.

It is always easier to believe than to deny. Our minds are naturally affirmative.

1898   Henry R. Luce: American publisher. With Briton Hadden founded weekly news magazine *Time* (1923), followed by *Fortune, Life, Sports Illustrated, Architectural Forum* and *House and Home.*

Show me a man who claims he is objective and I'll show you a man with illusions.

1924   Doris Day: U.S. singer, actress. Song hits: "It's Magic" and "Secret Love." Oscar nomination for *Pillow Talk.* After movie career went on to television success.

If a man does something silly, people say, "Isn't he silly?" If a woman does something silly, people say, "Aren't women silly?"

April 4

1802   Dorothea Dix: U.S. social reformer. Pioneer in movement for specialized treatment of the insane and the establishment of state hospitals for the insane.

In a world where there is so much to be done I felt strongly impressed that there must be something for me to do.

1810   James Freeman Clarke: American Unitarian clergyman, reformer, author. Wrote: *Ten Great Religions, Memorial and Biographical Sketches* and *Self-Culture.*

...A politician thinks of the next election and a statesman thinks of the next generation.

1828   Margaret Oliphant: Scottish novelist. Widowed at 31, she began a prolific writing career to support herself and her children. Wrote more than 100 books and more than 200 contributions to magazines. Major works: *Salem Chapel* and *Miss Majoribanks.*

Imagination is the first faculty wanting in those who do harm to their kind.

1858   Remy de Gourmont: French critic, essayist and novelist. Most contemporary critic of symbolism. Wrote 50 volumes, mainly collections of articles, including "Very Woman" and the novel *A Virgin Heart.*

Of all sexual aberrations, perhaps the most peculiar is chastity.

1896   Robert Sherwood: American playwright, editor. Plays: *Idiot's Delight* (Pulitzer Prize), *The Petrified Forest, Abe Lincoln in Illinois,* and *There Shall Be No Night* (Pulitzer Prize).

To be able to write a play ... a man must be sensitive, imaginative, naive, gullible, passionate; he must be something of an imbecile, something of a poet, something of a damn fool.

1928   Maya Angelou: American writer, singer, dancer and black activist. Toured Europe and Africa in *Porgy and Bess.* Autobiographical books chronicle her experiences growing up in Arkansas, *I Know Why the Caged Bird Sings* and *All God's Children Need Traveling Shoes.*

Children's talent to endure stems from their ignorance of alternatives.

1938   A. Bartlett Giamatti: U.S. scholar, president of Yale (1978–86), National Baseball League president and commissioner of baseball.

A liberal education is at the heart of a civil society, and at the heart of liberal education is the art of teaching.

April 5

1588   Thomas Hobbes: English philosopher. Father of materialism. Pioneer of modern political science. Leader of modern rationalism. His masterpiece, *Leviathan,* expresses his political philosophy.

Words are wise men's counters, they do but reckon with them, but they are the money of fools.

1837   Algernon Swinburne: English poet, man of letters. Known for his rebellion against Victorian social conventions and religion. Works: *Poems and Ballads, Songs Before Sunrise* and *Essays and Studies.*

For words divide and rend; / But silence is most noble till the end.

1856   **Booker T. Washington:** U.S. educator, social reformer. Established Tuskegee Institute (1881), which he headed until his death. Principal spokesman of black people. Wrote *Up from Slavery*.
No race can prosper till it learns that there is as much dignity in tilling a field as in writing a poem.

1871   **Glenn "Pop" Warner:** American football coach and innovator for over 49 years. His seven college teams had a total of 313 victories. He produced 47 All-Americans, most notably Jim Thorpe.
You play the way you practice.

1873   **Mistinguett:** Stage name of Jeanne Marie Bourgeois, the most famous comedienne of her time. Reached the height of her career with Maurice Chevalier at the Folies Bergère. Also successful in serious productions, *Madame Sans-Gene* and *Les Misérables*.
A kiss can be a comma, a question mark or an exclamation point. That's basic spelling that every woman ought to know.

1908   **Bette Davis:** U.S. actress. "First Lady of the American Screen." As independent in real life as her characters on screen. Oscar winner for *Dangerous* and *Jezebel*. Nominated for *Dark Victory, The Letter, The Little Foxes, Now, Voyager, Mr. Skeffington, All About Eve, The Star* and *What Ever Happened to Baby Jane?*
Strong women only marry weak men.

1937   **Colin L. Powell:** American Army general. Youngest and first black chairman of the Joint Chiefs of Staff. Advised George Bush on deployment of U.S. troops in "Operation Desert Storm," against Iraq.
Everyone says America isn't the world's policeman. But guess who gets called when somebody needs a cop.

April 6

1866   **Lincoln Steffens:** American journalist. Managing editor *McClure's Magazine* (1902–6). One of the first muckrakers. Exposed city corruption in "The Shame of the Cities." He saw the villain not as boss corruption but public apathy. In 1919 he visited post–Revolutionary Russia and announced:
I have seen the future and it works.

1888   **Emmanuel Celler:** U.S. politician, lawyer. U.S. congressman from New York (1922–72). Supported New Deal programs and fought Joe McCarthy. His recipe for success in Congress:
…The brashness of a sophomore … the perseverance of a bill collector.

1892   **Lowell Thomas:** U.S. author, radio news commentator. Filmed and narrated travelogues and wrote books about his travels. Books: *The Seven Wonders of the World* and *With Lawrence in Arabia*.
After the age of eighty, everything reminds you of something else.

1895   **Dudley Nichols:** American screenwriter, director. Highly regarded for his collaborations with John Ford on *The Lost Patrol, The Plough and the Stars* and *Stagecoach*. His screenplay for *The Informer* won an Oscar (1935).
A script is only a blueprint—the director is the one who makes the picture.

1928   **James D. Watson:** U.S. biochemist. With F.H.C. Crick worked out the structure of DNA. With Crick, awarded Nobel Prize (1962).
It's necessary to be slightly underemployed if you are to do something significant.

1929   **Andre Previn:** German-born U.S. composer, conductor, arranger, musical director, pianist. Won Academy Awards for the scores of *Gigi, Porgy and Bess, Irma La Douce,* and *My Fair Lady*.
The conductor is there … first of all for the oversimplified reason of just being the traffic cop, making sure everyone is playing at the same speed and the same volume.

1937   **Merle Haggard:** U.S. country and western singer. Has had 38 number one singles. Entertainer of the Year (1970). Hits: "Sing a Sad Song," "Okie from Muskogee," "The Fightin' Side of Me" and "That's the Way Love Goes."
I don't know if you could call my music Cowboy music. I don't sing about horses.

April 7

1506 **St. Francis Xavier:** Navarrese priest, missionary. "Apostle of the Indies." One of the original members of the Jesuits. Began his missionary work in Goa, India, 1534. Traveled to the Malay and Japan. Died while trying to enter China. Canonized (1622).
Give me the children until they are seven and anyone may have them after.

1770 **William Wordsworth:** English poet, known for his worship of nature, his humanitarianism and his interest in common people. Poetry: "Lyrical Ballads," "Tintern Abbey," "The Solitary Reaper," and the unfinished "The Recluse."
Minds that have nothing to confer / Find little to perceive.

1837 **John Pierpont Morgan:** U.S. financier, philanthropist. J.P. Morgan and Co. became world's most influential banking firm. Financed companies that became U.S. Steel and International Harvester. Donated art collection to New York's Metropolitan Museum of Art.
A man always has two reasons for what he does—a good one, and the real one.

1889 **Gabriela Mistral:** Pseudonym of Chilean poet Lucila Godoy de Alcayaga. All her poetry is a variation on the theme of love and sorrow. Poetry: "Sonnets of Death" and "Desolation." Nobel Prize for Literature (1945), first woman poet and first Latin American so honored.
I love the things I never had / Along with those I have no more.

1897 **Walter Winchell:** American journalist. Wrote an internationally famous syndicated gossip column. Hosted a long-running and very popular radio gossip program.
Good evening, Mr. and Mrs. North and South America and all the ships at sea ... let's go to press.

1915 **Billie Holiday:** "Lady Day." American jazz singer. Toured with Count Basie and Artie Shaw. Considered the finest interpreter of torch songs, jazz and ballads of her era. Hits: "God Bless the Child" and "Don't Explain."
Sometimes it's worse to win a fight than to lose.

1938 **Edmund G. "Jerry" Brown, Jr.:** U.S. politician. Governor of California (1975–82). Sought the Democratic nomination for president several times, refusing to accept political contributions of more than $100.
The insatiable appetite for campaign dollars has turned the government into a Stop and Shop for every greed and special interest in the country.

April 8

1582 **Phineas Fletcher:** English poet, best known for his religious and scientific poem, "The Purple Island, or The Isle of Man." Brother of poet Giles the Younger Fletcher.
Ah fool! Faint heart fair lady ne'er could win.

1894 **Mary Pickford:** "America's Sweetheart." Canadian-born U.S. silent screen star. Typical role was a sweet, innocent, loveable girl as in *Tess of the Storm Country*, *Rebecca of Sunnybrook Farm* and *Pollyanna*.
If you have made mistakes, even serious ones, there is always another choice for you. What we call failure is not falling down, but staying down.

1898 **E.Y. "Yip" Harburg:** U.S. lyricist. Collaborated with composers Vernon Duke, Arthur Schwartz, Jerome Kern and most often, Harold Arlen. Songs: "Brother Can You Spare a Dime?" "It's Only a Paper Moon" and "Over the Rainbow."
Virtue is its own revenge.

1912 **Sonja Henie:** Norwegian-born ice skater. Won gold medals in the 1928, 1932 and 1936 Olympics. Toured with an ice show before moving to a Hollywood career of films: *One in a Million*, *Sun Valley Serenade* and *The Countess of Monte Cristo*.
Jewelry takes people's minds off your wrinkles.

1918   Betty Ford: American first lady. Wife of Gerald R. Ford, 38th president of the U.S. Cofounder and president of the Betty Ford Center for Drug Rehabilitation.
Alcohol: Maybe it picks you up a little bit, but it sure lets you down in a hurry.

1919   Ian Smith: Rhodesian politician. Prime minister (1964–79). A founder of the Rhodesian Front, dedicated to immediate independence without African majority rule. Unilaterally declared independence (1965), which resulted in severe sanctions by the U.N. at Britain's request.
Don't forget that we have been killing each other for years.

1922   Carmen McRae: U.S. singer who worked with bands of Benny Carter, Count Basie and Mercer Ellington.
Blues is to jazz what yeast is to bread— without it, it's flat.

April 9

1758   Fischer Ames: American statesman, publicist and orator. Son of almanac maker Nathaniel Ames. Federalist congressman from Massachusetts (1789–97).
A monarchy is a merchantman which sails well, but will sometimes strike on a rock and go to the bottom; a republic is a raft which will never sink, but then your feet are always in the water.

1821   Charles Pierre Baudelaire: French poet. Important figure among the French symbolists. Published only a single volume of poetry, *Les Fleurs du Mal.*
Laughter is satanic, and, therefore, profoundly human. It is born of man's conception of his own superiority.

1865   Charles P. Steinmetz: German-born U.S. electrical engineer. Worked out the mathematics necessary to predict the efficiency of electrical motors and alternating current circuits.
No man really becomes a fool until he stops asking questions.

1898   Paul Robeson: U.S. actor singer, athlete. Phi Beta Kappa at Rutgers. Admitted to New York bar. Chose not to practice law. Starred on Broadway in *The Emperor Jones.* His vibrant bass voice is identified with the song "Ole Man River." Increasingly controversial, arguing that the Soviet Union was superior to the United States in the treatment of blacks.
The artist must elect to fight for Freedom or for Slavery.

1905   J. William Fulbright: U.S. politician, lawyer, teacher. Senator from Arkansas (1945–74). Chairman of Senate Foreign Relations Committee. Major critic of the Vietnam War. Founded the Fulbright scholarship program (1946).
We have the power to do any damn fool thing we want to do, and we seem to do it about every 10 minutes.

1926   Hugh Hefner: U.S. founder, editor and publisher of *Playboy* magazine. Used his magazine as a forum for his philosophy on sex and sexual freedom. His playmates of the month usually are buxom girl-next-door types.
The major civilizing force in the world is not religion, it's sex.

1932   Paul Krassner: American journalist. Writer for *Mad* magazine. Founder of Youth International Party (Yippies).
To have true justice we must have equal harassment under the law.

1933   Jean-Paul Belmondo: French stage and screen actor. Appealing sweet-and-sour personality fit in well with the "New Wave" films *Breathless, That Man from Rio* and *Borsalino.*
Women over thirty are at their best, but men over thirty are too old to recognize it.

April 10

1583   Hugo Grotius: Dutch jurist, statesman and theologian. His "De Jure Belli et Pacis" in which he appealed to "natural law" and the social contract as a basis for rational principles on which a system of laws could be formulated is regarded as the beginning of the science of international law.

For the mother of natural law is human nature itself.

1827 **Lew Wallace:** Major general of union volunteers during Civil War. Headed Andersonville court of inquiry. Governor of New Mexico (1878–81). Minister to Turkey (1881–85). Best known as author of *Ben Hur.*
Beauty is altogether in the eye of the beholder.

1847 **Joseph Pulitzer:** Hungarian-born American publisher. Bought the *St. Louis Post-Dispatch* and the *New York World.* Founded the *Evening World.* Pulitzer prizes, annual awards in journalism endowed by Pulitzer's will.
Publicity, publicity, publicity, is the greatest moral factor and force in our public life.

1882 **Frances Perkins:** U.S. government official. As U.S. secretary of labor (1933–45), the first woman to serve in a presidential cabinet. Chairwoman, U.S. Civil Service Commission (1946–53).
But with the slow menace of a glacier, depression came on. No one had any measure of its progress; no one had any plan for stopping it. Everyone tried to get out of its way.

1883 **Kahlil Gibran:** Syrian-U.S. writer, best known for the mystical prose poem, "The Prophet," which gained near cult status with the young in the twenties.
Evil is good tortured by its own hunger and thirst.

1903 **Clare Boothe Luce:** U.S. editor, playwright, politician and diplomat. Editor for *Vogue* and *Vanity Fair.* Married publisher Henry Luce. Best known for theatrical success *The Women.* Congress woman from Connecticut (1943–47). Ambassador to Italy (1953–57).
Censorship, like charity, should begin at home; but unlike charity, it should end there.

1936 **John Madden:** U.S. football coach. Won 112 games and a Super Bowl (1976) with Oakland Raiders. Has won 9 Emmy awards as football analyst with CBS and Fox.
If you see a defensive team with dirt and mud on their backs, they've had a bad day.

April 11

1770 **George Canning:** English statesman. Known for his liberal policies as foreign secretary (1822–27). Earnestly contended for Catholic Emancipation and repeal of the Corn Laws. Became prime minister in 1827, but died the same year.
Save me, oh, save me from the candid friend.

1794 **Edward Everett:** American Unitarian minister, masterful orator, educator and statesman. President of Harvard (1846–49). Governor of Massachusetts (1835–39). Ambassador to Great Britain (1841–45).
Education is a better safeguard of liberty than a standing army.

1862 **Charles Evans Hughes:** American jurist, lawyer. Chief Justice, Supreme Court (1930–41). Resisted attempts of Franklin D. Roosevelt to "pack" the court with justices favorable to his New Deal programs. Republican presidential nominee (1916).
We are under a Constitution, but the Constitution is what the judges say it is.

1893 **Dean Acheson:** American lawyer, statesman. Secretary of state (1949–53). Chief architect of the containment policy of communism expansion. Helped create NATO. Pulitzer Prize in history for *Present at the Creation.*
The first requirement of a statesman is that he be dull. This is not always easy.

1908 **Leo Rosten:** Polish-born American humorist, political scientist, teacher. Best known for *The Education of H*y*m*a*n K*a*p*l*a*n,* a series of humorous sketches of a night school for immigrants.
Extremists think "communication" means agreeing with them.

1914 **Norman McLaren:** Scottish-born animator. Joined the GPO Film Unit in London (1936). Put in charge of the National Film Board in Ottawa (1943). Oscar for cartoon "Neighbors" in which he animated live actors.
Animation is not the art of drawings that move, but the art of movements that are drawn.

1923   **Theodore Isaac Rubin:** U.S. psychoanalyst. Columnist with *Ladies' Home Journal.* Author of more than 20 books. Fiction deals with the lives of schizophrenics, catatonics and autistic children as in *Lisa and David* and *The Angry Book.*
All of us are crazy in one or another way.

April 12

1777   **Henry Clay:** "Great Pacificator." American politician, lawyer. U.S. congressman (1811–31) and senator from Kentucky (1831–42). Unsuccessful candidate for the presidency (1824, 1831 and 1844). U.S. secretary of state (1825–29). Drafted Missouri Compromise.
An oppressed people are authorized whenever they can to rise and break their fetters.

1823   **Aleksandr Ostrovsky:** Russian dramatist. Greatest representative of the Russian realistic period. Works: *Poverty Is No Crime, The Diary of a Scoundrel* and *The Storm.*
The entire civil service is like a fortress made of papers, forms and red tape.

1900   **Claire Leighton:** English illustrator and author. Created unique wood-engravings for classics and children's books, including *Four Hedges.*
Does one think the world wicked, or foolish, or falling to bits, then half an hour with a bulb catalogue will cure that nonsense.

1904   **Lily Pons:** French-born U.S. coloratura soprano with Metropolitan Opera (1931–56). During WWII, toured battle fronts in North Africa, India, China and Burma. Repertoire included. *Lakmé* and *Lucia di Lammermoor.* Her motto:
Earn a lot and give gloriously.

1909   **Lionel Hampton:** American jazz vibraphonist, pianist, drummer and bandleader. First to exploit the vibraphone in jazz. Played with Benny Goodman quartets and quintets (1936–40). Formed his own bands in the forties. Compositions: "Vibraphone Blues," "Flyin' Home" and "Hey-baba-re-bop."
All art is a communication of the artist's ideas, sounds, thoughts.

1919   **Ann Miller:** American dancer, actress. A zestful dancer with about the best legs in Hollywood. Appeared as the second female lead in MGM musicals *Easter Parade, On the Town,* and as a marvelous Bianca in *Kiss Me Kate.*
People are apt to overlook my face for my feet.

1947   **David Letterman:** American comedian and late-night talk show host. Star of NBC's "Late Night with David Letterman" which followed "The Tonight Show" (1982–93), before moving to CBS as a competitor with Jay Leno (1993). Noted for humorous lists of ten.
For New York City people [winter] is the worst time of year. While you're wearing mittens, it's virtually impossible to give somebody the finger.

April 13

1519   **Catherine de Medici:** Daughter of Lorenzo de Medici of Florence, Italy. Married Henry II of France. Regent (1560–74). Mother of Francis II and Charles IX. Nursed dynastic ambitions. Drawn into political and religious intrigues. Connived the infamous Massacre of St. Bartholomew.
Ah, sentiments of mercy are in union with a woman's heart.

1618   **Comte de Roger Bussy-Rabutin:** French courtier, soldier, satirist. Member of the Académie Française. Chiefly known for his urbane and malicious "Histoire amoureuse des Gaules," a partially fictitious tale of court scandals.
Where we have not what we like, we must like what we have.

1743   **Thomas Jefferson:** Third president of the U.S. (1801–9). As a delegate to the Continental Congress (1775–76), drafted the Declaration of Independence. Governor of Virginia and minister to France. John Adams' vice-president in 1800 election tied with Aaron Burr in electoral votes. Chosen president by House of Representatives. Established the University of Virginia.

The tree of liberty must be refreshed from time to time with the blood of patriots and tyrants. It is its natural manure.

1875　Ray L. Wilbur: American educator, cabinet official and author. Secretary of Interior (1929-33). President of Stanford University (1916-43).

The potential possibilities of any child are the most intriguing and stimulating in all creation.

1906　Samuel Beckett: Irish-born French novelist, dramatist, poet. Wrote most of his plays in French, then translated them to English. Best known for his literature of the absurd. Plays: *Waiting for Godot* and *Endgame.* Nobel Prize (1969).

We are all born mad. Some remain so.

1909　Eudora Welty: Pulitzer Prize-winning American novelist and short-story writer. Author of *The Robber Bridegroom, The Ponder Heart* and *The Optimist's Daughter.* Received two Guggenheim fellowships, three O. Henry awards and the National Medal for Literature.

Never think you've seen the last of anything…

1922　John Braine: One of the "angry young men" of English literature. Wrote *Room at the Top, Life at the Top* and *One and Last Love.*

Being a writer in a library is rather like being an eunuch in a harem.

April 14

1866　Anne Sullivan Macy: American educator. Nearly blind from a childhood fever, she was educated at the Perkins Institution. Returned there in 1887 to teach seven-year-old Helen Keller. Sullivan became able to communicate with Helen by spelling out words on her hand.

Children require guidance and sympathy far more than instruction.

1879　James Branch Cabell: American novelist, essayist and poet. Wrote: a sequence of 18 novels, collectively called *Biography of Michael* of which *Jurgen* is

the best known. They are set in an imaginary mediaeval kingdom.

The optimist proclaims that we live in the best of all possible worlds; and the pessimist fears this is true.

1889　Arnold Toynbee: English historian. His greatest work, the 12-volume *A Study of History,* a comparison of 21 different civilizations.

Always look ahead. Look far ahead as a racing motorist looks, through his telescopic sight, at the horizon which he will have reached before he knows it.

1899　Carlos P. Romulo: Philippine statesman, journalist. One of the founders of the United Nations First Asian to serve as president of U.N. General Assembly.

Literacy is a significant yardstick of the development of a nation.

1904　Sir John Gielgud: British actor of stage and screen. One of the most eminent interpreters of Shakespeare. Nominated for an Oscar for *Becket,* won one for *Arthur.*

Acting is half shame, half glory. Shame at exhibiting yourself, glory when you can forget yourself.

1923　John Caldwell Holt: American educator. Author of *How Children Fail, How Children Learn* and *The Underachieving School.*

Make a kid feel stupid and he'll act stupider.

1935　Loretta Lynn: U.S. country singer. Married at 14. Had 6 children, grandmother at 32. "Coal Miner's Daughter" is her nickname, one of her biggest hits, the title of her autobiography and also a film based on her life. Youngest person elected to the Country Hall of Fame (1988).

[I am] a spokesperson for every woman who had gotten married too early, gotten pregnant too often, and felt trapped by the tedium and drudgery of her life.

April 15

1452　Leonardo da Vinci: Italian painter, sculptor, architect, engineer. Archetypal

Renaissance man. Universal genius. One of the greatest intellects in the history of mankind. His *Notebooks* are a treasure of art criticism, scientific investigation and inventions centuries ahead of their time. Paintings: *The Adoration of the Magi, The Last Supper* and *Mona Lisa.*

O Lord / Thou givest us everything / At the price / Of our effort.

1814   **John Lothrop Motley:** U.S. diplomat, historian. Best remembered for the three-volume *The Rise of the Dutch Empire.* Minister to Austria (1861–67); to Great Britain (1869–70).

Give us the luxuries of life, and we will dispense with its necessities.

1832   **Wilhelm Busch:** German cartoonist and poet. Best known for wise, satiric drawings, accompanied by his own short rhymes, chastising human weaknesses. His "Max und Moritz" were the prototypes for Rudolph Dirks' "Katzenjammer Kids."

Becoming a father is easy enough / But being one can be rough.

1843   **Henry James:** American novelist, short-story writer, critic. Major figure in the history of the psychological novel. His early novels, *Portrait of a Lady* and *The Bostonians,* explored the relationship between innocence and experience, with Americans representing innocence and Europeans, experience. Other works: *The Turn of the Screw* and *The Ambassadors.*

It takes a great deal of history to produce a little literature.

1889   **A. Philip Randolph:** American black labor leader. Organized the Brotherhood of Sleeping Car Porters (1925). Directed the massive 1963 civil-rights march on Washington, D.C.

Violence seldom accomplishes permanent and desired results. Herein lies the futility of war.

1920   **Thomas Szasz:** Hungarian-born American psychiatrist, author. Wrote: *Pain and Pleasure, The Myth of Mental Illness* and *The Ethics of Psychoanalysis.*

The stupid neither forgive nor forget; the naive forgive and forget; the wise forgive but do not forget.

1951   **Heloise Cruse Evans:** American journalist. Took over her mother's nationally syndicated "Hints from Heloise" column, 1977.

The graveyards are full of women whose houses were so spotless you could eat off the floor. Remember the second wife always has a maid.

April 16

1844   **Anatole France:** Pseudonym of Jacques Anatole François Thibault. French poet, novelist and critic. Reached peak of his fame at the turn of the century. Dreyfus case stirred him to become a champion of internationalism. Nobel Prize (1921). Novels: *The Crime of Sylvester Bonnard, Penguin Island* and *The Gods Are Athirst.*

To die for an idea is to place a pretty high price upon conjecture.

1867   **Wilbur Wright:** U.S. aviation pioneer. With his brother Orville made the first powered, controlled and sustained airplane flight, December 17, 1903.

It is possible to fly without motors, but not without knowledge and skill.

1871   **John Millington Synge:** Foremost dramatist of Irish Renaissance. Claimed his works amounted to literal transcriptions of the language of Western Ireland's peasants. Plays: *Riders to the Sea* and *Playboy of the Western World.*

There is no language like the Irish for soothing and quieting.

1889   **Sir Charles Chaplin:** London-born actor, director, producer, screenwriter, composer. Chaplin developed the character of the "Little Tramp." Chaplin's genius was with pantomime. Cofounder of United Artists. Refused to cooperate with HUAC, causing him to be absent from U.S. for 20 years. Films: *The Tramp, The Kid, The Gold Rush, City Lights, Modern Times, The Great Dictator* and *Monsieur Verdoux.*

I don't mind coincidence—life is coincidence—but I hate convenience.

1900   **Polly Adler:** America's most famous madam. Began her career in 1920.

Operated very successful Broadway bordellos. Wrote a best-selling autobiography, *A House Is Not a Home*.

The degree to which a pimp, if he's clever, can confuse and delude a prostitute is very nearly unlimited.

1921 **Sir Peter Ustinov:** British actor, director, playwright, novelist, raconteur. Possesses a wonderfully mellifluous voice. Winner of a Tony, two Oscars, an Emmy and a Grammy. Directed an opera at Covent Garden (1962). Wrote best-selling memoir, *Dear Me.*

Parents are the bones on which children cut their teeth.

1947 **Kareem Abdul-Jabbar:** Born Ferdinand Lewis Alcindor, Jr., 7' 2" Kareem led UCLA to a 88-2 record and three national championships. Had his greatest pro success with L.A. Lakers, winning 5 NBA championships in 9 years.

A black man has to fight for respect in basketball, season after season. And I measure that respect in the figures on my contract.

April 17

1586 **John Ford:** English dramatist, known for his portrayal of passion and concentration on sexual abnormalities in works such as *Tis a Pity She's a Whore* and *The Lady's Trial.*

Glories / Of human greatness are but pleasing dreams / And shadows soon decaying.

1842 **Charles H. Parkhurst:** American Presbyterian clergyman, reformer and author. Books: *Our Fight with Tammany, A Little Lower Than the Angels* and *The Pulpit and the Pew.*

Purposelessness is the fruitful mother of crime.

1859 **Walter Camp:** "Father of American Football." One of founders of Intercollegiate Football Association, forerunner of Ivy League. Originated arrangement of seven linemen, four in the backfield. Named first All-American team (1889).

There is no substitute for hard work and

effort beyond the call of mere duty. That is what strengthens the soul and ennobles one's character.

1885 **Isak Dinesen:** Pseudonym of Karen Blixen. Danish novelist and short-story writer. From 1914 to 1931 lived on a coffee plantation in what is now Kenya. Wrote *Seven Gothic Tales, Out of Africa* and *Winter's Tales.*

We must leave our mark on life while we have it in our power, but it should close up, when we leave it; without a trace.

1894 **Nikita Khrushchev:** Soviet communist leader. As first secretary of the Soviet Communist Party and premier started a program of de-Stalinization. Enunciated a policy of peaceful coexistence with Western powers, strained with the Cuban missile crisis.

Economics is a subject that does not greatly respect one's wishes.

1897 **Thornton Wilder:** American novelist, playwright. Pulitzer Prize for *The Bridge of San Luis Rey. The Eighth Day* won the National Book Award (1968). Plays: *Our Town, The Skin of Our Teeth* and *The Matchmaker.*

The best thing about animals is that they don't talk much.

1923 **Harry Reasoner:** U.S. journalist. Principal anchorman for ABC (1970-78). Regular on television's "60 Minutes" (1968-70, 1978-91).

What youth is afraid of is that in old age strength to protest will be gone, but the terror of life will remain.

April 18

1480 **Lucrezia Borgia:** Roman-born noblewoman. Illegitimate daughter of Cardinal Borgia (later Pope Alexander VI). Sister of Cesare Borgia. Three times married to further her father's political ambitions. A patroness of art and education. Her reputation as a wanton and poisoner is probably unwarranted.

The more I try to do God's will the more he visits me with misfortune.

1570 **Thomas Middleton:** English dramatist. One of the most popular playwrights of his period. Often collaborated with Thomas Dekker or William Rowley. His masterpieces are *The Changeling* and *A Trick to Catch the Old One.*
A man is never too old to learn.

1817 **George Henry Lewes:** English philosophical writer, literary critic. Chiefly remembered for his theory of metaphysical development of positivism and his liaison with novelist George Eliot (Mary Ann Evans).
Many a genius has been slow of growth. Oaks that flourish for a thousand years do not spring up into beauty like a reed.

1857 **Clarence Darrow:** American lawyer, lecturer, writer. Categorically opposed to capital punishment. Lost the battle in the famous "Scopes Monkey Trail," but won the war by destroying his opponent William Jennings Bryan, when Bryan took the stand as an expert Bible witness.
The pursuit of truth will set you free, even if you never catch up with it.

1864 **Richard Harding Davis:** American journalist, novelist, short-story writer, war correspondent in six wars. Managing editor of *Harper's Weekly*. Author of *Soldiers of Fortune* and *The Bar Sinister.*
No civilized person goes to bed the same day he gets up.

1882 **Leopold Stokowski:** American Music director, Philadelphia Orchestra (1912–36). Organized All-American Youth Orchestra (1940–41). Helped popularize classics. Lecturing a talkative audience:
A painter paints his pictures on canvas. But musicians paint their pictures on silence. We provide the music and you provide the silence.

1917 **Frederika Louise:** German-born Queen of Greece (1947–64). Went into self-imposed exile when the monarchy was overthrown in 1973. When she married Constantine, she told the Greek people:
I was born a barbarian. I came to Greece to be civilized.

April 19

1721 **Roger Sherman:** U.S. statesman, lawyer, surveyor. Signer of the Declaration of Independence. Also signed the Articles of Association, Articles of Confederation and the Constitution, the only person to sign all four documents. U.S. senator from Connecticut (1791–93).
When you are in a minority, talk; when you are in a majority, vote.

1772 **David Ricardo:** English political economist. Proposed an iron law of wages, stating that wages tend to stabilize around the subsistence level. Most known for "Principles of Political Economy and Taxation."
Taxation under every form presents but a choice of evils.

1885 **Philip Curtiss:** U.S. novelist. Wrote *Between Two Worlds, The Gay Conspirators* and *The Honorable Charlie.*
Like many a race of persons or ideas, the race of smells has suffered cruelly on account of its lowest members.

1900 **Constance Talmadge:** American silent screen star. Her vivacity and sense of realism beguiled audiences. Adept at comedy. Films: *Intolerance, A Virtuous Vamp* and *Polly of the Follies.* She and sister Norma retired with the advent of sound.
I try to handle a comedy role the way a cartoonist handles his pencils ... One must leave a great deal to the imagination of the audience.

1901 **Edith Clara Summerskill:** English politician, gynecologist, member of Parliament and writer. Fought for women's welfare on all issues, often provoking hostility. Wrote *A Woman's World.*
... Governments still pin their faith to some new economic nostrum which is periodically produced by some bright young man. Only time proves that his alleged magic touch is illusory.

1932 **Jayne Mansfield:** Buxom sexpot of films in the fifties and sixties. Break came in Broadway production of *Will*

Success Spoil Rock Hunter? in which she appeared clad only in a Turkish towel. Killed in a car accident.

Men are those creatures with two legs and eight hands.

1935 **Dudley Moore:** London-born actor, musician, composer. The 5' 2" Moore is recognized as a fine jazz pianist and composer of music scores. Became a film star with *10*. Oscar nominated for *Arthur*.

What else is there to live for? Chinese food and women. There is nothing else!

April 20

0121 **Marcus Aurelius [Antoninus]:** Roman emperor, Stoic philosopher. Philosophical reflections contained in *The Meditations of Marcus Aurelius*.

The universe is change; our life is what our thoughts make of it.

1826 **Dinah Mulock Craik:** English poet and novelist. Author of Victorian best seller *John Halifax, Gentleman*. First published at 20 with *The Ogilvies*.

Believe only half of what you see and nothing that you hear.

1889 **Adolf Hitler:** "Der Fuhrer." Leader of National Socialist Party (Nazis) (1921-45). Dictator of Germany (1933-45). Instituted policies of anti–Semitism and German territorial expansion, seeking world domination, leading to WWII. Committed suicide in a Berlin bunker (1945).

The broad mass of a nation ... will more easily fall victim to a big lie than a small one.

1893 **Joan Miro:** Spanish artist. Became a member of the French school of surrealist painters. His works are predominantly abstract using curvilinear, fantastical forms in dreamlike settings. They are a mix of frivolous humor and nightmares.

Painting is made as we make love, a total embrace, prudence thrown to the wind, nothing held back.

1906 **Stanley Marcus:** U.S. merchant. President of Texas' Neiman-Marcus. Started the international fashion expositions and the Neiman-Marcus awards.

Any fine store can dress a few women beautifully. Our idea is to dress a whole community of women that way.

1920 **John Paul Stevens:** U.S. jurist. Judge of U.S. Court of Appeals for the Seventh District (Chicago) (1970–75). Appointed associate justice of the U.S. Supreme Court (1975). Considered a legal centrist.

It is not our job to apply laws that have not yet been written.

1949 **Jessica Lange:** U.S. actress. Made her debut as a toothsome foil in 1976 remake of *King Kong*. Developed into one of the screen's finest actresses. Oscar for her supporting role in *Tootsie*; the same year she was nominated in the Best Actress category for *Frances*. Best Actress Oscar winner for *Blue Sky*. Also nominated for *Country*, *Sweet Dreams* and *Music Box*.

When you learn not to want things so badly, life comes to you.

April 21

1729 **Catherine the Great:** German-born Sophia Frederike von Anhalt- Zerbst. Russian empress (1762–96). Overthrew neurotic husband Czar Peter III with help of the palace guard. Annexed Crimea. Divided Poland among Russia, Austria and Prussia (1795). One of Europe's most successful rulers.

I shall be an autocrat: that's my trade. And the good Lord will forgive me: that's his.

1816 **Charlotte Brontë:** English novelist. Her novel *Jane Eyre* was in part based on her unhappy experiences at the dreadful Clergy Daughters' School where her two eldest sisters died.

Conventionality is not morality. Self-righteousness is not a religion. To attack the first is not to assail the last.

1818 **Josh Billings:** Pseudonym of Henry Wheeler Shaw. American auctioneer, real-estate agent and humorist. Studied techniques of Artemus Ward. Turned his hand to writing humorous essays: *Josh Billings: His Book of Sayings* and annual volumes *Josh Billings' Farmer Allminax* (1870–90).

Nature never makes any blunders, when she makes a fool she means it.

1828 **Hippolyte A. Taine:** French literary and art critic, historian and intellectual leader. Known for emphasis on role of scientific determinism in literature. Greatest work: *The Origins of Contemporary France.*

There are four types of men in the world: lovers, opportunists, lookers-on, and imbeciles. The happiest are the imbeciles.

1882 **Percy Williams Bridgeman:** U.S. physicist. Nobel Prize winner (1946) pioneering for work in the development of high-pressure chambers for the study of matter at extreme pressures.

There is no adequate defence, except stupidity, against the impact of a new idea.

1896 **Henri de Montherlant:** French novelist and playwright. Advocated the overcoming of conflicts of life by vigorous action. Major work is a four-novel cycle, beginning with *Pity for Women*. Wrote several plays, including *Don Juan*.

Most affections are habits or duties we lack the courage to end.

1926 **Queen Elizabeth II:** British monarch. Succeeded father George VI, 1952. Richest woman in England. Saddened of late by the fire at Windsor castle and the unhappy marriages of her children.

The upward course of a nation's history is due in the long run to the soundness of heart of its average men and women.

April 22

1451 **Isabella of Spain:** Queen of Castile (1474–1505). Married King Ferdinand II of Aragon, jointly ruling both kingdoms. Patron of Christopher Columbus, financing his voyages to the New World.

Although I have never doubted it ... the distance is great from the firm belief to the realization from concrete experience.

1707 **Henry Fielding:** English novelist, playwright. Best known for picaresque novels. Organized the detective force that became Scotland Yard. Novels: *Tom Jones* and *Joseph Andrews*. Best known play: *Tom Thumb.*

Commend a fool for his wit, or a knave for his honesty, and they will receive you into their bosom.

1724 **Immanuel Kant:** German philosopher. Maintained that there are basic concepts, like cause and effect, which are not learned from experience but constitute the basic conceptual apparatus by which we make sense of experience and the world. Major works: *Critique of Pure Reason, Critique of Practical Reason* and *Critique of Judgment.*

Morality is not properly the doctrine of how we may make ourselves happy, but how we may make ourselves worthy of happiness.

1766 **Madame Germaine de Staël [-Holstein]:** Swiss-French novelist and woman of letters. Known for her salons which were attended by the leading literary and political figures of her day.

Politeness is the art of selecting among one's real thoughts.

1870 **Vladimir Ilyich Lenin:** Russian revolutionary. Spent many years in Western exile. After the overthrow of the Czar, led the Bolsheviks to power (1917). Became head of Soviet state, establishing the "dictatorship of the proletariat." Retained post until his death in 1924.

We are dead men on furlough.

1899 **Vladimir Nabokov:** Russian-born American novelist, poet. Became U.S. citizen (1945). Novels: *Invitation to a Beheading, Lolita, Laughter in the Dark, Pale Fire* and *The Gift.*

Our existence is but a brief crack of light between two eternities of darkness.

1904 **J. Robert Oppenheimer:** American physicist. Headed Los Alamos, New Mexico, laboratories during development of atomic bomb (1943–45). Proclaimed a security risk for his reluctance to proceed with its development. Fermi Award (1963).

Both the man of science and the man of action live always at the edge of mystery, surrounded by it.

April 23

1584 William Shakespeare: English poet, dramatist of the Elizabethan and early Jacobian period. Most widely known author in English literature. His plays have been performed almost continuously to this day. Wrote comedies, histories and tragedies, as well as 154 sonnets. Plays include: *Henry IV*, *Henry I*, and *Henry II*, *Richard III*, *A Midsummer Night's Dream*, *Romeo and Juliet*, *The Merchant of Venice*, *Henry V*, *Julius Caesar*, *Hamlet*, *Othello*, *King Lear*, *Macbeth* and *Antony and Cleopatra*.

This above all: to thine own self be true, / And it must follow, as the night the day, / Thou canst not then be false to any man.

1813 Stephen A. Douglas: U.S. politician and lawyer. Congressman from Illinois (1843–47), senator (1847–61). A great orator known for debates with Abraham Lincoln during 1858 Senate campaign on questions of slavery. Defeated for presidency by Lincoln (1860).

There can be no neutrals in this war— only patriots or traitors.

1852 Edwin Markham: American poet, lecturer. Best known for his poem, "The Man with a Hoe." Other works: *Lincoln and other Poems* and *Field Folk: Interpretations of Millet*.

He drew a circle that shut me out—Heretic, rebel, a thing to flaunt. / But love and I had the wit to win: / We drew a circle that took him in.

1858 Max Planck: German physicist. Modern physics began with his proposal of quantum theory, which states that electromagnetic radiation consists of quanta (particles of energy). 1918 Nobel Prize in physics.

A new scientific truth does not triumph by convincing its opponents, but rather because its opponents die, and a new generation grows up that is familiar with it.

1897 Lester Pearson: Canadian statesman, diplomat. Headed Canadian delegation to U.N. (1948–57). Awarded 1957 Nobel Peace Prize for work in Suez crisis of 1956. Prime minister (1963–68).

The grim fact is that we prepare for war like precocious giants and for peace like retarded pygmies.

1916 Charles W. "Bud" Wilkinson: U.S. football player and coach. Led Oklahoma to three national titles. His teams had a 47-game winning streak.

The man who tried and failed is superior to the man who never tried.

1947 Bernadette Devlin: Irish political activist. At 21, the youngest woman ever elected to British Parliament where she served 1969–74.

To gain that which is worth having, it may be necessary to lose everything else.

April 24

1815 Anthony Trollope: Prolific English writer of novels of Victorian life. Best known works are the two series, *Chronicles of Barsetshire* and the *Parliamentary* novels.

Love is like any other luxury. You have no right to it unless you can afford it.

1856 Henri Pétain: French Army marshal. Defense of Verdun made him a national hero. As French premier in 1940, negotiated armistice with Germany. Headed Vichy government of unoccupied France until 1944. Imprisoned as a collaborator after war.

To write one's memoirs is to speak ill of everybody except oneself.

1904 William de Kooning: Dutch-born American artist. His work had a strong influence on American Abstract Expressionism. Awarded Andrew W. Mellon Prize (1979). Noted for his controversial series of "Woman" (1950–53).

The trouble with being poor is that it takes up all your time.

1905 Robert Penn Warren: American poet, novelist. Coeditor of two anthologies of Southern writing. Poetry: *Promises* and *Now and Then Poems* both of which were awarded Pulitzer prizes. Became internationally famous for his political novel *All the King's Men*, loosely based on the life of Louisiana's Huey Long.

History is all explained by geography.

1930   **Dorothy Uhnak:** American mystery novelist and policewoman. Wrote bestselling novels *The Investigation* and *Law and Order*. New York City cop for 14 years. Received department's highest award for heroism.

I like to deliver more than I promise instead of the other way around, which is just one of my trade secrets.

1934   **Shirley MacLaine:** U.S. actress, at home in comedies and dramas. Oscar for *Terms of Endearment*. Nominated for *Some Came Running*, *The Apartment*, *Irma La Douce* and *Madame Sousatzka*. Wrote best selling books about her out-of-body experiences.

The best way to get most husbands to do something is to suggest that perhaps they're too old to do it.

1942   **Barbra Streisand:** U.S. singer, actress, producer, director, and songwriter. Conquered Broadway with *Funny Girl*. Song hits: "People," "The Way We Were," "Evergreen," and "Woman in Love." Oscar winner for *Funny Girl*. Nominated for *The Way We Were*.

The principal difference between a dog and a man is if you pick up a starving dog and make him prosperous, he will not bite you.

April 25

1533   **William I:** "The Silent." Prince of Orange, great leader in the struggle for the independence of the Netherlands from Spanish rule. Assassinated (1584).

It is not necessary to hope in order to act, or to succeed in order to persevere.

1599   **Oliver Cromwell:** English Puritan leader. Lord Protector of the Realm (1653–58). Commanded famous cavalry regiment Ironsides, parliamentary forces that defeated the Royalists, leading to the execution of King Charles I, making Cromwell virtually a dictator.

Do not trust to the cheering, for those persons would shout as much if ... I were going to be hanged.

1873   **Walter de La Mare:** English poet, novelist, anthropologist. Romantic writer with interests in childhood, nature, dreams and the uncanny. Works: *Songs of Childhood*, *The Return* and *The Veil*.

It is a very odd thing— / As odd as can be— / That whatever Miss T eats / Turns into Miss T.

1906   **William J. Brennan, Jr.:** U.S. jurist. Associate justice of Supreme Court (1956–1990). Wrote many majority decisions dealing with areas of obscenity and antitrust.

Law cannot stand aside from the social changes around it.

1908   **Edward R. Murrow:** Legendary journalist, fondly recalled for his inspirational reports from London before the U.S. entered WWII. Regular on television's "See It Now" (1951–58), "Person to Person" (1953–59), "Small World" (1958–60), and "CBS Reports" (1959–61).

Our major obligation is not to mistake slogans for solutions.

1918   **Ella Fitzgerald:** American singer, composer. Began singing at 16 with Chick Webb band. Became a star with "A-tisket, a-tasket," which she cowrote. Fitzgerald's wide-ranging voice and superb phrasing made her perhaps the greatest jazz ballad and scat singer.

Just don't give up trying to do what you really want to do. When there is love and inspiration, I don't think you can go wrong.

1940   **Al Pacino:** Intense, brooding American actor. Oscar winner for *Scent of a Woman*. Nominated for *The Godfather*, *The Godfather Part II*, *Serpico*, *Dog Day Afternoon*, *...And Justice for All*, *Dick Tracy* and *Glengarry Glen Ross*.

An actor becomes an emotional athlete. You work on yourself as an instrument.

April 26

1661 Daniel DeFoe: English author and adventurer. Won King William II's favor with his satirical poem "The True-born Englishman," an attack on xenophobic prejudice. Greatest fame is reserved for his best-known work *Robinson Crusoe.*

It is not the longest sword but the longest purse that conquers.

1711 David Hume: Scottish philosopher, historian. Restricted all knowledge to the experience of ideas or impressions. Maintained the mind consists only of accumulated perceptions. Wrote *A Treatise of Human Nature.*

Beauty in things exists in the mind which contemplates them.

1798 Eugène Delacroix: French painter. One of the great colorists of the Romantic movement. Used literary and historical subjects for his paintings, *Dante and Vergil in Hell, Massacre at Chios* and *Liberty Guiding the People.*

Experience has two things to teach: the first is that we must correct a great deal; the second, that we must not correct too much.

1834 Artemus Ward: Pen name of Charles Farrar Browne. American humorist from Maine. Works: *Artemus Ward: His Book* and *Artemus Ward: His Travels.*

Let us be happy and live within our means, even if we have to borrow the money to do it.

1886 Ma Rainey: Born Gertrude Pridgett. American blues singer and composer. One of the first to sing the blues on a stage. Began making recordings in 1923. Toured with her own company in vaudeville. Bessie Smith, a member of the troupe, became her pupil and protégée.

White folks hear the blues come out, but they don't know how it got there.

1893 Anita Loos: American novelist, scriptwriter. Wrote scripts for D.W. Griffith at 15. Plays: *Happy Birthday* and *Gigi.* Novel *Gentlemen Prefer Blondes* has been filmed twice and staged as a Broadway musical.

A girl with brains ought to do something else with them besides think.

1917 I.M. Pei: American architect known for innovative modernist structures. Buildings: National Airlines Terminal, Kennedy Airport; Herbert F. Johnson Museum of Art, Cornell University; National Gallery of Art, East Building, Washington, D.C.

Good architecture lets nature in.

April 27

1737 Edward Gibbon: English historian. Entered Parliament (1774). His masterpiece is *The History of the Decline and Fall of the Roman Empire,* which he was inspired to write during a tour of Italy.

History is indeed little more than the register of the crimes, follies and misfortunes of mankind.

1759 Mary Wollstonecraft Godwin: English author. Best know for the first great feminist manifesto, *Vindication of the Rights of Woman.* Died when her daughter Mary, later Mary Wollstonecraft Shelley, was born.

I do not wish [women] to have power over men, but over themselves.

1820 Herbert Spencer: English philosopher, social scientist. Applied the scientific principles of evolution to philosophy and ethics. Works: *Principles of Psychology* and *System of Synthetic Philosophy* (ten volumes).

Opinion is ultimately determined by the feelings, and not by the intellect.

1822 U.S. Grant: Eighteenth President of the United States. As Union Army general captured Vicksburg (1863). Made Commander-in-chief of Union Army (1864). Forced and accepted Robert E. Lee's surrender. Presidential administration beset by corruption and partisan politics.

I know no method to secure the repeal of bad or obnoxious laws so effective as their stringent execution.

1898 Ludwig Bemelmans: Austrian-born American writer, painter. Often illustrated his books with his own watercolors and drawings. Wrote books for children, most notably, *Madeleine.*

The true gourmet, like the true artist, is one of the unhappiest creatures existent. His trouble comes from so seldom finding what he constantly seeks: perfection.

1904 Cecil Day-Lewis: Irish-born British poet, critic, author. Wrote detective stories under pen name Nicholas Blake. Named Poet Laureate (1968). Father of actor Daniel Day Lewis. Collections: *The Magnetic Mountain* and *The Gate.*

We do not write in order to be understood; We write in order to understand.

1927 Coretta Scott King: American civil rights leader, lecturer, author. Widow of Martin Luther King, Jr. President Martin Luther King Center for Nonviolent Social Change.

When aroused, the American conscience is a powerful force for reform.

April 28

1758 James Monroe: Fifth U.S. president (1817–25). As minister to France, participated in the negotiations for the Louisiana Purchase. Secretary of state (1811–17). Established the Monroe Doctrine, warning Europe not to interfere in the Western Hemisphere.

National honor is national property of the highest value.

1874 Karl Kraus: Austrian journalist, critic and poet. Satirist compared to Juvenal and Jonathan Swift. Publisher and sole writer of the radical satirical magazine *The Torch* (1899–1936). Plays: *The Last Days of Mankind* and *The Unconquerable One.*

To be sure, the dog is loyal. But why, on that account, should we take him as an example? He is loyal to men, not to other dogs.

1878 Lionel Barrymore: American stage, screen and radio actor. First of the three Broadway Barrymore star siblings to appear on screen. Oscar winner for *A Free Soul.* Others: *Young Dr. Kildare* (14 more films in series) and *Key Largo.*

Even the catnip of hero-worship loses its effect eventually...

1901 George Crane: American psychologist. Author of *Radio Talks, Psychology Applied* and a syndicated column "The Worry Clinic."

There is no future in any job. The future lies in the man who holds the job.

1924 Kenneth Kaunda: Zambian politician. Founded the Zambian African National Congress (1958). Played a leading role in country's independence negotiations. Became first president (1964) when independence was obtained.

The power which establishes a state is violence; the power which maintains it is violence; the power which eventually overthrows it is violence.

1926 Harper Lee: American novelist. Her novel *To Kill a Mockingbird* won unanimous critical acclaim and a Pulitzer Prize (1961).

The one thing that doesn't abide by majority rule is a person's conscience.

1937 Saddam Hussein: Iraqui political leader. President of Iraq (1979–). His 1990 invasion of Kuwait prompted "Operation Desert Storm" during Persian Gulf war with U.S. and allies.

We would rather die than be humiliated, and we will pluck out the eyes of those who attack the Arab nation.

April 29

1833 Julia Louise Woodruff: American author. Used pen name W.M.L. Jay. Wrote, *Shiloh or, Without and Within, My Winter in Cuba* and *The Daisy Seekers.*

Out of the strain of the Doing, / Into the peace of the Done.

1854 Henri Poincaré: French mathematician. Made major contributions in most areas of mathematics, especially the three-body problem and tidal forces, opening up new directions in celestial mechanics.

Science is built up with facts, as a house is with stones. But a collection of facts is no more a science than a heap of stones is a house.

1863 William Randolph Hearst: American newspaper publisher. Built a vast newspaper and magazine empire. Name became synonymous with "yellow journalism." Helped launch the Spanish-American War. Served in Congress (1903–7).

A politician will do anything to keep his job—even become a patriot.

1879 Sir Thomas Beecham: British conductor. Founded British National Opera Company, the London Philharmonic and Royal Philharmonic. Artistic director of Covent Garden.

There are two golden rules for an orchestra: start together and finish together. The public doesn't give a damn what goes on in between.

1899 Duke Ellington: American jazz composer, bandleader, pianist. Major jazz influence. Led his orchestra (1923–74). Compositions: "Mood Indigo," "Satin Doll" and "Sophisticated Lady."

A Satin Doll is a woman who is as pretty on the inside as she is on the outside.

1901 Hirohito: Emperor of Japan (1926–89). Helped convince Japanese government to surrender to Allies (1945). Publicly renounced his imperial divinity. Wrote monographs on marine biology. After the attack on Hiroshima:

We have resolved to endure the unendurable and suffer what is unsufferable.

1933 Rod McKuen: American poet, singer, songwriter. Wrote popular song "Jean" for movie *The Prime of Miss Jean Brodie* (1963).

People are not born bastards. They have to work at it.

April 30

1771 Hoseau Ballou: American preacher. Originally a Baptist, he was the chief founder of Universalism. Editor of *The Universalist Magazine* (1819–28).

A religion that requires persecution to sustain it is of the devil's propagation.

1777 Karl Friedrich Gauss: German mathematician. Usually ranked with Archimedes and Newton as one of the three greatest mathematicians of all time. Often called the founder of modern mathematics. Did research in infinitesimal calculus, algebra and astronomy. A pioneer in topology His book on theory of numbers is generally considered his greatest accomplishment.

Mathematics is the queen of the sciences.

1870 Franz Lehár: Hungarian composer and conductor. Wrote popular operettas *The Merry Widow, The Count of Luxembourg* and *The Land of Smiles.* Last words:

Now I have finished with all earthly business, and high time too. Yes, yes, my dear child, now comes death.

1877 Alice B. Toklas: Expatriate American. Longtime secretary and companion of author Gertrude Stein who wrote *The Autobiography of Alice B. Toklas.*

Dawn comes slowly but dusk is rapid.

1909 Juliana: Queen of the Netherlands (1948–80). Became a lawyer. On the German invasion of Holland, she escaped to Britain and from there to Canada. Returned to Holland (1945). Became queen on the abdication of her mother Wilhelmina. Abdicated in favor of her daughter Beatrix.

You are interested in the kitchens of the world—you want to find out what is cooking ... who has a finger in the pie and who will burn his finger.

1933 Willie Nelson: American country and western singer, guitarist. Winner of three Grammys and eight Country Music Association Awards. Hits: "My Heroes Have Always Been Cowboys," "On the Road Again" and "Always on My Mind."

Life is just another scene from the world of broken dreams.

1961 Isiah Thomas: American basketball guard. All-American with University of Indiana. Led Detroit Pistons to two championships (1989, 1990).

When I was in high school and college, I thought the guys in the NBA always cooled it out until the fourth quarter. It was almost as if they didn't care. Well, it's true.

May 1

1672   **Joseph Addison:** English poet, essayist, critic. Helped perfect the essay as a literary form with his contributions to *The Tatler* and *The Spectator*. Works: "The Campaign" and "Cato."
Contentment is the utmost we can hope for in this world.

1769   **Arthur Wellesley, 1st Duke of Wellington:** "Iron Duke." English general, statesman. Represented England at the Congress of Vienna (1814–15). Defeated Napoleon at Waterloo. Prime Minister (1828–30).
Nothing except a battle lost can be half as melancholy as a battle won.

1830   **Mother Mary Jones:** Irish-born U.S. labor leader. Gained fame as agitator for Appalachian coal miners. Led children's march from Kensington, Pennsylvania, to the Sagamore Hill, New York, home of President Theodore Roosevelt to dramatize the evils of child labor.
Pray for the dead and fight like hell for the living.

1852   **Santiago Ramon y Cajal:** Spanish histologist. His basic study revealed the connection between the cells in the brain and the spinal cord.
That which enters the mind through reason can be corrected. That which is admitted through faith, hardly ever.

1881   **Pierre Teilhard de Chardin:** French Jesuit priest, theologian, paleontologist. Spent his life attempting to reconcile Christian beliefs with scientific knowledge.
Someday, after mastering the winds, the waves, the tides and gravity, we shall harvest for God the energies of love, and then, for a second time in the history of the world, man will have discovered fire.

1923   **Joseph Heller:** American novelist. Used his experiences as a WWII bombardier as the backdrop for his first and best known novel, *Catch-22*. He maintained he wrote it only to make money. Other novels: *Something Happened* and *Good as Gold*.

Some men are born mediocre, some men achieve mediocrity, and some men have mediocrity thrust upon them.

1926   **Terry Southern:** American novelist, short-story writer, screen-writer. Best known for his black comedy *Candy*, a parody of pornographic books. Screenplays: *Dr. Strangelove, The Loved One* and *Easy Rider*.
You've got to understand that it is not easy to make a bad movie—it requires a very special combination of talents and anti-talents.

May 2

1551   **William Camden:** English antiquary and historian. Headmaster of Westminster School. Compiled a pioneering topographical survey of the British Isles, "Britannia." Published a list of the epitaphs in Westminster Abbey. Also wrote *Annals of the Reign of Elizabeth to 1588*.
It is hard to teach an old dog tricks.

1859   **Jerome K. Jerome:** English humorist, novelist and playwright. Wrote the magnificently ridiculous *Three Men in a Boat* and his morality play *The Passing of the Third-Floor Back*.
Love is like the measles; we all have to go through it.

1860   **Theodor Herzl:** Hungarian-born journalist. Founder of Zionism. Negotiated with Turkey and Britain for a Jewish settlement in Palestine. Wrote *The Jewish State*.
A nation is a historical group of men of recognizable cohesion, held together by a common enemy.

1860   **Sir D'Arcy W. Thompson:** Scottish biologist. Wrote the classic *On Growth and Form* and *A Glossary of Greek Birds*, written in rich literary style, exemplifying his great erudition in physical and natural sciences.
Against a foe I can myself defend,—But heaven protect me from a blundering friend.

1879   **James S. Byrnes:** American politician, lawyer, editor. Senator from South

Carolina. Associate justice of the Supreme Court. Secretary of state. Governor of South Carolina.

Power intoxicates men. It is never voluntarily surrendered. It must be taken from them.

1903   Dr. Benjamin Spock: U.S. pediatrician and author. Major influence on modern American child-rearing practices and health care. *Common Sense Book of Baby and Child Care*, published in 1946, has sold over 30 million copies.

What good mothers and fathers instinctively feel like doing for their babies is usually best after all.

1921   Satyajit Ray: Indian film director. His film *Pather Panchali*, a human documentary dealing with a Bengali village, was a smash hit at the 1956 Cannes Film Festival. Ray made two sequels *Aparajito* and *World of Apu*.

In cinema, we must select everything for the camera according to the richness of its power to reveal.

May 3

1469   Niccolo Machiavelli: Florentine statesman, political philosopher. His masterpiece *The Prince* is regarded as a pioneer of political science. During his lifetime he had the reputation of being a teacher of treachery, intrigue and immortality. The term "Machiavellian" came to describe cynical and ruthless politics.

It is of great consequence to disguise your inclination, and to play the hypocrite well.

1748   Emmanuel Joseph Sieyes: French abbé and statesman. One of the chief theorists of the French Revolution. An architect of the coup that replaced the Directory by the Consulate.

They want to be free and they do not know how to be just.

1853   Edgar Watson Howe: "Sage of Potato Hill." American editor *Atchison Daily Globe* (1877–1911). Publisher, *E.W. Howe's Monthly* (1911–33). Author of novel *The Story of a Country Town*.

A modest man is usually admired—if people ever hear of him.

1874   Josephine Preston Peabody: American poet and playwright. Author of: *The Wayfarers, Fortune and Men's Eyes, The Singing Leaves* and *Harvest Moon*.

One does not expect in this world; one hopes and pays carfare.

1898   Golda Meir: Israeli stateswoman. First woman premier of Israeli (1969–74). A leader in the fight for a state of Israel. Worked to achieve peace with Arab neighbors through diplomacy, but the fourth Arab-Israeli war interfered.

Those who do not know how to weep with their whole heart don't know how to laugh either.

1913   William Inge: American dramatist. Wrote *Come Back Little Sheba, Bus Stop, The Dark at the Top of the Stairs* and *Picnic* (Pulitzer Prize). Transforms the lives or ordinary people living in drab surroundings into significant human experiences.

Theater is, of course, a reflection of life. Maybe we have to improve life before we can hope to improve theater.

1919   Pete Seeger: American folksinger, composer. Formed the Weavers with bass Lee Hays. Group's best-sellers: "Irene, Goodnight," "On Top of Old Smoky" and "Wimoweh." Hits as a soloist: "If I Had a Hammer," "Where Have All the Flowers Gone" and "Guantanamera."

Education is when you read the fine print. Experience is what you get if you don't.

May 4

1796   Horace Mann: "Father of American Public Education." U.S. lawyer, educator, legislator. As secretary of Massachusetts state board of education, labored to improve the public schools, increase teacher salaries and establish teacher training institutions.

In a republic, ignorance is a crime.

1825   Thomas H. Huxley: English biologist, teacher. Best known for his defense of Charles Darwin's theory of evolution. His lectures and writings helped popularize science. Writings: *Evidence as* *to Man's Place in Nature* and *Evolution and Ethics.*

Logical consequences are the scarecrows of fools and the beacons of wise men.

1896   Dr. Frank Baxter: U.S. educator who hosted television series "Now and Then" and "Gateways to the Mind" on such diverse subjects as Shakespeare, the sun, time and the human senses. His shows won 10 major awards, including an Emmy.

People who bring children into the world and are not prepared to feed their brains are ... ignoble.... For God's sake, take Hamlet's advice "Readiness is all."

1919   Heloise [Bowles Reese]: American journalist. Wrote syndicated column on household matters, "Hints from Heloise" (1961–77).

I think housework is the reason most women go to the office.

1929   Audrey Hepburn: Belgium-born actress. The radiant model-thin beauty won an Oscar for *Roman Holiday.* Nominated for *Sabrina, The Nun's Story, Breakfast at Tiffany's* and *Wait Until Dark.* Special Ambassador for UNICEF, devoting much of her free time to charity. Led a mission of mercy to famine- and war-torn Somalia. Died of colon cancer.

Only those people who are absolutely definite succeed.

1936   El Cordobes: Professional name of Manuel Benitez Perez. Spanish matador. Purists were shocked by his athleticism, but his theatrical style and disregard for danger made him an idol of the crowds and the highest paid matador in history. Gored 20 times.

Bravery is believing in yourself, and that thing nobody can teach you.

1941   George F. Will: American journalist, columnist. Conservative syndicated columnist. Won 1977 Pulitzer Prize. Political analysis for CBS.

Pessimism is as American as apple pie— frozen apple pie with a slice of processed cheese.

May 5

1802   Niels Henrik Abel: Norwegian mathematician whose great genius was cut short at age 26 years. Noted for his work in the theory of equations. His reply when asked how he had forged into the top rank of mathematicians so early in life:

By studying the masters, not their pupils.

1813   Søren Kierkegaard: Danish philosopher. Survived a gloomy early life which no doubt affected his thoughts on faith, knowledge, reality, free will and God. He believed that man's relation with God must be a lonely, agonizing experience. Books: *The Concept of Irony, Either-Or* and *Fear and Trembling.*

Life can only be understood backwards, but it must be lived forward.

1818   Karl Marx: German socialist. With Friedrich Engels, formulated principles of Dialectical Materialism, or economic determinism. Maintained that economic structure is the basis of all history and determines all social, political and intellectual aspects of life. Works: *The Communist Manifesto* and *Das Kapital.*

The ruling ideas of each age have ever been the ideas of the ruling class.

1882   Sylvia Pankhurst: English suffragist, editor, newspaper publisher and social reformer. Daughter of suffragist Emmeline Pankhurst and sister of evangelist Christabel Pankhurst. Sylvia diverged to pacifism, internationalism and labor politics.

I am going to fight capitalism even if it kills me. It is wrong that people like you should be comfortable and well fed while all around you people are starving.

1888   Paul Eldridge: American educator, novelist, poet. Wrote *My First Two Thousand Years, Men and Women, The Crown of Empire* and *The Tree of Ignorance.*

With the stones we cast at them, geniuses build new roads for us.

1890   Christopher Morley: American writer, editor. A founder of the *Saturday Review,* and editor (1924–41). Founder of dozens of clubs including the "Baker Street Irregulars." Wrote: *Tales from a Rolltop Desk* and *Kitty Foyle*.

There is only one success—to be able to spend your life in your own way.

1895   **Charles MacArthur:** American newspaperman, playwright. With Ben Hecht wrote plays *The Front Page* and *Twentieth Century*. Husband of Helen Hayes.

Complaints are only a sign you've been hurt. Keep the wounds out of sight.

1903   **James A. Beard:** American chef and author. Popularized American cooking. *Beard on Bread* is considered to be the definitive work on baking.

A gourmet who thinks of calories is like a tart who looks at her watch.

May 6

1758   **Maximilien Robespierre:** French revolutionist. Dominated the Committee of Public Safety which instituted the Reign of Terror (1793–94). Overthrown by the Convention of 1794 and was sent to the guillotine without a trial as he had sent so many others.

Pity is treason.

1856   **Sigmund Freud:** Austrian psychiatrist. Originated psychoanalysis. Postulated the existence of three internal forces governing a person's psychic life: the id, the instinctual force of life; the ego, the executive force that has contact with the real world; and the superego, or moral conscience.

I have found little that is good about human beings. It is my experience most of them are trash.

1861   **Sir Rabindranath Tagore:** Bengali poet, novelist, essayist and composer. Collected legends and tales which he included in *The Tragedy of Rudachandra, Binodini* and *Chitra*. Nobel Prize for literature (1913), the first Asiatic so honored.

"I am ashamed of my emptiness," said the Word to the Work. / "I know how poor I am when I see you," said the Work to the Word.

1895   **Rudolph Valentino:** Italian-born silent screen star, the leading heartthrob of his time. At his untimely death at 31, there was a wave of mass hysteria among female fans. Films: *The Four Horsemen of the Apocalypse, The Sheik, Blood and Sand,* and *Monsieur Beaucaire.*

To generalize on women is dangerous. To specialize on them is infinitely worse.

1914   **Randall Jarrell:** U.S. poet, critic and novelist. Author of *Blood for a Stranger, Poetry and the Age* and *The Gingerbread Rabbit.*

Nothing comes from nothing / The darkness from the darkness. / Pain comes from the darkness. / And we call it wisdom. / It is pain.

1915   **Orson Welles:** American actor, director and producer, screenwriter. His Mercury Theater radio production "The War of the Worlds," scared thousands one Halloween, who believed it a newscast. Collaborated with Herman Mankiewicz to create perhaps the greatest American film, *Citizen Kane,* shortly followed by another masterpiece, *The Magnificent Ambersons.* Spent his life trying to earn enough money to make movies the way he wished.

We should have the courage of our platitudes.

1915   **Theodore H. White:** American writer, journalist. Best known for his meticulously detailed chronicles of presidential campaigns. Pulitzer Prize for *The Making of the President: 1960.* As foreign correspondent, covered Europe, NATO and American politics (1955–78).

Politics in America is the binding secular religion.

May 7

1812   **Robert Browning:** English poet. Married poet Elizabeth Barrett and moved with her to Italy where they remained until her death in 1861. The story of their love was dramatized by Rudolf Beiser in *The Barretts of Wimpole Street.* Poems: "My Last Duchess," "The Pied Piper of Hamelin," and "The Ring and the Book."

All poetry is difficult to read, the sense of it is, anyhow.

1833　**Johannes Brahms:** German romantic composer. Wrote symphonies, chamber music, piano works, concerts, choral works, songs, leider. Works: *Hungarian Dances, Violin Concerto in D Major* and *Lullaby* and *A German Requiem.*

The fact that people do not understand and respect the very best things, such as Mozart's concertos, is what permits men like us to become famous.

1836　**Joseph G. Cannon:** "Uncle Joe." Illinois Republican congressman. Despotically ruled House of Representatives from his positions as chairman of the House Rules Committee and as Speaker of the House (1903–11).

Of all proposals for change fifty percent are harmful, the rest useless.

1892　**Archibald MacLeish:** American poet. Pulitzer Prize (1932) for narrative poem "Conquistador." His verse plays were political messages. *Panic* was about the Depression and *The Fall of the City,* was written during Hitler's rise to power. Won two more Pulitzers (1952 and 1958).

We have no choice but to be guilty / God is unthinkable if we are innocent.

1892　**Marshal Tito [Josip Broz]:** Led Yugoslav partisans against Nazis in WWII. Prime minister of Yugoslavia (1943–53). First communist leader to defy Soviet control. Worked for conciliation of country's diverse nationalities, which only postponed the bloody civil war until the manufactured nation came apart.

Any movement in history which attempts to perpetuate itself becomes reactionary.

1919　**Eva "Evita" Perón:** Argentine political figure. Active in the campaign to elect her husband Juan Perón president (1946). All but co-governed with him. Developed an adoring following among the poor whose enthusiasm for her did not end with her death of cancer at 33.

Without fanaticism we cannot accomplish anything.

1932　**Jenny Joseph:** English poet, ed-ucator, journalist. Best known for her poem "When I Am an Old Woman."

When I am an old woman, I shall wear purple / With a red hat which doesn't suit me, / And I shall spend my pension on brandy and summer gloves / And satin sandals, and say we've no money for butter.

May 8

1592　**Francis Quarles:** English religious poet. A churchman and royalist. Many of his books were destroyed during the Civil War. Best known works are *Emblems,* a series of symbolic pictures with verse commentary and a prose book of aphorisms, *Epigrams.*

He that begins to live, begins to die.

1668　**Alain René Lesage:** French novelist, dramatist. Early works are translations of Spanish authors. Celebrated for an animated style and dramatic presentations of human weaknesses. Best known works are *The Adventures of Gil Blas* and *Turcaret.*

Facts are stubborn things.

1884　**Harry S Truman:** Thirty-third president of the United States (1945–53). succeeding Franklin D. Roosevelt at the latter's death. Senator from Missouri (1933-45). Made decision to drop atom bomb on Japan to speed end of WWII. Decided to send troops to Korea. Announced policy of containment of communist influence in the world.

It's a recession when your neighbor loses his job; it's a depression when you lose your own.

1895　**Fulton J. Sheen:** Roman Catholic bishop and broadcaster. National director of the Society for the Propagation of the Faith. Internationally famous for his radio program *Catholic Hour* (1930–52) and the television show, "Life Is Worth Living" (1952–65).

An atheist is a man who has no invisible means of support.

1895　**Edmund Wilson:** American critic, novelist, short-story writer, poet. Editor and writer for *Vanity Fair*, *The New Republic* and *The New Yorker*. Books: *Axel's Castle* and *The Scrolls from the Dead Sea*.

In a sense, one can never read the book that the author originally wrote, and one can never read the same book twice.

1906   **Roberto Rossellini:** Italian director. After WWII, he burst onto the international scene as a leading neorealistic director. Had a scandalous affair with Ingrid Bergman which produced a son and twin girls. Films: *Open City*, *Paisan*, *General Della Rovere* and *The Rise of Louis XIV*.

To perceive evil where it exists is ... a form of optimism.

1920   **Sloan Wilson:** U.S. novelist. Wrote best-selling novels *The Man in the Gray Flannel Suit* and *A Summer Place.*

Success in almost any field depends more on energy and drive than it does on intelligence. This explains why we have so many stupid leaders.

May 9

1800   **John Brown:** "Old Brown of Osawatomie." U.S. abolitionist. Obsessed with fleeing slaves by force, with his five sons slaughtered settlers at Potwatomi Creek. Withstood an attack by proslavery forces at Osawatomie in bloody Kansas. Led a raid on the U.S. arsenal at Harper's Ferry, Virginia. Captured, convicted and hanged, he became a martyr to abolitionists.

Caution, caution, sir! It is nothing but the word of cowardice.

1860   **Sir James Barrie:** Scottish dramatist, novelist. Known for whimsy and sentimental fantasy in plays: *The Admirable Crichton* and *Peter Pan* and his novel *The Little Minister.*

I am not young enough to know everything.

1870   **Harry Vardon:** Amateur British golfing champion. One of the first to have a product tie-in, his "Vardon Flyer" guttie golf ball for A.G. Spalding.

Golfers find it a very trying matter to turn at the waist, more particularly if they have a lot of waist to turn.

1882   **Henry J. Kaiser:** American industrialist. His Bridge Builders, Inc. built the San Francisco Bay Bridge, the Bonneville Dam and the Grand Coulee Dam. Turned his attention to shipbuilding, constructing some 1,460 ships during WWII in record time.

Problems are only opportunities in work clothes.

1883   **José Ortega y Gasset:** Spanish philosopher, essayist, critic. Advocated Spain being ruled by a benevolent elite. His books: *Meditations on Quixote*, *Invertebrate Spain* and *The Revolt of the Masses.*

Nobility is defined by the demands it makes on us—by obligation, not by rights.

1921   **Daniel J. Berrigan:** U.S. Roman Catholic priest, political activist, poet. Convicted of destroying draft records in 1968 when he and his brother and fellow priest Philip protested the Vietnam War.

We shall see who emerges from the labyrinth: the minotaur or the man.

1949   **Billy Joel:** American singer, songwriter. Won Grammy's Legends Award (1990). Hits: "Piano Man," "It's Still Rock and Roll to Me," "Tell Her About It," "Uptown Girl" and "We Didn't Start the Fire."

The world doesn't need any more hip. The world doesn't need more cool, more clever.... The world needs Picassos, more Mozarts...

May 10

1760   **Claude Joseph Rouget de Lisle:** French songwriter. Wrote words and music of French national anthem "La Marseillaise."

Allons, enfants de la patrie, / Le jour, de gloire est arrivé!... / Aux armes, citoyens! / Formez vos bataillons! / Marchons! Marchons! Qu'un sang impur / abreuve nos sillons!

1838   **James Bryce:** British jurist and statesman. Irish secretary (1905-7). Ambassador to U.S. (1907-13). Took an active interest in university reform. Wrote the prize essay "The Holy Roman Empire."

Medicine is the only profession that labors to destroy the reason for its own existence.

1850 Sir Thomas Lipton: British merchant. A small Glasgow grocery owner started the Thomas J. Lipton Co. Ran his own tea, coffee and cocoa plantations to produce inexpensive products for his shops.

The man who on his trade relies / Must either bust or advertise.

1886 Karl Barth: Swiss theologian. Developed a "theology of the word of God." Led church opposition against Hitler and the Third Reich. Works include *Knowledge of God and the Service of God* and *Church Dogmatics.*

Men have never been good, they are not good and they never will be good.

1899 Fred Astaire: Premiere American film dancer. Danced with his sister Adele on Broadway before becoming a movie star when RKO teamed him with Ginger Rogers for a series of thirties' delights. Films: *The Gay Divorcee, Top Hat, Swing Time, Easter Parade, The Band Wagon* and *Funny Face.*

Old age is like everything else. To make a success of it, you've got to start young.

1902 David O. Selznick: American independent Hollywood producer. Founded his own company, Selznick International which produced quality films including: *Gone with the Wind, Rebecca, Since You Went Away, Duel in the Sun* and *Portrait of Jennie.*

There are only two classes—first class and no class.

1919 Ella T. Grasso: American politician. U.S. Representative (1971–74). Governor of Connecticut (1975–80). First woman elected governor in U.S.

I'm having trouble managing the [governor's] mansion. What I need is a wife.

May 11

1766 Isaac D'Israeli: English man of letters. Father of British statesman Benjamin Disraeli. Forte was literary illustrations of persons and history. Works: *Curiosities of Literature* and *Calamities of Authors.*

Beware the man of one book.

1888 Irving Berlin: Russian-born American composer, lyricist. Wrote more than 1000 songs and scores of Broadway musicals, including, "Alexander's Ragtime Band," "What'll I Do," "All Alone," "White Christmas," "God Bless America," "Easter Parade" and "Blue Skies."

We depend largely on tricks, we writers of songs. There is no such thing as a new melody.

1894 Martha Graham: American dancer, teacher, choreographer of modern dance. Founder and artistic director of Martha Graham School of Contemporary Dance (1927). Choreographed more than 150 works.

Nothing is more revealing than movement.

1895 William Grant Still: African American composer. Wrote five operas, four symphonies, three ballets, chamber and choral music and orchestral pieces.

A lot of those old Europeans are long-winded and dull. Yet they fill the programs. It is cruelly hard for modern composers to get a hearing.

1904 Salvador Dalí: Spanish painter, etcher. Disciple of surrealism. Experimented with pointillism, scientific cubism, futurism and constructivism. Most famous painting: *The Persistence of Memory,* limp, melting watches sagging over cliffs and leafless trees.

The thermometer of success is merely the jealousy of the malcontents.

1911 Phil Silvers: American vaudeville, movie and television fast-talking comic actor. Star of Broadway's *Top Banana,* repeating his success in film version. Enormously popular in television series, "You'll Never Get Rich" (1955–59).

I can make a villain loveable and sympathetic. Maybe it's because when I was a boy I wanted to grow up to be a man who could fix horse races or something.

1927 Mort Sahl: Canadian comedian, satirist, iconoclast. Popular in fifties

with the liberals by making fun of the conservatives. His fans were less amused when John F. Kennedy became president and Sahl continued to fire his zingers at those in power.
A conservative is someone who believes in reform. But not now.

May 12

1812   **Edward Lear:** English painter, writer. Known for his limericks and nonsense verse, including his best-known set of verses, "The Owl and the Pussycat."
They dined on mince, and slices of quince, / Which they ate with a runcible spoon; / And hand in hand, on the edge of the sand, / They danced by the light of the moon.

1820   **Florence Nightingale:** "Lady with the Lamp." English nurse and hospital reformer. Headed nurses who tended to the wounded in Crimean War. Founded the Nightingale School and Home for Nurses. Labored all her life for establishment of more nursing schools.
The very first requirement in a hospital is that it should do the sick no harm.

1828   **Dante Gabriel Rossetti:** English poet, painter. Driving force of Pre-Raphaelite Brotherhood. Wrote lyric poems, distinguished by mysticism and fantasy. Paintings: *The Girlhood of Mary Virgin* and *Ecce Ancilla Domini.* Poems: "The Blessed Damozel" and "My Sister's Sleep."
The worst moment for the atheist is when he is really thankful and has nobody to thank.

1888   **Theodor Reik:** Austrian-born U.S. psychoanalyst. Emphasized the role of intuition in treatment, diverging from orthodox Freudian views. Books: *Listening with the Third Ear* and *Curiosities of the Self.*
Women in general want to be loved for what they are and men for what they accomplish.

1915   **Mary Kay Ash:** American cosmetics executive. Founder and Chairman Emeritus of Mary Kay Cosmetics. Stressed positive attitude of the representatives who sold her products in cosmetic parties.
People fail forward to success.

1925   **Lawrence "Yogi" Berra:** Joined the New York Yankees as catcher-outfielder (1947). At the end of 17 years, he had hit 358 HRs. Appeared in the most World Series games (75). MVP (1951, 1954, 1955). Elected to Hall of Fame (1972). Managed Yankees and New York Mets to pennants.
You can observe a lot just by watching.

1933   **Andrei Voznesensky:** Soviet poet. Stressed the authors" right to freedom from ideological dogmatism and the right to explore new kinds of experience. Best known volume, *Antiworlds.*
The times spat on me. I spit back at the times.

May 13

1792   **Pope Pius IX:** Italian pope with the longest papacy (1846–78). Convened First Vatican Council. Defined dogma of Immaculate Conception.
The Church ought to be separated from the state, and the state from the Church.

1813   **John Sullivan Dwight:** U.S. music critic, editor, author. Member of the Transcendental Club and Brook Farm. Founder and editor *Dwight's Journal of Music.*
The Bible is a window in this prison of hope, through which we look into eternity.

1840   **Alphonse Daudet:** French novelist, short-story writer. Wrote humorous stories of provincial and Parisian life, "Letters from My Mill" and "Tartarin de Tarascon."
One who has a reputation for rising early can sleep until noon.

1882   **Georges Braque:** French painter, sculptor, stage, book and glass designer. Principle founder of modern art. With Picasso, developed cubism. Known for collage techniques. Paintings: *The Port of La Ciotat* and *The Black Birds.*
Truth exists, only falsehood has to be invented.

1907   **Dame Daphne du Maurier:** English novelist. Works of melodrama, period romances, Cornish settings and history.

Novels: *Rebecca, Jamaica Inn* and *French-man's Creek*.
Writers should be read, but neither seen nor heard.

1914   Joe Louis: American boxer. World heavyweight champion (1937–49), the longest reign in division history. Professional record, 63-3 with 49 KOs.
Everybody wants to go to heaven, but nobody wants to die.

1950   Stevie Wonder: Blind U.S. singer, songwriter, multi-instrumental artist, producer. Winner of 17 Grammy awards. Inducted into Rock 'n' Roll Hall of Fame (1989). Hits: "For Once in My Life," "You Are the Sunshine of My Life," and "I Just Called to Say I Love You."
Music can measure how broad our horizons are. My mind wants to see to infinity.

May 14

1686   Gabriel Fahrenheit: German physicist and instrument maker. Made important improvements in the construction of thermometers. Introduced the thermometric scale known by his name.
Pure water while freezing in the presence of pure ice always gives the same reading.

1727   Thomas Gainsborough: English painter, fashionable portraitist. Painted landscapes for his own pleasure. Most famous painting is *Blue Boy*. His great landscapes include *The Harvest Wagon* and *The Watering Place*.
We are all going to heaven, and Van Dyke is of the company.

1880   B.C. [Robert Charles] "Bertie" Forbes: Scottish-born American journalist, publisher and writer. Founder, publisher and editor of the business magazine bearing his name.
Information means money.

1925   Patrice Munsel: "Princess Pat." American operatic singer. At 18 the youngest singer ever accepted at the New York Met. Also appeared in films and Broadway musicals.

It thrills me no end when my own age group bursts out in whistles and cheers. Yet there is nothing in the world to compare with the feeling I get when I hear the "bravos" of that wonderful Metropolitan audience.

1936   Bobby Darin: American singer, pianist, guitarist, actor. Oscar nominated for film *Captain Newman M.D.* Song hits: "Splish Splash," "Mack the Knife," and "Beyond the Sea."
It's tough these days—the kids are fickle. They do more flipping over the songs that they do over any one singer.

1944   George Lucas: U.S. director, writer, producer. Heads Lucasfilms. Formed Industrial Light and Magic special effects company. Directed *Star Wars* and *American Graffiti*. Produced *The Empire Strikes Back, The Return of the Jedi* and *Indiana Jones* films.
Star Wars Is About 25 Percent of What I Wanted It to Be.

1952   David Byrne: Scottish-born American rock musician, composer. Lead singer and guitarist with new wave rock group "Talking Heads."
In a world where people have problems … compassion is a virtue, but I don't have the time … what are you, in love with your problems?…Don't expect me to explain your indecision…. Go talk to your analyst, isn't that what he's paid for?

May 15

1773   Prince Clemens Von Metternich: Chancellor of Austria (1809–48). His reactionary policies dominated Europe from the Congress of Vienna (1814–15) to the revolutions of 1848. He fled to England and retired to his castle on the Rhine in 1851.
Stability is not immobility.

1803   Edward George Bulwer-Lytton, Lord Lytton: British literary patron, novelist and dramatist. His enormous output of works, very popular in his day, are all but forgotten today. Works: *The Last Days of Pompeii* and *King Arthur*.
Genius does what it must, talent does what it can.

1894   Katherine Anne Porter: American short-story writer, novelist. Her best known work is the novel *Ship of Fools*, which received both a Pulitzer Prize and a National Book Award.
The real sin against life is to abuse and destroy beauty, even one's own—even more, one's own, for that had been put in our care and we are responsible for its well-being.

1902   Richard J. Daley: American political boss, mayor of Chicago (1955–76). Noted for making the Windy City run using an effective political machine and his mishandling of the protests at the Democratic National Convention (1968).
The party permits ordinary people to get ahead. Without the party, I couldn't be a mayor.

1904   Clifton Fadiman: American literary critic, author. Editor at Simon and Schuster (1929–35). Book editor of *The New Yorker* (1933–43). MC for radio program "Information Please" (1938–48).
Cheese is milk's leap toward immortality.

1915   Paul A. Samuelson: U.S. economist. Famed for his widely used textbook, *Economics, An Introductory Analysis*. Has made important contributions to mathematical structure of economic theory. Nobel Prize (1970).
Profits are the life blood of the economic system, the magic elixir upon which progress and all good things depend ultimately. But one man's life blood is another man's cancer.

1926   Peter Shaffer: British playwright. Wrote *Five Finger Exercise*, *Equus* and *Amadeus*. Wrote several novels in collaboration with his twin brother Anthony Shaffer, using the pseudonym Peter Anthony.
Everything we feel is made of Time. All the beauties of life are shaped by it.

May 16

1801   William H. Seward: U.S. politician and statesman. As Secretary of state (1861–69), purchased Alaska from Russia,

proclaimed at the time as "Seward's Folly." New York governor (1838–42) and senator (1849–61).
Revolutions never go backward.

1832   Philip D. Armour: U.S. meatpacking executive. Introduced on-premise slaughtering and utilization of animal waste. First to use refrigerator cars to transport meat cross-country and to make canned meat products.
I like to turn bristles, blood, and the inside and outside of pigs and bullocks into revenue.

1881   Anne O'Hara McCormick: U.S. foreign correspondent with *New York Times* (1922–54). First woman to receive Pulitzer Prize for journalism (1937).
The struggle to maintain peace is immeasurably more difficult than any military operation.

1928   Billy Martin: American baseball second baseman with four NY Yankees world champions in fifties. Five-time manager of Yankees, winning two pennants and a World Series. Also managed Minnesota, Detroit, Texas and Oakland.
When you're a professional you come back no matter what happened the day before.

1929   John Conyers, Jr.: Democratic congressman from Missouri from 1961. Author of *Anatomy of an Undeclared War* (1972).
The school, for a great many Black teenagers, is just another obstacle that society has put in their way.

1957   Joan Benoit Samuelson: U.S. track and field runner. Twice won the Boston marathon. Winner of first Olympic marathon. Sullivan Award winner (1985).
One hour with a child is like a ten-mile run.

1966   Janet Jackson: American singer, actress. Hits: "When I Think of You," "Miss You Much" and "Love Will Never Do (Without You)."
Beauty comes from within. It is sparked by an inner strength and radiance that goes far beyond physical appearance.

May 17

1805   **Robert Smith Surtees:** English sporting novelist. Creator of "Mr. Jorrocks," the fox hunting London grocer. Editor of the *New Sporting Magazine* (1831–36).
Women never look so well as when one comes in wet and dirty from hunting.

1875   **Joel E. Spingarn:** U.S. critic, author, educator. NAACP president (1930–39). In 1913 established the Spingarn medal, an annual award recognizing outstanding achievement by a black in service to his race.
Criticism is essentially an expression of taste, or that faculty of imaginative sympathy by which the reader or spectator is able to relive the vision created by the artist.

1900   **Ayatollah Ruhollah Khomeini:** Iranian religious and political leader. A Shiite Muslim who bitterly opposed the pro–Western regime of Shah Reza Pahlavi. Exiled from 1964 to 1979, Khomeini returned after the collapse of the Shah's government to be virtual head of a strict Muslim state.
Americans are the great Satan, the wounded snake.

1911   **Clark Kerr:** American educator and economist. Chancellor of the University of California (1952–58), president (1958–67). Fired by Governor Ronald Reagan. Chaired the Carnegie Commission on Higher Education (1967–73).
I find that the three major administrative problems on a campus are sex for the students, athletics for the alumni and parking for the faculty.

1911   **Maureen O'Sullivan:** Beautiful, demure brunette Irish-born actress. Mother of Mia Farrow. Best remembered for playing Jane to Johnny Weissmuller's Tarzan in the thirties.
Woman's greatest weapon is a man's imagination.

1912   **Archibald Cox:** U.S. lawyer, professor. Named Watergate special prosecutor, then fired by President Nixon when he rejected an administration compromise on disputed tapes.

I confess that I cannot understand how we can plot, lie, cheat and commit murder abroad and remain humane, honorable, trustworthy and trusted at home.

1914   **Stewart Alsop:** American journalist. With his brother Joseph, wrote the informative and opinionated syndicated column "Matter of Fact." He wrote of battling a rare blood disease in *Stay of Execution.*
Death is, after all, the only universal experience except birth.

1920   **Harriet Van Horne:** American newspaper columnist. Television and radio personality and critic.
Cooking is like love. It should be entered into with abandon, or not at all.

May 18

1862   **Josephus Daniels:** U.S. editor, publisher, diplomat. Secretary of the Navy during WWI. Ambassador to Mexico, 1933–42. Wrote *The Life of Woodrow Wilson* and *Editor in Politics.*
Defeat never comes to any man until he admits it.

1872   **Sir Bertrand Russell:** English philosopher, mathematician, social reformer. Wrote books on mathematics, philosophy, logic, war, politics, sociology, religion, education, sexual relations and marriage. Most famous scientific contribution is *Principia Mathematica*, with Alfred North Whitehead.
Mathematics may be defined as the subject in which we never know what we are talking about nor whether what we are saying is true.

1883   **Walter Gropius:** German architect. Founder and director of the Bauhaus until 1928. Designer of its second center in Dessau. Worked in U.S. (1937–69).
Architecture begins where engineering ends.

1892   **Frank Capra:** Populist-influenced Italian-born U.S. director. Oscar winner for *It Happened One Night, Mr. Deeds Goes to*

Town, You Can't Take It with You and the army documentary *Prelude to War.*

There are no rules in filmmaking, only sins. And the cardinal sin is Dullness.

1902 **Meredith Willson:** American composer, conductor. Flautist with John Philip Sousa's band and the New York Philharmonic. Appeared with Tallulah Bankhead on radio's "The Big Show." Wrote *The Music Man* and *The Unsinkable Molly Brown.*

Barbershop quartet singing is four guys tasting the holy essence of four individual mechanisms coming into complete agreement.

1919 **Margot Fonteyn:** English prima ballerina. Made debut at Vic-Wells Ballet in *Nutcracker* (1934). With Britain's Royal Ballet (1934–75). Formed partnership with Rudolf Nureyev (1962–79). President Royal Academy of Dancing from 1954 to 1991.

Great artists are people who find the way to be themselves in their art.

1920 **Pope John Paul II [Karol Jozef Wojtyla]:** Polish religious leader. First non-Italian pope since Renaissance (1978-). Author of an internationally best-selling book *Crossing the Threshold* (1994). Has traveled more than any other pope. Known for his doctrinal conservatism.

Man matures through work / Which inspires him to difficult good.

May 19

1762 **Johann Gottlieb Fichte:** German philosopher. Developed ethical idealism out of Immanuel Kant's work. Reputation rests mainly on *Addresses to the German Nation.*

It is a mistake to say that it is doubtful whether there is a God or not. It is not in the least doubtful, but the most certain thing in the world, nay, the foundation of all other certainty—the only solid absolute objectivity—that there is a moral government of the world.

1859 **Dame Nellie Melba:** Australian operatic soprano. Star of London's Covent Garden and New York Met, from 1890s. Best known for her roles in *Lakmé, Faust,*

and *La Traviata.* Famous for pure tone. Dessert "Peach Melba" named in her honor.

The first rule in opera is the first rule in life: see to everything yourself.

1879 **Lady Nancy Astor (Nancy Witcher Langhorne):** U.S.-born English politician. First woman to sit in the British House of Commons. Advocated women's rights, temperance. Opposed socialism. Wrote *My Two Countries.*

I married beneath me, all women do.

1890 **Ho Chi Minh:** Legendary Vietnamese leader, revolutionist. Founded Communist Party of Vietnam (1930). Organized Vietminh which fought Japanese in WWII. Played direct role in the Geneva Accord dividing Vietnam into North and South. President of Democratic Republic of Vietnam (North) (1954–69).

Military action without politics is like a tree without a root.

1925 **Malcolm X [Malcolm Little]:** American militant black activist. Spoke for racial pride and black nationalism. Joined Black Muslims while in prison. Rose to position of leadership. Suspended in 1964 by Elijah Muhammad. Malcolm X formed Organization for African American Unity. Assassinated (1965).

My alma mater was books, a good library … I could spend the rest of my life reading, just satisfying my curiosity.

1930 **Lorraine Hansberry:** Youngest U.S. playwright and first black to win Best Play Award from the New York Drama Critic's Circle for her first work, *A Raisin in the Sun. To Be Young, Gifted and Black* was completed by her husband Robert Nemiroff after her death at age 34 of cancer.

The thing that makes you exceptional, if you are at all, is eventually that which must also make you lonely.

1941 **Nora Ephron:** American author, screenwriter, director. Daughter of screenwriters Henry and Phoebe Ephron. Oscar nominated for screenplays for *Silkwood* and *When Harry Met Sally.* Directed 1993 hit *Sleepless in Seattle.*

Summer bachelors, like summer breezes, are never as cool as they pretend to be.

May 20

1768 Dolley Madison: American First Lady. Wife of President James Madison. Famous as Washington hostess while her husband was secretary of state (1801–9) and president (1809–17).
I would rather fight with my hands than my tongue.

1799 Honoré de Balzac: French novelist. Wrote more than 90 novels and tales. Considered a founder of the realistic school. Depicted ordinary and undistinguished lives in meticulous detail. Books: *The Last Chouans, The Human Comedy, Father Goriot* and *Lost Illusions.*
Behind every great fortune there is a crime.

1806 John Stuart Mill: English philosopher, economist. Leading proponent of Utilitarianism. Writings: *System of Logic, The Enfranchisement of Women, The Subjection of Women, On Liberty* and *Utilitarianism.*
Conservatives are not necessarily stupid, but most stupid people are conservatives.

1894 Adele Rogers St. Johns: American journalist. Star reporter of the William Randolph Hearst papers. Covered the Lindbergh baby kidnapping and Bruno Hauptman's trial. Books: *A Free Soul* and *Some Are Born Great.*
God made man, and then said I can do better than that and made woman.

1908 James Stewart: Perhaps the most popular actor to appear in films. The tall, gangling, long-faced star with a slow hesitant drawl projected sincerity, honesty and trustworthiness. Oscar winner for *The Philadelphia Story.* Nominated for *Mr. Smith Goes to Washington, It's a Wonderful Life* and *Anatomy of a Murder.* A bomber pilot during WWII, super-patriot and conservative Stewart stayed in reserves, rising to rank of brigadier general.
The secret of a happy life is to accept change gracefully.

1915 Moyshe Dayan: Israeli general, public official. Led invasion of Sinai Peninsula (1956). Agriculture minister (1959–64). Defense minister (1964–74). Led forces to victory in Six Day War (1967). Foreign minister (1977–79).
If you want to make peace, you don't talk to your friends. You talk to your enemies.

1946 Cher [Cherilyn Lapierre]: U.S. singer and actress. Had a successful television show with husband Sonny Bono (1971–77). Oscar winner for *Moonstruck.* Song Hits: "Gypsys, Tramps and Thieves," "Dark Lady" and "After All."
The trouble with some women is that they get all excited about nothing—and then marry them.

May 21

1688 Alexander Pope: "Wicked Wasp of Twickenham." English poet, satirist. Regarded as the epitome of English neoclassicism. Best Known Works: "Essay on Criticism," "Rape of the Lock," and translations of the *Iliad* and *The Odyssey.*
A little learning is a dang'rous thing; / Drink deep, or taste not the Pierian spring.

1780 Elizabeth Gurney Fry: English Quaker philanthropist. Dedicated her life to promoting wide-ranging prison reforms, particularly in the treatment of the poor and female prisoners.
Punishment is not for revenge, but to lessen crime and reform the criminal.

1793 Charles Paul de Kock: French novelist and dramatist. Established a reputation for an endless series of novels about contemporary Parisian life.
The best way to keep your friends is to never owe them anything and never lend them anything.

1868 Clarence Walworth Alvord: U.S. historian, editor. Founded *The Mississippi Valley Historical Review.* Editor of the 14-volume *Illinois Historical Collections.*
Historians take too eagerly an oath of allegiance to tradition and make only sporadic and halfhearted efforts to shake off the shackles laid on them by their forerunners.

1876 Cyrus S. Ching: U.S. government official, industrial relations executive. Director of Federal Mediation and Conciliation Service.

I learned long ago never to wrestle with a pig. You get dirty, and besides, the pig likes it.

1904   Thomas Wright "Fats" Waller: American composer, pianist. Played and recorded with Fletcher Henderson and Ted Lewis. Wrote score for Broadway musical *Early to Bed* and films *Hooray for Love* and *Stormy Weather*. Songs: "Ain't Misbehavin'," "Honeysuckle Rose" and "The Joint Is Jumpin'."
One never knows, do one?

1921   Andrei D. Sakharov: Nobel Peace Prize–winning physicist, mainly responsible for the development of the Soviet H-bomb. Became a symbol of Soviet dissidence, campaigning for a nuclear test-ban treaty, peaceful international coexistence and improved civil rights within the U.S.S.R. Forced into exile at Gorky.
Were there no ideals, there would be no hope whatsoever. Then everything would be hopelessness, darkness—a blind alley.

May 22

1813   Richard Wagner: German composer, conductor, librettist, author. The subject matter of most of his operas is drawn from Norse and Teutonic mythology and history. Works: *The Flying Dutchman, Tannhaüser, Lohengrin, Der Ring des Niebelunen, Tristan und Isolde* and *Der Meistersinger von Nürnberg.*
To be German means to carry on a matter for its own sake.

1844   Mary Cassatt: American impressionist artist. Noted for paintings of mother and child. Also renown for her etching and drypoint studies of domestic scenes.
Why do people so love to wander? I think the civilized parts of the world will suffice for me in the future.

1859   Sir Arthur Conan Doyle: English novelist. Known chiefly for his popular series of tales concerning Sherlock Holmes and his good-natured companion, Dr. Watson: *A Study in Scarlet, The Sign of the Four, The Memoirs of Sherlock Holmes* and *Hound of the Baskervilles.*
When you have eliminated the impossible, whatever remains, however improbable, must be the truth.

1907   Lord Laurence Olivier: Generally regarded as the finest British actor of his generation. His first love always was the stage, especially in Shakespearean roles. Oscar for *Hamlet* and special Oscars for *Henry V* and Life Achievement. Nominated for *Wuthering Heights, Rebecca, Richard III, The Entertainer, Othello, Sleuth, Marathon Man* and *The Boys from Brazil.*
A comedian is closer to humanity than a tragedian. He learns not to take himself seriously.

1914   Vance Packard: American nonfiction writer. Author of popular sociological books, including *The Hidden Persuaders, The Status Seekers* and *The Waste Makers.*
Leadership appears to be the art of getting others to want to do something you are convinced should be done.

1922   Judith Crist: American film and drama critic. Journalism professor, Columbia University. Books: *The Private Eye* and *The Cowboy and the Very Naked Girl.*
To be a critic, you have to have maybe three percent education, five percent intelligence, two percent style, and ninety percent gall and egomania in equal parts.

1924   Charles Aznavour: French-born Armenian foggy-voiced singer and actor. Toured with Edith Piaf and Les Compagnons de la Chanson. Gained fame in fifties for the motion picture *Shoot the Piano Player.*
Success is the result of a collective hallucination simulated by the artist.

May 23

1707   Carolus Von Linnaeus: Swedish botanist. His classification or artificial system of plants, known as the "sexual system," superseded Jussieu's natural system. His *Species plantarum* is considered the foundation of modern botanical nomenclature.
Nature does not proceed by leaps.

1734 **Franz Anton Mesmer:** German physician. Discoverer of cure by suggestion, which he attributed to magnetic force. Although his work has been discredited, it prepared the way for the use of hypnotism in medicine and investigation of hysterical symptoms.
There is only one illness and one cure.

1810 **[Sarah] Margaret Fuller:** U.S. editor, essayist, poet and teacher. First female journalist for the *New York Tribune*. Author of the remarkable feminist tract "Women in the Nineteenth Century," envisioning America as the one place where women might rise above men's tyranny.
'Tis an evil to have a man's ambition and a woman's heart.

1854 **Edgar Smith:** American educator, chemist, author. Wrote *The Life of Robin Hare* and *Chemistry in Old Philadelphia*.
You may tempt the upper class with your villainous demitasses / But Heaven will protect the working girl.

1875 **Alfred P. Sloan, Jr.:** U.S. automobile executive. President of General Motors (1923–37). Chairman of the Board (1937–56). The Alfred P. Sloan Foundation started the cancer research center Sloan-Kettering Institute.
We never give an order at GM. We "sell" the idea to those who must carry it out.

1914 **Barbara Mary Ward:** Baroness Jackson of Lodsworth: English economist. Advocated European economic unity and help for the underdeveloped countries. Books: *The Rich Nations and the Poor Nations* and *Spaceship Earth*.
It is very much easier for a rich man to invest and grow richer than for the poor man to begin investing at all. And this is also true of nations.

1933 **Joan Collins:** British-born stage, film and television actress. Films: *The Girl in the Red Velvet Swing* and *Rally 'Round the Flag Boys*. Found her niche playing evil Alexis on television's "Dynasty."
The easiest way to convince my kids that they don't really need something is to get it for them.

May 24

1544 **William Gilbert:** English physician, physicist. Coined terms "electric" and "magnetic poles." First to suggest the earth acted like a giant magnet and heavenly bodies were kept in place by magnetism.
Philosophy is for the few.

1743 **Jean-Paul Marat:** French revolutionary. Advocated extreme violence during the French Revolution. Leader of the Montagnard faction. Assassinated by Charlotte Corday in his bath.
God has always been hard on the poor, and He always will be.

1819 **Queen Victoria I:** British monarch. Queen of Great Britain and Ireland (1837–1901). Restored dignity to the crown. Devoted to her husband Prince Albert with whom she had nine children.
Great events make me quiet and calm; it is only trifles that irritate my nerves.

1870 **Jan C. Smuts:** South African statesman, soldier. Boer guerrilla leader in the South African War (1899–1902). Prime Minister of Union of South Africa.
Democracy, with its promises of international peace, has been no better guarantee against war than the old dynastic rule of kings.

1887 **Mother Mary Madeleva, CSC:** American author, educator and poet. President of St. Mary's College, Notre Dame, Indiana (1934–60). Author of: *Knights Errant and Other Poems, My First Seventy Years* and *Conversations with Cassandra*.
Indoors I have a small world of good and, so far as possible, old books and pictures.

1918 **Coleman Young:** U.S. politician. First black mayor of Detroit (1974–92). Served longer than any other mayor in city's history. Won Spingarn Award (1980).
We must take the profit out of prejudice.

1941 **Bob Dylan:** American singer, songwriter, guitarist and harmonica player. Born Robert Allen Zimmerman, he took his stage name from poet Dylan Thomas. Innovator of folk-rock style. Songs: "A

Hard Rain's Gonna Fall," "Blowin' in the Wind," "Mr. Tambourine Man" and "Like a Rollin' Stone."

No one's free, even the birds are chained to the sky.

May 25

1803   Ralph Waldo Emerson: "The Sage of Concord." U.S. poet, essayist, philosopher. Known for challenging traditional thought in his essays and lectures. Works: *Nature, The American Scholar* and *Poems.*

A foolish consistency is the hobgoblin of little mind.... With consistency a great soul has simply nothing to do.

1878   Bill Robinson: "Bojangles." U.S. dancer, actor. Best known for appearances in films with Shirley Temple.

Most of all I want to help my homeland realize that it will grow only as it lets all its people do their full part in making it rich and strong.

1879   Lord Beaverbrook: William Maxwell Aitken. Canadian-born British publisher, statesman and financier. Played a major role in building Great Britain's popular press.

Buy old masters. They fetch better prices than old mistresses.

1889   Igor Sikorsky: American aviation engineer. Built and flew first multimotored plane. Developed first successful helicopter.

The helicopter ... approaches closer than any other vehicle to the fulfillness of mankind's ancient ideas of the flying horse and the magic carpet.

1917   Theodore Hesburgh: American priest, educator. President of the University of Notre Dame for 30 plus years. A crusader for civil rights. Chaired Commission on Civil Rights (1969–72). Awarded Presidential Medal of Freedom and more than 100 honorary degrees.

Anyone who refuses to speak out off campus does not deserve to be listened to on campus.

1926   Miles Davis: American jazz trumpeter. Prophet of the "cool" school. Albums: *The Birth of the Cool, Miles Ahead* and *We Want Miles.*

An artist's first responsibility is to himself.

1929   Beverly Sills: "Bubbles." American coloratura soprano. With New York City Opera (1955–79). Director (1979–88). Medal of Freedom (1980). Repertoire: *Manon, La Traviata* and *Lucia di Lammermoor.*

I'm cheerful. I'm not happy, but I'm cheerful. There's a big difference ... A happy woman has no cares at all; a cheerful woman has cares and learns to ignore that.

May 26

1689   Lady Mary Wortley Montagu: English author, traveler, medical pioneer, poet, essayist and eccentric. Her witty letters of Middle Eastern life were published posthumously.

I give myself admirable advice, but I am incapable of taking it.

1886   Al Jolson: American singer, actor. Rose to stardom on Broadway stage, becoming America's most popular entertainer. Jolson ushered in the sound era with *The Jazz Singer* (1927). He was never as good in films as when facing the adoring crowds whom he loved.

Wait a minute, wait a minute. You ain't heard nothin' yet, folks.

1907   John Wayne: Legendary U.S. film actor, personified for some the American ideals of loyalty, integrity, honesty and self-reliance. Others objected to his super-patriot pose. Won an Oscar for *True Grit.* Other films: *Stagecoach, Red River* and *The Quiet Man.*

Nobody should come to the movies unless he believes in heroes.

1908   Robert Morley: Rotund British actor, playwright. The delightful character actor is at his best being jovial or pompous. Oscar nominated for his first film, *Marie Antoinette.* Others: *Major Barbara, The Story of Gilbert and Sullivan* and *Oscar Wilde.*

Beware of the conversationalist who adds "In other words." He is merely starting afresh.

1920   **Peggy Lee:** American singer, songwriter and actress. Oscar nominated for performance in *Pete Kelly's Blues.* Hits: "Manana," "Lover," "Fever" and "Is That All There Is."
I learned courage from Buddha, Jesus, Lincoln, Einstein and Cary Grant.

1928   **Jack Kevorkian:** "Dr. Death." Retired American pathologist, writer and inventor. Has assisted more than 20 people with incurable diseases to commit suicide.
I want to use death to benefit humanity. Now, it's just a total waste.

1951   **Sally Ride:** U.S. astronaut and astrophysicist. First American woman in space on Space Shuttle *Challenger* (June 18-24, 1983).
I came into this because I wanted to fly in space. My intention after the flight is to come back to the astronaut office and get back in line and try to fly again.

May 27

1265   **Dante Alighieri:** Italian poet. His most famous work is the masterpiece *The Divine Comedy*, the story of his imaginary journey through hell, purgatory and heaven with guides Vergil and Beatrice.
The hottest places in hell are reserved for those who in time of great moral crises maintain their neutrality.

1794   **Cornelius Vanderbilt:** "The Commodore." U.S. financier, transport executive. Formed Hudson River steamboat line. Owned a New York–to–California steamship line. Bought controlling interest in New York and Harlem Railroad, New York Central Railroad and Hudson Railroad. Left $100 million at his death.
If I had learned education I would not have had time to learn anything else.

1818   **Amelia Jenks Bloomer:** American social reformer. Campaigned for temperance and women's rights. Advocated dress reform which led to her wearing full trousers, nicknamed "bloomers."

The costume of women should be suited to her wants and necessities. It should conduce at once to her health, comfort and usefulness; and, while it should not fail to conduce to her personal adornment, it should make that end of secondary importance.

1878   **Isadora Duncan:** U.S. dancer. One of the first to interpret dance as a free form of art. Found great success in Europe. Free spirit who believed in free love. Strangled by her own scarf in a freakish accident.
Any intelligent woman who reads the marriage contract, and then goes into it deserves all the consequences.

1907   **Rachel Carson:** U.S. marine biologist. Her books *The Sea Around Us*, *The Edge of the Sea* and particularly *The Silent Spring* are known for their literary merit as well as their scientific content. She warned of the hazards to wildlife and humans of the indiscriminate use of insecticides.
The most alarming of all man's assaults upon the environment is the contamination of air, earth, rivers and sea.... This pollution for the most part is irreversible.

1911   **Hubert H. Humphrey:** American politician. Outstanding liberal Democratic party leader. U.S. senator from Minnesota. U.S. vice president. Democratic presidential candidate (1968).
The right to be heard does not automatically include the right to be taken seriously.

1923   **Henry Kissinger:** U.S. government official. Secretary of state for presidents Nixon and Ford. Nobel Peace Prize winner (1973), shared with Le Duc Tho of North Vietnam. Attempted to negotiate an Arab-Israeli peace agreement (1973-75). Initiated SALT talks (1969).
In crises the most daring course is often the safest.

May 28

1759   **William Pitt the Younger:** English statesman. Prime minister of England (1783–1801). Cited as England's greatest prime minister. Clamped down on radical agitation during French Revolutionary wars.

Necessity is the plea of every infringement of human freedom. It is the argument of tyrants; it is the creed of slaves.

1779 Thomas Moore: Irish poet. Known for Irish folk songs, "The Minstrel Boy" and "Believe Me, if All Those Enduring Young Charms." Also wrote satires, a novel, *History of Ireland,* and several biographies.
Tis the last rose of summer, / Left blooming alone; / All her lovely companions / Are faded and gone.

1807 Jean Louis Rodolphe Agassiz: Swiss-born U.S. naturalist, author. Founder of the Marine Biological Laboratory at Woods Hole, Massachusetts. Major work: *Contributions to the Natural History of the United States of America.*
Go to Nature; take the facts in your own hands; look and see for yourself.

1884 Edvard Beneš: A founder of Czechoslovakia. President (1935–38). Led exile regime in London during WWII. Returned home in 1945, serving as president until communist takeover of 1948.
I never feel sure of myself except when I am speaking the truth.

1888 Jim Thorpe: U.S. athlete. Declared a pro, he was stripped of 1912 gold medals in Olympic pentathlon and decathlon. All-American running back at Carlisle Indian School. Played major league football and baseball. Named Outstanding Athlete of 20th Century (1950). After decking Knute Rockne who once tried to tackle him, Thorpe said:
Son, they came to see old Jim play.

1908 Ian Fleming: English writer. Created the character of James Bond, Agent 007, licensed to kill for the British government. Books include: *From Russia with Love* and *Goldfinger.*
...Vodka dry Martini—with a slice of lemon peel. Shaken and not stirred, please. I would prefer Russian or Polish vodka!

1917 Barry Commoner: American biologist, environmentalist. Advocated environmental protection and use of solar energy. Books: *Science and Survival* and *The Politics of Energy.*

If you can see the light at the end of the tunnel you are looking the wrong way.

May 29

1736 Patrick Henry: American patriot, lawyer, merchant. Delegate to Continental Congress. Governor of Virginia. Great orator whose stirring call to arms brought many to the struggle against the British.
I know not what course others may take but as for me, give me liberty or give me death.

1874 G.K. Chesterton: English essayist, novelist, journalist, poet. Father Brown was his detective creation, appearing in a series of books.
Courage is a contradiction in terms. It means the strong desire to live taking the form of readiness to die.

1880 Oswald Spengler: German philosopher of history. Maintained that every culture is a distinct organic form that grows, matures and decays. Author of the morbidly prophetic *The Decline of the West.*
Socialism is nothing but the capitalism of the lower classes.

1892 Max Brand: Pseudonym of Frederick Faust. "King of the pulp writers." U.S. novelist and screenwriter. Wrote the Dr. Kildare series and *Destry Rides Again.*
There has to be a woman, but not much of a one. A good horse is much more important.

1903 Bob Hope: "Old Ski Nose." U.S. actor, comedian. Got his start in vaudeville in the twenties, where he perfected the character of the none-too-bright, not-too-brave, know-it-all who at the first sign of danger is apt to hide behind some female's skirt. Movies: *The Cat and the Canary, Road to Singapore, My Favorite Blonde* and *The Paleface.*
If you watch a game, it's fun. If you play it, it's recreation. If you work at it, it's golf.

1917 John F. Kennedy: Thirty-fifth U.S. president (1961–63). Assassinated by

Lee Harvey Oswald in Dallas, Texas, November 22, 1963, ending a thousand days in office, often referred to as "Camelot." First and thus far only Roman Catholic president. WWII hero. Congressman from Massachusetts (1947–53), senator (1953–60). Forced U.S.S.R to pull missiles from Cuba (1962).

Those who make peaceful revolution impossible will make violent revolution inevitable.

1939   **Al Unser:** U.S. automobile racer. Three-time USAC / CART national champion. Four-time Indy winner. Brother of Bobby Unser, father of Al, Jr.

You may drive the freeways daily at top speeds with confidence and skill. But that doesn't qualify you as a race driver. Put an ordinary driver in an Indy-type race car and he'd probably crash before he got out of the pit area.

May 30

1814   **Mikhail Bakunin:** Russian revolutionary and anarchist leader took part in revolutionary agitation in Germany, Austria and France before being extradited to Russia and exiled to Siberia. Founder of Nihilism.

The passion for destruction is also a creative passion.

1888   **James A. Farley:** U.S. political leader, businessman. Managed Franklin D. Roosevelt's 1932 and 36 presidential campaigns. Powerful chairman of Democratic National Committee (1932–40). U.S. postmaster general (1933–40).

A rigged convention is one with the other man's delegates in control. An open convention is when your delegates are in control.

1891   **Ben Bernie:** U.S. radio bandleader. Known for mellifluous and humorous introductions and his trademark radio sign-off:

And now the time has come to lend an ear to au revoir. Pleasant dreams. Think of us … when requesting your themes. Until the next time when … possibly you may all tune in again. Keep the Old Maestro always … in your schemes. Yowsah, yowsah, yowsah.

1892   **Stepin Fetchit [Lincoln Theodore Perry]:** U.S. actor. First black to receive featured billing. Played lazy, easily frightened comic characters now labeled as insulting stereotypes in *Show Boat, David Harum* and *Dimples.* First black entertainer to earn a million.

All the things that Bill Cosby and Sidney Poitier have done wouldn't be possible if I hadn't broken that law. I set up thrones for them to come and sit on.

1898   **Howard Hawks:** Considered the first American "auteur," having control of films from start to finish as screenwriter, producer and director. Films: *Scarface, Bringing Up Baby, Only Angels Have Wings, Sergeant York, Red River* and *Gentlemen Prefer Blondes.*

For me the best drama is one that deals with a man in danger.

1901   **Cornelia Otis Skinner:** American stage actress. Daughter of tragedian Otis Skinner. Best known for one-woman shows and her monologues. Co-wrote the play *The Pleasure of His Company* and the book *Our Hearts Were Young and Gay.*

Woman's virtue is man's greatest invention.

1903   **Countee Cullen:** Black American poet. A leader of the so-called Harlem Renaissance. Author of *The Black Christ, The Ballad of the Brown Girl* and *Color.*

Never love with all your heart / It only ends in aching.

1909   **Benny Goodman:** "The King of Swing." U.S. clarinetist, bandleader. Song hits: "Stompin' at the Savoy," "Don't Be That Way," Let's Dance," "Sing, Sing, Sing" and "Taking a Chance on Love." One of the first white bandleaders to include blacks in bands.

If a guy's got it, let him give it. I'm selling music not prejudice.

1926   **Christine Jorgenson:** An Ex-GI, named George, she became one of the first to have a sex-change operation.

While I'm not a complete woman, no one is a complete anything—male or female—including myself. But I still consider myself a woman.

May 31

1819 Walt Whitman: "The Good Gray Poet." "The Bard of Democracy." U.S. poet, journalist, essayist. His *Leaves of Grass* was initially condemned as a vulgar, immoral book. Other works: "Drum Taps," "Crossing Brooklyn Ferry," "Song of Myself," and "Out of the Cradle Endlessly Rocking."
To have great poets, there must be great audiences, too.

1857 Pope Pius XI [Ambrogio Damiano Ratti]: Italian religious leader. Papacy (1922–39). Best known for negotiating Lateran Treaty (1929), establishing the Vatican's independence from Italy.
To suffer and to endure is the lot of humanity.

1860 Walter Sickert: British painter. Pupil of Whistler. Influenced by Degas. Used the latter's style to illustrate London low life. Painting: *Ennui*.
Nothing links man to man like the frequent passage from hand to hand of a good book.

1894 Fred Allen: U.S. comedian, humorist started in vaudeville. Became a national institution on several witty and popular radio series featuring the famous Allen's Alley of colorful characters.
Committee—a group of men who individually can do nothing but as a group decide that nothing can be done.

1898 Norman Vincent Peale: U.S. clergyman. Prominent religious author and radio preacher on national program *The Art of Living*. Wrote *The Power of Positive Thinking*.
Getting people to like you is merely the other side of liking them.

1920 Edward Bennett Williams: Top U.S. criminal lawyers whose clients included Adam Clayton Powell, Jimmy Hoffa and Senator Joseph McCarthy.
The lawyer is neither expected nor qualified to make a moral judgment of the person seeking his help.

1943 Joe Namath: U.S. football New York Jets' quarterback. Two-time All-AFL, and once All-NFL. Promised and delivered a Super Bowl victory for the Jets in 1969. Pro Hall of Fame (1985).
When you win, nothing hurts.

June 1

1780 Carl Von Clausewitz: Prussian general and military historian. Wrote *War* which expounded philosophy of war. His work had a tremendous effect on military strategies during the World Wars.
There is only one decisive victory; the last.

1801 Brigham Young: Assumed leadership of the Mormons after the murder of founder Joseph Smith. Led followers to the Great Salt Lake Basin in Utah, arriving July 24, 1847.
Sin consists in doing wrong when we know and can do better, and it will be punished with a just retribution, in the due time of the Lord.

1804 Mikhail Glinka: Russian civil servant and composer. Wrote opera, *Life for the Tsar*. His *Ruslan and Lyudmila* pioneered the style of the Russian national school of composers.
A nation creates music—the composer only arranges it.

1878 John Masefield: English poet, dramatist, novelist. From 1930 until his death in 1967, poet laureate of London. Best known for his sea poems, *Salt Water Ballads* and the narrative poem "Reynard the Fox." His novels are romantic adventure stories. Also wrote literary criticism.
The days that make us happy make us wise.

1924 William Sloane Coffin, Jr.: American clergyman. Leader in Vietnam peace movement. Chaplain, Yale University (1958–75). Pastor, Riverside Church, New York City (1977–).
The word of the Lord falls with the force of a snowflake.

1926 Marilyn Monroe: Hollywood's most glamorous blonde sex symbol since

Jean Harlow. A sense of tragedy surrounded the vulnerable star who came to hate the image she and the studios created for her. Married three times, her husband included Joe DiMaggio and Arthur Miller. Films: *The Asphalt Jungle, Bus Stop, Some Like It Hot* and *The Misfits*.

Husbands are chiefly good lovers when they are betraying their wives.

1937   **Morgan Freeman:** U.S. actor. "Easy Reader" on television's "The Electric Company." Moved on to Broadway and films. Oscar nominated for *Street Smart* and for *Driving Miss Daisy*.

Never let pride be your guiding principle. Let your accomplishments speak for you.

June 2

1730   **Martha Washington:** American widow who married George Washington, first president of the United States.

I have learned too much of the vanity of human affairs to expect felicity from the scenes of public life.

1740   **Donatien Alphonse François, Marquis de Sade:** French nobleman. Imprisoned for 12½ years by royal decree for staging orgies during which he whipped and sodomized prostitutes. His life spawned the word "sadism," deriving pleasure from inflicting pain.

It is not my mode of thought that has caused my misfortunes, but the mode of thoughts of others.

1840   **Thomas Hardy:** English novelist, poet and dramatist. Novels: *Far from the Madding Crowd, The Return of the Native, Tess of the D'Urbervilles* and *Jude the Obscure*. Poetry: *Wessex Poems* and *Winter Words*.

A story must be exceptional enough to justify its telling.

1890   **Hedda Hopper:** U.S. actress, gossip columnist. Wife of matinee idol DeWolf Hopper. She appeared in more than 50 films. During her 28-year career as a radio columnist, she rivaled Louella Parsons in fame and power. Noted for her hats.

Our town worships success, the bitch goddess whose smile hides a taste for blood.

1899   **Edwin Way Teale:** U.S. naturalist and author. Won Pulitzer Prize for *Wandering Through Winter* (1966). Other works: *The Lost Woods* and *Autumn Across America*.

How sad would be November if we had no knowledge of the spring!

1904   **Johnny Weissmuller:** U.S. actor. Most famous and popular Tarzan of them all. Former gold medal–winning Olympic swimmer appeared as "The Ape Man" in 12 films.

The main thing is not to let go of the vine.

1913   **Barbara Mary Crampton Pym:** English novelist. Wrote seven popular novels, including: *Quartet in Autumn, A Very Private Eye* and *Crampton's Hodnet*.

How absurd and delicious it is to be in love with someone younger than yourself. Everybody should try it.

June 3

1635   **Philippe Quinault:** French dramatist. Collaborated with Jean-Baptise Lully in the creation of the form of the "tragédie-lyrique" which became the model for French opera. Among his popular librettos are *Amadis, Roland* and *Armida*.

It is not wise to be wiser than is necessary.

1726   **James Hutton:** Scottish geologist. Founded the science of geology. Anticipated Darwin's idea of organic evolution by natural selection. Wrote *A Theory of the Earth*.

The result, therefore, of our present inquiry is that we find no vestige of a beginning—no prospect of an end.

1808   **Jefferson Davis:** American political leader, soldier, farmer. Senator from Mississippi (1847–51 and 1857–61). U.S. secretary of war (1853–57). President of the Confederate States of America (1861-65). Imprisoned and indicted for treason, but case was dropped.

Neither current events nor history show that the majority rules, or ever did rule.

1816   Alfred Mercier: Louisiana-born U.S. author of poems, novels and plays written in French. Founded a French literary society in New Orleans, L'Athénée Louisianais which published *Compte Rendu*, a periodical which contained the best of the French literature published in Louisiana at the time.

There was a wise man in the East whose constant prayer was that he might see today with the eyes of tomorrow.

1906   Josephine Baker: U.S. black singer, dancer. Made her reputation mainly in Paris, touring with the Revue Nègre. Joined French Resistance, earning several medals. Tireless campaigner for Civil Rights in the U.S. Of her somewhat scandalous stage image:

I wasn't really naked. I simply didn't have any clothes on.

1926   Allen Ginsberg: U.S. beat movement poet. Verses are loosely structured and spontaneous, largely drawn from experiments with hallucinogenic drugs and vision, as well as the teachings of Zen Buddhism. Poems: "The Howl," "Kaddish" and "Reality Sandwiches."

I saw the best minds of my generation destroyed by madness.

1931   Bert Lance: U.S. government official. President Carter's director of U.S. Office of Management and the Budget. Forced to resign because of questionable banking practices.

If it ain't broken, don't fix it.

June 4

1843   Charles C. Abbott: U.S. naturalist. Author of *Days Out of Doors* and *Notes of the Night*. Abbott's laws:

(1) If you have to ask, you're not entitled to know. (2) If you didn't like the answer, you shouldn't have asked the question.

1863   Robert Fitzsimmons: U.S. boxer. At 160 pounds took the world heavyweight championship from James J. Corbett. Lost it to James J. Jeffries.

The bigger they come, the harder they fall.

1878   Frank Buchman: U.S. clergyman called "a surgeon of souls." Founder of the Moral Re-Armament movement, a non-sectarian international attempt to change the world by changing one person at a time.

With all the sincerity of my eighty years— I say God is the answer to the modern confusion that dogs us.

1894   Gabriel Pascal: Transylvanian-born producer, director. Stage actor in Vienna. Entrusted by George Bernard Shaw with the filming of Shavian plays.

Vestal virgins half-nude in a steambath. That is Hollywood's idea of sex. They must think the American male is so tired and impotent that he has to have a vast exposure of female flesh to excite him.

1908   Rosalind Russell: U.S. actress. Graduate of American Academy of Dramatic Arts. Played strong-willed career women. Oscar nominated for *Mourning Becomes Electra, My Sister Eileen, Sister Kenny* and *Auntie Mame*.

Acting is standing up naked and turning around very slowly.

1919   Robert Merrill: U.S. operatic baritone. First performer to sing 500 performances at the Met. Roles: Escamillo (*Carmen*), Germont (*La Traviata*), Marcello (*La Bohème*) and Iago (*Otello*).

If you think you've hit a false note, sing loud. When in doubt, sing loud.

1937   Robert Fulghum: U.S. author. First to simultaneously have the number one and two spots on hardcover best-seller list with *All I Really Need to Know I Learned in Kindergarten* and *It Was on Fire When I Lay Down on It*.

Always trust your fellow man and always cut the cards.

June 5

1723   Adam Smith: Scottish moral philosopher, political economist. His major work, *The Wealth of Nations* was the first systematic formulation of classical English economics. Advocated a laissez-faire economy.

There is no art which one government sooner learns of another than that of draining money from the pockets of the people.

1883 **John Maynard Keynes:** English economist. Originator of so-called New Economics. Advised wide government expenditure as a counter measure to deflation and depression. Works: *The End of Laissez-faire, A Treatise on Money* and *How to Pay for the War.*

The avoidance of taxes is the only intelligent pursuit that still carries any reward.

1887 **Ruth Fulton Benedict:** American anthropologist. A leading member of the culture-and-personality movement in U.S. anthropology of the 1930s. Best known works: *Patterns of Culture* and *Race: Science and Politics.*

The trouble is not that we are never happy—it is that happiness is so episodical.

1897 **Madame Chiang Kai-shek:** Wife of Generalissimo Chiang Kai-shek. Phi Beta Kappa graduate of Wellesley College. Sister-in-law of Sun Yat-sen, founder of the Chinese Republic. She was most instrumental in enlisting U.S. sympathy and relief for China.

China colors all seas that wash her shores.

1934 **Bill Moyers:** U.S. broadcast journalist. Personal assistant to Lyndon B. Johnson. White house press secretary. Publisher of *Newsday.* Contributing editor to *Newsweek.* Editor-in-chief of television's "Bill Moyers' Journal."

Ideas are great arrows, but there has to be a bow. And politics is the bow of idealism.

1939 **Margaret Drabble:** English author whose novels include the espionage thriller *The Needle's Eye* and *The Middle Ground.*

On one thing professionals and amateurs agree: mothers can't win.

1947 **David Hare:** Award-winning English playwright and director. Founded the Portable Theatre and became resident playwright at the Royal Court (1969–71). Plays, *Slag, Teeth 'n' Smiles* and *Plenty.*

The art of writing is the art of discovering what you believe.

June 6

1755 **Nathan Hale:** American schoolteacher and patriot, Revolutionary hero. Hanged by British as a spy. Gained immortality with his familiar last words, "I only regret that I have but one life to lose for my country." His words, upon being warned by a friend against taking the assignment that led to his arrest:

Every kind of service necessary to the public good becomes honorable by being necessary.

1799 **Aleksandr Pushkin:** Russian poet, playwright, novelist, short-story writer. Russia's greatest poet. In his country he holds the same place that Shakespeare does in England and Goethe does in Germany. Works: *Ruslan and Lyudmilla, Eugene Onegin, Boris Godunov* and *The Queen of Spades.*

Blessed is the man who to himself has kept the high creation of his soul.

1860 **William R. Inge:** "The Gloomy Dean." Pessimistic English theologian and dean of St. Paul's Cathedral. Explored mystical aspects of Christianity in sermons and newspaper articles. Wrote *Outspoken Essays* and *Lay Thoughts of a Dean.*

Worry is interest paid on trouble before it falls due.

1875 **Thomas Mann:** German novelist, essayist. Nobel Prize winner for literature (1929). Forced into exile by Nazis (1939). Became a U.S. citizen (1944). Works: *Buddenbrooks, Death in Venice, The Magic Mountain* and *Doctor Faustus.*

Beauty can pierce one like a pain.

1898 **Dame Ninette De Valois:** Irish-born dancer, choreographer, ballet director. First English dancer accepted by Diaghileff for his Ballet Russes. Founder and director of Sadler's Wells Ballet School, now Royal Ballet School.

You cannot create genius. All you can do is nurture it.

1909 Sir Isaiah Berlin: Latvian-born British philosopher. Director of the Royal Opera House, president of the British Academy, translator of Turgenev, activist in Jewish affairs and first president of Wolfson College, Oxford.
Man cannot live without seeking to describe and explain the universe.

1925 Maxine Kumin: American poet, novelist and essayist. Author of: *No One Writes a Letter to a Snail, The Nightmare Factory* and *A Way of Staying Sane.* Won Pulitzer Prize for *Up Country* (1973).
Nature is a catchment of sorrows.

June 7

1778 George Bryan "Beau" Brummell: English dandy, wit. Influenced men toward simplicity and moderation in dress. Credited with inventing trousers to replace breeches.
I always like to have the morning well-aired before I get up.

1848 Paul Gauguin: French painter. Abandoned his family to devote himself completely to his art. Set out for Tahiti, where he spent the rest of his life. A highly original painter who had a great influence on impressionists.
Art is either a revolutionist or a plagiarist.

1897 George Szell: Hungarian-born U.S. conductor with Berlin State Opera, German Opera, Metropolitan Opera and Cleveland Orchestra.
In music one must think with the heart and feel with the brain.

1899 Elizabeth [Dorothea Cole] Bowen: Irish novelist and short-story writer. Explored psychological relationships in the upper class. Works: *Encounters, The Death of the Heart* and *The Heat of the Day.*
Jealousy is no more than feeling alone against smiling enemies.

1909 Jessica Tandy: English-born actress. Teamed with husband Hume Cronyn in plays such as *The Fourposter* and *The Gin Game,* for which she won a Tony. Most celebrated stage performance was as the original Blanche DuBois in *A Streetcar Named Desire* (1947). Oscar winner at 81 for *Driving Miss Daisy.*
When I'm ready to stop acting, you'll read about it in the obituaries.

1917 Gwendolyn Brooks: One of foremost African American poets of the 20th century. Poems depict the wounds and inequities inflicted on blacks. Pulitzer Prize for poetry for her verse narrative, "Annie Allen" (1950), the first awarded to an African American woman. Succeeded Carl Sandburg as poet laureate of Illinois.
It is brave to be involved / To be fearful to be unresolved.

1922 Rocky Graziano: U.S. boxer. World middleweight champion (1946-47). Fought Tony Zale for title three times in 21 months, losing twice. Pro record 67-10-6 with 52 knockouts.
Fighting is the only racket where you're almost guaranteed to end up as a bum.

June 8

1810 Robert Schumann: German composer. Husband of pianist, teacher and composer Clara Wieck. Parallel to his piano work, he produced some of the finest lieder. Compositions: *Carnaval, Myrthen, Liederkreise, Papillons* and four symphonies.
In order to compose, all you need to do is to remember a tune that no one else has thought of.

1814 Charles Reade: English novelist. Noted for historical romances and novels that exposed social injustice that led to reforms. His masterpiece was the long historical novel of the 15th century, *The Cloister and the Hearth.* His recipe for a successful novel:
Make 'em laugh; make 'em cry; make 'em wait.

1869   **Frank Lloyd Wright:** U.S. architect, writer. Created what he called "organic architecture," using natural materials, and a low, gently spreading profile, known as the Prairie Style. Projects: Guggenheim Museum, New York City; Kaufmann House, Bear Run, Pennsylvania; and Robie House, Chicago, Illinois.
Youth is a quality, not a matter of circumstances.

1903   **Marguerite Yourcenar:** French novelist, poet, critic, classical scholar. First woman elected to the Académie Française. Novels: *Memoirs of Hadrian* and *The Abyss.*
I have never seasoned a truth with the sauce of a lie in order to digest it more easily.

1917   **Byron R. "Whizzer" White:** All-American running back with University of Colorado. Played pro football with Pittsburgh and Detroit. Football Hall of Fame (1954). Lawyer, jurist. Associate justice of U.S. Supreme Court (1962–).
We're the only branch of government that explains itself every time it makes a decision.

1923   **Malcolm Boyd:** U.S. Episcopal priest, author. Activist in civil and gay rights movements. Books: *Are You Running with Me Jesus?* and *Free to Live, Free to Die.*
Prayer represents commitment. To pray is to say "I'm willing to get with it—love, responsibility, action."

1925   **Barbara Bush:** American first lady. Wife of George Bush, the 41st U.S. president. Probably more popular than her husband. Co-wrote *Millie's Book*, with the White House pet.
As you grow older, I think you need to put your arms around each other more.

June 9

1672   **Peter I:** "The Great." Russian Czar (1682–1725). Modernized Russia. Embarked on a series of sweeping military, fiscal, educational, administrative and ecclesiastical reforms, many based on Western

models. Moved his capital to the new city he built, St. Petersberg, his "window to the West." Views on taxation:
Ask the impossible so to receive as much as possible.

1791   **John Howard Payne:** American actor, playwright, editor and poet. Plays: *Love in Humble Life, The Signet Ring* and *The Wife and the Widow.* Most famous poem is "Home, Sweet Home."
'Mid pleasures and palaces though we may roam, / Be it ever so humble, there's no place like home.

1892   **Cole Porter:** U.S. composer and lyricist. His style was clever and sophisticated. Musical comedies: *Jubilee, Kiss Me Kate* and *Can-Can.* Songs: "Night and Day," "Begin the Beguine," "You're the Tops" and "I Get a Kick Out of You."
All the imagination I ever needed was a phone call from a producer.

1900   **Fred Waring:** U.S. conductor. His chorus, the Pennsylvanians, have made many tours and radio and television appearances since 1923.
Poems can be read or spoken, melodies can be played or whistled, but words and music were blended into song, and a song was written to be sung.

1916   **Les Paul:** U.S. guitarist. With wife Mary Ford had numerous hits, including "How High the Moon" and "The World Is Waiting for the Sunrise" as a multi-recording guitarist. Popularized the electric guitar.
Heavy metal music is five guys on the stage sounding like WWIII.

1922   **George Axelrod:** U.S. dramatist. Plays: *The Seven Year Itch* and *Breakfast at Tiffany's.*
A humorist ... can himself be horrified out of laughter, which is a terrible thing. We're not seeing things funny, partly because we're scared to death. In a grotesque horrible way, life itself has become pretty much of a joke. And you can't make a joke on a joke.

1931   **Jackie Mason:** Rabbi U.S. comedian. Delights in being "politically incorrect."

Starred in successful Broadway one-man show, *The World According to Me.*
Did you ever hear of a kid playing accountant—even if he wanted to be one?

June 10

1895 Hattie McDaniel: U.S. character actress. Oscar winner for *Gone with the Wind,* first black to do so. Her roles were mainly maids.
Why should I complain about making $7000 a week playing a maid? If I didn't, I'd be making seven dollars a week actually being one!

1911 Terence Rattigan: English playwright. Wrote *French Without Tears, The Winslow Boy, The Browning Version* and *Separate Tables.*
A novelist may lose his reader for a few pages; a playwright never dares lose his audience for a minute.

1921 Prince Philip: Duke of Edinburgh. Greek-born consort of Queen Elizabeth II of England.
Dontopedology is the science of opening your mouth and putting your foot in it. I've been practicing it for years.

1922 Judy Garland: U.S. actress, singer. Fondly remembered by many singing "Over the Rainbow" in *The Wizard of Oz.* Among her most successful films in her troubled life: *Meet Me in St. Louis, Easter Parade* and *A Star Is Born.* Mother of entertainer Liza Minnelli.
How strange when an illusion dies / It's as though you've lost a child...

1926 Nat Hentoff: U.S. newspaper columnist, editor. Author of *The Jazz Life, Our Children Are Dying* and *Journey Into Jazz.*
It's not only that you can't go home again; you can't pretend to be from a place you only visited.

1928 Maurice Sendak: American children's book author and illustrator. Wrote and illustrated *Where the Wild Things Are,* which won the Carnegie Medal. It perturbed parents but delighted children and sold hugely all over the world.

You cannot write for children ... They're much too complicated. You can only write books that are of interest to them.

1933 F. Lee Bailey: U.S. attorney and author. Represented Albert DeSalvo (the Boston Strangler), Patty Hearst, Dr. Sam Sheppard, Capt. Ernest Medina and was a member of the O.J. Simpson defense team.
I use the rules to frustrate the law. But I didn't set up the ground rules.

June 11

1572 Ben Jonson: English dramatist, poet. Best known for his dramatic satires *Volpone, Epicoene, The Alchemist* and *Bartholomew Fair.* His lyric genius is ranked second only to Shakespeare.
Talking and eloquence are not the same: to speak, and to speak well, are two things. A fool may talk, but a wise man speaks.

1776 John Constable: English painter. Noted for Romantic views of the English countryside. Paintings: *Salisbury Cathedral* and *Waterloo Bridge.*
There has never been a boy painter, nor can there be. The art requires a long apprenticeship, being mechanical as well as intellectual.

1888 Anna Akhmatova: Pseudonym of Anna Andreeyevna Gorenko. Ukrainian-born poet. With her husband Nicholas Gumilev started the Neo-classicist Acmeist movement. Works: *Evening, Beads, Anno Domini* and *Requiem.*
No foreign sky protected me, / no stranger's wings shielded my face, / I stand as witness to the common lot, / survivor of that time, that place.

1910 Jacques Cousteau: French ocean explorer, filmmaker, author. Invented the aqualung, which has made possible the sport of scuba diving. Wrote *The Silent World* and *The Living Sea.*
Biological sciences will in the end take the lead, for without life, there is no science.

1913 Vince Lombardi: Legendary U.S. football coach of the Green Bay Packers.

He led them to victory in the first two Super Bowls.

There is nothing that stokes the fire like hate.

1920   **Hazel Scott:** West Indian–born U.S. jazz pianist, singer, actor and feminist. Married to politician Adam Clayton Powell (1945–60). A popular entertainer in Paris (1965–67).

Any woman who has a great deal to offer the world is in trouble.

1925   **William Stryon:** American author concerned with oppression in its myriad forms. Author of Pulitzer-winning *The Confessions of Nat Turner* and *Sophie's Choice.*

Depression is a howling tempest in the brain.

June 12

1802   **Harriet Martineau:** English social and historical writer. Works: *Illustrations of Political Economy, Poor Laws and Paupers Illustrated* and *Society in America.*

Anyone must see at a glance that if men and women marry those whom they do not love, they must love those whom they do not marry.

1819   **Charles Kingsley:** English clergyman, poet and novelist. Deeply involved in social reform. Wrote: *The Saint's Tragedy, Yeast* and *Adam Locke.*

The age of chivalry is never past, as long as there is a wrong left unaddressed on earth.

1827   **Johanna Spyri:** Swiss author, best known for her novel *Heidi,* the story of a young girl who leaves her cozy home in the Swiss Alps for adventures in the world below.

Anger makes us all stupid.

1892   **Djuna Barnes:** American novelist, poet and illustrator. Began her career as a reporter and illustrator for magazines. Her works, many of which she illustrated, include the outstanding novel *Nightwood* and her verse play *The Antiphon.*

A strong sense of identity gives man an idea he can do no wrong; too little accomplishes the same.

1897   **Sir Anthony Eden:** English statesman. Foreign secretary (1935–38, 1940–45 and 1951–55). Prime minister (1955–57). Helped establish the Southeast Asia Treaty Organization.

Everybody is always in favor of general economy and particular expenditures.

1924   **George Bush:** Forty-first U.S. president and 43rd vice president. Texas congressman, youngest WWII fighter pilot. Ambassador to the U.N. (1971–73). Republican National Chairman (1973–74). Headed the CIA (1976).

Don't try to fine tune somebody's else's view.

1929   **Anne Frank:** German-Jewish girl. Kept a diary later published as *The Diary of a Young Girl* during two years of hiding from the Nazis. Was captured and sent to a concentration camp where she died.

How wonderful it is that nobody need wait a single moment before starting to improve the world.

June 13

1752   **Fanny Burney:** Madame d'Arblay. english novelist. Chiefly known for her *Diaries and Letters* and novels *Evelina, Cecilia* and *Camilla.*

Traveling is the ruin of all happiness! There's no looking at a building here after seeing Italy.

1795   **Thomas Arnold:** English educator. Set the pattern for English public-school system while headmaster at Rugby. Introduced "muscular Christianity." Father of poet Matthew Arnold.

My object will be, if possible, to form Christian men, for Christian boys I can scarcely hope to make.

1865   **William Butler Yeats:** Irish poet, dramatist. Son of J.B. Yeats, a well-known Irish painter. Cofounder of a theater society that would become the Abbey Theatre. Best known poems: "Bzyantium," "Easter 1916," "Leda and the Swan" and "Among School Children."

No man has ever lived that had enough / Of children's gratitude or woman's love.

1893 **Dorothy Sayers:** English mystery novelist. Created sophisticated amateur detective Lord Peter Wimsey. Earned a reputation as a leading Christian apologist with her plays *The Zeal of Thy House* and *The Devil to Pay.*
The worst sin—perhaps the only sin— passion can commit, is to be joyless.

1894 **Mark Van Doren:** American poet, critic and novelist. His *Collected Poems 1922-38* earned him a Pulitzer Prize. Also wrote critical biographies of Thoreau, Dryden, Shakespeare and Hawthorne.
Wit is the only wall / Between us and the dark.

1903 **Harold "Red" Grange:** "The Galloping Ghost." All-American football running back at the University of Illinois. Played pro ball with the Chicago Bears and New York Yankees. Against Michigan in 1924, he accumulated 402 total yards and 5 touchdowns. On his trademark ability to evade tacklers:
If you can't explain it, how can you take credit for it?

1911 **Luis Alvarez:** U.S. experimental nuclear physicist. During WWII developed radar navigation and landing systems for aircraft. Developed the bubble-chamber which allowed him to discover new sub-atomic particles. Won Nobel Prize (1968).
Nuclear physicists are in the position of a boy who finds a penny and thinks he is on his way to becoming a millionaire.

June 14

1811 **Harriet Beecher Stowe:** U.S. novelist. Best known as the author of *Uncle Tom's Cabin* which aroused considerable anti-slavery feelings prior to the Civil War.
No one is as thoroughly superstitious as the godless man.

1855 **Robert M. Lafollette, Sr.:** U.S. politician, lawyer. Leader of the Progressive movement which championed the little guy against established interests. Wisconsin congressman (1885–91), reform governor (1900–6) and senator (1907–25). Progressive Party presidential candidate (1924).
Politics is economics in action.

1904 **Margaret Bourke-White:** U.S. photo-journalist. An innovator in photo essays with *Life* magazine (1936–69). Covered WWII for *Life* magazine. First woman photographer to be attached to the U.S. armed forces. An official U.N. correspondent during the Korean War. Books: *Eyes on Russia* and *Halfway to Freedom.*
The beauty of the past belongs to the past.

1909 **Burl Ives:** U.S. folk singer, actor. Oscar winner for *The Big Country.* Memorable as "Big Daddy" in *Cat on a Hot Tin Roof.* Songs: "Blue Tail Fly," "The Foggy, Foggy Dew" and "Big Rock Candy Mountain."
Ballad singing has been going on ever since people sang at all. It comes up like an underground stream and then goes back again. But it always exists.

1928 **Ernesto "Che" Guevara:** Argentine-born Latin American guerrilla and revolutionary. Trusted aide of Fidel Castro in the Cuban revolution. Left Cuba in 1965 to become a guerrilla leader in South America. Captured and executed in Bolivia.
Silence is an argument carried on by other means.

1933 **Jerzy Kosinski:** Polish-born U.S. author. His novels espouse a belief in survival at any cost. Wrote *The Painted Bird, Being There* and *Passion Play.*
You don't die in the United States, you underachieve.

1946 **Donald Trump:** U.S. real estate tycoon. Built New York's Trump Tower and Atlantic City casinos. His enthusiastic self-promotion made him a celebrity of the eighties. Faced near bankruptcy in 1990.
As long as you're going to be thinking anyway, think big.

June 15

1767 **Rachel Robards Jackson:** U.S. first lady. Caused a scandal by marrying Andrew Jackson before divorcing her first husband.
Believe me, this country [Florida] has been greatly overrated. One acre of our fine Tennessee land is worth a thousand here.

1843 Edvard Grieg: Norwegian composer of choral works, dances and sonatas for various instruments. Best known for his *Peer Gynt Suite.*
I am sure my music has a taste of codfish in it.

1884 Harry Langdon: U.S. actor in minstrel shows, circuses, burlesque, vaudeville and silent films. His baby face was featured in the likes of *Tramp, Tramp, Tramp, The Strong Man* and *Long Pants.*
Comedy is the satire of tragedy.

1902 Erik Ericson: Danish-born psychologist, writer, educator. Opened new relationship between psychoanalysis and social sciences. Introduced term "identity crisis." Books: *Childhood and Society, Gandhi's Truth* and *Young Man Luther.*
Doubt is the brother of shame.

1914 Saul Steinberg: U.S. artist and cartoonist. Known for his *New Yorker* magazine covers combining styles of cubism and pointillism.
Every explanation is an over explanation.

1922 Morris K. Udall: "Mo." U.S. politician, lawyer. Arizona U.S. representative from 1961. Chairman of House Interior and Insular Affairs Committee. Sought Democratic presidential nomination (1976). Brother of Stewart L. Udall.
Old prayer for politicians: Teach us to utter words that are tender and gentle. Tomorrow we may have to eat them.

1932 Mario Cuomo: U.S. politician. Governor of New York (1982–94). Often mentioned as a Democratic presidential candidate, but has declined to make a run.
You campaign in poetry. You govern in prose.

June 16

1583 Count Axel Oxenstierna: Swedish statesman. Chancellor of Sweden for 42 years. His country's greatest civil servant. Negotiated favorable peace treaties with Denmark, Sweden and Poland. Regent for Queen Christina.
Behold, my son, with what little wisdom the world is ruled.

1890 Stan Laurel: British-born U.S. comedian, teamed with Oliver Hardy to form a beloved comedy team in more than 100 films, 27 of which were features. Laurel was the featherbrained member of the team, characteristically scratching his head and at the first sign of trouble, sobbing uncontrollably.
All I know is just how to make people laugh.

1912 Enoch Powell: English conservative politician and scholar. Enlisted in WWII as a private, rose to the rank of brigadier. Minister of housing and minister of health. Held controversial views in opposition to black immigration and the common market.
History is littered with wars which everybody knew would never happen.

1917 Katharine Graham: U.S. publisher. Consistently voted one of the most influential women in the United States. President of the *Washington Post* (1963–67); publisher (1968–78); chairman and CEO from 1973.
I always thought if you worked hard enough and tried hard enough, things would work out. I was wrong.

1938 Joyce Carol Oates: U.S. writer, university professor. Winner of the National Book Award for 1970 novel *Them.* Also received four O. Henry awards.
The use of language is all we have to pit against death and silence.

1954 Howard Stern: U.S. radio shock personality. His programs are offensive to many people, most particularly women and gays whom he makes primary targets of his politically incorrect comments. As many others are delighted with his outrageous behavior.
The rule I follow is this: I should say anything I think is funny.

June 17

1703 John Wesley: English evangelist, theologian. Founder of Methodist movement. In 1738 during the reading of Luther's preface to the Epistle to the Romans, he experienced an assurance of salvation which he felt driven to bring to others.

Make all you can, save all you can, give all you can.

1860   Charles Frohman: American theatrical manager and impresario. He introduced Maude Adams in *Peter Pan* in 1905. Helped create the "star" system. His last words before going down with the *Lusitania*, May 7, 1915:

Why fear death? It is the most beautiful adventure in life.

1871   James Welden Johnson: American black poet and novelist. Wrote *The Autobiography of an Ex-Colored Man, Black Manhattan* and edited *American Negro Poetry.*

You are young, gifted and Black. We must begin to tell our young. There's a world waiting for you. Yours is the quest that's just begun.

1882   Igor Stravinsky: Russian-born U.S. composer. Best known for ballets, *The Firebird, Petrouchka* and *The Rite of Spring.* Essentially an experimenter, he also composed *Oedipus Rex*, an opera-oratorio, and the choral *Symphony of Psalms.*

Too many pieces of music finish too long after the end.

1914   John Hersey: American novelist, journalist. Pulitzer Prize for *A Bell for Adano.* Others: *The Wall* and *The War Lover.*

Journalism allows its readers to witness history. Fiction gives its readers an opportunity to live it.

1919   Kingman Brewster: U.S. educator, diplomat. President of Yale University (1963–77). U.S. Ambassador to Great Britain.

There is no greater challenge than to have someone relying upon you; no greater satisfaction than to vindicate his expectation.

1943   Newt Gingrich: Republican congressman from Georgia. G.O.P. minority whip. Speaker of the House (1995–). Loves to tweak Democrats and liberals.

I understand my critics are fixated and pathologically disoriented, but they're my opponents. Why should I try to correct that?

June 18

1581   Sir Thomas Overbury: English poet and courtier. Became involved in numerous court intrigues and scandals, one of which resulted in his death in the Tower of London. Posthumously published works: "The Wife" and "Crumm's Fal'n from King James's Table."

The man who has nothing to boast of but his illustrious ancestors, is like the potato— the best part under ground.

1812   Ivan Goncharov: Russian novelist. Best known for the novel *Oblomov,* one of the greatest and most typical examples of Russian realism.

It is a trick among the dishonest to offer sacrifices that are not needed, or not possible, to avoid making those that are required.

1869   Carolyn Wells: U.S. writer, humorist, poet, playwright and anthologist. Books: *At the Sign of the Sphinx, A Satire Anthology* and *Book of Limericks.*

There is one thing I can't get in my head— Why do people marry the people they wed?

1877   James Montgomery Flagg: American artist and author. Created the WWI recruiting poster of Uncle Sam, pointing his finger, with the caption "I Want You."

…If there be no beauty in women the race goes hungry and is not fed.

1913   Sylvia Field Porter: U.S. financial reporter and author of *Money Book.* Leading financial columnist with the *New York Post* (1935–77) and the *New York Daily News* since 1978. *Sylvia Porter's Income Tax Guide* has been published annually since 1960.

Beware of the danger signals that flag problems: silence, secretiveness, or sudden outbursts.

1926   Tom Wicker: Pseudonym of Paul Connolly. Nationally syndicated American columnist. Chief of the Washington Bureau of the *New York Times* (1964–68). Wrote *A Time to Die* about the riots at Attica prison.

Government expands to absorb revenues and then some.

1937   **Gail Godwin:** U.S. novelist and short-story writer. Author of *Glass People.* Author of *Dream Children* and *The Odd Woman.*
Good teaching is one-fourth preparation and three-fourths theatre.

June 19

1566   **James I:** King of England (1603-25). Son of Mary, Queen of Scots. On her forced abdication became James VI, King of Scots (1567–1625). Succeeded Elizabeth I as English monarch.
[Smoking is] a custom loathsome to the eye, hateful to the nose, harmful to the brain, dangerous to the lungs, and in the black stinking fume thereof nearest resembles the horrible Stygian smoke of the pit that is bottomless.

1608   **Thomas Fuller:** English clergyman, scholar and writer. One of the wittiest and most prolific authors of the 17th century. Works: *The Holy State, the Profane State* and his most famous work, *History of the Worthies of Britain.*
Security is the mother of danger and the grandmother of destruction.

1623   **Blaise Pascal:** French philosopher, scientist, mathematician and writer. Formulated the first laws of atmospheric pressure, equilibrium of liquids and probability. *Les Pensées*, projected apology for the Christian religion appeared in their entirety only after his death.
The heart has its reasons which reason knows nothing of.

1856   **Elbert Hubbard:** U.S. writer, essayist, lecturer, editor. After years as a successful businessman, established in 1893 the Roycrofters, a craft community in East Aurora, N.Y. Best known as the author of *A Message to Garcia*, which embodied his ideas about a community of workers.
A compliment is a sarcastic remark with a flavor of truth.

1881   **James J. Walker:** "Jimmy." Dapper, debonair and flamboyant, fun-loving mayor of New York City (1925–32). Forced to resign as a result of an investigation into widespread corruption in his administration.
A reformer is a guy who rides through a sewer in a glass bottom boat.

1903   **Lou Gehrig:** U.S. baseball first baseman with the New York Yankees who set a record for consecutive games played (2,130). Gehrig died of a muscle wasting disease, now known by his name. He demonstrated his bravery at a Yankee stadium ceremony to honor him, saying:
Two weeks ago, I got a bad break. Yet today, I count myself the luckiest man on the face of the earth.

1919   **Pauline Kael:** American film critic, author. Columnist for *The New Yorker* magazine. Books: *I Lost It at the Movies, Kiss Kiss Bang Bang* and *5001 Nights at the Movies.*
The first prerogative of an artist in any medium is to make a fool of himself.

June 20

1723   **Adam Ferguson:** Scottish man of letters, philosopher, historian, and patriot. Member of the Scottish common sense school of philosophy. Works: *Essay on the History of Civil Society* and *Principles of Moral and Political Science.*
We mistake human nature if we wish for a termination of labor, or a sense of repose.

1852   **George Iles:** Gibraltar-born U.S. author. Editor: *Little Masterpieces of Science* and *Little Masterpieces of Autobiography.*
Doubt is the beginning, not the end of wisdom.

1858   **Charles W. Chestnutt:** American writer, school principal, attorney and founder of a legal stenography firm. Son of emancipated blacks, he wrote works on social justice. His story "The Goophered Grapevine" was the first published work of a black fiction writer.
We are all puppets in the hands of Fate and seldom see the strings that move us.

1878   Arthur E. Morgan: U.S. civil engineer, educator, author of *Nowhere Was Somewhere*. President of Antioch College (1920–36).
Lack of something to feel important about is almost the greatest tragedy a man may have.

1905   Lillian Hellman: American dramatist. Plays include: *The Children's Hour, Watch on the Rhine, Another Part of the Forest* and *The Little Foxes*. A left-winged activist and one of the most persuasive voices in American theater.
Cynicism is an unpleasant way of saying the truth.

1909   Errol Flynn: Hard-living Tasmanian-born roguish actor who starred in many swashbuckling films, including *Captain Blood, The Charge of the Light Brigade* and *The Adventures of Robin Hood*.
It isn't what they say about you—it's what they whisper about you.

1946   Andre Watts: German-born U.S. pianist who appeared with the Philadelphia Orchestra at age nine. An international favorite, known for his 19th century repertoire.
It must be hard for people who don't have great joy or great sorrows to get any emotion across....

June 21

1639   Increase Mather: American colonial clergyman. Pastor of Second Church of Boston. President of Harvard (1685-1701). Criticized the extremism of the Salem witchcraft trials.
It were better that ten suspected witches should escape, than that one innocent person should be condemned.

1806   Augustus De Morgan: English mathematician, logician and bibliographer. Helped develop the notion of different kinds of algebra. With Boyle developed symbolic logic. His name is given to De Morgan's law of logic.
Great fleas have little fleas upon their back to bite 'em. / And little fleas have lesser fleas, and so on ad infinitum.

1892   Reinhold Niebuhr: American theologian. He dealt with the failure of Christianity to confront social problems. Writings: *Moral Man and Immoral Society, Christian Realism and Political Problems* and *Essays in Applied Christianity*.
Life has no meaning except in terms of responsibility.

1905   Jean-Paul Sartre: French philosopher, dramatist, novelist and critic. His works dramatize the discovery of the meaningless of life, the precondition for his philosophy of Existentialism. Works: *Nausea, The Flies, No Exit,* and *The Roads to Freedom*.
Hell is—other people.

1912   Mary McCarthy: American writer, reviewer, critic, satirist. Works: *Memories of a Catholic Girlhood, The Company She Keeps, The Groves of Academe* and *The Group*.
There are no new truths but only truths that have not been recognized by those who have perceived them without noticing.

1931   Margaret Heckler: U.S. government official, diplomat. Secretary of Health and Human Services in the Reagan administration. Ambassador to Ireland.
A country that can put men on the moon can put women in the Constitution.

1935   Françoise Sagan: French novelist. Best known for her earliest work *Bonjour Tristesse*, written in four weeks when she was just 18. It was followed by *A Certain Smile*. Both novels are direct testaments of adolescent wisdom and precocity.
I like men to behave like men—strong and childish.

June 22

1844   Margaret Sidney: Pen name of Harriet Mulford Stone Lothrup. U.S. author of *Five Little Peppers and How They Grew* and others in the series.
Corners are for little people; but when people who know better do wrong, there aren't any corners they can creep into, or they'd get into them pretty quick.

June 23

1887   **Sir Julian Huxley:** British biologist, writer. Secretary of the Zoological Society of London (1935–42). Applied his scientific knowledge to politics and social problems. First director-general of UNESCO.
Operationally, God is beginning to resemble not a ruler but the last fading smile of a cosmic Cheshire cat.

1898   **Erich Maria Remarque:** German-U.S. novelist. Best known for his anti-war novel *All Quiet on the Western Front.* Also wrote *Three Comrades* and *A Time to Live and a Time to Die.*
The simple fact that a man has survived the war ... makes him, after a short time, remember war as a grand adventure.

1906   **Anne Morrow Lindbergh:** U.S. author. Wrote *The Gift from the Sea.* Wife of famed aviator Charles Lindbergh.
By and large, mothers and housewives are the only workers who do not have regular time off. They're the great vacationless class.

1906   **Billy Wilder:** Vienna-born U.S. director, screenwriter, producer. Oscar winner as best director and screenwriter for *The Lost Weekend* and *The Apartment* (which also earned Best Picture Oscar). Oscar for directing *Stalag 17* and for screenwriter for *Sunset Boulevard.* Nominated either as director or screenwriter 13 other times.
Hindsight is always twenty-twenty.

1910   **Katherine Dunham:** U.S. dancer and choreographer. Organized first professional African American dance troupe. Choreographed for opera and wrote several books about her field.
You dance because you have to. Dance is an essential part of life that has always been with me.

1922   **Bill Blass:** American fashion designer. Noted for his men and women's clothes, furs, luggage, grooming products and chocolates.
When in doubt, wear red.

1668   **Giovanni Battista Vico:** Italian jurist, philosopher of law and cultural history. Exponent of a new science of humanity. Influenced many later scholars including Goethe and Marx.
Common sense is judgement without reflection which is shared by an entire class, a people, a nation, or the whole human race.

1876   **Irvin S. Cobb:** U.S. playwright, novelist, journalist, editor, actor. Noted for his "Judge Priest" stories.
Middle age is when you begin to exchange your emotions for symptoms.

1894   **Edward VIII [Duke of Windsor]:** King of England who resigned in 1936, abdicating his throne for twice married American Wallis Simpson.
The thing that impresses me most about America is the way parents obey their children.

1894   **Dr. Alfred Kinsey:** American zoologist who authored several studies of the sexual life of human beings. Books: *Sexual Behavior of the Human Male* and *Sexual Behavior of the Human Female.*
The only unnatural sex act is that which you cannot perform.

1910   **Jean Anouilh:** French dramatist, screenwriter. Influenced by the neoclassicism inspired by Giraudoux. Wrote *Antigone, The Waltz of the Toreadors* and *Becket.*
Talent is like a faucet, while it is open, one must write.

1927   **Bob Fosse:** U.S. dance, choreographer, director. Tony winner for *Pippin, Pajama Game, Dancin', Damn Yankees, Sweet Charity* and *Redhead.* Oscar winner for *Cabaret.*
My friends know that to me happiness is when I am merely miserable and not suicidal.

1940   **Wilma Rudolph:** American runner. Winner of three Olympic Gold medals for track in 1960: 100 meters, 200 meters and 4×400 meter relay.
When the sun is shining I can do anything; no mountain is too high, no trouble too difficult to overcome.

June 24

1763 **Joséphine:** Born Marie Josephe Rose Tascher de la Pagerie. Wife of Vicompte de Beauharnais. He was executed during the French Revolution. First wife of Napoléon Bonaparte (1796), and French Empress. The childless marriage was dissolved in 1809.

Trust to me, ladies, and do not envy a splendor which does not constitute happiness.

1813 **Henry Ward Beecher:** U.S. clergyman, social reformer. Spoke out against slavery, the Civil War and Reconstruction. Wrote for *The Independent*, and after 1870 edited *The Christian Union*.

All words are pegs to hang ideas on.

1842 **Ambrose Bierce:** American journalist, author and editor. His often vitriolic wit, fascination with the supernatural and precise use of language won him the nickname "Bitter Bierce." Works: *The Fiend's Delight, Can Such Things Be?* and *The Devil's Dictionary.*

Certainty is being mistaken at the top of one's voice.

1848 **Brooks Adams:** American geopolitical historian. Son of Charles Francis Adams. Grandson of John Quincy Adams. Traveled extensively in Europe, the Middle East and India. Major work, *The Law of Civilization and Decay.* A prophet of American doom, he saw the wave of new immigrants as a corruption of the nation.

A man must not swallow more beliefs than he can digest.

1895 **Jack Dempsey:** U.S. boxer. World heavyweight champion (1919–26). Lost title to Gene Tunney. Career record 62-1-0 with 49 KOs.

Nobody owes anybody a living, but everybody is entitled to a chance.

1899 **Chief Dan George:** Native Canadian Indian actor. Served 12 years as the chief of his tribe, the Tse-lat-watt Sioux. Best known for his Oscar winning role as Old Lodge Skins in the film *Little Big Man.*

If the very old remember, the very young will listen.

1912 **Norman Cousins:** U.S. editor of *Saturday Review* (1937–72). Wrote *Anatomy of an Illness as Perceived by the Patient.*

Death is not the greatest loss in life. The greatest loss is what dies inside us while we live.

June 25

1834 **Henry Codman Potter:** American Protestant Episcopal bishop, social reformer and author. Books: *Sisterhoods and Deaconesses, The Scholar and the State, and Other Orations and Addresses* and *The Modern Man and His Fellow Man.*

The supreme vice of commercialism is that it is without an ideal.

1865 **Robert Henri:** American realist painter. Major influence in what has come to be called the Ashcan movement. Established his own influential art school in New York City (1908). Formed the group known as *The Eight.*

If you want to know how to do a thing you must first have a complete desire to do that thing.

1873 **Arthur Chapman:** U.S. journalist, historical writer, poet. Author of *The Story of Colorado* and *The Pony Express.*

Out where the handclasp's a little stronger, / Out where the smile dwells a little longer, / That's where the West begins.

1887 **George Abbott:** U.S. playwright, director, producer, screenwriter. Remained active at 100 years of age. Plays: *Three Men on a Horse* and *The Boys from Syracuse.* Stage musicals: *The Pajama Game* and *Damn Yankees.*

The greatest temptation is to have an alibi.

1900 **V.F. Calverton:** U.S. novelist, critic, lecturer. Editor of *Anthropology of American Negro Literature.* Founder of *The Modern Quarterly.*

Jesus to the Negro is no simple religious savior, worshipped on Sundays and forgotten during the week. He is the incarnation of the suffering soul of a race.

1903   George Orwell: Pen name of Eric Arthur Blair. English novelist, essayist and critic. War correspondent in WWII for the BBC and *The Observor.* Most remembered for his novels attacking totalitarianism, *1984* and *Animal Farm.*
All animals are equal, but some animals are more equal than others.

1945   Carly Simon: U.S. vocalist, songwriter. Best New Artist Grammy (1971). Hits: "You're So Vain," "Mockingbird" and "Nobody Does It Better."
Performing wouldn't be so bad if everyone could come up onstage and I could kiss them beforehand. As it is, it's like making love without any preliminary kissing.

June 26

1753   Comte De Antoine Rivarol: French writer. Remembered for his pithy wit and maxims. Wrote the sarcastic *Petit Almanach de nos grands hommes.*
Man spends his life in reasoning on the past, in complaining of the present, in fearing for the future.

1824   William Thompson, Lord Kelvin: British physicist, mathematician. Devised a temperature scale named for him based on absolute zero. Coined term "kinetic energy."
When you can measure what you are speaking about, and express it in numbers, you know something about it....

1865   Bernard Berenson: American-born art critic and historian. Wrote *Aesthetics and History* and *The Italian Painters of the Renaissance.*
Consistency requires you to be as ignorant today as you were a year ago.

1892   Pearl Buck: U.S. novelist raised in China by her missionary parents. Pulitzer Prize for *The Good Earth.* Nobel Prize in Literature (1938). Other novels: *A House Divided, Dragon Seed* and *The Time is Noon.*

Every great mistake has a halfway moment, a split second when it can be recalled and perhaps remedied.

1912   Babe Didrickson Zaharias: All-around athlete. Chosen female Athlete of the Year six times. Excelled in track and field and golf. Helped found the Ladies Professional Golf Association. Voted female "Athlete of the Half Century" in 1950.
Boy, don't you men wish you could hit a ball like that!

1931   Colin Wilson: British author of *The Outsider.* One of the angriest of Britain's Angry Young Men.
Now, as far as I'm concerned our civilization is an appalling stinking thing, materialistic, drifting, second-rate.

1961   Greg Lemond: U.S. cyclist. Called "Huck Finn with steel thighs" by *Sports Illustrated.* Three-time winner of the Tour de France.
The first four or five years, I was crazy about cycling. It's hard to have that same enthusiasm.

June 27

1846   Charles S. Parnell: Ardent Irish nationalist. First president of the Home Rule Party. His influence and his cause was harmed when he was named as corespondent in a divorce case and was forced to retire.
No man has a right to fix the boundary of the march of a nation; no man has a right to say to his country—this far and no further.

1869   Emma Goldman: Lithuanian-born U.S. anarchist, feminist and birth control advocate. Imprisoned in 1893 for inciting a riot in New York City and during WWI for opposing and obstructing the military draft. Deported to the U.S.S.R. (1919).
Idealists ... foolish enough to throw caution to the winds ... have advanced mankind and have enriched the world.

1880   Helen Keller: American educator, author. Born deaf and blind. Learned to communicate with the help of teacher Anne Sullivan. Became an example of achievement despite supreme handicaps. Her autobiography is titled *The Story of My Life.*

Death ... is no more than passing from one room into another. But there's a difference for me, you know. Because in that other room I shall be able to see.

1900   Lorenzo Tucker: One of America's first major black screen actors. Handsome star of many all-black films (1920-40). Called the "Black Clark Gable."

I've lived long enough to see that everything goes in cycles. Light-skinned blacks will be acceptable again. Really it's all so silly and just shows the ignorance that is always the basis of racial discrimination.

1927   Bob Keeshan: American television actor. Star of longest-running children's program, "Captain Kangaroo" (1955-81). Appeared as the clown Clarabelle on television's "Howdy Doody Show."

...we aren't playing to small animals, but to young humans of potentially great taste.

1930   H. [Henry] Ross Perot: U.S. multi-millionaire businessman and politician who spent a large amount of his fortune on an unsuccessful presidential bid in 1992. Founder of Electronic Data Systems. Chairman and CEO until he was bought out by GM in 1986.

This will probably cause you to faint because you never heard anybody in public life say they made a mistake.

1946   Sally Priesand: American religious leader. First ordained female rabbi (1972). Wrote *Judaism and the New Woman.*

Clergy are father figures to many women, and sometimes they are threatened by another woman accomplishing what they see is strictly male goals. But I can see them replacing that feeling with a sense of pride that women can have that role.

June 28

1491   Henry VIII: King of England. Founded the Church of England with himself as head when the Catholic Church

denied him a divorce from his wife who gave him no heir. He divorced her and married five more times. Two of his wives were beheaded for adultery. Father of Elizabeth I.

He who I favor wins.

1712   Jean-Jacques Rousseau: Swiss-born French philosopher, author, political theorist and composer. Father of French Romanticism. His most famous and influential work, *The Social Contract.*

People who know little are usually great talkers, while men who know much say little.

1867   Luigi Pirandello: Italian dramatist and novelist. A major figure of modern theater. Known for symbolic dramas and satires. Wrote, *Six Characters in Search of an Author* and *Right You Are if You Think You Are.*

Life is full of infinite absurdities, which strangely enough, do not even need to appear plausible, since they are true.

1873   Alexis Carrel: French biologist, surgeon. Received Nobel Prize (1912) for development of blood vessel suture technique.

Man cannot remake himself without suffering. For he is both the marble and the sculptor.

1892   E.H. Carr: British historian. Author of *The History of Russia, The Moral Foundation for World Order* and *What Is History?*

Change is certain. Progress is not.

1905   Ashley Montagu: British–U.S. anthropologist and author. Wrote: *The Natural Supremacy of Women* and *The Prevalence of Nonsense.*

Human beings are the only creatures who are able to behave irrationally in the name of reason.

1928   Mel Brooks: American actor, director, screenwriter and producer. Writer for Sid Caesar's television "Show of Shows." Best-known films: *The Producers, Blazing Saddles* and *Young Frankenstein,* each earning him an Oscar nomination for story or screenplay.

Bad taste is simply saying the truth before it should be said.

June 29

1798 Giacomo Leopardi: Italian poet. Self-taught prodigy. A gifted congenitally handicapped (hunchbacked) child who by 16 had read all the Latin and Greek classics. Among his most noted lyric poems are those collected under the title *I canti*.

The surest way of concealing from others the boundaries of one's own knowledge is not to overstep them.

1858 George W. Goethals: American engineer and administrator of the Panama Canal project (1907–14). The first civil governor of the Canal Zone.

Knowledge of our duties is the most essential part of the philosophy of life. If you escape duty, you avoid action. The world demands results.

1861 William James Mayo: American surgeon. Cofounder with his brother Charles of the Mayo Clinic at the University of Minnesota. A specialist in stomach surgery.

A specialist is a man who knows more and more about less and less.

1865 William Borah: U.S. politician, lawyer. Republican senator from Idaho. An isolationist. Played a major role in preventing the U.S. from joining the League of Nations.

The marvel of all history is the patience with which men and women submit to burdens unnecessarily laid upon them by their governments.

1900 Antoine de St. Exupery: French author and aviator. Wrote *The Little Prince*. Opened transatlantic airmail routes to South America and Africa.

Experience shows us that love does not consist in gazing at each other but in looking together in the same direction.

1903 Robert Traver: Pseudonym of John Donaldson Voelker. U.S. jurist, author. Best known for his novel *Anatomy of a Murder*.

Judges ... may be divided roughly into four classes, judges with neither head nor heart—they are to be avoided at all costs; judges with head but no heart—they are almost as bad; then judges with heart but no head—risky but better than the first two; and finally, those rare judges who possess both head and heart—thanks to blind luck, that's our judge.

1941 Stokely Carmichael: African American civil rights activist. Developed the Black Power concept. Elected leader of the Student Noviolent Coordinating Committee. Changed the group's focus from integration to black liberation.

For a real end to exclusion in American society, that society would have to be so radically changed that the goal cannot really be defined as inclusion.

June 30

1685 John Gay: English playwright, poet. Best known for his satire, *The Beggar's Opera*, whose target was Sir Robert Walpole and the court of George II.

The comfortable estate of widowhood is the only hope that keeps up a wife's spirits.

1884 Georges Duhamel: French author and novelist. Sought to uphold traditional values and safeguard individual liberties. Best known works are his novel cycles *Salavin* and *The Pasquier Chronicles*.

I have too much respect for the idea of God to make it responsible for such an absurd world as this one is.

1893 Harold Laski: English political scientist. A Marxist although not a Communist. Believed the state responsible for social reform. Books: *Authority in the Modern State*, *A Grammar of Politics* and *The American Presidency*.

The only real security for social well-being is the free exercise of men's minds.

1903 Robert E. Hannegan: U.S. lawyer, politician. Chairman of the National Democratic Committee.

Ideals are the "incentive payment" of practical men. The opportunity to strive for them is the currency that has ennobled America through the centuries.

1906 **Anthony Mann:** U.S. director of films *The Naked Spur, The Far Country* and *Man of the West.*

If you're going to tell a story, instead of telling an intellectual story—which by necessity requires a tremendous number of words—you should pick one that has pictorial qualities to start with.

1917 **Lena Horne:** U.S. singer, actress. Began her career as a dancer. Still possesses her stunning good looks and attractive husky voice. Film appearances: *Cabin in the Sky, Stormy Weather* and *Death of a Gunfighter.*

All they knew about blacks in Hollywood was what Tarzan told them and Tarzan was not the brightest in that outfit!

1934 **Harry Blackstone, Jr.:** U.S. magician like his father before him. Quite adept at sleight-of-hand and card tricks.

Nothing I do can't be done by a 10-year-old ... with 15 years of practice.

July 1

1646 **Gottfried Von Leibniz:** German philosopher and mathematician. Made major contributions to mathematical logic and metaphysics. Independently of Isaac Newton, invented calculus. Perhaps the last universal genius, spanning the whole of contemporary knowledge.

It is easier to be original and foolish than original and wise.

1804 **George Sand:** (*Pseudonym of Amandine Aurore Lucille Dupin*) French novelist of tales of love that transcend convention. Her lovers included Merimee, de Musset and Chopin. Works: *Valentine, La Mare au diable* and *La Petite Fadette.*

Happiness lies in the consciousness we have of it, and by no means in the way the future keeps its promises.

1882 **Susan Glaspell:** American novelist, playwright. Wrote *The Glory of the Conquered, The Road to Temple* and the Pulitzer Prize–winning play *Alison's House.*

I can't think of any sorrow in the world that a hot bath wouldn't help, just a little bit.

1892 **James M. Cain:** American novelist of hard-boiled fiction that was the basis for some remarkable film noir movies: *The Postman Always Rings Twice, Double Indemnity* and *Mildred Pierce.*

I write of the wish that comes true—for some reason, a terrifying concept.

1908 **Estee Lauder:** American cosmetics executive. Founder Estee Lauder, Inc. in 1946. Had great success with Youth Dew bath oil in the fifties. Named one of the Ten Top outstanding women in business in 1970.

The best way to apply a fragrance ... is to spray it into the air ... and walk into it.

1915 **Jean Stafford:** American author of *Children Are Bored on Sunday* and *A Mother in History.* Her *Collected Stories* won a Pulitzer Prize (1970).

Whiskey and music, I reflected, especially when taken together, make time fly incredibly fast.

1941 **Twyla Tharp:** American dancer and choreographer. Organized a modern dance troupe in 1965. Her works include *The Bix Pieces, Bach Partita* and the dance numbers for films *Hair* and *White Nights.*

Art is the only way to run away without leaving home.

July 2

1714 **Christoph Willibald Gluck:** German composer. Best known for operas based on simplicity: *Orfeo ed Eurydice, Alceste* and *Paride ed Elena.* Paris was divided in the famous Gluck and Niccolò Piccinni controversy, between supporters of French and Italian operatic styles.

The language of nature is the universal language.

1877 **Herman Hesse:** German-Swiss novelist. Nobel prize winner in 1946. Author of lyrical, symbolic, ironic novels, *Steppenwolf* and *Magister Ludi.*

If you hate a person, you hate something in him that is part of yourself. What isn't part of ourselves doesn't disturb us.

1903   Sir Alec Douglas-Home: British politician. Member of the House of Lords. Disclaimed peerages for life. Held several cabinet posts as well as becoming leader of the House of Lords (1957–60). Foreign secretary (1960–63) and premier (1963).
There are two problems in my life. The political ones are insoluble and the economic ones are incomprehensible.

1908   Thurgood Marshall: American Supreme Court Justice. The first black justice, appointed in 1967 by Lyndon Johnson. As chief of the legal staff of the NAACP, argued the case of *Brown vs. Board of Education of Topeka* before the Supreme Court.
Our whole constitutional heritage rebels at the thought of giving government the power to control men's minds.

1918   Robert W. Sarnoff: U.S. communications executive. President of NBC who converted network to first all-color television station (1956).
Finance is the art of passing currency from hand to hand until it finally disappears.

1925   Patrice Lumumba: Congolese (now Zaire) leader. First prime minister of the Congo. Leading negotiator with Belgium for independence as premier. Removed from office and killed.
When you civilize a man, you only civilized an individual, but when you civilize a woman, you civilize a whole people.

1926   Medgar Evers: American civil rights martyr. Shot to death in front of his home (1963). Awarded Spingarn Medal (1963).
You can kill a man but you can't kill an idea.

July 3

1683   Edward Young: English poet, dramatist, literary critic. Author of *Night Thoughts*, occasioned by, among other sorrows, the death of his wife. Many of its lines have passed into proverbial use.
Like our shadows, / Our wishes lengthen as the sun declines.

1860   Charlotte Perkins Gilman: American lecturer, author, poet. Wrote *In This Our World, Women and Economics* and *The Man-Made World.*
There is no female mind. The brain is not an organ of sex.

1878   George M. Cohan: American entertainer. Actor, singer, dancer, songwriter, producer. Starred in numerous Broadway musicals. His songs include: "I'm a Yankee Doodle Dandy," "Give My Regards to Broadway" and "You're a Grand Old Flag."
Always leave them wanting more.

1883   Franz Kafka: Prague-born German novelist and short-story writer. Wrote of guilt-ridden, isolated men in an aimless world. Author of *The Metamorphosis, The Trial* and *Amerika.*
A book must be an ice ax to break the frozen sea within us.

1900   John Mason Brown: America's outstanding lecturer and critic-at-large. Drama critic and editor for *Saturday Review* (1944-55). Author of *Letters From Greenroom Ghosts, Two on the Aisle* and *Through These Men.*
A good conversationalist is not one who remembers what was said, but says what someone wants to remember.

1927   Ken Russell: Controversial British director noted for his excesses in his films which include Oscar nominated *Women in Love, The Devils, Lisztomania, Tommy, Altered States* and *Gothic.*
This isn't the age of manners, it is the age of kicking people in the crotch.

1937   Tom Stoppard: British author and dramatist. Plays include *Rosencrantz and Guildenstern Are Dead* and *The Real Thing.*
Every exit is an entry somewhere else.

July 4

1804   Nathaniel Hawthorne: American novelist and short-story writer. Best known for *Twice-Told Tales, Mosses from an Old Manse, The Scarlet Letter,* and *The House of the Seven Gables.*

What other dungeon is so dark as one's own heart? What jailer so inexorable as one's self.

1807   Giuseppe Garibaldi: Italian military leader in the movement for Italian unification and independence. Conquered the Kingdom of the Two Sicilies and captured Naples. Defeated in an attempt to capture Rome.

Man created God, not God man. The priest is the personification of falsehood.

1872   Calvin Coolidge: U.S. politician. Thirtieth president of the United States, succeeding Warren G. Harding who died in office (1923). Reelected by a large majority in 1924. Famous for his taciturn nature.

I have noticed that nothing I never said ever did me any harm.

1900   Louis Armstrong: "Satchmo." American musician, bandleader, composer, singer, actor. Leading trumpeter in jazz history. Made more than 1,500 recordings. Originated the "scat" vocal. Hit songs include: "Potato Head Blues," "Struttin' with Some Barbecue," "A Kiss to Build a Dream On" and "Hello Dolly."

There are some people that if they don't know, you can't tell 'em.

1905   Lionel Trilling: American critic, scholar. His essays combined social, psychological and political insights with literary criticism. Author of *The Liberal Imagination, The Opposing Self* and *Mind in the Modern World.*

It is now life and not art that requires the willing suspension of disbelief.

1918   Ann Landers and **Abigail Van Buren:** Pseudonyms of twins Pauline Esther and Esther Pauline Friedman. Syndicated advice columnists whose columns appear in 1,000 newspapers around the country.

Says Ann: *Keep in mind that the true measure of an individual is how he treats a person who can do him absolutely no good.*

Says Abby: *If you want a place in the sun, you've got to put up with a few blisters.*

1927   Neil Simon: American playwright. Probably the most commercially successful playwright in Broadway history. His plays include *Come Blow Your Horn, Barefoot in the Park, The Odd Couple, Biloxi Blues* and *Lost in Yonkers.*

Too much of a good thing can be wonderful.

July 5

1755   Sarah Siddons: Welsh actress. Best known for her performances as tragic-heroine's Isabella in *The Fatal Marriage* and Lady Macbeth in *Macbeth.*

...I believe one half of the world is born for the convenience of the other half.

1810   P.T. Barnum: American showman. Extraordinary entrepreneur. Opened the New York City museum in 1842 where for the next 27 years he featured freaks and wonders, including midget Tom Thumb and the Swedish Nightingale, Jenny Lind. In 1871 he formed the Barnum and Bailey Circus.

More persons ... are humbugged by believing nothing, than by believing too much.

1843   Mandell Creighton: English historian and bishop of London. Chief works are *Simon de Montfort, History of the Papacy During the Reformation Period* and *Queen Elizabeth.*

The real object of education is to leave a man in the condition of continually asking questions.

1889   Jean Cocteau: French poet, novelist, dramatist, essayist, filmmaker and director. Most famous of his modernistic ballets are *Parade* and *Le Boeuf sur le toit.* Plays include *Antigone* and *Orphée.* Novels: *La Belle et la bête* and *Les Enfants terribles.*

Mirrors should reflect a little before throwing back images.

1899   Marcel Achard: French playwright, screenwriter, director. Presided over the Cannes Film Festival (1958–59) and the Venice Festival (1960). Films: *The Merry Widow, Mayerling* and *The Earrings of Madame De.*

Women like silent men. They think they're listening.

1911   **Georges Pompidou:** French politician and statesman. Prime minister in 1962. Dismissed by his patron Charles de Gaulle after the 1968 general elections. Following de Gaulle's resignation in 1969 he was elected president.

A statesman is a politician who places himself at the service of the nation. A politician is a statesman who places the nation at his service.

1915   **Barbara "Babe" Paley:** American model, editor of a high fashion magazine, socialite and charity worker. Wife of William S. Paley. Frequently chosen by the New York Dress Institute as one of the best dressed.

No woman is ever too slim or too rich.

July 6

1747   **John Paul Jones:** Scottish naval hero of the American Revolution. Commanded the *Bonhomme Richard* in celebrated victory over the British ship *Serapis*. Later became an admiral with the Russian navy, winning victories over Turks.

Love ... may be considered as the cordial that Providence has bestowed on mortals to help them digest the nauseous draught of life.

1875   **Roger W. Babson:** American educator, moralist and columnist. Founded the Babson Report Service and other stock market counseling services.

Eat fresh air and store up sleep.

1899   **Mignon Good Eberhart:** American novelist. Author of *Case of Susan Dare, Dead Man's Plans* and *R.S.V.P. Murder.*

A request not to worry ... is perhaps the least soothing message capable of human utterance.

1913   **Gwyn Thomas:** Welsh author. Wrote *The Keep, The Love Man* and *Where Did I Put My Pity?*

Poetry is trouble dunked in tears.

1921   **Nancy Davis Reagan:** American actress and wife of Ronald Reagan, former actor and president of the United States. She had great influence on her husband

with whom she appeared in the film *Hellcats of the Navy.*

A woman is like a teabag—only in hot water do you realize how strong she is.

1927   **Bill Haley:** U.S. musician and singer. Formed various country and western groups with a touch of rhythm and blues. With the Comets his hits included: "Rock Around the Clock" and "See You Later, Alligator."

It wasn't something we planned, it just evolved. We got to where we weren't accepted as country-western or rhythm and blues. ... We didn't call it that at the time but we were playing rock 'n' roll.

1935   **Dalai Lama (Tenzin Gyatso):** Spiritual and temporal head of Tibet. Worshipped by the adherents of Lamaism as a living God. Exiled, now living in India. Nobel Peace Prize winner (1989), in recognition of his nonviolent campaign to end China's domination of Tibet.

Sleep is the best meditation.

July 7

1860   **Gustav Mahler:** Czechoslovakian-born Austrian composer. Conductor and artistic director of Vienna State Opera House. Resigned after ten years to devote himself to composition and the concert. An important bridge between the late romantic 19th century style and the revolutionary work of Schoenberg. Works include, *Das Leid von der Erde.*

A symphony must be like the world. It must contain everything.

1887   **Marc Chagall:** Russian-born French painter. Developed a style of great poetry and brightness. Noted for his illustrations for Gogol's novel *Dead Souls.* Painted a ceiling at the Paris Opera and a massive mural for the Metropolitan Opera at Lincoln Center in New York.

To call anything that appears illogical a fantasy or a fairy tale is to admit that one does not understand nature.

1899   **George Cukor:** American director. Famous as a woman's director for

the sensitivity he showed in portraying strong intelligent female characters in films such as *Little Women, Dinner at Eight, Camille, The Women, The Philadelphia Story, Adam's Rib, Born Yesterday* and *My Fair Lady*, the latter his only Oscar after five nominations.
Real talent is a mystery, and people who've got it know it.

1906 **Leroy "Satchel" Paige:** Legendary American baseball pitcher with the Negro Leagues. At age 42 he made it to the Major Leagues where he gave strong evidence of what he might have done had the color ban been lifted when he was a young man.
Don't look back, something might be gaining on you.

1911 **Gian Carlo Menotti:** Italian-born American composer and librettist. His best known operas are *The Medium, Amahl and the Night Visitors* and *The Saint of Bleecker Street.*
A man only becomes wise when he begins to calculate the approximate depth of his ignorance.

1915 **Margaret Walker:** American writer, poet and educator. Wrote *For My People*, which celebrated the black identity. Other works: *Prophets for a New Day* and *October Journey.*
Love stretches your heart and makes you big inside.

1940 **Ringo Starr:** British drummer with the Beatles. With their breakup his solo work included "It Don't Come Easy," "Photograph" and "You're Sixteen."
I always thought we were five. Us four— and we weren't the greatest players—and something else: magic!

July 8

1621 **Jean La Fontaine:** French author. Writer of comedies, lyrics, elegies, ballads and licentious tales. Best remembered for his *Fables.*
Be advised that all flatterers live at the expense of those who listen to them.

1839 **John D. Rockefeller:** American financier, philanthropist. Founded an oil company that became Standard Oil Trust. Founded the University of Chicago and Rockefeller Foundation. Gave over $500 million in aid of medical research, universities and Baptist churches.
The growth of a large business is merely a survival of the fittest.

1867 **Käthe Kollwitz:** German sculptor and graphic artist. Chose serious tragic subjects, with strong social or political content. Works, etchings: *Weaver's Revolt* and *Peasant's War*, and a series of eight prints on the theme of *Death.*
Every war already carries within it the war which will answer it. Every war is answered by a new war, until everything, everything is smashed.

1898 **Alec Waugh:** English novelist and journalist. Brother of Evelyn Waugh. Author of *Island in the Sun, The Mule on the Minaret* and *A Spy in the Family.*
I am prepared to believe that a dry martini slightly impairs the palate, but think what it does for the soul.

1907 **George W. Romney:** U.S. automobile executive with American Motors. A one-time Mormon missionary. Governor of Michigan. His quest for the Republican presidential nomination ended when he admitted to being "brainwashed" about Vietnam.
I didn't say that I didn't say it. I said that I didn't say that I said it. I want to make that perfectly clear.

1913 **Walter Kerr:** American journalist, playwright. Drama critic for the *New York Herald Tribune* and *New York Times.* Husband of playwright Jean Kerr with whom he coauthored the play *Murder in Reverse.*
Half the world is composed of idiots, the other half of people clever enough to take indecent advantage of them.

1926 **Elisabeth Kübler-Ross:** Swiss-born American psychiatrist, thanatologist and writer.
Dying nowdays is more gruesome in many ways, namely, more lonely, mechanical, and

dehumanized; at times it is even difficult to determine technically when the time of death has occurred.

July 9

1764   **Ann Radcliffe:** English novelist wrote Gothic romances set in Italy: *The Romance of the Forest, The Mysteries of Udolpho* and *The Italian.*
Fate sits on these dark battlements, and frowns; / And as the portals open to receive me, / Her voice, in sullen echoes, through the courts, / Tells of a nameless deed.

1811   **Sara Pyson Parton:** Pen Name "Fanny Fern." American author. Wrote weekly for Bonner's *New York Ledger* (1856-72). Highest paid author of her day. Books: *Fern Leaves from Fanny's Portfolio* and *Ginger-Snaps.*
The way to a man's heart is through his stomach.

1858   **Franz Boas:** German-born American anthropologist. His lifelong work was the study of the Indian tribes of the Pacific Northwest. Established newer and simpler concepts of race and culture, outlined in *Race, Language and Culture.*
When we think of the past we forget the fools and remember the sages.

1894   **Dorothy Thompson:** American journalist, writer, radio commentator and activist. Author of *The Courage to Be Happy, Political Guide* and *I Saw Hitler!*
They have not wanted "Peace" at all; they have wanted to be spared war—as though the absence of war was the same as peace.

1901   **Barbara Cartland:** Prolific British author of more than 400 books, mostly Gothic romances, that have sold over 100 million copies. Step-grandmother of Princes Diane. Earned a place in *Guinness Book of Records* for writing 26 books in 1983.
The virgin ... is not only an attribute of the body, it is a state of mind.

1908   **Paul Brown:** American football coach and executive. One of the most innovative coaches of all time. Coached Cleveland

Browns (1946–62) and Cincinnati Bengals (1968–76). Elected to Hall of Fame (1967).
A winner never whines.

1937   **David Hockney:** English graphic and pop artist. His work includes a set of satirical etchings, *The Rake's Progress.*
It is very good advice to believe only what an artist does, rather than what he says about his work.

July 10

1509   **John Calvin:** French theologian. Founder of Calvinism. Promulgated the doctrine of divine election. His views and writings did much to propel the Protestant Reformation. In 1559 founded a theological seminary at Geneva that became the university.
God cannot be conceived without his eternity, power, wisdom, goodness, truth, right and mercy.

1723   **Sir William Blackstone:** English jurist and writer. Best known for *Commentaries on the Laws of England.* Advocated prison reform.
It is better that ten guilty persons escape than one innocent suffer.

1834   **James Abbott McNeil Whistler:** Expatriate American painter, etcher and lithographer. President of Royal Society of British Artists. Best known for *Arrangement in Gray and Black No. 1, The Artist's Mother.*
Art happens—no hovel is safe from it, no prince may depend upon it, the vastest intelligence cannot bring it about.

1867   **Finlay Peter Dunne:** American humorist. Creator of the Irish bartender "Mr. Dooley," who comments on everything happening to the United States. Author of *Mr. Dooley in Peace and War, Mr. Dooley's Philosophy* and *Mr. Dooley Says.*
The past always looks better than it was; its only pleasant because it ain't here.

1915   **Saul Bellow:** Canadian-born American writer of Jewish moral and social alarm. Received the National Book

Award for *The Adventures of Augie March* and a Pulitzer Prize for *Humboldt's Gift*. Awarded a Nobel Prize in 1976.
The two real problems in life are boredom and death.

1927 **David Dinkins:** American politician. First African American mayor of New York City (1989). Lost in 1993 to Rudolph Guiliani, the first Republican mayor since 1965.
Ellis Island is for the people who came over on ships. My people came in chains.

1943 **Arthur Ashe:** American tennis player. First black to win U.S. Championship and Wimbledon. Wrote black sports history *Hard Road to Glory*. In 1992 announced that he had been infected with AIDs from a blood transfusion during heart surgery. Died in 1993.
Every time you win, it eliminates the fear a little bit. You never really cancel the fear of losing, you keep challenging it.

July 11

1754 **Thomas Bowdler:** English author who wrote expurgated editions of Shakespeare's works and Gibbon's *Decline and Fall*. The term "bowdlerize" has been with us since.
Those expressions are omitted which can not with propriety be read aloud in the family.

1767 **John Quincy Adams:** Sixth U.S. president (1825–29). Son of John Adams. Returned to the House of Representatives after his term of office and served from 1831 to 1848. Secretary of state under James Monroe. Negotiated the Treaty of Ghent, ending the War of 1812.
America with the same voice which spoke herself into existence as a nation, proclaimed to mankind the inextinguishable rights of human nature, and the only lawful foundation of government.

1838 **John Wanamaker:** U.S. merchant and government official. Founded a Philadelphia department store bearing his name. Postmaster General (1889–93).

Half the money I spend on advertising is wasted and the trouble is I don't know which half.

1876 **Max Jacob:** French Jewish poet and artist. Convert to Catholicism. Wrote in a surrealistic style. Author of *Le Cornet à dés*.
When you get to the point where you cheat for the sake of beauty, you are an artist.

1880 **Jeannette Rankin:** American politician, pacifist, suffragist and activist. Republican congresswoman from Montana (1917–19 and 1941–43), first woman to do so. Voted against U.S. participation in both world wars. In 1968, she led 5,000 women to Capital Hill to protest the Vietnam War.
You can no more win a war than you can win an earthquake.

1888 **Bartolomeo Vanzetti:** Italian anarchist, who with Nicola Sacco was convicted and executed for murders during a robbery. Doubt of their guilt created an international storm of protest. They were vindicated by a proclamation of Governor Dukakis (1977). Vanzetti's final statement:
Our words—our lives—our pains; nothing! The taking of our lives, lives of a good shoemaker and a poor fish peddler—all! That last moment belongs to us—that agony is our triumph.

1899 **E.B. White:** American humorist, essayist, novelist. Author of the classic children's books, *Stuart Little* and *Charlotte's Web*.
A sarong is a simple garment carrying the implicit promise that it will not long stay in place.

July 12

100 B.C. **Gaius Julius Caesar:** Roman general, statesman, orator and writer. Formed the first triumvirate with Pompey and Crassus. Conquered all Gaul and Britain. Roman dictator (49–44 B.C.). Assassinated on the Ides of March.
All bad precedents began as justifiable measures.

1817   **Henry David Thoreau:** American essayist, naturalist and poet. Part of the Transcendentalist circle. Editor of *The Dial*. Built a cabin at Walden Pond, living there for two years and later wrote his most famous work *Walden*.

If a man does not keep pace with his companions, perhaps it is because he hears a different drummer. Let him step to the music he hears, however measured or far away.

1884   **Amadeo Modigliani:** Italian painter and sculptor. Painted his subjects, usually the poor of Montmartre in elongated, mannerist style. His health was delicate and his life was marked by poverty, drink and drug addiction.

A beefsteak is more important than a drawing. I can easily make a drawing, but I cannot make a beefsteak.

1895   **R. [Richard] Buckminster Fuller:** American architect, engineer and theoretician. He sought solutions to global living by gaining the maximum benefits from a minimum expenditure of energy and materials. Developed the Dymaxion House in 1927 and the Dymaxion streamlined omnidirectional car in 1932. His most famous creation is the geodesic dome.

Pollution is nothing but resources we're not harvesting.

1908   **Milton Berle:** "Uncle Miltie." U.S. comedian. Star of one of the most popular television shows of all time in the golden age of television. Began his career in vaudeville. Also worked on radio and in films.

The only thing that bothers me about growing older is that when I see a pretty girl now it arouses my memory instead of my hopes.

1917   **Andrew Wyeth:** American artist. Painter of people and places of the northeastern states. Best-known work is *Christina's World*.

Christina's a close friend of mind and crippled. Every other day she drags herself over the field from her house to visit the graves of her family. ... The field in Christina's world is not really that large, but I felt it that way.

1934   **Van Cliburn:** American concert pianist. Gained international fame by winning first prize at the international Tchaikovsky Piano Competition, Moscow (1958).

An artist can be truly evaluated only after he is dead. At the very 11th hour, he might do something that will eclipse everything else.

July 13

1793   **John Clare:** English poet. Supported himself as a farm laborer. Plagued by poor health, poverty and finally madness. Wrote *Poems Descriptive of Rural Life and Scenery* and *The Rural Muse*.

If life had a second edition, how I would correct the proofs.

1886   **Father Edward J. Flanagan:** American Roman Catholic priest who founded Boys Town where vocational training was supplemented with religious and social education.

There isn't any such thing in the world as a bad boy ... but a boy left alone, frightened, bewildered ... the wrong hand reaches for him ... he needs a friend ... that's all he needs.

1903   **Sir Kenneth Clark:** English art historian. Leading scholar of the Italian Renaissance. Widely known for his popular BBC television series "Civilization" and a book of the same name. His massive *Catalogue of Drawings of Leonardo da Vinci...* was the first chronological record of the artist's work.

We can destroy ourselves by cynicism and disillusion, just as effectively as by bombs.

1913   **Dave Garroway:** Low key television personality. Host of popular "Garroway at Large" (1949–54). Frequently appeared on the "Today Show" in partnership with chimpanzee J. Fred Muggs.

I'm curious about people. I talk as if there were two or three friends out there. ... I think you have to be pretty easygoing.

1934   **Wole Soyinka:** Pen name of Akinwande Oluwole Soyinka. Nigerian poet, playwright and essayist. Nobel Prize winner (1986). Works: *The Lion and the Jewel* and *Poems from Prison*.

Fame is a flippant lover.

1935   Jack Kemp: American professional football quarterback, politician and government official. Played for the Buffalo Bills. U.S. congressman from New York.

Pro football gave me a good sense of perspective to enter politics. I'd already been booed, cheered, cut, sold, traded and hung in effigy.

1942   Harrison Ford: Extremely popular American film actor in *Star Wars, Raiders of the Lost Ark, Witness* (Oscar Nomination) and *The Fugitive*.

Failures are inevitable. Unfortunately, in film they live forever and they're 40 ft. wide and 20 ft. high.

July 14

1858   Emmeline Pankhurst: English suffragist. Founded the Women's Social and Political Union (1903). Conducted hunger strikes when arrested for arson and bombings.

Trust in God. She will provide.

1860   Owen Wister: American novelist. Author of the prototypal Western, *The Virginian.* He wrote more than "When you call me that, smile."

When yu' can't have what you choose, yu' just choose what yu' have.

1898   Albert "Happy" Chandler: U.S. politician and baseball executive. Governor of Kentucky and second commissioner of baseball. Backed Branch Rickey's move to make Jackie Robinson the first black in the major leagues.

We Americans are a peculiar people. We are for the underdog no matter how much of a dog he is.

1904   Isaac Bashevis Singer: Yiddish novelist, short-story writer, critic and journalist. Written in Yiddish, his stories often are set in Poland of the past. Nobel Prize (1978). Works: *The Magician of Lublin, Enemies, Lost in America* and *The Golem.*

The wastepaper basket is a writer's best friend.

1912   Woodrow Wilson "Woody" Guthrie: American folksinger. Father of Arlo Guthrie. Able to put over songs of social significance with true feeling. Most famous for his "Dust Bowl Ballads," describing the forced migration of Oklahoma families from their barren land. Hits: "This Land Is Your Land" and "Pastures of Plenty." To his working class audience:

I am out to sing the songs that will make you take pride in yourself and your work.

1913   Gerald Ford: U.S. politician. Congressman from Michigan (1949–73). Appointed vice president by Nixon, succeeding him as president when he resigned. Ford later pardoned Nixon.

Truth is the glue that holds governments together. Compromise is the oil that makes governments go.

1937   Jerry Rubin: American political activist and author. Original "yippie." Convicted under anti-riot provision in 1968 Civil Rights Act.

...Everyone had a label—pig, liberal, radical, revolutionary.... If you had everything but a gun, you were a radical but not a revolutionary.

July 15

1573   Inigo Jones: English architect. Well known for his designs of sets, costumes and stage machinery for court "Masques" of Ben Jonson, Thomas Heywood and William Davenant. Earned the title of "the English Palladio."

I find no other pleasure than learning.

1779   Clement Moore: American Hebraist, poet and educator. A Hebrew scholar and a founder of the General Theological Seminary, New York City (1823–50). Best known as the author of *A Visit from St. Nicholas.*

He had a broad face and a little round belly, / That shook, when he laughed, like a bowl full of jelly.

1836 **William Winter:** American drama critic, historian, essayist and poet. Drama critic with the *New York Times* (1861-66) and *New York Tribune* (1866-1909).
Ambition has but one reward for all: / A little power, a little transient fame, / A grave to rest in, and a fading name!

1850 **Mother Francis Xavier (Maria Francesca) Cabrini:** Italian-born nun. First American saint. Canonized (1946). Founder of convents, orphanages and hospitals in Europe and the U.S.
I want all of you to take on wings and fly swiftly to repose in that blessed peace possessed by a soul that is all for God.

1906 **Richard W. Armour:** The American humorist is noted for historical satires and literary scholarship. His books include *It All Started with Columbus* and *Twisted Tales from Shakespeare.*
Until Eve arrived, this was a man's world.

1933 **Julian Bream:** English-born guitarist and lutenist. A protégé of Andrés Segovia. He edited much music for guitar and lute. Specialized in early ensemble music.
The great secret of Elizabethan music is that it is meant to be enjoyed. ... The Elizabethan wanted fun from music.

1953 **Jean-Bertrand Aristide:** Haitian priest and political leader. Elected president of Haiti. Deposed by a military coup d'état. Returned to office through the intervention and efforts of the U.S. Forced to renounce his priesthood.
Jesus was not a priest, he was a lay worker.

July 16

1723 **Sir Joshua Reynolds:** English painter, known for his portraits. President of Royal Academy (1768-1792). Works include *Dr. Samuel Johnson* and *Sarah Siddons as the Tragic Muse.* Left well over 2,000 works.
Simplicity is an exact medium between too little and too much.

1821 **Mary Baker Eddy:** U.S. religious leader. Founder of the Christian Science movement and the *Christian Science Monitor* newspaper. Author of *Science and Health* and *Rudimental Divine Science.*
Health is not a condition of matter but of mind.

1862 **Ida Bell Wells:** American journalist, reformer, civil rights activist, and publisher. Launched anti-lynching campaign. First president, American Negro League.
One had better die fighting against injustice than to die like a dog or a rat in a trap.

1880 **Kathleen Norris:** American author of over 80 wholesome novels whose formula usually was "get a girl into trouble, then get her out again." It allowed her to sell more than 10 million copies. They include: *Certain People of Importance* and *Over at the Crowleys.*
Over and over again mediocrity is promoted because real worth isn't to be found.

1896 **Trygve Lie:** Norwegian government official. First secretary general of the United Nations. Dealt with Arab intervention in Israel and the Korean War.
War occurs because people prepare for conflict, rather than for peace.

1907 **Barbara Stanwyck:** Remarkably popular American actress in films: *Meet John Doe, Ball of Fire, Stella Dallas, Double Indemnity* and *Sorry, Wrong Number,* the last four for which she received Oscar nominations.
Put me in the last 15 minutes of a picture, and I don't care what happened before. I don't even care if I was in the rest of the damn thing—I'll take it in those fifteen minutes.

1948 **Pinchas Zuckerman:** Outstanding Israeli violinist and conductor. Child prodigy. Soloist with major American and European orchestras. Guest conductor all over the world.
It's like walking in a desert and all of a sudden you need water. If you can transmit this to the audience, this wonderful need for music. Well, that is what you are always trying to do.

July 17

1674 **Isaac Watts:** English Nonconformist minister. Regarded as the father of English hymnody. Wrote hymns, "Behold the Glories of the Lamb" and "Jesus Shall Reign."
So when a raging fever burns, / We shift from side to side by turns; / And 'tis poor relief we gain / To change the place, but keep the pain.

1763 **John Jacob Astor:** U.S. businessman. Amassed a fortune trading furs all over North America. At his death he was the richest man in the country.
A man who has a million dollars is as well off as if he was rich.

1810 **Martin Farquhar Tupper:** English moralist. Author of *Proverbial Philosophy*, a series of moralizing commonplaces in free verse, which achieved huge, worldwide popularity.
To be accurate, write, to remember, write, to know thine own mind, write.

1889 **Erle Stanley Gardner:** U.S. detective story writer. A trial lawyer by profession he created the character of lawyer Perry Mason. Wrote well over 100 books, beginning with *The Case of the Velvet Claws*.
All I ask of life is that it keep moving.

1898 **Berenice Abbott:** American photographer. Her best known works are black and white architectural, documentary images of New York City.
Photography can never grow up if it imitates some other medium. It has to walk alone; it has to be itself.

1902 **Christina E. Stead:** Australian-born novelist and Hollywood screenwriter. Her best known work *The Man Who Loved Children*, depicts marriage as savage warfare between love and independence.
Charm is a cunning self-forgetfulness.

1912 **Art Linkletter:** Canadian-born U.S. broadcaster. Hosted popular radio and television shows, "House Party" and "People Are Funny." Author of best-selling "Kids Say the Darndest Things."
The four stages of man are infancy, childhood, adolescence and obsolescence.

July 18

1811 **William Makepeace Thackeray:** India-born English novelist and satirist. From 1842 to 1851 he was on the staff of *Punch*. Most of his major novels were published as monthly serials. Novels: *Vanity Fair*, *The Memories of Barry Lyndon* and *The Rose and the Ring*.
Remember it is as easy to marry a rich woman as a poor woman.

1890 **Charles Eugene Wilson:** U.S. industrialist, engineer. Designed Westinghouse's first auto starter. Became president of General Motors. U.S. secretary of defense (1953–57).
An expert is a mechanic away from home.

1906 **Clifford Odets:** American playwright. Outstanding proletarian dramatist. First an actor in the Theater Group. One of the founders of the Group Theatre. Plays: *Waiting for Lefty*, *Golden Boy* and *The Country Girl*.
There are two kinds of marriage—where the husband quotes the wife, or where the wife quotes the husband.

1913 **[Richard] "Red" Skelton:** American comedian and actor. Very popular on radio, television and in movies. Created characters "The Mean Widdle Kid," "Clem Kadiddlehopper," "Deadeye" and "Freddie the Freeloader."
All men make mistakes, but those who are married find out about them sooner.

1918 **Nelson Mandela:** South African political Leader of African National Congress. Sentenced to life imprisonment (1964), for conspiracy to overthrow South African government. Released from prison (1990). Became the first black president of South Africa (1993).
I have cherished the ideal of a democratic and free society … it is an ideal for which I am prepared to die.

1921 **John Glenn, Jr.:** U.S. astronaut and politician. First man to orbit the Earth (1962). U.S. senator from Ohio since 1975.
Knowledge begets knowledge. The more I see, the more impressed I am—not with

what we know — but with how tremendous the areas are that are yet unexplored.

1933 Yevegny Aleksandrovich Yevtushenko: Soviet poet. Much of his poetry expressed the impatience of the younger Soviet generation with the society of Stalin. He had some trouble with Soviet officials, especially with the publication of "Babi Yar," which charged the Soviet Union with anti-Semitism.
Poetry is like a bird, it ignores all frontiers.

July 19

1799 Sophie Rostopchine Segur: Russian-born French writer of famous books for children based on stories told her children and grandchildren. Her central character was "Sophie," a girl with many trials and tribulations.
God keeps the wicked to give them time to repent.

1834 Edgar Degas: French painter. Associated with the Impressionists. Known for his mastery of motion. His most famous medium was pastels. He portrayed ballet dancers at work and women at their toilette.
Art is vice. One does not wed it, one rapes it.

1865 Charles Horace Mayo: American surgeon. Cofounder with brother William James of the Mayo Clinic Foundation for Medical Education and Research (1915).
Worry affects the circulation, the heart, the glands, the whole nervous system. I have never known a man who died from overwork, but many who died from doubt.

1896 A.J. [Archibald Joseph] Cronin: Scottish-born physician and author of best-selling novels *Hatter's Castle, The Stars Look Down, The Citadel* and *The Keys of the Kingdom.*
Worry never robs tomorrow of its sorrow; it only saps today of its strength.

1898 Herbert Marcuse: German-born American political philosopher and sociologist. Fled Hitler's Germany in 1934. In the U.S. he argued that mass materialism stifles all diversity. Author of *Eros and Civilization* and *One-Dimensional Man.*
Most people are afraid of freedom. They are conditioned to be afraid of it.

1922 George McGovern: U.S. politician and historian from South Dakota. As Democratic candidate for president in 1972 campaigned on an immediate end of the war in Vietnam and a broad program of social reform.
The longer the title, the less important the job.

1946 Ilie Nastase: Romanian tennis player. Twice number one in the world (1972, 1973). Won U.S. Open (1972), French Open (1973).
If you have confidence, you have patience. Confidence, that is everything.

July 20

1304 Francesco Petrarch: Italian poet and scholar. Primary interest was Latin and Greek literature. Founder of Renaissance Humanism. His beloved was Laura, the subject of his collection of lyrics called "Rime" (verses) or "Canzoniere" (song book).
Rarely do great beauty and great virtue dwell together.

1591 Anne Hutchinson: American colonial religious liberal. Banished from the Massachusetts Bay Colony for her religious views. Emigrated to Rhode Island where she was killed in an Indian massacre.
What from the Church of Boston? I know no such church, neither will I own it. Call it the whore and strumpet of Boston, no Church of Christ!

1850 John Graves Shedd: American merchant. As president of Marshall Field and Co. (1906–22), developed it into a retail chain. First Chicago merchant to give employees a half-day holiday on Saturdays. Endowed Shedd Aquarium in Chicago's Grant Park.
It is the sick oyster which possesses the pearl.

1880 **Hermann Keyserling:** "The wandering philosopher." Estonian-born German philosophical writer and mystic. Ideas centered on the theme of spiritual regeneration. Books: *The Travel Diary of a Philosopher* and *Creative Understanding*. *The majority of great men are the offspring of unhappy marriages.*

1890 **Theda Bara:** American stage and silent screen femme fatale. The greatest of film vamps wore indigo makeup to emphasis her pallor. She surrounded herself with symbols of death. It was claimed that her name was an anagram of "Arab Death," although she was a Jewish girl, Theodosia Goodman, born in Cincinnati. Films: *A Fool There Was, Carmen, Camille* and *Cleopatra*.
I'm going to continue doing vampires as long as people sin.

1895 **Laszlo Moholy-Nagy:** Hungarian-born American painter, photographer and art teacher. Worked primarily with light. Became recognized as a leading avant-garde artist in the New Photographers movement in Europe. Headed the new Bahhaus school in Chicago.
...Photography is not primarily important as a picture maker but as a means of extending human vision.

1919 **Sir Edmund Hillary:** New Zealand mountain climber and Arctic explorer. With Tenzing Norgay, he was the first to reach the summit of Mt. Everest.
It is not the mountain we conquer, but ourselves.

1938 **Diana Rigg:** Attractive British actress who established her reputation in Shakespeare but found her greatest fame and popularity as the lithe, jumpsuited secret agent Mrs. Emma Peel on television's "The Avengers."
Escapist stuff of course, but really pointing toward the future, because women today have become more realistic and self-sufficient. They are moving in the direction of Emma Peel.

July 21

1664 **Matthew Prior:** English poet and diplomat. Chiefly known for his epigrams, satires and society verse. Works: "A Better Answer (to Chloe Jealous)," "A Letter to the Lady Margaret Cavendish when a Child," and "The Secretary."
They never taste who always drink; / They always talk, who never think.

1899 **Ernest Hemingway:** Macho American novelist and short-story writer. The former newspaperman and foreign correspondent wrote superb dialogue. Awarded a Nobel Prize (1954). Committed suicide (1961). Works: *In Our Time, The Sun Also Rises, A Farewell to Arms, For Whom the Bell Tolls* and *The Old Man and the Sea* (Pulitzer).
A man can be destroyed but not defeated.

1911 **Marshall McLuhan:** Canadian cultural critic and communication theorist. Studied the cultural and psychological consequences of mass media and technology. Author, *The Medium Is the Message*.
We march backwards into the future.

1920 **Isaac Stern:** Outstanding Russian-born American violinist. His Carnegie Hall debut in 1943 was a triumph. His honors include: Officer of the Légion d'honneur of France, Kennedy Center Honors Award, and Wolf Prize of Israel. Energetic worker for the cause of human rights.
Music is not an acquired culture ... it is an active part of natural life.

1930 **Gene Littler:** "Gene the Machine." American golfer. Elected to the PGA / World Golf Hall of Fame (1990).
Golf is not a game of great shots. It's a game of the most accurate misses. The people who win make the smallest mistakes.

1934 **Jonathan Miller:** British physician, writer, actor and director. Appeared in the play *Beyond the Fringe*, which he co-authored. Directed films, television and plays. Research fellow, history of medicine, University College.
Illness is not something a person has. It's another way of being.

1952 **Robin Williams:** Talented American comedian and actor. Star of television

series "Mork and Mindy." Has uncanny improvisational skills. Films: *The World According to Garp, Good Morning, Vietnam* and *Mrs. Doubtfire.*
Cocaine is God's way of saying you're making too much money.

July 22

1849   **Emma Lazarus:** American poet and essayist. Poetry: *Admetus and Other Poems* and *Songs of a Semite.* Best known for "The New Colossus," inscribed on the Statue of Liberty.
Give me your tired, your poor, / Your huddled masses yearning to breathe free, / The wretched refuse of your teeming shore, / Send these the homeless, temptest-tossed, to me: / I lift my lamp beside the golden door.

1890   **Rose Kennedy:** American public figure, philanthropist, mental health activist. Wife of Joseph P. Kennedy. Mother of president John F. Kennedy and senators Bobby and Teddy Kennedy.
Birds sing after a storm; why shouldn't people feel as free to delight in whatever remains to them?

1891   **Ely Culbertson:** American bridge expert. Inventor and popularizer of contract bridge. Devoted his later years to working for world peace. Author of *Contract Bridge Complete* and *Total Peace.*
The bizarre world of cards is a world of pure power politics where rewards and punishments are meted out immediately.

1893   **Karl Menninger:** American psychiatrist. Cofounder of the Menninger Foundation, a major center for the study and treatment of mental health problems.
You can almost be certain that the man who commits violent crimes has been treated violently as a child.

1898   **Stephen Vincent Benét:** American poet, short-story writer and novelist. His most famous poem, "John Brown's Body," won a Pulitzer Prize (1929). His unfinished American epic "Western Stars" earned him a posthumous Pulitzer (1944).
We thought we were done with these things but we were wrong / We thought, because we had power, we had wisdom.

1908   **Amy Vanderbilt:** American journalist. Etiquette expert who wrote a syndicated newspaper column and regular revision of her 1952 *Complete Book of Etiquette.*
Parents must get across the idea that "I love you always, but sometimes I do not love your behavior."

1923   **Robert Dole:** U.S. politician. Senator from Kansas. Senate minority leader (1987–94). Majority leader (1985-87 and 1995–96).
If you're hanging around with nothing to do and the zoo is closed, come over to the Senate. You'll get the same kind of feeling and you won't have to pay.

July 23

1823   **Coventry [Kersey Dighton] Patmore:** English poet and librarian at the British Museum. Associated with the Pre-Raphaelite brotherhood. Best known works are "The Angel in the House," a long poetic celebration of married life, and "The Unknown Eros."
Love is sure to be something less than human if it is not something more.

1834   **James Gibbons:** American religious leader. In 1886, appointed the country's second cardinal. Held that the Constitution was man's greatest governmental achievement. Founded and was first chancellor of Catholic University. Author of *The Faith of Our Fathers.*
Reform must come from within, not from without. You cannot legislate for virtue.

1874   **"Sunny Jim" Fitzsimmons:** Horse racing trainer of steeds that won over 2,275 races, including two Triple Crown winners, Gallant Fox in 1930 and Omaha in 1935.
I'll be around as long as the horses think I'm smarter than they are.

1888   **Raymond Chandler:** American detective story writer. Master of hardboiled fiction. Created brash private eye

Philip Marlowe. Books: *The Big Sleep, Farewell, My Lovely* and *The Lady in the Lake.*

Down these mean streets a man must go who is not himself mean; who is neither tarnished nor afraid.

1891 Haile Selassie I: Emperor of Ethiopia. Descendent of the Queen of Sheba. First ruler to address both the League of Nations and the United Nations. His pleas for help to the League against the invasion of Mussolini's troops were ignored.

Outside the kingdom of the Lord there is no nation which is greater than any other. God and history will remember your judgment.

1906 Marston Bates: American zoologist and author. Wrote *The Prevalence of People, Man in Nature* and *The Nature of Natural History.*

Research is the process of going up alleys to see if they are blind.

1907 Elspeth Josceline Grant Huxley: Kenyan-born English novelist. Has written many novels and essays on her native land and its problems, including, *The Flame Trees of Thika.*

It [Africa] is a cruel country: it takes your heart and grinds it into powdered stone— and no one minds.

July 24

1783 Simón Bolívar: "The Liberator." South American statesman and soldier. Leader in the liberation of northern South America from the control of Spain, leading to the freedom of Columbia, Venezuela, Peru and Bolivia. President of Columbia and Peru.

I plowed furrows in the ocean.

1802 Alexandre Dumas (Père): French novelist and dramatist. Wrote nearly 300 volumes. Author of *The Count of Monte Cristo, The Three Musketeers* and plays *Napoleon Bonaparte* and *Antony.* Lived a life of gusto with many mistresses.

The chain of wedlock is so heavy that it takes two to carry it, sometimes three.

1819 Josiah Gilbert Holland: U.S. editor, poet and novelist. His works, popular in his day, include: *Single and Married, Garnered Sheaves* and *The Mistress of the Manse.* Cofounder of *Scribner's Monthly,* editor (1870–81).

God gives every bird its food, but He does not throw it into the nest.

1878 Baron Edward J.M. Dunsany: Irish author, playwright and poet. Active in the Abbey Theatre. Best known works: *The Glittering Gates, A Night at an Inn* and *The Laughter of the Gods.*

…No man is entirely unmoved by being asked for information upon his particular subject…

1898 Amelia Earhart: American aviatrix. First woman to make a solo flight across the Atlantic Ocean. Disappeared in the South Pacific while attempting to fly around the world.

Courage is the price that Life exhorts for granting peace.

1916 John D. MacDonald: American mystery writer. Created the character Travis McGee. All his McGee novels have a color in the title. *A Flash of Green, Bright Orange for the Shroud* and *Pale Gray for Guilt.*

Friendships, like marriages, are dependent on avoiding the unforgivable.

1920 Bella Abzug: American politician, lawyer. Founder of the New Democratic Coalition. First Jewish woman elected U.S. representative (Democrat from New York, 1971–77).

Congress is a middle-aged, middle-class, white male power structure.… No wonder it's been so totally unresponsive to the needs of the country.

July 25

1848 Arthur James Balfour: English statesman. Major force in the Conservative party for 50 years. Prime minister (1902–5). As foreign secretary is known for the Balfour Declaration which expressed official approval of Zionism.

It has always been desirable to tell the truth, but seldom if ever necessary.

1853   **David Belasco:** U.S. producer, playwright. A theatrical giant who made major innovations in staging. Important influence on standards of theatrical production. Associated with 374 plays.
Never let yourself be seen in public unless they pay for it.

1880   **Morris Raphael Cohen:** Russian-born U.S. philosopher and mathematician. Author of *Reason and Nature: Logic in the Scientific Method.*
The business of the philosopher is well done if he succeeds in raising genuine doubts.

1902   **Eric Hoffer:** U.S. philosopher who received no formal education because of a temporary blindness. Worked as a longshoreman. Author of *The True Believer, The Passionate State of Mind* and *In Our Time.*
It is easier to love humanity as a whole than to love one's neighbor.

1905   **Elias Canetti:** Bulgarian author. Wrote novel *Auto-da-Fé* and nonfiction *Crowds and Power.* Nobel Prize in 1981.
Whenever you observe an animal closely, you feel as if a human being sitting inside were making fun of you.

1935   **Barbara Harris:** U.S. stage and screen actress. Member of Chicago's Second City Improvisation troupe. Tony award winner for *The Apple Tree.* Films, *A Thousand Clowns* and *Family Plot.* Her description of director Alfred Hitchcock:
The man with the navy-blue voice.

1956   **Iman:** Beautiful and mysterious black model and actress.
People think of me as close to royalty ... I carry the way I do because I am royalty within myself.

July 26

1856   **George Bernard Shaw:** Irish dramatist, critic and social reformer. His plays and essays were his way of promoting his theories. A member of the Fabian Society from its founding (1883). Plays: *Arms and the Man, Mrs. Warren's Profession, Man and Superman, Major Barbara, Pygmalion* and *Saint Joan.*
Martyrdom ... is the only way in which a man can become famous without ability.

1875   **Carl Jung:** Swiss analytical psychologist. He broke from Sigmund Freud in 1913 and went into a long period of self-analysis, described in his autobiographical *Memories, Dreams, and Reflections.* He formulated the introvert and extrovert types.
Show me a sane man and I will cure him for you.

1893   **George Grosz:** German-American artist. Known for his venomous satirical caricatures and lithographs which attack militarism, the bourgeois and capitalists. *Ecce Homo* is a collection of his works.
They are a fine people but quick to catch the disease of anti-humanity. I think it's because of their poor elimination. Germany is a headquarters for constipation.

1895   **Robert Graves:** English poet, novelist and critic. Works include: *Fairies and Fusiliers, I, Claudius* and *The White Goddess.*
As you are woman, so be lovely: / As you are lovely, so be various, / Merciful as constant, constant as various, / So be mine, as I yours for ever.

1906   **Gracie Allen:** Delightfully zany comedienne in films and on radio and television with her husband and partner straight-man George Burns. Noted for her scatterbrain answers to his questions.
When I was born, I was so surprised I couldn't talk for a year and a half.

1928   **Stanley Kubrick:** American director whose films have received extremely divided opinions of their value. Notable works; *Paths of Glory, Spartacus, Lolita, Dr. Strangelove, 2001: A Space Odyssey* and *A Clockwork Orange.*
The great nations have always acted like gangsters, and the small ones like prostitutes.

1943   **Mick Jagger:** English rock star. Lead singer with the Rolling Stones. Biggest hits: "I Can't Get No Satisfaction," "Ruby Tuesday," "Honky Tonk Woman," "Angie" and "Miss You."
All dancing is a replacement for sex.

July 27

1768 Charlotte Corday: French patriot. An aristocrat who assassinated the French revolutionary Jean Paul Marat because she saw him as the persecutor of the Girondists. She was executed for the crime.

In Paris, they cannot understand how a useless woman, whose longer life could have been of no good, could sacrifice herself to save her country.

1824 Alexandre Dumas (Fils): French dramatist. Bastard son of the novelist Alexandre Dumas. His works include: *La Dame aux camelias* and *Le Demi-monde.*

I prefer rogues to imbeciles because they sometimes take a rest.

1852 George Foster Peabody: U.S. banker and philanthropist. Director of Federal Reserve Bank of New York (1914–21). Donated his estate, Yaddo, Saratoga Springs, New York, for an arts center. Peabody Awards for excellence in broadcasting are named for him.

Education is a debt due from present to future generations.

1870 Hilaire Belloc: French-born English poet, historian and essayist. Author of *The Bad Child's Book of Beasts, Cautionary Tales* and *On Nothing.*

The grace of God is courtesy.

1906 Leo Durocher: American baseball player with the St. Louis Cardinals' Gashouse Gang. Manager of Dodgers and Giants, leading the former to one pennant in 1941 and the latter to two in 1951 and 1954, winning the World Series in 1954.

Use your best pitcher today. Tomorrow it may rain.

1916 Elizabeth Hardwick: American critic, novelist and educator. Author of *The Simple Truth* and *A View of My Own.* Editor: *Selected Letters of William James.*

The greatest gift is a passion for reading. It is cheap, it consoles, it distracts, it excites, it gives you knowledge of the world and experience of a wide kind. It is a moral illumination.

1924 Vincent Canby: American journalist and film critic with the *New York Times* from 1969.

Hack fiction exploits curiosity without really satisfying it or making connections between it and anything else in the world.

July 28

1804 Ludwig Andreas Feuerbach: German philosopher. Analyzed religion from a psychological and anthropological viewpoint in *The Essence of Christianity* and *The Essence of Religion.*

In practice all men are atheists, they deny their faith by their actions.

1844 Gerard Manley Hopkins: English poet and Jesuit priest. Known for his poems on religion and nature. Author of "The Windhover," "The Caged Skylark," "Spring and Fall" and "The Leaden Echo and the Golden Echo."

Glory be to God for dappled things.

1866 Beatrix Potter: English writer and illustrator of stories for children. Her drawings and watercolors made her stories all the more enchanting. They include: *The Tale of Peter Rabbit, The Roly-Poly Pudding* and *Jemima Puddleduck.*

Once upon a time there were four little rabbits, and their names were Flopsy, Mopsy, Cottontail and Peter.

1901 Harry Bridges: Australian-born U.S. labor leader. Controversial head of the West Coast longshoremen's union. The government tried on two occasions to have him deported for being intent on overthrowing the U.S. government by force.

No man has ever been born a Negro hater, a Jew hater, or any kind of hater. Nature refuses to be involved in such suicidal practices.

1909 Malcolm Lowry: English novelist. His reputation is based on his autobiographical novel *Under the Volcano,* set in Mexico, where he lived (1936–37). Also wrote *Dark Is the Grave Wherein My Friend Is Laid.*

God has little patience with remorse.

1929   **Jacqueline Bouvier Kennedy Onassis:** American first lady. Wife of President John F. Kennedy. Later married Aristotle Onassis. Editor with Doubleday at the time of her death. Of JFK:
Now he is a legend when he would have preferred to be a man.

1943   **Bill Bradley:** U.S. senator from New York. All-American basketball player at Princeton. Rhodes Scholar at Oxford. Olympic Gold Medal winner. All-Star small forward with the New York Knicks.
The taste of defeat has a richness of experience all its own.

July 29

1805   **Alexis de Tocqueville:** French historian. Known for his studies of nature and the operations of democracy. Best known works: *Democracy in America* and *The Old Regime and the Revolution.*
The health of a democratic society may be measured by the quality of functions performed by private citizens.

1869   **Booth Tarkington:** American novelist and playwright. Served in the Indiana House of Representatives (1902–3). His novels include *Penrod* and *Seventeen* and his two Pulitzer winners, *The Magnificent Ambersons* and *Alice Adams.*
Arguments only confirm people in their own opinions.

1877   **Charles William Beebe:** American naturalist and explorer. Curator from 1899 of ornithology for the New York Zoological Society. Explored ocean depths down to almost 1000 meters in a bathysphere. Books: *Galapagos, World's End* and *Beneath Tropic Seas.*
One thing we cannot escape—forever afterward, throughout all of life, the memory of the magic of water and its life, of the home which was once our own—this will never leave us.

1878   **Don [Donald R.P.] Marquis:** American newspaperman and humorist. Known for his columns "The Sun Dial" in the *New York Sun* and "The Lantern" in the *New York Tribune.* Created the character of Clem Hawley, the Old Soak.
An optimist is a guy that has never had much experience.

1883   **Benito Mussolini:** Italian fascist leader. Became Italian dictator in 1922. Attacked Ethiopia (1935). Made an alliance with Hitler (1939). Entered WWII with the fall of France. Killed by Italian partisans.
Blood alone moves the wheels of history.

1905   **Dag Hammarskjöld:** Swedish diplomat and political economist. Secretary general of the United Nations (1953-61). Awarded Nobel Peace Prize (1961).
Do not seek death. Death will find you. But seek the road which makes death a fulfillment.

1907   **Melvin Belli:** American lawyer and writer. Silver-haired and silver-tongued headline-making trial lawyer. Clients: Lenny Bruce, Martha Mitchell and Jack Ruby.
A lawyer's performance in the courtroom is responsible for about 25 percent of the outcome; the remaining 75 percent depends on the facts.

July 30

1818   **Emily Brontë:** One of three English sister novelists. Based on her novel *Wuthering Heights* and her poetry she is generally agreed to be the greater talent in the family. Poems: "The Prisoner," "Remembrance" and "The Visionary."
Proud people breed sad sorrows for themselves.

1857   **Thorstein B. Veblen:** American economist and social philosopher. Known for his criticism of 19th century capitalism. Author of *The Theory of the Leisure Class* and *The Instinct of Workmanship.*
Conspicuous consumption of valuable goods is a means of reputability to the gentleman of leisure.

1863   **Henry Ford:** U.S. auto manufacturer. Created the mass-produced automobile and introduced the assembly line. With the Model T, produced a car that sold for $500 allowing working people to afford cars. Signed first union-shop contract in the industry (1941).

Money is like an arm or leg—use it or lose it.

1889   **Casey Stengel:** U.S. baseball player. Best known as manager of the New York Yankees whom he led to ten world series and the hapless expansion team the New York Mets who were loved for their futility. Known for his garbled but colorful explanations to the press.

Can't anyone here play the game?

1898   **Henry Moore:** English sculptor who developed his style of bold, smooth usually human forms. Worked with bronze, stone, concrete and wood. He often would group together two or more forms to create one sculptural entity.

I can see a reclining figure in anything, a smudge on the wall, an ink blot, a pebble.

1940   **Patricia Schroeder:** American lawyer and politician. Democratic congresswoman from Colorado.

Most companies still are much more likely to give employees a parking space for a car than to provide a child-care slot for a son or daughter.

1947   **Arnold Schwarzenegger:** Austrian-born U.S. bodybuilder and screen star. Best known for box-office hits: *Conan the Barbarian, The Terminator* and *True Lies.*

I just use my muscles as a conversation piece, like someone walking a cheetah down 42nd Street.

July 31

1689   **Samuel Richardson:** English novelist. Known for his expansion of the novel and for his interest in the psychological aspects of character. Author of *Pamela, or Virtue Rewarded* and *Clarissa Harlow.*

Calamity is the test of integrity.

1867   **S.S. Kresge:** American businessman who made his fortune with a chain of five and ten stores across the country.

Hard work and the Bible can bring any youngster to that glorious sunset—success.

1901   **Jean Dubuffet:** French painter. Champion of "art brut," the naive and powerful artwork of prisoners, psychotics and other unusual amateurs.

For me insanity is super-sanity. The normal is psychotic—a collective psychosis. Normal means lack of imagination, lack of creativity.

1912   **Milton Friedman:** U.S. economist and professor with the University of Chicago. Served on the research staff of the National Bureau of Economic Research. Leading conservative economist. Author of *Studies in the Quantity Theory of Money* and *Monetary History of the United States, 1867–1960.* Nobel Prize (1976).

The government solution to a problem is usually as bad as the problem.

1921   **Whitney Young, Jr.:** U.S. civil rights leader. Executive director of the National Urban League. Called for a "Marshall Plan" for the nation's blacks to help them catch up after generations of discrimination. Author of *To Be Equal* and *Beyond Racism.*

Our ability to create has outreached our ability to use wisely the products of our inventions.

1944   **Sherry Lee Lansing:** U.S. producer and motion picture executive. Films as producer: *Fatal Attraction, The Accused* and *Indecent Proposal.* On her appointment as senior vice president of production at Columbia pictures:

I just hope this is maybe the last time a woman holding a position such as this will be newsworthy. It should be natural.

1951   **Evonne Goolagong:** Australian tennis star. First aborigine in international sports. Annoyed by constant references to her aboriginal background:

It began to upset me. I just want to be myself and be accepted for what I am.

August 1

10 B.C. **Emperor Claudius:** Roman emperor. Implemented administrative reforms. Extended Roman rule over North Africa and made Britain a Roman province.

As for being half-witted, well, what can I say except that I have survived to middle age with half my wits, while thousands have died with theirs intact. Evidently quality of wit is more important than quantity.

1779 **Francis Scott Key:** American poet and attorney. After watching the bombardment of Ft. McHenry during the War of 1812, wrote "The Star-spangled Banner."

'Tis the star-spangled banner; O long may it wave / O'er the land of the free, and the home of the brave.

1815 **Richard Henry Dana, Jr.:** American lawyer and writer. Shipped aboard the brig *Pilgrim* from Cape Horn to California. He wrote of his experiences in *Two Years Before the Mast.*

Six days shalt thou labor and do all thou art able, / And on the seventh—holystone the decks and scrape the cable.

1818 **Maria Mitchell:** First woman astronomer in the United States. First woman member of American Academy of Arts and Sciences. Discovered a new comet. Her words inscribed beneath her bust in the Hall of Fame:

Every formula which expresses a law of nature is a hymn of praise to God.

1819 **Herman Melville:** American author. Spent his youth aboard ships which formed the basis for his books *Typee, Omoo* and his masterpiece *Moby Dick.* A critical and popular failure at the time of its publication, it has become recognized as one of the best, truly American novels.

To scale great heights, we must come out of the lowermost depths. The way to heaven is through hell.

1936 **Yves St. Laurent:** French fashion designer. Responsible for the "chic beatnik" and "little boy" looks in the 1960s. Produces perfumes Opium and Paris.

Fashions fade, style is eternal.

1942 **Jerry Garcia:** American guitarist. Cofounder of the Grateful Dead, an influential rock band that emerged from various San Francisco groups. Albums: *Grateful Dead, Anthem of the Sun, American Beauty* and *Live Dead.*

Truth is something you stumble into when you think you're going someplace else.

August 2

1754 **Pierre Charles L'Enfant:** French engineer, architect and urban planner. Moved to America in 1777 to fight the British in the Revolutionary War. Designed ceremonial and monumental works introducing symbolic and allegorical European decorative motifs to America. Designed basic plan for Washington, D.C. (1791–92).

[It is a] city of magnificent vistas.

1820 **John Tyndall:** Largely self-educated British physicist and natural philosopher. Best known for his research on radiant heat, the acoustics properties of the atmosphere and the blue color of the sky.

Life is a wave, which in no two consecutive moments of its existence is composed of the same particles.

1865 **Irving Babbitt:** U.S. educator, scholar and literary critic. Founded modern humanistic movement with Paul E. Moore. Author of *Rousseau and Romanticism* and *Democracy and Leadership.*

It is well to open one's mind but only as a preliminary to closing it ... for the supreme act of judgment and selection.

1867 **Ernest Dowson:** English poet of the decadent school. Part of the Rhymers' Club group at Oxford. His most famous poem is "Non Sum Qualis Eram Bonae sub Regno Cynarae" (in verses), containing the familiar refrain:

I have been faithful to thee, Cynara! in my fashion.

1894 **Westbrook Pegler:** American newspaper columnist. Wrote a nationally syndicated sports feature for the *Chicago Tribune.* In 1933, he joined the *New York*

World-Telegram to write the column "Fair Enough," venting the opinions of the "average man" on the world of international events.

I am a member of the rabble in good standing.

1924 **James Baldwin:** American author. At fourteen preached in Harlem storefront churches. The leading black spokesman's works include: *Go Tell It on the Mountain, Notes of a Native Son, Nobody Knows My Name* and *The Fire the Next Time.*

Anyone who has ever struggled with poverty knows how extremely expensive it is to be poor.

1933 **Peter O'Toole:** Talented and eccentric Irish actor. Academy Award nominated for performances in *Lawrence of Arabia, Beckett, The Lion in Winter, Goodbye, Mr. Chips, The Ruling Class, The Stunt Man* and *My Favorite Year.*

For me, life has either been a wake or a wedding.

August 3

1867 **Stanley Baldwin:** British statesman. Conservative prime minister during the general strike of 1926 and at the time of Edward VIII's abdication.

The attainment of an ideal is often the beginning of a disillusion.

1887 **Rupert Brooke:** English poet. Wrote two volumes of romantic and patriotic poetry in the early years of WWI. Died at 28 of blood poisoning on his way to the Dardanelles and was buried there.

If I should die, think only this of me; / That there's some corner of a foreign field / That is forever England.

1900 **Ernie Pyle:** American war correspondent during WWII who wrote about the everyday trials and tribulations of the ordinary soldier. Pulitzer Prize winner (1944). Killed by Japanese machine gun fire (1945).

I write from the worm's-eye point of view.

1905 **Dolores Del Rio:** Beautiful Mexican movie star in numerous U.S. films, including, *What Price Glory, Bird of Paradise* and *Flying Down to Rio.*

So long as a woman has twinkles in her eyes, no man notices whether she has wrinkles under them.

1905 **Maggie Kuhn:** American social activist and writer. Founder of the senior citizen's political activist group "The Gray Panthers."

Old age is not a disease—it is a struggle and survivorship triumph over all kinds of vicissitudes and disappointments, trials and illnesses.

1920 **Phyllis Dorothy "P.D." James:** English mystery writer who created intelligent, perceptive, poet Inspector Adam Dalgleish. Books: *Cover Her Face* and *An Unsuitable Job for a Woman.*

Life had taught him that the unforgivable was usually the most easily forgiven.

1937 **Diane Wakoski:** American poet. Author of *Coins and Coffins, Greed, Parts I and II* and *Motorcycle Betrayal Poems.*

Justice is / reason enough for anything ugly. It balances the beauty in the world.

August 4

1792 **Percy Bysshe Shelley:** English poet. Championed liberty and rebelled against the strictures of English politics and religion. Author of "Prometheus UnBound," "The Cloud," "Ode to the West Wind," "Ozymandias" and "Epipsychidion."

Poetry is the record of the best and happiest moments of the happiest and best minds.

1805 **William Rowan Hamilton:** The greatest man of science ever produced by Ireland and among the greatest mathematicians of his day. A master of languages, he made significant contributions in the study of optics and applications of algebra to geometry.

I have very long admired Ptolemy's description of his great astronomical master, Hipparchus; a labor-loving and truth-loving man. Be such my epitaph.

1839　Walter Pater: English man of letters, critic and essayist. Became known with his *Studies in the History of the Renaissance* and for his philosophical romance, *Marius the Epicurean.*
All art constantly aspires towards the conditions of music.

1870　Sir Harry Lauder: Scottish entertainer. Beloved star of the British music hall and American vaudeville known for his recitations while dressed in traditional kilt.
The future is not a gift—it is an achievement.

1899　Ezra Taft Benson: American cabinet official and religious leader. Eisenhower's controversial secretary of agriculture and head of the Mormon Church. Strong supporter of the John Birch Society.
Every man should have the courage of his convictions, no matter what the odds.

1912　Raoul Wallenberg: Swedish diplomat. Responsible for saving nearly 100,000 Budapest Jews during WWII by designing a Swedish protection passport and arranged Swedish houses offering Jews refuge. Arrested by the Soviets in 1945, never to be seen again.
When there is suffering without limits, there can be no limits to the methods one should use to alleviate it.

1958　Mary Decker Slaney: American middle distance runner. Held seven different track and field records. Won both 1,500 and 3,000 meters at 1983 World Championship in Helinski.
No coach could ever make me do anything I physically didn't want to do.

August 5

1850　Guy de Maupassant: French short-story writer and novelist. Member of the naturalist school. His style is direct and simple. Stories: "The Necklace" and "The Umbrella." Novels: *Bel-Ami* and *Pierre et Jean.*
The bed encompasses our whole life, for we were born in it, we live in it, and we shall die in it.

1876　Mary Ritter Beard: American historian and writer. Married to historian Charles A. Beard with whom she wrote: *Rise of American Civilization* and *The American Spirit: A Study of the Idea of Civilization in the United States.* She also wrote *On Understanding Women* and *Women as a Force in History.*
Viewed narrowly, all life is universal hunger and an expression of energy associated with it.

1886　Bruce Barton: American author, advertising executive and congressman. Wrote *The Book Nobody Knows* and *What Can a Man Believe?*
If advertising encourages people to live beyond their means, so does matrimony.

1899　Conrad Potter Aiken: American poet, novelist and critic. Pulitzer Prize in 1929 for *Selected Poems* and a National Book Award in 1953 for *Collected Poems.* Novels: *Blue Voyage* and *King Coffin.*
Let us go in and dance once more / On the dream's glimmering floor.

1906　John Huston: U.S. film director, screenwriter and actor. Son of actor Walter Huston. Father of Anjelica Huston. Oscar winner as director and screenwriter for *The Treasure of the Sierra Madre.* Nominated as director for *The Asphalt Jungle, Moulin Rouge* and *Prizzi's Honor.* Eight other nominations for Best Screenwriting.
The director is the actor's sole audience.

1923　Richard G. Kleindienst: American government official. Played important role getting Nixon elected in 1968. U.S. attorney general (1972–73).
If people demonstrate in a manner to interfere with others, they should be rounded up and put in a detention camp.

1930　Neil Armstrong: U.S. astronaut. Served as command pilot of *Gemini 8.* On the *Apollo 11* mission, he became the first man to step on the moon.
That's one small step for a man, one giant leap for mankind.

August 6

1809 Alfred, Lord Tennyson: English poet. Appointed poet laureate (1850). Although very popular in his lifetime, his work has been criticized for shallowness and sentimentality. Works: "Locksley Hall," "The Charge of the Light Brigade," "In Memoriam" and "Enoch Arden."

In the spring a young man's fancy lightly turns to love.

1868 Paul Claudel: French author, diplomat and poet. French ambassador to the United States. Wrote poetic dramas *The Hostage* and *Satin Slipper*.

You explain nothing, O poet, but thanks to you all things become explicable.

1881 Alexander Fleming: Scottish bacteriologist. The discoverer of penicillin in 1928. He shared the 1945 Nobel Prize for physiology of medicine with Howard Florey and Ernst Chain, who perfected a method of producing the volatile drug.

It is the lone worker who makes the first advance in a subject; the details may be worked out by a team, but the principle idea is due to the enterprise, thought and perception of an individual.

1883 Scott Nearing: American sociologist and radical who fought against child labor and abuses of big business. Books: *Poverty and Riches, Democracy Is Not Enough* and *The Conscience of a Radical*.

During the whole period of written history it is not the worker but the robbers who have been in control of the world.

1911 Lucille Ball: U.S. actress, comedienne and astute businesswoman. Appeared in over 70 films. Made her greatest mark with television series "I Love Lucy," with then-husband Desi Arnaz and her solo shows that followed. President of Desilu, one of the world's largest television production companies.

The secret of staying young is to live honestly, eat slowly, and lie about your age.

1916 Richard Hofstadter: U.S. physicist. Did basic studies in the structure of neutrons and protons. Nobel prize winner (1961).

No one who lives among intellectuals is likely to idolize them unduly.

1927 Andy Warhol: Leader of the American pop artists. Known for paintings of soup cans and celebrities. Made several avant-garde films.

Sex is the biggest nothing of all time.

August 7

1876 Mata Hari: Pseudonym of Margaretha G. Macleod. Dutch dancer and courtesan. Joined the German Secret Service during WWI. Passed on military secrets that she wormed our of her Allied lovers. Convicted of spying, she was executed by the French.

I never could dance well. People came to see me because I was the first who dared to show myself naked to the public.

1885 Billie Burke: American actress. The toast of Broadway in the early part of the century. Married Florenz Ziegfeld. Starred in numerous silent films, but is best remembered as a flittery matron in a number of films and as Glinda, the good witch in *The Wizard of Oz*.

Ah, that sad and bewildering moment when you are no longer the cherished darling, but must turn the corner and try to be funny.

1903 Louis B. Leakey: British anthropologist, archaeologist and paleontologist. He was convinced that Africa and not Asia was the cradle of mankind. In 1959, together with his wife Mary, he unearthed the skull of "Zinjanthropus." In 1964, he found remains of *Homo habilis* and in 1967 discovered *Kenyapithecus africanus*.

Theories on prehistoric and early man constantly change as new evidence comes to light. A single find such as **Homo habilis** *can upset long-held—and reluctantly discarded concepts.*

1904 Dr. Ralph Bunche: U.S. diplomat and educator. Principal secretary of U.N. Palestine Commission. Nobel Prize for mediating Palestine conflict (1948–49).

We must fight as a race for everything that makes for a better country and a better world. We are dreaming idiots and trusting fools to do anything less.

1911 **Nicholas Ray:** U.S. director, who concentrated on disaffected loners in films such as: *Knock on Any Door, In a Lonely Place, Johnny Guitar* and *Rebel Without a Cause.*

There is no formula for success. But there is a formula for failure and that is to try to please everybody.

1927 **Edwin W. Edwards:** U.S. politician. Controversial governor of Louisiana. Reelected in 1992 by defeating KKK officer David Duke. Speaking of the 1983 gubernatorial race:

[I could not lose unless I was] caught in bed with a dead girl or a live boy.

1942 **Garrison Keillor:** American entertainer and story teller. His public radio show "Prairie Home Companion," featuring his stories from fictional Lake Wobegon, Minnesota captivates a wide audience.

Cats are intended to teach us that not everything in nature has a purpose.

August 8

1694 **Francis Hutchinson:** British philosopher. Exponent of the moral-sense theory of ethics. His main work, *A System of Moral Philosophy*, was published posthumously.

Wisdom denotes the pursuing of the best ends by the best means.

1866 **Matthew Henson:** American Black explorer who accompanied Admiral Peary on all his polar expeditions. Placed U.S. flag at the North Pole.

As I stood there at the top of the world and thought of the hundreds of men who had lost their lives in the effort to reach it, I felt profoundly grateful that I had the honor of representing my race.

1883 **Emilano Zapata:** Mexican revolutionary leader of a Mexican agrarian movement. Supported Francisco Madero's overthrow of Porfirio Díaz. Occupied Mexico City three times. Assassinated.

Men of the South! It is better to die on your feet than to live on your knees.

1884 **Sara Teasdale:** American poet. Received a special Pulitzer Prize for her *Love Songs* (1917). Other collections of her poems: *Helen of Troy and Other Poems* and *Dark of the Moon.*

No one worth possessing / Can be quite possessed.

1908 **Arthur J. Goldberg:** U.S. government official, jurist and labor lawyer. Played an important role in the merger of the CIO and AFL. U.S. secretary of labor (1961–62). Associate justice of the Supreme Court (1962–65). U.S. delegate to the U.N. (1965–68).

Modern diplomats approach every problem with an open mouth.

1922 **Rudi Gernreich:** U.S. fashion designer. Introduced plastic fabrics in futuristic modes. Most famous for designing topless bathing suits and evening gowns.

It was just a whimsical idea that escalated when so many crazy ladies took it up.

1937 **Dustin Hoffman:** U.S. actor on stage and screen. Academy Award nominated for *The Graduate, Midnight Cowboy, Lenny* and *Tootsie.* Won Oscars for *Kramer vs. Kramer* and *Rain Man.*

Life is really a game and you must treat it as a game…. Life stinks, but that doesn't mean you don't enjoy it.

August 9

1593 **Izaak Walton:** English writer. Best known for *The Compleat Angler*, a discourse on the pleasures of fishing. He also wrote biographies of Sir Henry Wotton, Richard Hooker and George Herbert.

Angling may be said to be so like the mathematics that it can never be fully learnt.

1631 **John Dryden:** English poet, dramatist and critic. Noted for his satiric verse. Poet laureate (1668–1700). Works: "All for Love," "The Conquest of Granada,"

"Annus Mirabilis" and "Absalom and Achitophel."

Beware the fury of a patient man.

1896 **Jean Piaget:** Swiss psychologist. Pioneer investigator of the origin and development of children's intellectual faculties.

At the age of eleven or twelve a child becomes capable of certain formal or abstract operations of thought which before were possible only as concrete operations or properties of the immediately precise object world. This provides the last of three mental revolutions during development.

1913 **Herman Talmadge:** U.S. politician and lawyer. Democratic governor of Georgia (1948–55). Elected to the U.S. Senate in 1957.

Virtually everything is under federal control nowadays except the federal budget.

1922 **Philip Larkin:** British writer, librarian and poet. Turned down the post of poet laureate after the death of Sir John Betjeman. Poetry: *The North Ship, The Whitsun Weddings* and *High Windows.*

Nothing, like something, happens anywhere.

1928 **Bob Cousy:** U.S. basketball player and coach. Led Boston Celtics to six NBA championships. Ten times all-star. Elected to Hall of Fame (1970).

I like the purity of the pros. They tell everybody that they want to win and make money, and that's what they do.

1963 **Whitney Houston:** U.S. pop singer and actress. Platinum hits: "I Wanna Dance with Somebody" and "I Will Always Love You," from her starring movie *The Bodyguard.*

Gospel music was my greatest influence…. It gave me emotion and spiritual things, and it helped me to know what I was singing about because in gospel music the words mean everything.

August 10

1753 **Edmund Jennings Randolph:** American public official and lawyer. Governor of Virginia. First U.S. attorney general (1789–94). U.S. secretary of state (1794–95).

Our chief danger arises from the democratic parts of our constitution.

1810 **Camillo di Cavour:** Italian statesman. Helped bring about the unification of Italy under the House of Saxony.

I have discovered the art of deceiving diplomats. I speak the truth, and they never believe me.

1874 **Herbert C. Hoover:** Thirty-first president of the U.S. An engineer, he headed Allied relief operations during WWI. Participated in famine relief work after WWII. As president, he was done in by the Great Depression.

Blessed are the young, for they shall inherit the national debt.

1881 **Witter Bynner:** American poet and playwright. Author of *The New World, The Persistence of Poetry* and *A Book of Lyrics.*

The biggest problem in the world / Could have been solved when it was small.

1897 **Reuben Nakian:** "Grand Old Man of American Sculpture." Used Greek and Roman mythology in his works: *Voyage to Crete, Rape of Lucrece, Mars, Venus* and *Birds in Flight.*

Sculpture should have a powerful human content. Sculpture should be poetry.

1928 **Eddie Fisher:** U.S. singer. Husband of Debbie Reynolds, Elizabeth Taylor and Connie Stevens. Hit songs: "I'm Walking Behind You," "Oh! My Pa-Pa" and "Heart."

Women would be the most enchanting creatures on earth if, in falling into their arms, one didn't fall into their hands.

1942 **Betsey Johnson:** American fashion designer. Dubbed "The Madwoman of Seventh Avenue."

Real success is being totally indulgent about your own trip.

August 11

1833 **Robert G. Ingersoll:** U.S. lawyer, agnostic, orator and writer. Powerful advocate of scientific rationalism and a humanistic philosophy. Books: *The Gods* and *Why I Am an Agnostic.*

In nature there are neither rewards nor punishments—there are consequences.

1882 Horace Meyer Kallen: German-born U.S. educator and philosopher. Author of *The Education of Free Men* and *Liberty, Laughter and Tears.*
Education is the first resort as well as the last for worldwide solution of the problems of freedom.

1892 Hugh MacDiarmid: Pseudonym of Christopher Murray Grieve. Scottish poet and critic. Founded the Scottish Nationalist Party. Author of *A Drunk Man Looks at the Thistle* and *At the Sign of the Thistle.*
Our principal writers have nearly all been fortunate in escaping regular education.

1921 Alex Haley: American writer. Collaborated on *The Autobiography of Malcolm X.* Best known for *Roots,* which traced his ancestry back to its origins in Africa. He calls the work, a mixture of fact and fiction, "faction."
Roots is not just the saga of my family. It is the symbolic saga of a people.

1925 Carl T. Rowan, Jr.: Nationally syndicated African-American newspaper columnist. Ambassador to Finland (1963-64). Director of the U.S. Information Agency (1964-65).
Men are more inclined to hate trouble than to hate injustice.

1933 Jerry Falwell: U.S. clergyman and political lobbyist. Leading exponent of the so-called "electronic church." Founded the conservative political lobbying organization, Moral Majority.
I believe in the separation of church and state, but not the separation of God and government.

1946 Marilyn Vos Savant: American journalist with an IQ of 228, the highest ever recorded. Her column "Ask Marilyn" appears in *Parade* magazine.
If you want a better body, you must exercise more. If you want a better mind, you must read more.

August 12

1774 Robert Southey: English poet and author. Poet laureate (1813-43). One of the Lake Poets. Best remembered for the ballad "The Battle of Blenheim."
It is not for man to rest in absolute contentment.

1859 Katherine Lee Bates: American poet, educator, editor and writer. Best known as the author of "America the Beautiful."
America! America! / God shed His grace on thee / And crown thy good with brotherhood / From sea to shining sea!

1876 Mary Roberts Rinehart: U.S. novelist, mystery story writer, journalist, playwright and suffragist. Invented the "Had I But Known" school of detective fiction. Author of *The Circular Staircase, Tish* and the play *The Bat.*
Love is like the measles. The older you get it, the worse the attack.

1880 Christy Mathewson: "Big Six." Hall of Fame righthanded pitcher with the New York Giants. Won 30 or more games three consecutive years (1903-5). Had 373 career victories.
You can learn little from victory. You can learn everything from defeat.

1881 Cecil B. DeMille: U.S. director, producer and screenwriter. Most closely identified with epic spectacles such as: *The Ten Commandments* (1923 and 1956), *The King of Kings, The Sign of the Cross, Cleopatra* (1934) and *The Greatest Show on Earth.*
The way to make a film is to begin with an earthquake and work up to a climax.

1882 George Wesley Bellows: American artist. Painted boxing scenes and landscapes. Paintings: *Stag at Sharkeys* and *The Cliff Dwellers.*
Art strives for form, and hopes for beauty.

1911 Cantinflas: Mexican circus clown, acrobat and actor. One of the most-beloved comics of the Spanish-speaking world. Won International recognition with *Around the World in 80 Days.*
Always I project optimism.... Chaplin makes sometimes to cry. Cantinflas makes only to laugh—never to cry.

August 13

1818   **Lucy Stone:** U.S. suffragist, abolitionist, woman's rights activist, social reformer and editor. Married a fellow radical, but maintained her maiden name as a symbol of equality. Founded and edited *Woman's Journal* (1870).
"We, the people of the United States." Which "We, the people"? The women were not included.

1851   **Felix Adler:** U.S. educator and founder of the New York Society for Ethical Culture. Author of *Creed and Deed, Life and Destiny* and *An Ethical Philosophy of Life.*
Love of country is like love of a woman— he loves her best who seeks to bestow on her the highest good.

1895   **Bert Lahr:** U.S. comedian in vaudeville and on radio. Best remembered for his performance as the Cowardly Lion in *The Wizard of Oz.*
I think you laugh at a great comedian because you want to cry. Laughter is never too far from tears.

1899   **Alfred Hitchcock:** British film director of suspense films including: The *39 Steps, The Lady Vanishes, Rebecca, Notorious, Strangers on a Train, Rear Window* and *Psycho.* He made a cameo appearance in each of his movies, something fans always looked for.
What is drama but life with the dull bits cut out.

1912   **Ben Hogan:** One of the most prominent U.S. golfers. Four-time PGA Player of the Year. Of the major tournaments, he won four U.S. Opens, two Masters, two PGA and one British Open. Sixty-three career wins.
Management—placing the ball in the right position for the next shot, knowing exactly where to be on the green—is eighty percent of winning golf.

1916   **Daniel Schorr:** American radio and television correspondent. Dismissed from CBS-TV news for leaking a secret House Intelligence Commission report on the CIA to the *Village Voice.*

I'm fighting for freedom of the press, and maybe I should also be fighting for freedom from the press.

1926   **Fidel Castro:** Cuban revolutionary leader who led his guerrillas to victory over Fulgencio Batista in 1959. Transformed his nation into the first communist state in the Western hemisphere.
Men do not shape destiny. Destiny produces the man for the hour.

August 14

1840   **Baron Richard Krafft-Ebbing:** German neurologist. Professor of psychiatry, Vienna. Initiated study of sexual deviation. Coined terms paranoia, sadism, masochism in his *Psychopathia Sexualis.*
Woman loves with her whole soul. To woman love is life, to man it is the joy of life.

1863   **Ernest L. Thayer:** American author of "Casey at the Bat," which appeared in the *San Francisco Examiner,* June 3, 1888.
Oh! somewhere in this favored land the sun is shining bright; / The band is playing somewhere, and somewhere hearts are light; / And somewhere men are laughing and somewhere children shout, / But there is no joy in Mudville—mighty Casey has struck out.

1867   **John Galsworthy:** English novelist and playwright. Known for his social satire and portrayal of the British upper middle class. Best known for his novel series, *The Forsythe Saga.* Awarded Nobel Prize in 1932.
If you do not think about the future, you cannot have one.

1925   **Russell Baker:** American columnist with the *New York Times.* Pulitzer Prize for his autobiography *Growing Up.* Host of "Masterpiece Theatre" (1993).
Americans like fat books and thin women.

1928   **Lina Wertmuller:** Italian actress, director and playwright in the legitimate theater before turning to movies. Films directed include: *The Seduction of Mimi, Swept Away* and *Seven Beauties,* all starring Giancarlo Giannini.

Laughter is the vaseline that makes the ideas penetrate better.

1945   Steve Martin: U.S. comedian, actor and screenwriter. Popularity soared with guest appearances and hosting "The Tonight Show" and "Saturday Night Live." Films: *The Jerk, Roxanne* and *Father of the Bride.*

Making yourself look stupid seems much more human. Making other people look stupid just seems cheap.

1947   Danielle Steel: U.S. author of romantic best-sellers including *Full Circle, Daddy, Vanished* and *Wings.*

A bad review is like baking a cake with all the best ingredients and having someone sit on it.

August 15

1769   Napoléon Bonaparte: Emperor of France (1804–15). In 1799 launched a successful coup d'état. As emperor enacted many internal reforms in the economy and legal system. His conquests were put to an end by Wellington and the English fleet at Trafalgar. He escaped his exile at Elba and enjoyed a brief triumph but he was crushed at the Battle of Waterloo.

What is history but a fable agreed upon?

1771   Sir Walter Scott: Scottish novelist and poet. Derived most of his material from Scottish history and legend. His ballads include "Marmion" and "The Lady of the Lake." Novels: *Rob Roy, Ivanhoe* and *Quentin Durward.*

O what a tangled web we weave, / When first we practice to deceive.

1887   Edna Ferber: American novelist and short-story writer. Her novels include the Pulitzer Prize–winning *So Big, Show Boat* and *Giant.* She wrote several plays: *The Royal Family, Dinner at Eight* and *Stage Door.*

A woman can look both moral and exciting—if she also looks as if it were quite a struggle.

1888   T.E. Lawrence: "Lawrence of Arabia." British archaeologist, military strategist and author. Aided Arabs in a revolt against the Turks during WWI. Took part in the conquest of Palestine. Author of *The Seven Pillars of Wisdom.*

Many men would take the death sentence without a whimper to escape the life sentence which fate carries in her other hand.

1912   Julia Child: American chef, cooking consultant, writer and television personality. Author of *Mastering the Art of French Cooking* and *The French Cookbook.*

In France, cooking is a serious art form and a national sport.

1924   Phyllis Schlafly: American political activist. Foe of the Equal Rights Amendment. Champion of conservative causes. Author of *A Choice Not an Echo.*

Marriage is like panty-hose. It all depends upon what you put into it.

1944   Linda Ellerbee: American broadcast journalist and writer. With NBC News (1978–86), ABC News from 1986. Cohost of television's "Our World."

I want to know why, if men rule the world, they don't stop wearing neckties.

August 16

1645   Jean de la Bruyère: French writer and moralist. His sympathies lay with the ancients in their literary battle with the moderns. His most famous work: *Characters of Theophrastus* translated from the Greek, with *Characters, or the Manners of the Century.*

If poverty is the mother of crimes, want of sense is the father of them.

1862   Amos Alonzo Stagg: U.S. football innovator. Coached the University of Chicago for 41 years and 14 more years at College of the Pacific. Teams won 314 games.

No coach ever won a game by what he knows; it's what his players have learned.

1868   Bernarr McFadden: American publisher. Responsible for magazines *True Story, True Romances,* etc. A health fanatic, he parachuted from a plane on his 81st, 83rd and 84th birthdays.

If you feed a cold, as is often done, you frequently have to starve a fever.

1894   George Meany: American labor leader. President of AFL–CIO (1955–79). Helped reunify labor by bringing together the AFL and CIO. Awarded Presidential Medal of Freedom (1964).

The most persistent threat to freedom, to the rights of Americans, is fear.

1913   Menachem Begin: Israeli political leader. Prime minister (1977–83). Shared 1978 Nobel Peace Prize with Anwar Sadat for signing historic Camp David accord.

Israel is still the only country in the world against which there is a written document to the effect that it must disappear.

1920   Charles Bukowski: "The Laureate of the Low Life." American author and poet. A literary savage who wrote of the seamy side of life where he lived. Works: *Ham on Rye* and *Confessions of a Man Insane Enough to Live with Beasts.*

That's what friendship means: sharing the prejudice of experience.

1958   Madonna [Ciccone]: American entertainer and singer. Great self-promoter of limited talent who constantly reinvents herself to maintain an audience who wonders what shocking thing she will do next. Biggest record, "Like a Virgin." Films: *Desperately Seeking Susan, Dick Tracy* and *A League of Their Own.*

I lost my virginity as a career move.

August 17

1601   Pierre de Fermat: "The Prince of Amateurs." French mathematician. Regarded as the greatest mathematician of the 17th century. Shared with Pascal the creation of the mathematical theory of probability.

I have found a very great number of exceedingly beautiful theorems.

1786   Davy Crockett: U.S. frontiersman and politician. Fought in the Creek War. Elected to Tennessee legislature and to Congress. Killed in the defense of the Alamo.

I leave this rule for others when I'm dead. Be sure you're right—then go ahead.

1887   Marcus M. Garvey: U.S. black nationalist leader. Advocated separatism and racial pride. Promoted a "Back to Africa" movement. Editor of *Negro World.*

Up, you mighty race, you can accomplish what you will.

1890   Harry L. Hopkins: U.S. public official. Administrator of the Federal Emergency Relief Administration. Organized the Works Projects Administration during Roosevelt's first term.

People don't eat in the long run—they eat every day.

1892   Mae West: U.S. actress in stock, burlesque, vaudeville, Broadway and the movies. Wrote suggestive plays, often condemned as being obscene. The show business legend's movies include: *She Done Him Wrong, I'm No Angel, Belle of the Nineties* and *My Little Chickadee.* Famed for her double-entendre wisecracks.

I used to be Snow White, but I drifted.

1904   John Hay Whitney: "Jock." American publisher and diplomat. Owner of the New York *Herald Tribune.* Ambassador to Great Britain. Funded the J.H. Whitney Foundation which set up "Opportunity Fellowships" for people with exceptional promise who had not had the fullest opportunity to develop their abilities.

To be fair is not enough anymore. We must be ferociously fair.

1932   V.S. Naipaul: West Indian novelist and journalist. Writes satirical stories of the vanishing culture of the East Indian in Trinidad. Author of *In a Free State* and *A Bend in the River.*

Ignorant people in preppy clothes are more dangerous to America than oil embargoes.

August 18

1792   Lord John Russell: British statesman. Prime Minister (1846–52 and 1865–66). Champion of liberal measures and parliamentary reform.

If peace cannot be maintained with honor, it is no longer peace.

1807   **Charles F. Adams:** U.S. diplomat and public official. Grandson of John Adams and son of John Quincy Adams. Minister to Great Britain (1861–68). Published the life and works of his father and grandfather and edited the letters of his grandmother, Abigail Adams.

All education is self-acquired, since no one can educate another.

1834   **Marshall Field:** American merchant and philanthropist. Founder of Chicago's premier department store, Marshall Field and Co. Left a large part of his fortune to the University of Chicago and the Field Museum of Natural History.

Goodwill is the one and only asset that competition cannot undersell or destroy.

1922   **Shelley Winters:** The American actress began her career as a sexpot, but as her looks were more common than sultry, she was allowed to prove her worth as an actress. She won Academy Awards for *The Diary of Anne Frank* and *A Patch of Blue*, and was nominated for *A Place in the Sun* and *The Poseidon Adventure.*

Nudity on the stage? I think it's disgusting, shameful and unpatriotic. But if I were 22 with a great body, it would be artistic, tasteful, patriotic and a progressive, religious experience.

1922   **Alain Robbe-Grillet:** French novelist. Originator of the "antinovel" which described images without commentary. Author of *The Voyeur, Jealousy* and *Last Year at Marienbad.*

The true writer has nothing to say. What counts is the way he says it.

1925   **Brian Wilson Aldiss:** English science fiction writer and novelist. Literary editor of the *Oxford Mail* (1958–69). Best known for *Non-stop, The Moment of Eclipse* and *The Helliconia Spring.*

When childhood dies, its corpses are called adults.

1933   **Roman Polanski:** French-born Polish film director. Had a terrifying WWII childhood in Poland. His eight-month pregnant wife Sharon Tate was murdered by the Manson family. He fled the United States to escape conviction of raping a 13-year-old. Films: *Knife in the Water, Repulsion, Rosemary's Baby* and *Chinatown.*

Cinema should make you forget you are sitting in the theater.

August 19

1686   **Eustace Budgell:** English miscellaneous writer. A principal contributor to *The Spectator.* Signed some 37 papers with an X. Founded the weekly *Bee* (1733–35). Drowned himself.

When an argument is over, how many weighty reasons does a man recollect which his heat and violence made him utterly forget?

1870   **Bernard Baruch:** American businessman and statesman. Became wealthy while still in his 20s through shrewd financial deals. Held several key government posts including U.S. representative to the U.N. Atomic Energy Commission. Author of *American Industry in the War* and *A Philosophy of Our Time.*

Never follow the crowd.

1883   **Gabrielle "Coco" Chanel:** French fashion designer. Revolutionized women's fashions after WWII with straight, simple lines. Her world famous perfume Chanel No. 5 brought her great wealth and a dazzling social life.

Nature gave you the face you have at 20; it is up to you to merit the face you have at 50.

1902   **Ogden Nash:** American poet who wrote humorous and satirical verse. Much of his work was originally published in the *New Yorker* magazine. Wrote lyrics for *One Touch of Venus,* and *Two's Company.*

There is only one way to achieve happiness on this terrestrial ball, / And that is to have either a clear conscience or none at all.

1919   **Malcolm Forbes:** American publisher and editor of *Forbes* magazine (1957–90). Notorious for his extravagance and elaborate parties. Had a passionate interest in ballooning and Fabergé eggs. His collection of the latter was one of the finest in the world.

Nothing confers freedom like a buck in the bank.

1921 Gene Roddenberry: American writer and producer. Best known as the creator of the television series "Star Trek."
Space—the final frontier...These are the voyages of the starship Enterprise. Its five-year mission: to explore strange new worlds, to seek out new life and new civilizations, to boldly go where no man has gone before.

1946 Bill Clinton: U.S. politician. Governor of Arkansas. Became 42nd president of the United States in a three-man election race with former president Bush and maverick Ross Perot. Beset by charges of draft-dodging and womanizing.
There is nothing wrong with America that cannot be cured by what is right with America.

August 20

1881 Edgar A. Guest: U.S. poet. Syndicated author of sentimental verse for the *Detroit Free Press*. Wrote "A Heap o' Livin'" and "Life's Highway."
He started to sing as he tackled the thing / That couldn't be done, and he did it.

1886 Paul Tillich: German-born American theologian and philosopher. Applied aspects of depth psychology and existentialism to his interpretation of Christian doctrine. Major work: *Systematic Theology.*
The first duty of love is to listen.

1890 H.P. Lovecraft: American author of horror tales in the Poe tradition. Works include: *The Shadow Over Innsmouth, The Color Out of Space* and *The Case of Charles Dexter Ward.*
The most merciful thing in the world, I think, is the inability of the human mind to correlate all its contents.

1910 Eero Saarinen: U.S. architect. Buildings include: General Motors Technical Center, U.S. Embassy in London, Trans World Airline terminal in New York's Kennedy Airport. Also responsible for the parabolic "Gateway to the West" in St. Louis.
The purpose of architecture is to shelter and enhance man's life on earth and to fulfill his belief in the nobility of his existence.

1921 Jacqueline Susann: U.S. best-selling author of novels *Valley of the Dolls* and *The Love Machine.* She made no literary claims for her works, admitting they were to provide her readers with access to the sensational world of show business.
I've made characters live, so that people talk about them at cocktail parties, and that, to me, is what counts.

1944 Craig Nettles: All-Star baseball third baseman with the Indians and Yankees. Commenting on the constant state of unrest on his team caused by the battles between team owner George Steinbrenner and his managers and players:
Some kids want to join the circus when they grow up. Others want to be big-league baseball players. I feel lucky. When I came to the Yankees I got to do both.

August 21

1789 Augustin-Louis Cauchy: First of the great French mathematicians. He introduced rigor into mathematical analysis and began the systematic creation of the abstract theory of equations. His last words:
Men pass away but their deeds abide.

1798 Jules Michelet: French historian. Noted for his vivid accounts of French history. Greatest works, the 24-volume *Histoire de France* and the 7-volume *Histoire de la Révolution.*
He who knows how to be poor knows everything.

1887 Carmel White Snow: American fashion editor with *Harper's Bazaar* (1932–57). Promoted Parisian designers.
Elegance is good taste plus a dash of daring.

1890 William M. Henry: American journalist. Award-winning columnist with Los Angeles *Times* (1911–70).
What is research, but a blind date with knowledge.

1904 [William] "Count" Basie: American pianist, bandleader and composer. Led big bands from 1935 until his death in 1984. Hits: "One o'Clock Jump," "Basie Boogie" and "I Left My Baby."

...a band has to keep on trying and to keep that feeling that they just want to play and drive.... I think I'm happiest with my band when they're still not sure they're the greatest.

1931   Don King: U.S. boxing promoter. Controlled heavyweight titles from 1978–90 with Larry Holmes and Mike Tyson as champs.
A sportsman: a hustler with a Ph.D.

1936   Wilt Chamberlain: U.S. basketball center, 7' 4". Led NBA in scoring seven times and rebounding eleven times. Four-time MVP; 31,419 career points. Led Philadelphia 76ers and LA Lakers to NBA titles.
Nobody roots for Goliath.

August 22

1862   Claude Debussy: French composer. Identified with impressionism. Best known pieces include *Claire de lune, Prélude a l'Après-midi d'un Faun, La Mer* and his only opera *Péleas et Mélisande.*
Music is the arithmetic of sounds as optics is the geometry of light.

1891   Jacques Lipchitz: French sculptor. One of the founders of the Cubist school of sculptor. His work is noted for heavy stone abstractions and monumental figures.
Copy nature and you infringe on the work of our Lord. Interpret nature and you are an artist.

1893   Dorothy Parker: U.S. poet, satirist, short-story writer and book reviewer for *The New Yorker* and screenwriter. A celebrated wit in American literary circles. Member of the Algonquin Round Table group.
Brevity is the soul of lingerie, as the Petticoat said to her Chemise.

1902   Leni Riefenstahl: German director and actress. The former ballet and modern dancer and painter became Adolf Hitler's favorite director. Best known films: *Triumph of Will* and *Olympiad.* Claimed political ignorance not sympathy for the Nazis was behind her wartime activities.

I filmed the truth as it was then. Nothing more.

1904   Deng Xiaoping: Chinese leader and vice premier (1949–76, 1977–87). Most powerful leader of the Communist party.
It doesn't matter if a cat is black or white, so long as it catches mice.

1920   Ray Bradbury: American science-fiction writer. Best known for short-story collections: *The Martian Chronicles* and *I Sing the Body Electric!* as well as novels *Fahrenheit 451* and *Something Wicked This Way Comes.*
We are anthill men upon an anthill world.

1934   H. Norman Schwarzkopf: American general. Commanded troops of Desert Storm in the Persian Gulf war with Iraq.
It doesn't take a hero to order men into battle. It takes a hero to be one of those men who goes into battle.

August 23

1754   Louis XVI: King of France (1774–93). The reforms of his ministers failed to prevent the revolution. His allowance of France to become involved in the American Revolution exacerbated the national debt. Convicted of treason by the National Convention which abolished the monarchy, his last words before being guillotined:
May my blood cement your happiness!

1849   William E. Henley: English poet, playwright, critic and editor. While recovering from having a leg amputated, he wrote *A Book of Verses.* Became a friend of Robert Louis Stevenson who used him as a model for Long John Silver in *Treasure Island.* Henley's best known poem "Invictus" concludes with the lines:
I am the master of my fate; / I am the captain of my soul.

1869   Edgar Lee Masters: American lawyer, poet and novelist. Member of the Chicago literary renaissance, the Chicago Group. Best known work is *Spoon River Anthology.* Also wrote biographies of Vachel

Lindsay, Walt Whitman, Mark Twain and Abraham Lincoln.

Immortality is not a gift, / Immortality is an achievement; / And only those who strive mightily / Shall possess it.

1883   Jonathan Wainwright: "Skinny." U.S. army general who defended Corregidor. Forced to surrender, he survived the infamous "Death March."

There is no such thing as bravery; only degrees of fear.

1888   Morris L. Ernst: U.S. lawyer, author, editor. Author of *Hold Your Tongue!*, *Adventures on Libel and Slander, How High Is Up* and *A Love Affair with the Law.*

A sound marriage is not based on complete frankness; it is based on a sensible reticence.

1912   Gene Kelly: U.S. dancer, actor, director and choreographer. Athletic dancer in movies such as *On the Town, An American in Paris* and *Singing in the Rain.* Received a special Oscar for his versatility and his achievements in the art of choreography.

A choreographer takes an idea out of his head and transposes it on people's anatomy.

1932   Mark Russell: U.S. political satirist who rose to popularity at the time of the Watergate scandal. He has continued to spoof politicians, particularly presidents.

...after he [Richard Nixon] resigned, I had to go back to writing my own material.

August 24

1591   Robert Herrick: English clergyman and poet. Known for pastoral and love lyrics. Author of "To the Virgins," "To Make Much of Time" and "Hesperides."

Gather ye rose-buds while ye may, / old time is still a flying: / And the same flower that smiles today, / Tomorrow will be dying.

1810   Theodore Parker: American religious leader, abolitionist, reformer and author. Leader of the anti-slavery movement. Founded *Massachusetts Quarterly Review.*

As society advances, the standard of poverty rises.

1872   Max Beerbohm: English essayist and caricaturist. Legendary for his wit and powers of satire. Caricatures published in *The Poet's Corner.* Author of *A Christmas Garland,* the novel *Zuleika Dobson* and *A Defense of Cosmetics,* a collection of essays.

Only mediocrity can be trusted to be always at its best.

1895   Richard J. Cushing: American Roman Catholic Cardinal. Archbishop of Boston (1944–70). Director of the Boston office of the Society for the Propagation of the Faith.

Saints are all right in Heaven, but they're hell on Earth.

1898   Malcolm Cowley: U.S. editor, poet and translator. Literary editor of *The New Republic* (1929–44). Books include *Exile's Return* and *The Dream of the Golden Mountains.*

Talent is what you possess; genius is what possesses you.

1899   Jorge Luis Borges: Argentine poet, critic, and short-story writer. Noted for highly original fictional narratives: *Historia universal de la infamia* and *Extraordinary Tales.*

To die for a religion is easier than to live it absolutely.

1929   Yasir Arafat: Palestinian political leader. Head of PLO. Shared 1994 Nobel Peace Prize with Israeli leaders Yitzhak Rabin and Shimon Peres.

Chaos. Catastrophe. Bloodshed. Complete confusion. If you ask me honestly what is most likely to happen in the future, that is my answer.

August 25

1836   Bret Harte: U.S. short-story writer, novelist, poet and humorist. Helped found and edit *The Overland Monthly.* Stories include "The Luck of the Roaring Camp," "The Outcasts of Poker Flat" and "Plain Language from Truthful James."

Give me a man that is capable of a devotion to anything, rather than a cold, calculating average of all the virtues.

1905   Clara Bow: U.S. actress. The famous "It" girl, so called for her starring role in the film *It* written by Elinor Glyn. The title referred to that "something extra" she possessed, which later would be identified as "sex appeal."

The more I know about men, the more I like dogs.

1913   Walt Kelly: U.S. cartoonist. Creator of the comic strip "Pogo," whose message was a satirical and penetrating look at American society and its problems.

We have met the enemy and he is us.

1918   Leonard Bernstein: Gifted American conductor and composer. Equally at home with symphonic music and Broadway shows. Initiated a television series, "Young People's Concerts" with the New York Philharmonic. Compositions: *The Age of Anxiety, Mass* and *West Side Story.*

Music ... can name the unnamable and communicate the unknowable.

1919   George C. Wallace: U.S. politician. Leader of the South's fight against federally ordered racial integration as governor of Alabama. American Independent Party presidential candidate. Shot campaigning in 1972. Paralyzed from his waist down.

Segregation now, segregation tomorrow and segregation forever!

1927   Althea Gibson: U.S. tennis player. First African-American to win a major tournament. U.S. singles champ (1957 and 1958). Wimbledon champ the same years.

No matter what accomplishments you make, somebody helps you.

1930   Sean Connery: Scottish actor. Best known in the role of James Bond in several popular 007 films. Other movies: *The Man Who Would Be King, The Name of the Rose* and *The Hunt for Red October.*

To get anywhere in life you have to be antisocial. Otherwise you'll end up being devoured.

August 26

1676   Sir Robert Walpole: English statesman. Regarded as the first British prime minister (1721–42). Made the cabinet system effective and powerful for the first time. Regarded as indispensable by both George I and George II.

Gratitude is a lively sense of future favors.

1743   Antoine Laurent Lavoisier: French father of modern chemistry. Defined the role of oxygen, which he named. Concluded that human energy was derived from oxidation of hydrogen and carbon. Instrumental in establishing chemical nomenclature.

To call forth a concept a word is needed; to portray a phenomenon, a concept is needed. All three mirror one and the same reality.

1873   May Lambeton Becker: American editor and writer. Author of *Books as Windows, Adventures in Reading* and *Choosing Books for Children.*

We grow neither better nor worse as we get old, but more like ourselves.

1875   John Buchan, Lord Tweedsmuir: Scottish writer and governor general of Canada. Author of *Prester John* and *The Thirty-Nine Steps.*

We can only pay our debt to the past by putting the future in debt to ourselves.

1904   Christopher Isherwood: English novelist, short-story writer, playwright and memoirist. Described the social corruption and disintegration of Germany during Hitler's rise to power in *Berlin Stories,* the basis later of the Broadway and film musical *Cabaret.*

I am a camera with its shutter open, quite passive, recording, not thinking.

1914   Julio Cortázar: Argentine-born author who lived in exile in Paris after the election of Juan Perón. Author of *Rayuela* and *A Change of Light.*

After the age of 50 we begin to die little by little in the deaths of others.

1921   Benjamin Bradlee: American journalist and editor of the *Washington*

Post. Supported the Watergate investigation of reporters Woodward and Bernstein.
News is the first rough draft of history.

August 27

1770   Georg Wilhelm Hegel: German idealist philosopher. Had great influence on modern movements of existentialism, Marxism, positivism and analytical philosophy. Author of *The Science of Logic* and *Philosophy of Right and Law.*
The basis of the State is the power of Reason actualizing itself as Will.

1871   Theodore Dreiser: U.S. novelist. Pioneered naturalism in American literature. A leading light of the Chicago Group. Author of *Sister Carrie, Jennie Gerhardt* and *An American Tragedy.*
Our civilization is still in a middle stage, scarcely beast, in that it is no longer wholly guided by instinct; scarcely human, in that it is not yet wholly guided by reason.

1882   Samuel Goldwyn: Polish-born U.S. producer. Formed the Goldwyn film company with Edgar Selwyn. His knack was to bring together talented movie teams. Noted for his many malapropisms.
Let's have some new clichés.

1890   Man Ray: U.S. painter, sculptor and photographer. One of the founders of the Dada group. Developed the rayograph technique in photography.
Pleasure and the pursuit of freedom are the guiding motives of all human activity.

1908   Lyndon B. Johnson: Thirty-sixth U.S. president, succeeded assassinated John F. Kennedy. Exercised his political skill learned as a senator from Texas and majority leader to pass civil rights and antipoverty legislation. Anti-Vietnam War sentiment caused him not to seek renomination in 1968.
Politics is the art of the possible.

1910   Mother Teresa: Born Agnes Gonxha Bojaxhiu in Yugoslavia. Founded the Missionaries of Charity in Calcutta. Also opened facilities for the poor in New York and New Jersey. Nobel Peace Prize (1979).

Loneliness and the feeling of being unwanted is the most terrible poverty.

1932   Antonia Fraser: English author of mysteries featuring Jemima Shore. Wrote *Mary Queen of Scots* and *Quiet as a Nun.*
I decided as usual justice lay in the middle—that is to say nowhere.

August 28

1749   Johann Wolfgang von Goethe: German poet, playwright and novelist. Also held a cabinet post in the ducal court of Weimar, directed the city's theater and did research in science. Leading "Strum und Drang" ("Storm and Stress") dramatist. Best known for *Faust* and *The Sorrows of Young Werther.*
Knowing is not enough; we must apply. Willing is not enough, we must do.

1774   Elizabeth Ann Seton: U.S. educator and religious leader. Founded the Sisters of St. Joseph, a teaching order instrumental in establishing American parochial schools. Canonized in 1975, becoming the first U.S.–born saint.
It is seldom in life that one knows a coming event is to be of crucial importance.

1882   Belle Benchley: Director of Zoological Gardens of San Diego (1922–47). The "Zoo Lady," was the only female zoo director in the world.
Animals have their moods just as we do and do not always desire attention.

1899   Charles Boyer: French actor in many fine romantic film roles, such as: *Algiers, All This and Heaven Too* and *Gaslight.*
A Frenchwoman, when double-crossed, will kill her rival, the Italian woman rather kill her deceitful lover, the English woman simply breaks off relations—but they all will console themselves with another man.

1903   Bruno Bettelheim: Austrian-U.S. psychologist and educator. Authority on children, especially the emotionally disturbed. Author of *Love Is Not Enough* and *The Uses of Enchantment.*
Anxious mothers make insane kids.

1906   John Betejeman: English poet and architectural authority. Poet laureate

(1972–84). His poems celebrate the English countryside. Author of *New Bats in Old Belfries* and *A Pictorial History of English Architecture*.

History must not be written with bias, and both sides must be given, even if there is only one side.

1913   Robinson Davies: One of Canada's most read and popular authors. Novelist, playwright, essayist and critic. Known for *Deptford Trilogy*, *Fifth Business*, *The Manticore* and *World of Wonders*.

Fanaticism is … over-compensation for doubt.

August 29

1619   Jean Baptiste Colbert: French government official and businessman. Finance minister to Louis XIV (1665–85). Built French navy and initiated state manufactures.

The art of taxation consists in so plucking the goose as to get the most feathers with the least hissing.

1632   John Locke: English philosopher. Founder of British empiricism. Leading proponent of liberalism. His most famous treatise, *An Essay Concerning Human Understanding*, is an inquiry into the nature of knowledge. Also wrote *Two Treatises on Civil Government*. Great influence on the framers of the U.S. Constitution.

It is one thing to show a man he is in error, and another thing to put him in possession of the truth.

1809   Oliver Wendell Holmes, Sr.: U.S. poet and essayist. Father of jurist Oliver Wendell Holmes, Jr. First dean of the Harvard Medical School. Author of "Old Ironsides" and "The Deacon's Masterpiece." Contributed "The Autocrat of the Breakfast Table" to the *Atlantic Monthly*.

Man has his will—but woman has her way.

1876   Charles Franklin Kettering: U.S. engineer, inventor and manufacturer in the automobile industry. Designed the motor for the first electric starter for gasoline motors.

It's amazing what ordinary people can do if they set out without preconceived notions.

1915   Ingrid Bergman: Swedish-born actress of incredible beauty and remarkable radiance and vitality. Winner of Oscars for *Gaslight*, *Anastasia* and *Murder on the Orient Express*. Superb in *Casablanca*, *Gaslight*, *The Bells of St. Mary's* and *Notorious*.

My recipe for happiness? Good health and a bad memory.

1920   Charlie "Bird" Parker: Self-taught American jazz saxophonist. The leading spirit of modern jazz, pioneering new "cool" movement. Alcohol and heroin took his life at 35.

Music is your own experience, your thoughts, your wisdom. If you don't live it, it won't come out of your horn.

1958   Michael Jackson: Incredibly successful entertainer. Made over $70 million with his *Thriller* album. Numerous single hits include: "Ben," "Beat It," "Bad" and "The Way You Make Me Feel."

I am very uncomfortable around others in a social situation: people don't treat me as a person. I'm really only at ease on the stage.

August 30

1797   Mary Wollstonecraft Shelley: English novelist, daughter of William Godwin and Mary Wollstonecraft. Second wife of poet Percy Bysshe Shelley. Best known for her Gothic novel *Frankenstein, or the Modern Prometheus*.

To examine the causes of life, we must first have recourse to death.

1871   Ernest Rutherford: British physicist. He discovered and named alpha, beta and gamma radiation. Discovered and named "half-life" phenomenon of radioactivity. First to achieve a man-made nuclear reaction. Nobel Prize in chemistry (1908).

All science is either physics or stamp collecting.

1893   Huey P. Long: "The Kingfish." American politician and lawyer. Demagogic political boss of Louisiana in the

1930s. Governor (1928–32); U.S. senator (1932–35). Assassinated in 1935.

If Fascism comes to America it would be on a program of Americanism.

1901 **John Gunther:** U.S. foreign correspondent and author. Books include: *Inside Europe, Inside Asia, Death Be Not Proud* and *Inside Africa.*

Ours is the only country deliberately founded on a good idea.

1901 **Roy Wilkins:** American civil rights leader. Executive director of the NAACP (1965–77). Sought equal rights through changes in laws.

The man who shoots and burns and drowns us is surely our enemy, but so is he who cripples our children for life with inferior public education.

1907 **Shirley Booth:** U.S. stage, screen and television actress. Academy Award for recreating her Broadway role in *Come Back Little Sheba.* Best remembered for television series, "Hazel," as a wisecracking maid.

Success doesn't necessarily bring complete confidence.

1918 **Ted Williams:** U.S. outfielder with the Boston Red Sox. One of the greatest hitters of all time, the Hall of Famer is the last man to hit .400 in a season (.406 in 1941).

All I want out of life is that when I walk down the street, folks will say, "There goes the greatest hitter who ever lived."

August 31

1811 **Théophile Gautier:** French poet and novelist. Stressed perfection of form. Forerunner of the Parnassian school. Author of *Art for Art's Sake, La Comédie de la mort* and *Albertus.*

To love is to admire with the heart; / To admire is to love with the mind.

1870 **Maria Montessori:** Italian educator. Originated a method of education that stresses development of initiative, and sense and muscle training as well as the freedom of the child.

Never help a child with a task at which he feels he can succeed.

1885 **Dubose Heyward:** American novelist, poet and dramatist. Best known for his first novel *Porgy,* which became the basis for George Gershwin's opera *Porgy and Bess.*

A woman is a sometime thing.

1903 **Arthur Godfrey:** U.S. entertainer. One of television's most successful personalities in the 1950s. First established himself on radio with folksy variety programs.

Even if you're on the right track—you'll get run over if you just sit there.

1908 **William Saroyan:** U.S. author and playwright. Noted for optimism and mastery of the vernacular. Wrote *The Daring Young Man on the Flying Trapeze, The Human Comedy* and *The Time of Your Life,* for which he was awarded a Pulitzer Prize that he turned down.

Good people are good because they've come to wisdom through failure.

1935 **Eldridge Cleaver:** American political activist and author. Civil rights radical wrote *Soul on Ice* while in prison. Later wrote *Soul on Fire.*

The price of hating other human beings is loving oneself less.

1936 **Marva Collins:** American teacher and educational reformer. Started Chicago's one-room school, Westside Preparatory (1975).

When someone is taught the joy of learning, it becomes a lifelong process that never stops, a process that creates a logical individual. That is the challenge and joy of teaching.

September 1

1789 **Lady Marguerite Blessington:** Irish-born English socialite and writer. Known for her great beauty. She headed an intellectual salon and wrote a memoir of Lord Byron.

There is no cosmetic for beauty like happiness.

1868   Frank McKinney "Kin" Hubbard: U.S. humorist and caricaturist. Created the character "Abe Martin," who was featured in 26 books written by Hubbard. Spent most of his career on the staff of the *Indianapolis News* (1891–1930).
We'd all like to vote for the best man, but he's never a candidate.

1875   Edgar Rice Burroughs: U.S. novelist. Best known as the creator of Tarzan, the Ape Man, whom he featured in 23 books.
As the body rolled to the ground Tarzan of the Apes placed his foot upon the neck of his lifelong enemy, and raising his eyes to the full moon threw back his fierce young head and voiced the wild and terrible cry of his people.

1907   Walter Reuther: American labor leader. President of the U.S Auto Workers (1946–70). President of the CIO (1952-55). Leading anticommunist. Architect of merger of the AFL with the CIO (1955).
If it walks like a duck, and quacks like a duck, then it just may be a duck.

1935   Seiji Ozawa: Japanese-born conductor. Music director of the Boston Symphony Orchestra since 1973.
To make music, all the members of the orchestra must have the same idea about the music. Only the conductor can decide that one idea, and I think that is his most important job.

1938   Alan Dershowitz: U.S. lawyer and law professor at Harvard. Represents controversial defendants which included Claus von Bulow.
All sides in a trial want to hide at least some of the truth.

1939   Lily Tomlin: U.S. comedian and actor. Got her break with television's "Laugh-In," creating characters such as Edith Ann, the devilish little girl in the big rocking chair and Ernestine, the sarcastic nasal telephone operator. Films: *9 to 5* and *Nashville.*
We're all in this together—by ourselves.

September 2

1838   Lydia Kamekeha Liliuokalani: Hawaiian queen. Last sovereign to rule before annexation of the islands by the U. S. Composed the song, "Aloha Oe."
The Hawaiian people have been from time immemorial lovers of poetry and music, and have been apt in improvising historic poems, songs of love, and chants of warship, so that praises of the living or wails over the dead were with them but the natural expression of their feelings.

1850   Eugene Field: American poet and journalist. Wrote column "Sharps and Flats," for the *Chicago Daily News.* Known for children's poems "Little Boy Blue" and "Wynken, Blynken and Nod."
The best of all physicians / Is apple pie and cheese.

1852   Paul Bourget: French Catholic and conservative writer of novels, short-stories, plays, poetry, criticism and travel books. Works: *Edel, Nouveaux Essais de psychologie contemporaine* and *L'Étape.*
One must live the way one thinks or end up thinking the way one has lived.

1901   Adolph Rupp: Legendary U.S. basketball coach with the University of Kentucky. Holds the record for career victories (876).
Success is the best builder of character.

1904   Elizabeth Borton de Trevino: American children's author and journalist. Newberry Medal winner for *I, Juan de Pareja* (1966).
Slaves learn to fear the master who prefaces his remarks with tributes to his own virtues.

1918   Martha Mitchell: Outspoken wife of Attorney General John Mitchell. Called reporters in the middle of the night to spread Washington gossip.
Nixon bleeds people. He draws every drop of blood and then drops them from a cliff. He'll blame any person he can put his foot on.

1948   Christa McAuliffe: U.S. astronaut. A New Hampshire schoolteacher. The first ordinary citizen chosen to travel in space. Perished with six crew members in the January 28, 1986, *Challenger* explosion.
I touch the future, I teach.

September 3

1811   John Humphrey Noyes: U.S. religious leader. Founded Bible Communists community in Putney, Vermont. Practiced polygamy. Forced to flee to New York, he established the prosperous Oneida Community.

There is no more reason why sexual intercourse should be restrained by law, than why eating and drinking should be—and there is little occasion for shame in the one case as in the other.

1849   Sarah Orne Jewett: U.S. writer and hostess. Author of *Country Byways, The King of Folly Island and Other People* and *Tales of New England.*

Tact is after all a kind of mind reading.

1856   Louis H. Sullivan: U.S. architect. Founder of Chicago School. Gained international fame with the Chicago Auditorium Theater building. Others: St. Louis' Wainwright Building, the first skyscraper, and the Carson, Pirie, Scott department store in Chicago.

Form ever follows function.

1914   Dixie Lee Ray: U.S. politician and marine biologist. Chairperson of Atomic Energy Commission. U.S. assistant secretary of state for oceans and international environment and science affairs. Governor of Washington (1977–80). Received U.N. Peace Prize (1977).

Anything that the private sector can do, government can do it worse.

1927   Hugh Sidey: U.S. correspondent and author. Chief of Washington Bureau. Wrote *John F. Kennedy, President* and *Lyndon Johnson in the White House.*

Bureaucrats are the only people in the world who can say absolutely nothing and mean it.

1931   Dick Motta: U.S. basketball coach with several pro teams. His 1978 Washington Bullets won the NBA championship. Ranks third in career victories behind Lenny Wilkins and Red Auerbach.

The opera ain't over till the fat lady sings.

1938   Caryl Churchill: English dramatist. Her greatest commercial success has been *Serious Money,* a satire of the world of financial brokers. Also wrote: *Cloud Nine, Top Girls* and *Mad Forest.*

England, that little gray island in the clouds where governments don't fall overnight and children don't sell themselves in the street and my money is safe.

September 4

1768   Vicomte François René de Chateaubriand: French writer. Interested in exotic locations and primitive tribes. Author of novels of North and South American Indians: *Atala* and *Rene.* Also set his work in Greece, the Holy Land and the Near East.

An original writer is not one who imitates nobody, but one nobody can imitate.

1824   Phoebe Cary: American poet. Wrote hymn, "Nearer Home." Other works: "Suppose," "The Lovers" and "Dreams and Realities."

And though hard be the task, / Keep a stiff upper lip.

1905   Mary Renault: Pen name of English novelist Mary Challans. Early works based on her experiences as a wartime nurse. She moved on to historical novels, including *The Last of the Wine, The King Must Die* and *Fire from Heaven.*

Go with your fate, but not beyond. Beyond leads to dark places.

1908   Richard Wright: American novelist. Wrote powerful books exploring the way blacks were mistreated and shaped by white society. His most famous work is *Native Son.* His autobiographies: *Black Boy* and *American Hunger.*

Men can starve from a lack of self-realization as they can from a lack of bread.

1917   Henry Ford, II: U.S. automobile executive. CEO of Ford Motor Company. Grandson of Henry Ford. Son of Edsel Ford.

Don't complain. Don't explain.

1918 Paul Harvey: "Voice of U.S. Heartland." Conservative American radio commentator with ABC news since 1957. Syndicated columnist for *Los Angeles Times* since 1954.
In times like these, it helps to recall that there have always been times like these.

1926 Ivan Illich: Austrian-born American social critic and theorist. Ordained a Roman Catholic priest in 1951. Made Monsignor in 1957. Resigned priestly duties. Cofounder and director, Center for Intercultural Documentation (1961–76). Author of *De-Schooling Society* and *Toward a History of Needs.*
Leadership does not depend on being right.

September 5

1568 Tommasso Campanella: Italian philosopher and poet. Tried to reconcile the naturalistic themes of the Renaissance with Counter-Reformation orthodoxy. Imprisoned by the Spanish Inquisition for heresy. In prison wrote his famous utopian work *City of the Sun.*
The people is a beast of muddy brain / That knows not its own strength.

1638 Louis XIV: "The Sun King." King of France (1643–1715). Made the state an absolute monarchy. Ruled during a period of French greatness. Expanded French territory, persecuted Huguenots, built the palace at Versailles and sowed the seeds of the Revolution during his grandson's reign.
Every time I bestow a vacant office I make a hundred discontented persons and one ingrate.

1888 Sir Savrepalli Radhakrishnan: Indian statesman and philosopher. Ambassador to U.S.S.R. (1949–52). President of India (1962–67). Author of *The Religion We Need* and *Religion in a Changing World.*
Every sinner should be vouchsafed a future, as every saint has had a past.

1905 Arthur Koestler: Hungarian-born English novelist and essayist. An idealist, he has been disillusioned by communism, science, Yoga and Zen, to name a few. Author of *Darkness at Noon, Scum of the Earth* and *The Ghost in the Machine.*
Scientists are peeping Toms at the keyhole of eternity.

1912 John Cage: Highly inventive U.S. composer, writer, philosopher and artist. All his work since the 1950s is influenced solely by his idea that Zen and other Eastern philosophies are more relevant in art than Western traditions. Compositions: *Music for Wind Instruments, Music of Changes* and *Fontana Mix.*
Try as we may to make a silence, we cannot.

1936 Jonathan Kozol: American educator and author. Wrote *Death at an Early Age*, a probing criticism of American education. It won the National Book Award (1968).
Pick battles big enough to matter, small enough to win.

1950 Cathy Lee Guisewitz: American cartoonist. Creator of the "Cathy" cartoon strip, which amusingly shows how difficult it is to be an independent career woman today.
Even when I know it isn't true, some little part of me always clings to the hope that everything would be different if I just had a new color of lipstick.

September 6

1656 Guillaume Dubois: French cardinal, statesman and leading minister of the regent Philippe, duc d'Orleans. Virtually all powerful, he was appointed foreign minister in 1720 and prime minister in 1722.
To become a great man it is necessary to be a great rascal.

1757 Marie Joseph du Motier, Marquis de LaFayette: French soldier and statesman. Hero of the American Revolution. Negotiated French military support for American cause. Aided victory at Yorktown, remarking on British surrender:
The play is over. The fifth act has come to an end.

1800   Catherine Esther Beecher: American educator who promoted higher education for women. Daughter of Lyman Beecher. Sister of Harriet Beecher Stowe.
The delicate and infirm go for sympathy, not to the well and buoyant, but to those who have suffered like themselves.

1860   Jane Addams: American social worker. Founded Chicago's Hull House, one of first American social settlements (1889). Active in pacifist and suffrage movements. First woman to win Nobel Peace Prize (1931).
Civilization is a method of living, an attitude of equal respect for all men.

1875   Arthur Train: American lawyer and writer. Author of *The Prisoner at the Bar, On the Trail of Bad Men* and *The Adventures of Ephraim Tutt.*
A court is a place where they dispense with justice.

1899   Billy Rose: U.S. entrepreneur and songwriter. Owner of several New York theaters and night clubs. Produced shows: *Jumbo, Aquacade* and *Carmen Jones.* Songs: "It's Only a Paper Moon" and "Me and My Shadow."
Never put your money in anything that eats or needs repainting.

1917   Barbara "Bobo" Rockefeller: American model, actress and socialite, born Jievute Paulekiute. Married Winthrop Rockefeller after divorce from proper Bostonian Richard Sears, Jr.
...I think that each of us is more than we are portrayed and less than we believe.

September 7

1533   Elizabeth I: English Queen (1558-1603). Daughter of Henry VII and Anne Boleyn. Led her nation in one of its greatest periods. Encouraged exportations in the New World. Fought Spain's world empire. Her fleet defeated the Spanish Armada (1588).
I have the heart of a man, not a woman, and I am not afraid of anything.

1707   Georges-Louis Leclerc de Buffon: French naturalist. Curator of the Jardin du Roi. Best known for his 36-volume *Histoire naturalle* (1749–88).
Genius is only a great aptitude for patience.

1860   Anna Mary "Grandma" Moses: American folk painter. Best known for paintings of rural life. Started painting in her late 70s. Paintings: *Black Horses* and *From My Window.*
A primitive artist is an amateur whose work sells.

1887   Dame Edith Sitwell: English poet and prose writer. An eccentric who habitually dressed in medieval costume. Known for her experimental patterns of sound and imagery. Poems: "Daphne," "The Strawberry" and "The Little Ghost Who Died for Love."
The aim of flattery is to soothe and encourage us by assuring us of the truth of an opinion we have already formed about ourselves.

1900   Taylor Caldwell: English-born U.S. novelist. Her best-selling novels include: *Dynasty of Death, Dear and Glorious Physician* and *Captains and the Kings.*
He that hath no rule over his own spirit is like a city that is broken down and without walls.

1909   Elia Kazan: "Gadge." U.S. actor, screenwriter, producer and director. Oscar winner as director for *Gentleman's Agreement* and *On the Waterfront.* Nominated for *A Streetcar Named Desire, East of Eden* and *America, America.*
Criticism—a bite out of someone's back.

1931   Al McGuire: U.S. basketball coach and television color commentator. Led Marquette to an NCAA championship (1977) and then quit coaching.
I think the world is run by C students.

September 8

1841   Antonín Dvořák: Czech composer whose musical style was eclectic. In the U.S. from 1892, he suggested the way to develop a truly national American style of music was to base it on the melodies of Negroes and Indians. Major works: *Carnival Overture, From the New World Symphony, Te Deum* and *Rusalka*.

In the Negro melodies of America I find all that is needed for a great and noble school of music.

1889　**Robert A. Taft:** "Mr. Republican." U.S. politician. Son of William Howard Taft. U.S. senator from Ohio (1939–53). Unsuccessfully sought presidential nomination (1952). Helped write Taft-Hartley Act (1947).

The only method by which people can be supported is out of the effort of those who are earning their own way. We must not create a deterrent to hard work.

1900　**Claude Pepper:** U.S. politician. Democratic senator from Florida (1936-51); congressman (1963–89). Champion for senior citizens. Instrumental in passage of law against mandatory retirement based solely on age.

Ageism is as odious as racism and sexism.

1911　**Euell Gibbons:** U.S. naturalist. Author of books promoting eating wild foods, including *Stalking the Good Life*.

Supermarkets are all right, but it's much more fun to shop for food in nature.

1915　**Duffy Daugherty:** American football coach with Michigan State. His team tied Notre Dame both in a game and for the national championship (1966). FWAA coach of the year (1965).

A tie is like kissing your sister.

1922　**Sid Caesar:** American comedian. Best work done on television with "The Admiral Broadway Review," "Your Show of Shows," "Caesar's Hour" and "The Sid Caesar Show." Emmy winner (1952, 1957).

The trouble with telling a good story is that it invariably reminds the other fellow of a dull one.

1924　**Grace Metalious:** American author. Best known for her steamy novels of small-town life, *Peyton Place* and *Return to Peyton Place*.

Didn't you ever notice how it's always people who wish they had somethin' or had done somethin' that hate the hardest?

September 9

1585　**Duc Armand Jean du Plessis de Richelieu:** French cardinal and statesman. Chief minister to Louis XIII (1624-42). Built France into a world power. Centralized the government. Made alliances with the Netherlands and German Protestant powers.

To deceive a rival, artifice is permitted. One may employ everything against one's enemies.

1828　**Count Leo Tolstoy:** Russian novelist and moral philosopher. Also wrote short-stories, plays and essays. With Dostoyevsky made the realistic novel an important literary genre. Novels: *The Cossacks, War and Peace, Anna Karenina* and *Resurrection.*

Happy families are all alike, but an unhappy family is unhappy in its own way.

1887　**Alfred M. Landon:** U.S. politician and oilman. Governor of Kansas (1933-37). Carried only two states in his overwhelming defeat for the presidency by Franklin D. Roosevelt in 1936.

Don't spend what you don't have.

1890　**Colonel Harland Sanders:** U.S. restaurateur. Originator of Kentucky Fried Chicken. He had his first restaurant in Corbin, Kentucky.

There's no reason to be the richest man in the cemetery. You can't do any business from there.

1900　**James Hilton:** English novelist and journalist. Produced best-selling novels *Lost Horizon, Goodbye Mr. Chips* and *Random Harvest*.

If you forgive people enough you belong to them, and they to you, whether either person likes it or not—squatter's rights of the heart.

1908　**Cesare Pavese:** Italian novelist, poet, editor and translator. Translated the work of many major American writers.

His work: *The Political Prisoner, The Harvesters* and *The Moon and the Bonfires.*

One ceases to be a child when one realizes that telling one's troubles does not make it any better.

1932   Sylvia Miles: Stage-trained U.S. actress who often beautifully plays brassy, vulgar types. Films: *Midnight Cowboy* and *Farewell My Lovely* (both gained her Oscar nominations), *Wall Street* and *Crossing Delancey.*

Only the untalented can afford to be humble.

September 10

1487   Julius III: Born Giammaria Ciocchi del Monte. Italian pope (1550–55). Promoted Jesuits and initiated church reforms. Founded Collegium Germanicum.

Do you not know, my son, with what little understanding the world is ruled?

1885   Carl Van Doren: American editor, critic and biographer. Brother of poet Mark Van Doren. Managing editor of the *Cambridge History of American Literature.* His biography *Benjamin Franklin* won a Pulitzer Prize (1938).

The race of men, while sheep in credulity, are wolves for conformity.

1892   Arthur Holly Compton: U.S. physicist and professor. Made key contribution to the development of the quantum theory of energy. Nobel Prize winner (1927).

Learn the truth that we may be freer to develop ourselves in the best possible ways. Learn the need for good will among men that we may cooperate. Learn the means of cooperation.

1896   Elsa Schiaparelli: Italian-French fashion designer. Noted for her daring innovations and brilliant colors, such as shocking pink.

Women dress alike all over the world. They dress to be annoying to other women.

1903   Cyril Connolly: English essayist, critic and novelist. Founded and edited the magazine *Horizon* (1939–50). Author of *Enemies of Promise, The Unquiet Grave* and *The Evening Colonnade.*

Whom the gods wish to destroy they first call promising.

1929   Arnold Palmer: U.S. golfer. Won four Masters, two British Opens and one U.S. Open. Two-time PGA Player of the Year. First player to win over $1 million in career.

What other people may find in poetry or art museums, I find in the flight of a good drive—the white ball sails up into the blue sky, growing smaller and smaller, then suddenly reaching its apex, curving, falling and finally dropping to the turf to roll some more, just the way I planned it.

1934   Charles Kuralt: Likeable U.S. newsman with CBS. Host of television's "On the Road with Charles Kuralt" and "Sunday Morning." Tells the story of remarkably interesting ordinary Americans.

Thanks to the interstate highway system, it is now possible to travel across the country from coast to coast without seeing anything.

September 11

1700   James Thomson: Scottish-born poet. Author of "A Poem to the Memory of Sir Isaac Newton." Wrote the ode "Rule, Britannia!" that appeared originally in the last scene of the dramatic piece *Alfred, a Masque.*

For loveliness / Needs not the foreign aid of ornament, / But is when unadorned the most.

1862   O. Henry: Pen name of William Sydney Porter. U.S. short-story writer. Noted for his popular sentimental tales of ordinary people. Spent over three years in prison for embezzlement. Stories: "The Gift of the Magi," "The Last Leaf" and "Cabbages and Kings."

Life is made up of sobs, sniffles and smiles, with sniffles predominating.

1885   D.H. Lawrence: English novelist, short-story writer, poet and essayist.

Known for his idealistic theories about sexual relations. Many of his books were banned as obscene. He was persecuted during WWI for supposed pro–German sympathies. Novels: *Women in Love, Lady Chatterley's Lover* and *Sons and Lovers.*

I never saw a wild thing / Sorry for itself.

1913   **Hedy Lamarr:** Austrian-born actress. Gained worldwide notoriety in 1933 as Hedwig Keisler by appearing completely nude in the film *Ecstasy.* In Hollywood the exquisite brunette beauty appeared in *Algiers, White Cargo* and *Samson and Delilah.*

Any girl can be glamorous. All you have to do is stand still and look stupid.

1917   **Jessica Mitford:** English-born American writer. Sister of Nancy Mitford. Lifelong champion of civil rights. Best-known book: *The American Way of Death.*

Gracious dying is a huge, macabre and expensive joke on the American people.

1924   **Tom Landry:** Former Dallas Cowboys football coach. The only coach the team had from its formation in 1960 until he was fired and replaced in 1989 by the new owner. Won two Super Bowls. Had 271 career victories.

A team that has character doesn't need stimulation.

1946   **Lola Falana:** "First Lady of Las Vegas." U.S. entertainer. Returned to the Las Vegas stage in 1989 after an 18-month absence due to her battle with multiple sclerosis.

Dignity is fighting weakness and winning.

September 12

1829   **Charles Dudley Warner:** American essayist, editor and novelist. Collaborated with Mark Twain on the novel *The Gilded Age.* Editor of the multi-volume *Library of the World's Best Literature.*

Everyone talks about the weather, but nobody does anything about it.

1852   **Herbert Henry Asquith:** Earl of Oxford and Asquith. English statesman. Liberal Party prime minister (1908–16). Championed the Parliament Act of 1911 that limited the powers of the House of Lords.

Youth would be an ideal state if it came a little later in life.

1880   **H.L. Mencken:** American newspaperman, editor and critic. With the *Baltimore Sun* (1908–56). Literary editor of the *Smart Set.* Editor (1914–23). With George Jean Nathan founded the iconoclastic *The American Mercury* magazine (1924). Author of *The American Language.* A bad-tempered, crude and intolerant writer.

Love is the delusion that one woman differs from another.

1888   **Maurice Chevalier:** French singer and musical comedy star. His many films in the U.S. include *The Love Parade, Love in the Afternoon* and *Gigi.* Even in old age he usually played a charming rogue who couldn't resist women who couldn't resist him.

The French are true romantics. They feel the only difference between a man of forty and one of seventy is thirty years of experience.

1891   **Arthur Hays Sulzberger:** American journalist. Publisher of the *New York Times.* Married Iphigene Ochs, daughter of publisher of the *Times,* Adolph Ochs.

We tell the public which way the cat is jumping. The public will take care of the cat.

1892   **Alfred A. Knopf:** American publisher. With his wife Blanche W. Knopf founded Alfred A. Knopf, Inc., publishers (1915).

An economist is a man who states the obvious in terms of the incomprehensible.

1913   **Jesse Owens:** U.S. track and field athlete. Won four gold medals for the 100 meter, 200 meter, 4 by 100 relay and the long jump at the Berlin Olympics in 1936. Snubbed by Hitler because of his race.

I wasn't invited to shake hands with Hitler, but I wasn't invited to the White House to shake hands with the President either.

September 13

1819　Clara Wieck Schumann: Brilliant German pianist. Teacher and composer. Wife of composer Robert Schumann. After his death she toured widely as a pianist. Wrote a piano concerto and "Drei Romanzen" for violin and piano.
I always wish that the last movement [of the "Renjenlieder Sonata"] might accompany me in my journey from here to the next world.

1830　Marie Ebner-Eschenbach: Austrian novelist. Known for sensitive portrayals of life in Austrian villages and castles. Masterpiece is *The Child of the Parent.*
In youth we learn; in age we understand.

1860　John J. Pershing: "Black Jack." American general. Led campaign against Pancho Villa in Mexico. Head of the United States Expeditionary Force in Europe during WWI. Pulitzer Prize winner (1932) for *My Experiences in the World War.* Pronounced at the grave of the Marquis de Lafayette:
Lafayette, we are here.

1876　Sherwood Anderson: American short-story writer, novelist, poet and journalist. Major work: *Winesburg, Ohio*, a collection of stories about small-town life.
Everyone in the world is Christ and they are all crucified.

1894　J.B. Priestley: English novelist, dramatist and essayist. Noted for distorting the past, present and future in works such as *The Good Companions, Dangerous Corner* and *When We Are Married.*
Marriage is like paying an endless visit in your worst clothes.

1905　Claudette Colbert: French-born U.S. actress at her best in sophisticated comedy. Oscar winner for *It Happened One Night.* Nominated for *Private Worlds* and *Since You Went Away.*
Why do grandparents and grandchildren get along so well? They have the same enemy—the mother.

1938　Judith Martin: Etiquette expert, columnist and author. Her amusing advice appears under the name Miss Manners. Her column appears in more than 300 newspapers.
It is far more impressive when others discover your good qualities without your help.

September 14

1769　Baron Freidrich von Humboldt: German naturalist and explorer. Traveled throughout Europe, the Americas and Russian Asia collecting plants, studying rivers and ocean currents. Made the first isothermic and isobaric maps.
True enjoyment comes from activity of the mind and exercise of the body, the two are ever united.

1849　Ivan Pavlov: Russian physiologist. Researched blood circulation and conditioned reflects. His study with dogs is known to every student in a general psychology course. Nobel Prize (1904).
Facts are the air of scientists. Without them you can never fly.

1864　Lord Robert Cecil: English conservative statesman and author. One of the leading architects of the League of Nations. President of the League of Nations Union (1923–45). Awarded Nobel Peace Prize (1937). Wrote books on commercial law, the church and peace.
Old age is the Outpatient's Department of purgatory.

1883　Margaret Sanger: American founder of the birth control movement in the U.S. Founded the National Birth Control League (1914) and Planned Parenthood Foundation (1953). Served as its first president.
No woman can call herself free who does not own and control her body. No woman can call herself free until she can choose consciously whether she will or will not be a mother.

1899　Hal B. Wallis: U.S. producer. As executive producer in charge of production at Warner Brothers and as the head of his own company he was responsible for the production of more than 400

films. Some of the best: *Little Caesar, The Adventures of Robin Hood, The Maltese Falcon* and *Barefoot in the Park.*
I wonder if this business will ever turn honest.

1917 **Sydney J. Harris:** English-born U.S. author and journalist. With the *Chicago Daily News,* from 1941 to 1986. Wrote syndicated column, "Strictly Personal" (1944–86). Author of *A Majority of One, Last Things First* and *Pieces of Eight.*
Happiness is a direction and not a place.

1934 **Kate Millet:** American writer, critic, sculptor, philosopher and feminist. Champions women's issues groups. Member of CORE since 1965. Author of *Sexual Politics.*
Hostility is expressed in a number of ways. One is laughter.

September 15

1613 **François de la Rochefoucauld:** French writer. Author of five editions of *Réflexions ou sentences et maximes morales,* pessimistic epigrams which owed their origin to his belief that human behavior is based on self-love.
Hypocrisy is a tribute vice pays to virtue.

1789 **James Fenimore Cooper:** American novelist. Best known for the adventure stories featuring frontiersman Natty Bumpo, a natural man uncorrupted by civilization. Novels: *The Pioneers, The Pilot, The Last of the Mohicans, The Pathfinder* and *The Deerslayer.*
Ignorance and superstition ever bear a close and even a mathematical relation to each other.

1876 **Bruno Walter:** German-born American conductor. Concert pianist at 9, but at 13 turned to conducting. Achieved the reputation as the perfect classicist among contemporary conductors. Foremost conductor of Mahler's symphonies. Composed two symphonies.
I hate shyness in art as much as I approve of it in life.

1889 **Robert Benchley:** American humorist and critic. His classic comedy monologue *The Treasurer's Report* launched his comedy career. Made more than 40 movie shorts including *How to Sleep.* Wrote drama criticism for the *New Yorker.*
A dog teaches a boy fidelity, perseverance, and to turn around three times before sitting down.

1890 **Agatha Christie:** English novelist and playwright. Mystery writer who has sold more than 100 million copies featuring Belgian detective Hercule Poirot and eccentric amateur detective, the spinster Miss Marple. Author of novels *Death on the Nile* and *And Then There Were None.* Plays: *The Mousetrap* and *Witness for the Prosecution.*
In my experience, pride is a word often on women's lips—but they display little sign of it where love affairs are concerned.

1894 **Jean Renoir:** French motion picture director. Son of painter Pierre Auguste Renoir. Among his most famous films are the moving anti-war *Grand Illusion, The Rules of the Game, The Diary of a Chambermaid* and *The River.*
Life itself is an infinitely more rewarding spectacle than all the inventions of the mind.

1945 **Jessye Norman:** Exceptionally gifted African-American soprano. Made her operatic debut as Elizabeth in *Tannhaüser,* in 1969. Met debut as Cassandra in 1983. Repertory includes classical German pieces and French moderns.
I love beautiful things, beauty in anything, beauty in an athlete, or just getting up very early in the morning for rehearsals.

September 16

1678 **Henry St. John, Viscount Bolinbroke:** English statesman, orator and man of letters. Leader of Tory party during reign of Queen Anne. Major works: *Dissertation Upon Parties* and *Letters on the Study of History.*
History is philosophy teaching by examples.

1875 **James Cash Penney:** American businessman. Founder and board chairman of the J.C. Penney Company, which once operated more than 1700 department stores nationally. He lost a fortune in 1929, but bounced back.

Golden Rule principles are just as necessary for operating a business profitably as are trucks, typewriters and twine.

1885 **Karen Horney:** German-born American psychoanalyst. Outgrew Freud's concepts, adopting principles similar to those of Adler. Best know for exposing the male chauvinist bias in Freudian analysis of women. Author of *Our Inner Conflicts* and *Neuroses and Human Growth.*

A perfectly normal person is rare in our civilization.

1887 **Nadia Juliette Boulanger:** French composer, conductor and teacher. Studied at the Conservatorie (1897–1904), where she won several prizes. Went on to write many vocal and instrumental works. Later devoted herself to teaching at the Conservatorie and the École Normale de Musique, where she had international influence.

I'm lucky I'm so old and I live always with young people.

1893 **Albert Szent-Gyorgyi:** Hungarian-born American biochemist. First to isolate vitamin C. Awarded Nobel prize in physiology (1937).

Discovery consists of seeing what everybody has seen and thinking what nobody has thought.

1924 **Lauren Bacall:** U.S. actress. Dubbed "The Look" after the former model costarred with Humphrey Bogart in the film *To Have and Have Not.* Married Bogart and later Jason Robards, Jr. Other films include: *The Big Sleep, Key Largo* and *How to Marry a Millionaire.*

I hope my daughter will know that the passion of anger is also a part of love and that the opposite of love is not hate but indifference.

1926 **Robert H. Schuller:** American clergyman who invented the drive-in church. Preaches each Sunday to nearly 10,000 people, some sitting in pews, some in cars. His television program "The Hour of Power" has an audience of more than 3 million.

When you can't solve the problem, manage it.

September 17

1743 **Marquis Marie Jean de Condorcet:** French mathematician and philosopher. Leading thinker of the Enlightenment. Made contributions to the theory of probability. Devised a state education system.

Enjoy your own life without comparing it with that of another.

1883 **William Carlos Williams:** American poet, playwright, essayist and fiction writer. Maintained a lifelong medical practice. Considered patron saint of American poets. Pulitzer Prize for *Pictures from Brueghel and Other Poems.* Other works: 5-volume epic *Paterson* and *In the American Grain.*

The better work men do is always done under stress and at great personal cost.

1890 **Gabriel Heatter:** American radio performer and journalist. Began his news broadcasts with "Ah yes. There's good news tonight."

Mere longevity is a good thing for those who watch life from the side lines. For those who play the game, an hour may be a year, a single day's work an achievement for eternity.

1907 **Warren E. Burger:** American jurist and lawyer. Appointed chief justice of the Supreme Court (1969). A strict constructionist in criminal matters.

The right of every person "to be let alone" must be placed on the scales with the right of others to communicate.

1916 **Mary Florence Stewart:** English author of the trilogy *The Last Enchantment* about King Arthur and Merlin. Also wrote *Nine Coaches Waiting* and *This Rough Magic.*

The best way of forgetting how you think you feel is to concentrate on what you know you know.

1923 **Hank Williams, Sr.:** American singer, guitarist and songwriter. Most famous songs: "Lonesome Blues," "My Bucket's Got a Hole in It," "Cold, Cold Heart," "Jambalaya" and "Your Cheatin' Heart." Died of a drug and alcohol overdose.

You got to have smelt a lot of mule manure before you can sing like a hillbilly.

1935   **Ken Kesey:** American author. Associated with the "Beat" movement. Worked as a ward attendant in a mental hospital and used the experience to write his most famous work, *One Flew Over the Cuckoo Nest.*

Take what you can use and let the rest go by.

September 18

1709   **Samuel Johnson:** English lexicographer, essayist, poet and moralist. The major literary figure of the second half of the 18th century. Best known works include the pioneering *Dictionary of the English Language*, an edition of Shakespeare's works, 10-volume *Lives of the Poets, The Rambler, The Adventurer* and *The Idler.*

Marriage has many pains, but celibacy has no pleasures.

1779   **Joseph Story:** U.S. jurist. Pioneer in founding and directing Harvard Law School. Associate justice of the Supreme Court (1811–45).

[The law] is a jealous mistress and requires a long and constant courtship. It is not to be won by trifling favors, but by lavish homage.

1827   **John Townsend Trowbridge:** American poet, editor and author of books for boys. Pen name: Paul Creyton. Contributing and managing editor of *Our Young Folks* (1865–73). Wrote *Jack Hazard* and *Toby Trafford* series. Best known poem: "Darius Green and His Flying Machine."

The birds can fly, / An' why can't I?

1895   **John G. Diefenbaker:** Canadian politician. Leader of Progressive Conservative Party. Prime minister (1957–63). Suffered political downfall over controversy of producing nuclear weapons.

I am not anti–American. But I am strongly pro–Canadian.

1905   **Agnes de Mille:** American dancer and choreographer. Toured with humorous mime-dancers (1929–40). Choreographed ballet *Rodeo*, the first to include tap dancing. Choreographed for films *Carousel, Gentlemen Prefer Blondes* and *Oklahoma!* Tony Award winner (1947 and 1962).

Ballet technique is arbitrary and very difficult. It never becomes easy; it becomes possible.

1905   **Greta Garbo:** Swedish-born actress. Twice nominated for Academy awards for *Anna Christie* and *Ninotchka*. The remarkable beauty retired from films at the age of 36 in 1939. Other films: *Flesh and the Devil, Mata Hari, Grand Hotel, Queen Christina, Anna Karenina* and *Camille.*

I never said "I want to be alone." I only said, "I want to be let alone." There is all the difference.

1933   **Robert Blake:** U.S. actor who started his career as a child, appearing as Little Beaver in the *Red Ryder* Westerns. Best known films: *In Cold Blood* and *Tell Them Willie Boy Is Here*. Star of television's "Baretta" (1975–78). Emmy winner (1975).

Every time you think you got it made, old Mother Nature kicks you in the scrotum.

September 19

1737   **Charles Carroll:** American revolutionary leader. Helped draft Maryland constitution. U.S. senator (1789–92). Only Roman Catholic signer of the Declaration of Independence.

When I signed the Declaration of Independence I had in view not only our independence from England but the toleration of all sects.

1778   **Lord Henry Peter Brougham:** English statesmen. Lord Chancellor of England, 1833–34. Played an important role in the improvement of education, law reform and the abolition of slavery.

Education makes people easy to lead, but difficult to drive; easy to govern, but impossible to enslave.

1894   Rachel Field: American novelist, playwright and poet. Editor of several collections of fairy tales. Author of *Hitty, Her First Hundred Years, Calico Bush, All This and Heaven Too* and *And Now Tomorrow*.
I've seen public opinion shift like a wind and put out the very fire it lighted.

1904   Bergen Evans: American educator and author. Wrote "The Skeptic's Corner" for *American Mercury* (1946–50). Author of "The Last Word," a syndicated daily newspaper feature. Host of several language-oriented television shows. Works: *Dictionary of Contemporary American Usage* and *Dictionary of Quotations*.
Lying is an indispensable part of making life tolerable.

1911   William Golding: English novelist. A master of strange situations and ironic twists. Nobel Prize winner (1983). Author of the contemporary classic *Lord of the Flies, Pincher Martin* and *Rites of Passage*.
My yesterdays walk with me. They keep step, they are gray faces that peer over my shoulder.

1921   Charlie Conerly: American Hall of Fame quarterback with the New York Giants (1948–61). Completed 36 of 53 passes against the Pittsburgh Steelers in 1948.
When you win, you're an old pro. When you lose, you're an old man.

1932   Mike Royko: U.S. newspaper syndicated columnist. Reporter with Chicago newspapers since 1959. Pulitzer Prize winner for commentary (1972). His one-rule diet:
...if you enjoy it, you can't eat it. If you don't like it, you can eat all you want.

September 20

1842   Lord James Dewar: British-Scottish physicist. First to liquefy and then solidify hydrogen. Research in low-temperature preservation led to the Thermos bottle. Invented cordite, first smokeless powder.
Minds are like parachutes. They only function when they are open.

1851   Henry Arthur Jones: English playwright. Achieved prominence in the field of melodrama. Also contributed greatly to Victorian society drama. Author of *The Silver King, The Dancing Girl* and *The Liars*.
O God! Put back Thy universe and give me yesterday.

1878   Upton Sinclair: U.S. muckraking author of novels and nonfiction. Wrote over 80 books. Espoused socialism and concern for social and political problems. Books: *The Jungle, King Coal, Oil!* and *Boston*.
Is it altogether a Utopian dream, that once in history, a ruling class might be willing to make the great surrender, and permit social change to come about without hatred, turmoil, and waste of human life.

1885   Ferdinand "Jelly Roll" Morton: American jazz pianist, singer, bandleader, arranger and composer. His style was tinged with Creole elements and ragtime. Compositions: "New Orleans Blues," "Jelly Roll Blues" and "King Porter Stomp." Disputed W.C. Handy's claim as the originator of jazz and the blues.
New Orleans is the cradle of jazz, and I myself happened to be the creator in the year 1902.

1901   Charles Abrams: American lawyer and author. Wrote: *The Future of Housing, Forbidden Neighbors* and *The City Is the Frontier*.
The Ghetto—particularly the Negro ghetto—a peculiarly American institution, its boundaries set by force of deed, covenants, statues, or simple duress.

1902   Stevie [Florence Margaret] Smith: English poet and novelist. Author of "Me Again," "Not Waving but Drowning," *A Good Time Was Had by All* and *Novel on Yellow Paper*.
If there was no death I think you couldn't go on.

1917   Arnold "Red" Auerbach: Second winningest basketball coach in history, 1,037 victories, including playoff games in 20 years. Led Boston Celtics as general manager-coach to nine NBA titles, eight in a row. Club president since 1970.
When people are used to winning, they put out more.

1934   **Sophia Loren:** Italian actress. Tall, statuesque, sensuous star of films *Desire Under the Elms, Two Women* (Oscar winner), *Yesterday, Today and Tomorrow* and *Marriage Italian Style.*
A woman's dress should be like a barbed wire fence; serving its purpose without obstructing the view.

September 21

1849   **Sir Edmund William Gosse:** English man of letters. Translated Ibsen's works. Wrote critical essays of English literature of the 17th and 18th century and Scandinavian and French literature.
My faith in beauty shall not fail / Because I fail to understand.

1863   **John Bunny:** U.S. actor in minstrel shows, legitimate theater and films as the first comic star of American screen. Made more than 160 comedy shorts.
Here's to our wives and sweethearts— may they never meet.

1866   **Charles Jean Henri Nicolle:** French bacteriologist. Nobel Prize winner in medicine (1928) for discovering that typhus fever is transmitted by the body louse.
Chance favors only those who know how to court her.

1866   **H.G. Wells:** English science-fiction author of *The Time Machine, The Invisible Man* and *The War of the Worlds.* Also wrote the realistic novel *Kipps* and *Outline of History.*
Human history becomes more and more a race between education and catastrophe.

1909   **Kwame Nkrumah:** African founder of the nation of Ghana. Formed Convention People's Party to fight for independence of Gold Coast. First prime minister of Ghana (1957–66). Suppressed dissent and was overthrown.
We prefer self-government with danger to servitude with tranquillity.

1916   **Françoise Giroud:** Swiss-French politician, journalist, editor. French Minister of Women. Cofounder of *Elle* and *L'Express.*

To live several lives, you have to die several deaths.

1947   **Stephen King:** Best-selling American author of horror novels, most of whom have been adapted to film. They include: *Carrie, The Shining, The Dead Zone, Stand By Me* and *Misery.*
We make up horrors to help us cope with the real ones.

September 22

1694   **Philip Dormer Stanhope, 4th Earl of Chesterfield:** English statesman and man of letters. He is best known for his letters to his son, written between 1737 and 1768, which provide a classic portrayal of an ideal 18th century gentleman.
When a man seeks your advice he generally wants your praise.

1788   **Theodore Hook:** English novelist and wit. Author of *Impromptu at Fulham, Gilbert Gurney* and *William Weare.*
My little dears, who learn to read, / Pray early learn to shun / That very foolish thing indeed / The people call a pun.

1847   **Alice Meynell:** English poet, literary critic and essayist. Author of "A Thrush Before Dawn," "The Laws of Verse," "The Poet to the Birds" and "In Early Spring."
The sense of humor has other things to do than to make itself conspicuous in the act of laughter.

1885   **Erich Von Stroheim:** Austrian-born director, actor and screenwriter. As an actor he played mainly villains, dubbed "the man you love to hate." As a director he made costly, lengthy films including his masterwork *Greed.* Others: *The Merry Widow, The Wedding March* and *Queen Kelly.*
In Hollywood, you're only as good as your last picture. If you haven't got a last picture, you're no good.

1902   **Howard Jarvis:** U.S. political activist and politician. An anti-tax crusader. Was successful in getting California voters to approve Proposition 21, which led to lower property taxes but also resulted in a loss of many services that citizens had grown accustomed to having.

The only way to cut government spending is not to give them the money to spend in the first place.

1910 **Marjorie Holmes:** U.S. novelist. Author of *World by the Tail, Follow Your Dream* and *I've Got to Talk to Somebody, God.*

The man who treasures his friends is usually solid gold himself.

1927 **Tommy Lasorda:** American baseball manager with the L.A. Dodgers since 1975. Led his team to two World Series victories, 1981 and 1988.

There are three types of baseball players: those who make it happen, those who watch it happen, and those who wonder what happened.

September 23

63 B.C. **Augustus Caesar:** First Roman Emperor. Adopted son of Julius Caesar. As emperor centralized power. Introduced Pax Romana, an era of peace. Accomplished much construction. His excellent advice:

Make haste slowly.

1800 **William Holmes McGuffey:** American educator. Wrote and published his *Eclectic Readers*, which made him famous and are still yearned for by some backward-looking educational reformers.

Shall birds, and bees, and ants, be wise, / While I my mo-ments waste? / O let me with the morn-ing rise, / And to my du-ty haste.

1838 **Victoria Claflin Woodhull:** American writer, editor and reformer. Opened a stock brokerage office in 1868. Founded *Woodhull and Claflin's Weekly* advocating equal rights for women, free love and a single moral standard. First woman candidate for U.S. presidency.

I have an inalienable constitutional and natural right to love whom I may, to love as long or as short a period as I can, to change that love every day if I please.

1889 **Walter Lippmann:** U.S. journalist. Syndicated political columnist for the *New York Herald-Tribune* (1931–62) and *The Washington Post* (1962–67). Author of *A Preface to Politics, The Good Society,* and *Unity and the Common Market.*

Men who are orthodox when they are young are in danger of being middle aged all their lives.

1899 **Louise Nevelson:** Russian-born American sculptor and printmaker. Famed for her environmental sculptures: abstract, wooden, box-like shapes stacked up to form walls and painted white or gold.

I never feel age.... If you have creative work, you don't have age or time.

1930 **Ray Charles:** American pianist and singer, blind since the age of six. Wrote songs in the rhythm 'n' blues style in the 1950s, but later delved into jazz, soul and country. A great musical genius. Songs: "What'd I Say," "Georgia on My Mind," "Hit the Road Jack," "I Can't Stop Loving You," "Busted" and "Crying Time."

Soul is a way of life, but it is always the hard way.

1949 **Bruce Springsteen:** "The Boss." American singer and songwriter. A leader in the rock and roll field and voice of dissident youth. Hits: "Hungry Heart," "Dancing in the Dark," "Born in the U.S.A.," "My Hometown," "War" and "Philadelphia."

Talk about a dream, try to make it real.

September 24

1717 **Horace Walpole:** Fourth Earl of Oxford. English politician, author, man of letters, connoisseur, collector and memorialist. Works: *Memoirs, Anecdotes of Painting in England* and *The Castle of Otranto.*

The world is a comedy to those that think, a tragedy to those who feel.

1755 **John Marshall:** U.S. jurist. Fourth chief justice of the Supreme Court (1801–35). Instrumental in molding the court and establishing its function. U.S. secretary of state (1800–1).

The power to tax involves the power to destroy.

1825 Frances Ellen Watkins Harper: American writer, poet and abolitionist. Author of *Poems on Miscellaneous Subjects, Idylls of the Bible* and *The Sparrow's Fall and Other Poems.*

The respect that is only bought by gold is not worth much.

1843 Samuel Willoughby Duffield: American Presbyterian clergyman, hymnologist and poet. Author of *The Heavenly Land* and *English Hymns: Their Authors and History.*

A mind without occupation is like a cat without a ball of yarn.

1895 Tommy Armour: U.S. golf professional and teaching pro. Member of the PGA / World Golf Hall of Fame. Won U.S. Open in 1927, PGA Championship in 1930 and British Open in 1931.

Golf is an awkward set of bodily contortions designed to produce a graceful result.

1896 F. Scott Fitzgerald: American novelist, short-story writer and screenwriter. Spokesman for the "Jazz Age," which he named. Author of *This Side of Paradise, The Great Gatsby* and *The Last Tycoon.*

At eighteen our convictions are hills from which we look; at forty-five they are caves in which we hide.

1936 Jim Henson: American puppeteer. Created the Muppets in 1954, who appeared as regulars on television's "Sesame Street" and in a series of movies. Henson was the voice of Kermit the Frog and created Miss Piggy.

I believe in taking a positive attitude toward the world. My hope still is to leave the world a little better than when I got here.

September 25

1793 Felicia Dorthea Hemans: English poet. Author of 24 volumes of verse which expressed romantic themes of childhood, innocence, liberty, inspiration and nature. Best known for *The Homes of England, The Landing of the Pilgrim Fathers* and *Casabianca.*

The boy stood on the burning deck, / Whence all but he had fled.

1897 William Faulkner: Among the greatest American writers. Most of his novels are set in imaginary Yoknapatawpha County, Mississippi. Author of *The Sound and the Fury, Sanctuary, Intruder in the Dust, Requiem for a Nun* and *A Fable.* In his 1949 Nobel Prize for literature speech he declared:

I believe man will not merely endure, he will prevail. He is immortal, not because he, alone among creatures, has an inexhaustible voice but because he has a soul, a spirit capable of compassion and sacrifice and endurance.

1905 Walter "Red" Smith: American sportswriter for Philadelphia and New York newspapers from 1936 to 1982. Won Pulitzer Prize for commentary in 1976.

There is nothing to writing. All you do is sit down at a typewriter and open a vein.

1906 Dmitri Shostakovich: Preeminent Russian composer of the Soviet generation. His style and compositions largely defined the nature of new Russian music. Wrote 15 symphonies, chamber music, concerti and film scores.

A creative artist works on his next composition because he was not satisfied with his previous one.

1931 Barbara Walters: American television personality. Appears regularly on "20 / 20." One of the highest paid journalists in America. Television's first anchorwoman. Best known for her interviews with personalities in the world of entertainment and politics.

Show me someone who never gossips and I'll show you someone who isn't interested in people.

1932 Glenn Gould: Canadian concert pianist. Debuted at age 15 with Toronto Symphony. Known for his Bach interpretations.

A record is a concert without halls and a museum whose curator is the owner.

1944 Michael Douglas: U.S. actor, director and producer. Son of actor Kirk Douglas. Oscar winner for *Wall Street.* Other films: *Fatal Attraction, Basic Instinct* and *Disclosure.*

The exciting thing about making movies today is that everything is up for grabs. And you had better grab.

September 26

1783   **Jane Taylor:** English children's writer. Best known as the author of "Twinkle, twinkle, little star."

Then let me to the valley go, / This pretty flower to see, / That I may also learn to grow in sweet humility.

1888   **J. Frank Dobie:** American educator, folklorist and author. Maverick Texas historian. Author of *The Flavor of Texas, Guide to Life and Literature of the Southwest* and *Tales of Old-Time Texas*.

Conform and be dull.

1888   **T.S. Eliot:** American-born English poet, critic and dramatist. Recognized as one of the major poets of the 20th century. His poetry revolutionized the literary conventions of the Romantics and Victorians. Received a Nobel Prize in 1948. Works: "The Love Song of J. Alfred Prufrock," "The Waste Land," "The Hollow Men," "Ash Wednesday," *Old Possum's Book of Practical Cats* and plays *Murder in the Cathedral* and *The Cocktail Party*.

This is the way the world ends / Not with a bang but a whimper.

1892   **Robert S. Lynd:** U.S. sociologist, educator and author. Wrote *Middletown: A Study in Contemporary American Culture* with wife Helen Merrill Lynd. Managing editor of *Publisher's Weekly*.

Life is worth living, but only if we avoid the amusements of grown-up people.

1895   **George Raft:** U.S. dancer and actor. Worked his way up from movie hoofer to tough guy and mobster in films such as *Scarface, Bolero, Each Dawn I Die* and *Some Like It Hot*.

Part of the $10,000,000 I've made in my career went for gambling, part for horses and part for women. The rest I spent foolishly.

1897   **Paul VI [Giovanni Batista Montini]:** Catholic Pope from 1963 to 1978. Carried through the Vatican II reforms. Issued the encyclical *Humanae Vitae*, condemning birth control.

Chastity is not acquired all at once but results from a laborious conquest and daily affirmation.

1898   **George Gershwin:** Foremost American composer. Wrote many popular songs and musicals with his lyricist brother Ira. Also known for his more serious music such as *Rhapsody in Blue*. Songs: "I Got Rhythm," "Summertime," "Someone to Watch Over Me," "But Not for Me," and "They Can't Take That from Me."

True music ... must repeat the thought and inspiration of the people and the time. My people are Americans. My time is today.

September 27

1722   **Samuel Adams:** American revolutionary patriot and statesman. Helped organize the Boston Tea Party and the Sons of Liberty. Wrote pamphlets against the British. Member of the Continental Congress (1774–81). Signer of the Declaration of Independence. Governor of Massachusetts (1794–97).

The country shall be independent, and we will be satisfied with nothing short of it.

1821   **Henri Frédéric Amiel:** Swiss writer whose 16,900 page *Journal intime* is a masterpiece of self-analysis.

Destiny has two ways of crushing us—by refusing our wishes and by fulfilling them.

1840   **Alfred Thayer Mahan:** U.S. admiral and naval theorist. Wrote 20 books on naval history and global strategy, which greatly influenced the policies of the super powers during the late 19th and early 20th centuries.

Force is never more operative than when it is known to exist but is not brandished.

1874   **Myrtle Reed:** American novelist, essayist and poet. Author of *Lavender and Old Lace, Love Affairs of Literary Men* and *A Weaver of Dreams*.

It is bad manners to contradict a guest. You must never insult people in your own house—always go to theirs.

1896   **Sam Ervin:** American politician and lawyer. U.S. senator from North Carolina (1954–75). Headed the Senate Select Committee on Presidential Campaign Activities investigating the Watergate scandal.

I've always been worried about people who are willing to work for nothing. Sometimes that's all you get from them, nothing.

1917 Louis S. Auchincloss: American novelist, short-story writer, essayist and biographer. Author of *The Rector of Justin, Powers of Attorney,* and *The Cat and the King.*
Perfection irritates as well as it attracts, in fiction as in life.

1949 Mike Schmidt: Hall of Fame third baseman with the Philadelphia Phillies. Perhaps the best to have ever played the game. Led national league in home runs eight times; 548 career home runs; 3-time MVP and 10-time golden glove winner.
Philadelphia is the only city in the world where you can experience the thrill of victory and the agony of reading about it the next day.

September 28

1820 Friedrich Engels: German socialist and collaborator with Karl Marx on *The Communist Manifesto.* Engels completed Marx's *Das Kapital* after Marx's death.
From the first day to this, sheer greed was the driving force of civilization.

1841 Georges Clemenceau: French politician and statesman. Helped overthrow Napoleon III. A defender of Alfred Dreyfuss. Premier (1906–9 and 1917–20).
War is a series of catastrophes which result in victory.

1856 Kate Douglas Wiggin: American editor and novelist. Best known for *Rebecca of Sunnybrook Farm.* Also wrote: *A Cathedral Courtship* and *Ladies in Waiting.*
Most of all the other beautiful things in life come by twos and threes, by dozens and hundreds. Plenty of roses, stars, sunsets, rainbows, brothers and sisters, aunts and cousins, but only one mother in the whole world.

1887 Avery Brundage: American sports figure. President of U.S. Olympic Committee (1929–53). President of the International Olympic Committee (1952–73). Champion of the superiority of amateur sports.

Sport must be amateur or it is not sport. Sports played professionally are entertainment.

1909 Al Capp: U.S. cartoonist. Creator of "Li'l Abner," a comic strip noted for broad satire of the mores and politics of the country.
Abstract art is a product of the untalented, sold by the unprincipled to the utterly bewildered.

1915 Ethel Rosenberg: With her husband Julius, the first American civilians executed for espionage. Although a dedicated Communist, there is serious doubt that she actually was a spy. Her last words:
We are the first victims of American fascism.

1934 Brigitte Bardot: French actress. A blonde sex-kitten as a pouting child-woman in films directed by her husband Roger Vadim: *And God Created Woman* and *The Bride Is Much Too Beautiful.*
Men are beasts, and even beasts don't behave as they do.

September 29

1547 Miguel de Cervantes [Saavedra]: Spanish novelist, dramatist and poet. His reputation as one of history's greatest novelists rests almost entirely on *Don Quixote* and twelve short stories known as the *Exemplary Tales.*
There are only two families in the world, the Haves and the Have-Nots.

1758 Lord Horatio Nelson: British naval commander. Defeated French in the Battle of the Nile (1798). Killed during the Battle of Trafalgar, in which the French fleet was destroyed. His long romance with Lady Emma Hamilton caused a scandal.
...In case signals can neither be seen or perfectly understood, no captain can do very wrong if he places his ship alongside that of the enemy.

1810 Elizabeth Cleghorn Gaskell: English novelist. Her stories were of English country life and the problems of the working class. Author of *Mary Barton, Ruth* and *North and South*.

I'll not listen to reason. Reason always means what someone else has to say.

1901 Enrico Fermi: Italian-born U.S. physicist. Pioneered the study of neutrons and neutron bombardment. Led the group which made the first man-made nuclear chain reaction at the University of Chicago's Stagg Field in 1942. Nobel Prize (1938).

Whatever nature has in store for mankind, unpleasant as it may be, men must accept, for ignorance is never better than knowledge.

1935 Jerry Lee Lewis: American rock 'n' roll singer and piano player. Biggest hit: "Great Balls of Fire." Married seven times. Cousin of evangelist Jimmy Swaggart and country and western singer Mickey Gilley.

Either be hot or cold. If you are lukewarm, the Lord will spew you forth from his mouth.

1942 Madeline Kahn: U.S. actress in crazy, quirky roles. Oscar nominations for *Paper Moon* and *Blazing Saddles*. Also appeared in *Young Frankenstein* and *High Anxiety*.

It's acceptable for men to act the fool. When women try, they're considered aggressive and opinionated.

1943 Lech Wałesa: Polish political leader and labor union official. Founded Solidarity, the only independent trade union in the Communist world (1980). Won Nobel Peace Prize (1983). Elected president in 1990.

Freedom is a food which must be carefully administered when people are too hungry for it.

September 30

1861 William Wrigley, Jr.: American manufacturer. Founded Wrigley chewing gum empire. President of the company from 1891 to 1932. Owner of the Chicago Cubs baseball team.

When two men in business always agree, one of them is unnecessary.

1895 Lewis Milestone: Russian-born American director and screenwriter. Best known films: *All Quiet on the Western Front, The Front Page, Of Mice and Men* and *A Walk in the Sun.* When told by a studio executive that the ending of *All Quiet on the Western Front* was too depressing:

I've got your happy ending. We'll let the Germans win the war.

1921 Deborah Kerr: English actress. Oscar nomination for *Edward, My Son, From Here to Eternity, The King and I, Heaven Knows, Mr. Allison, Separate Tables* and *The Sundowners.*

I don't think anybody knew I could act until I put on a bathing suit in From Here to Eternity.

1922 Jesse Unruh: American political leader. Powerful and influential California assemblyman. Aided the presidential campaigns of John F. Kennedy and Robert Kennedy.

Money is the mother's milk of politics.

1924 Truman Capote: American author and playwright. Wrote of alienated individuals in slightly surreal stories. Works include: *Other Voices, Other Rooms, Breakfast at Tiffany's* and *In Cold Blood.*

Finishing a book is just like you took a child out in the yard and shot it.

1928 Elie Wiesel: Hungarian-born journalist and author. A survivor of Auschwitz concentration camp, his books deal with the Holocaust. In 1986 he won the Nobel Peace Prize.

Because of indifference, one dies before one actually dies.

1931 Angie Dickinson: Long-legged, beautiful U.S. actress. Best known for her television series "Police Woman" (1974-78) and films *Rio Bravo, The Sins of Rachel Cade* and *Dressed to Kill.*

I dress for women and I undress for men.

October 1

1799 Rufus Choate: American lawyer, author, statesman and notable orator. Leader of the New England bar. Preeminent among

American advocates. Elected to Hall of Fame of Great Americans (1915).

The final end of government is not to exercise restraint but to do good.

1837   Robert Gould Shaw: Young white U.S. colonel chosen to lead the 54th Regiment of Massachusetts Volunteer Infantry, the first unit of black soldiers during the Civil War. He and most of his command were killed in a suicide charge against South Carolina's impregnable harbor fortification, Fort Wagner.

We are fighting for men and women whose poetry has not yet been written.

1893   Faith Baldwin: American writer of popular romantic novels, including: *Office Wife, Skyscraper, They Who Love* and *Evening Star.*

Time is a dressmaker specializing in alterations.

1904   Vladimir Horowitz: Russian-born American virtuoso pianist. Best know for his interpretations of Rachmaninoff, Chopin, Liszt, Prokofiev, Scriabin and Schumann. Multi–Emmy winner for classical recordings.

Never be afraid to dare. And never imitate. Play without asking advice.

1907   Helen Brown Lawrenson: American editor and author. First woman to write for *Esquire* magazine with her article "Latins Are Lousy Lovers."

Whatever else can be said about sex, it cannot be called a dignified performance.

1911   Fletcher Knebel: American author of novels *Seven Days in May, Convention* and *Night of Camp David.*

It is now proved beyond a shadow of a doubt that smoking is one of the leading causes of statistics.

1924   Jimmy Carter: Democratic 39th president of the U.S. (1971–81), first to be elected from the Deep South (Georgia). The Iran hostage crisis contributed to his defeat in 1980 by Ronald Reagan. Many say he has been a better president since he left office than when he served in it.

We should live our lives as though Christ were coming this afternoon.

October 2

1847   Paul von Hindenburg: German statesman and soldier. Field Marshal during WWI, scoring brilliant victories on the Eastern Front. Second president of the Weimar Republic. Pressured into appointing Adolf Hitler as Chancellor.

In war, there is only one alternative: either you must be a hammer, or you will be made into an anvil.

1869   Mahatma Mohandas Gandhi: Indian political leader. Leader of the Indian nationalist movement against the British. Espoused nonviolent civil disobedience to achieve political and social changes. His threatened "fasts to the death" were effective because of his international reputation as a holy man. Assassinated in 1948.

Non-violence is the first article of my faith. It is also the last article of my creed.

1871   Cordell Hull: American statesman and diplomat. U.S. secretary of state (1933–44). Developed the Good Neighbor policy with Latin America. Promoted cooperation with the Soviet Union against Hitler. Nobel Peace Prize (1945).

War is the great failure of man.

1879   Wallace Stevens: American poet. Pulitzer Prize winner for his *Collected Poems* (1954). Spent nearly forty years with the Hartford Accident and Indemnity Co., serving as vice president (1934–55). Other works: "Peter Quince at the Clavier," "Sunday Morning" and "Le Monocle de Mon Oncle."

The poet is the priest of the invisible.

1890   Groucho Marx: Fast-thinking, master of the ad-lib, American comedian, who with his brothers Chico and Harpo (sometimes Zeppo) were delightfully zany in Broadway shows and films. Groucho hosted the popular television quiz show, "You Bet Your Life." Films: *Animal Crackers, Duck Soup, A Night at the Opera* and *A Day at the Races.*

Politics is the art of looking for trouble, finding it everywhere, diagnosing it incorrectly and applying the wrong remedies.

1904   Graham Greene: English novelist, short-story writer and playwright. Novels are psychological studies, adventure thrillers and stories of moral dilemmas. Works: *The Power and the Glory, The Heart of the Matter* and *Our Man in Havana.*

There is always one moment in childhood when the door is open and lets the future in.

1951   Sting [Gordon Sumner]: English singer, songwriter and actor. Bass guitarist for the Police. Took his nickname from the yellow and black jersey he wore. He appeared as Baron Frankenstein in the film *The Bride.*

Success always necessitates a degree of ruthlessness. Given the choice of friendship or success, I'd probably choose success.

October 3

1800   George Bancroft: American historian and diplomat. Called the "Father of American History." Author of the 10-volume *A History of the United States.* U.S. secretary of state (1845–46). Minister to England (1846–49).

Where the people possess no authority, their rights obtain no respect.

1858   Eleanora Duse: Internationally acclaimed Italian stage actress. A rival of Sarah Bernhardt. She had a thousand faces and provided psychological motivation for her roles. Her great powers were best shown in the works of her lover Gabriele D'Annunzio and Henrik Ibsen.

Suspicion is the friendship one actress has for another.

1897   Louis Aragon: French poet, novelist and critic. Early on associated with Cubism and Dada. Influenced by surrealism to write *Nightwalker.* After becoming a Communist, he devoted his art to social revolution. Poem: "The Red Front." Novel: *The Century Was Young.*

The function of genius is to furnish cretins with ideas twenty years later.

1898   Leo McCarey: U.S. director, producer and screenwriter. Oscars for directing *The Awful Truth* and both for directing and writing *Going My Way.* Others: *Duck Soup, Ruggles of Red Gap* and *An Affair to Remember.*

I never made a picture that fell off the screen.

1899   Gertrude Berg: American comedic actress and writer. Wrote and starred (as Molly Goldberg) in the radio and television series "The Goldbergs." Won 1959 Tony award for her performance in "A Majority of One."

I'm a firm believer in anxiety and the power of negative thinking.

1900   Thomas C. Wolfe: American author. His autobiographical novel *Look Homeward Angel* was rejected by publishers until Maxwell Perkins of Scribner's, recognizing its virtues, helped cut the *and the River* and *You Can't Go Home Again.*

Loneliness ... is and always has been the central and inevitable experience of every man.

1925   Gore Vidal: U.S. novelist, playwright and critic. Novels: *Myra Breckinridge* and *Burr.* Screenplay: *Suddenly Last Summer.* Television play: *Visit to a Small Planet.* Play: *The Best Man.*

All children alarm their parents, if only because you are forever expecting to encounter yourself.

October 4

1542   St. Robert Bellarmine: Italian cardinal and theologian. Writer and lecturer on controversial subjects. Considered to be one of the most powerful defenders of the teachings of the Roman Catholic Church.

Freedom of belief is pernicious, it is nothing but the freedom to be wrong.

1814   Jean François Millet: French painter. Painted landscapes and rural scenes. Among his best known works are *Angelus* and *The Man with the Hoe.*

It is the treating of the commonplace with the feeling of the sublime that gives to art its true power.

1884   Damon Runyon: U.S. journalist and author. Sportswriter for papers in

Denver, San Francisco and New York. Wrote syndicated sports column, "Both Barrels," and more general column, "The Brighter Side."

The race is not always to the swift, nor the battle to the strong, but that's the way to bet.

1895 [Joseph F.] Buster Keaton: Among the greatest screen comedians. Typically portrayed a dignified, restrained young man with a deadpan "stone face." Silent movies: *Sherlock, Jr., The General, Steamboat Bill, Jr.,* and *The Cameraman.*

People may talk it up or talk it down, but my face has been a valuable trademark for me during my sixty years in show business.

1928 Alvin Toffler: U.S. author. Wrote: *The Culture Consumers, Future Shock* and *The Third Wave.*

Future shock ... the shattering stress and disorientation that we induce in individuals by subjecting them to too much change in too short a time.

1943 H. Rap Brown: American civil rights leader. Chairman SNCC in 1967. Converted to Islam while in prison.

I say violence is necessary. It is as American as cherry pie.

1946 Susan Sarandon: Talented and intelligent U.S. actress with great large expressive eyes. Most memorable in *The Rocky Horror Show, Pretty Baby, Atlantic City* (Oscar), *Bull Durham, Thelma and Louise* and *Dead Man Walking* (Oscar).

It is not difficult to be successful. But it is difficult to remain human.

October 5

1703 Jonathan Edwards: American Presbyterian clergyman, educator, philosopher and theologian. Third president of Princeton. His theology was highly influenced by Newtonian science and Lockean psychology. Best known sermon: "Sinners in the Hands of an Angry God."

Resolved, never to do anything which I should be afraid to do if it were the last hour of my life.

1713 Denis Diderot: French encyclopedist, materialistic philosopher, novelist, satirist, dramatist and art critic. Mainly known for having compiled and edited with others, the 28-volume *Encyclopédie ou Dictionnaire Raisonné des Sciences, des Arts et des Métiers.*

Ignorance is less remote from truth than prejudice.

1879 John Erskine: American educator, author and musician. English professor at Columbia, 28 years. Students included Mark Van Doren, Mortimer J. Adler, Clifton Fadiman and Rexford G. Tugwell. Works: *The Private Life of Helen of Troy, The Delight of Great Books, What Is Music?* and *My Life as a Teacher.*

Nature is everything man is born to, and art is the difference he makes in it.

1882 Robert H. Goddard: U.S. physicist and rocketry pioneer. In 1919, published the classic report, *A Method of Reaching Extreme Altitudes,* in which he predicted the breaking free of earth's gravity and traveling to the moon and beyond. Had more than 200 rocketry patents.

It is difficult to say what is impossible, for the dream of yesterday is the hope of today and the reality of tomorrow.

1908 Joshua Logan: U.S. producer and director of many Broadway shows, including *Mr. Roberts, South Pacific* and *Fanny.* Directed films *Bus Stop, Picnic* and *Paint Your Wagon.*

Music has a poetry of its own, and that poetry is called melody.

1936 Václav Havel: Czech dissident dramatist and political leader. Obie winner for "The Increased Difficulty of Concentration." First freely elected president of Czechoslovakia in 55 years (1990).

Even a simple, apparently powerless man who dares to tell the truth and is prepared to sacrifice his life wields surprisingly more power than thousands of anonymous voters under different conditions.

1959 Maya Lin: American architect. Designed the Vietnam Memorial in Washington, D.C.

It terrified me to have an idea that was solely mine to be no longer a part of my mind, but totally public.

October 6

1820 **Jenny Lind:** "The Swedish Nightingale." Swedish opera star. Sang her first opera at age 18. Brought to the U.S. by P.T. Barnum.
My voice is still the same, and this makes me beside myself with joy! Oh, Mon Dieu, when I think what I might be able to do with it.

1868 **George H. Lorimer:** American editor. Literary editor-in-chief for *Saturday Evening Post* (1899–1937). Author of *Old Gorgon Graham, The False Gods* and *Jack Spurlock, Prodigal.*
Putting off an easy thing makes it hard, and putting off a hard one makes it impossible.

1887 **"Le Corbusier" [Charles Edouard Jeanneret]:** Swiss architect and city planner. A founder of modern fundamentalist architecture. Buildings: Palace of the League of Nations, Geneva; National Museum of Western Art, Tokyo; and Carpenter Visual Art Center, Harvard University.
A house is a machine for living in.

1905 **Helen Willis Moody:** American tennis player. Won eight Wimbledon, seven U.S. and four French single titles (1923-38). Female Athlete of the Year (1935).
If you see a tennis player who looks as if he is working very hard then that means he isn't very good.

1908 **Carole Lombard:** U.S. actress. Beautiful blonde comedienne in films *Twentieth Century, My Man Godfrey* (Oscar nomination), *Nothing Sacred* and *To Be or Not to Be.* At the time of her death in a plane crash she was married to Clark Gable. Previously married to William Powell.
Hollywood is where they write the alibis before they write the story.

1914 **Thor Heyerdahl:** Norwegian entomologist and adventurer. His Kon-Tiki expedition established the possibility that Polynesians may have originated in South America. His Ra expedition confirmed the possibility that pre–Columbia cultures may have been influenced by Egyptian civilization.

Progress is man's ability to complicate simplicity.

1929 **Shana Alexander:** U.S. author and journalist. Appeared in the "Count Counterpoint" of television's "60 Minutes" (1975–79). Columnist of "The Feminine Eye" for *Life* (1961–64). Editor of *McCall's* (1969–71).
The sad truth is that excellence makes people nervous.

October 7

1849 **James Whitcomb Riley:** "The Hoosier Poet." Wrote poems rich in the habits, speech and outlook of rural and small-town Indiana folk. Poems: "When the Frost Is on the Punkin," "The Old Swimming Hole," "Little Orphant Annie" and "The Raggedy Man."
The ripest peach is highest on the tree.

1879 **Joe Hill:** Swedish-born U.S. labor organizer and songwriter. Joined the Industrial Workers of the World (IWW) in 1910. Took part in organizing and in strike activities for the radial labor organization. Songs: "The Preacher and the Slave" and "There Is Power in Union." Executed in Utah for a murder he probably didn't commit.
I die like a true rebel. Don't waste any time mourning—organize!

1885 **Niels Bohr:** Danish physicist. Revolutionized physics by combining elements of quantum theory with classic mechanics. Worked on U.S. atom bomb project. Organized first Atoms for Peace conference (1955). Nobel Prize in physics (1922).
An expert is a man who has made all the mistakes which can be made in a narrow field.

1907 **Helen Clark MacInnes:** Scottish-born American writer. Author of *Above Suspicion, Decision at Delphi, Home Is the Hunter* and *The Salzburg Connection.*
It's the educated barbarian who is the worst; he knows what to destroy.

1927 **R.D. Laing:** Scottish psychiatrist and author. Counterculture guru in

the 1960s. Held controversial views of schizophrenia, outlined in his book *The Divided Self.*
Insanity—a perfectly rational adjustment to an insane world.

1931 **Desmond Tutu:** South African Black archbishop. First native African Anglican bishop of Johannesburg. Nobel Peace winner (1984).
You don't choose your family. They are God's gift to you, as you are to them.

1934 **Inamu Baraka:** American poet and playwright, born LeRoi Jones. Published his first book of poems, *Preface to a Twenty-Volume Suicide Note* (1961). Won an Obie Award for the play *The Dutchman* (1964). Active in organizing blacks for social and political action.
A man is either free or he is not. There cannot be any apprenticeship for freedom.

October 8

1713 **Alison Cockburn:** Scottish poet. Famous for her wit and brilliance as a hostess. Queen of Endinburgh society for 60 years. Best known for the first version of the ballad "The Flowers of the Forest."
I've seen the smiling of Fortune beguiling, / I've felt all its favours and found its decay.

1833 **E.C. [Edmund Clarence] Stedman:** American author, poet, journalist and editor. War correspondent of the New York World (1861-63). He published *Victorian Poets, Poets of America* and *Nature of Poetry.*
Fashion is a potency in art, making it hard to judge between the temporary and the lasting.

1873 **Alfred Jarry:** French dramatist and novelist. Most famous for epic burlesques *Ubu Roi* and its sequels and the novel *The Supermale.*
God is the tangential point between zero and infinity.

1895 **Juan Perón:** Argentine political leader. Virtual dictator as president (1946-55). Wife Evita, beloved by the peasants, died of cancer. Attempted to make Argentina economically self-sufficient. Repressed opposition, overthrown and forced into exile. Returned in 1973. Followed as president by his second wife, Isabel.
We are no longer interested in elections except as a means to reach our objectives.

1912 **John W. Gardner:** U.S. educator, public official and reformer. President of the Carnegie Foundation for the Advancement of Teaching. U.S. secretary of health, education and welfare (1965), directing Lyndon B. Johnson's various "war on poverty" programs. Organized and Chaired "Common Cause," a citizens' lobbying group.
A good man isn't good for everything.

1922 **Christian N. Barnard:** South African surgeon. Performed first heart transplant in 1967. Arthritis prevented him from further operations.
Suffering isn't ennobling, recovery is.

1941 **Jesse Jackson:** U.S. clergyman and civil rights leader. Joined Martin Luther King in civil rights marches and protests. Named national director of Operation Breadbasket. Charismatic orator sought Democratic presidential nomination.
Our flag is red, white and blue, but our nation is a rainbow—red, yellow, brown, black and white—and we're all precious in God's sight.

October 9

1884 **Helene Deutsch:** American psychologist. Pioneer in the Freudian movement. Last of the original Freudians. Author of *The Psychology of Women.*
After all, the ultimate goal of all research is not objectivity, but truth.

1890 **Aimee Semple McPherson:** U.S. religious leader. Best known female evangelist of her day. Founded the International Church of the Foursquare Gospel. Built the Angelus Temple in Los Angeles, serving as its minister (1923–44).
O Hope! dazzling, radiant Hope!—What a change thou bringest to the hopeless; brightening the darkened paths, and cheering the lonely way.

1899 **Bruce Catton:** U.S. historian and journalist. Reporter for several newspapers. Information director for several governmental agencies. Author of *Mr. Lincoln's Army, A Stillness at Appomattox* and *America Goes to War.*

What both the reporter and the historians are really looking at are people on the march ... the sum of many small victories won by individual human beings is a victory for all of us.

1900 **Alistair Sim:** British actor. For many the definitive Ebenezer Scrooge, in a classic 1951 film. Former elocution professor was delightful in eccentric roles in *Laughter in Paradise, The Belles of St. Trinan's* and *The Green Man.*

It was revealed to me many years ago with conclusive certainly that I was a fool and that I had always been a fool. Since then I have been as happy as any man has a right to be.

1908 **Jacques Tati:** French director and actor. Best known for his delightful *Mr. Hulot's Holiday,* in which he created a gangling, awkward character who had a series of misadventures in a gadget-obsessed world. Other films: *Mon Oncle* and *Playtime.*

It is necessary for my characters to evolve, not for my camera to move.

1934 **Jill Ker Conway:** Australian-born U.S. historian, educator and writer. Author of *The Female Experience in 18th and 19th Century America: A Guide to the History of American Women.*

It is essential for women students to have female role models of innovative, progressive professors. They don't get this in seven-eighths of their courses.

1940 **John Lennon:** English musician, singer and songwriter. Founding member of the Beatles. He and Paul McCartney wrote most of the hit songs of the group. Songs after the groups breakup: "Imagine" and "Starting Over." He was murdered December 8, 1980.

Life is what happens while you are making other plans.

October 10

1791 **Henry L. Ellsworth:** American public official and agriculturist. First commissioner of patents.

The advancement of the arts from year to year taxes our credulity, and seems to presage the arrival of that period when human improvement must end.

1813 **Giuseppi Verdi:** Italian musician and composer. Before turning to writing opera he was a farmer. He had a genius for dramatic, lyric and tragic stage music. His operas include: *Rigoletto, Il Trovatore, La Traviata, Aïda* and *Otello.*

I adore [music] ... when I am alone with my notes, my heart pounds and the tears stream from my eyes, and my emotions and my joys are too much to bear.

1895 **Lin Yutang:** Chinese-born government official, writer, speaker, philosopher and university chancellor. Author of *My Country and My People, Wisdom of Confucius* and *On the Wisdom of America.*

... Science is but a sense of curiosity about life, religion is a sense of wonder at life, art is a taste for life, philosophy is an attitude toward life.

1900 **Helen Hayes:** American stage and screen actress. Her legitimate stage triumphs include: *Caesar and Cleopatra, What Every Woman Knows, Victoria Regina* and *Mrs. McThing.* Oscar winner for *The Sin of Madelon Claudet* and *Airport.*

If you rest, you rust.

1913 **Claude Simon:** French novelist. The absence of story, time and punctuation is his hallmark. Most important novels, *The Wind* and *The Road to Flanders.* Nobel Prize for literature (1985).

To begin with, our perspective of the world is deformed, incomplete. Then our memory is selective. Finally, writing transforms.

1930 **Harold Pinter:** English playwright, screenwriter, novelist, poet, director and actor. Plays: *The Caretaker* and *The Dumb Waiter.* Oscar nominated for screenplays *The French Lieutenant's Woman* and *Betrayal.*

In other words, apart from the known and the unknown, what else is there?

1946 Ben Vereen: U.S. entertainer. Tony winner for *Pippin* (1972). Probably best known as *Chicken George*, in television miniseries, *Roots*. Made a comeback from serious injuries incurred in a car accident to appear in Broadway's *Jelly's Last Jam*.
At the end of the day, give up your worries and give thanks for the journey.

October 11

1872 Harlan Fiske Stone: U.S. jurist. Associate justice of the Supreme Court (1925–41) and chief justice (1941–46). A liberal who believed in judicial restraint.
I have nothing personally against the world in which I grew up.... But I don't see why I should let my social predilections interfere with experimental legislation that is not prohibited by the Constitution.

1884 Eleanor Roosevelt: Wife of Franklin D. Roosevelt, 32nd U.S. president. Affectionately called "The First Lady of the World." She often served as her husband's legs and ears, bringing to his attention the problems of the nation that she saw in her far flung-travels. Wrote the column, "My Day." U.S. representative to the U.N. (1945, 1947–52, 1961). Named "World's Most Influential Woman."
The giving of love is an education in itself.

1897 Nathan Twining: U.S. Air Force General. Directed air assaults against Solomon Islands and New Guinea during WWII. Chairman, Joint Chiefs of Staff (1957–60).
If our air forces are never used, they have achieved their finest goal.

1906 Charles Revson: U.S. cosmetics manufacturer. Served as president, chairman and CEO of Revlon, Inc., which he founded in 1932, the largest cosmetics and fragrance manufacturer.
I don't meet competition. I crush it.

1910 Joseph Alsop, Jr.: U.S. political columnist. With his brother, Stewart Alsop, wrote the syndicated column "Matter of Fact." Passionate anti-communist. Strong supporter of U.S. policies in Vietnam. Wrote *We Accuse* with his brother.
Gratitude, like love, is never a dependable international emotion.

1917 Thelonious Monk: American jazz pianist and composer. Formed his own big band in 1959, but mainly led his quartet. Compositions: "Straight No Chaser," "Round About Midnight," "Off Minor" and "Introspection."
There are no wrong notes.

1918 Jerome Robbins: American choreographer, dancer and ballet master and director. Choreographed film *The King and I.* Choreographed and codirected *West Side Story* (Oscar). Broadway shows include: *Gypsy* and *Fiddler on the Roof.*
I don't see why people are so amazed that ballet can entertain them. To me "ballet" means "dance," any kind of dance.

October 12

1775 Lyman Beecher: American preacher and author. Opposed Catholicism. Supported traditional Calvinism. Father of Henry Ward Beecher and Harriet Beecher Stowe. Wrote *A Plea for the West* and *Works.*
Eloquence is logic on fire.

1866 James Ramsey MacDonald: British politician and statesman. One of the founders of the British Labor Party. Became the first Labor Prime Minister in 1924. Also served 1929–34.
We hear war called murder. It is not: it is suicide.

1872 Ralph Vaughan Williams: English composer. Considered to be the most important of his generation. His music is derived from English folk and classical tradition. Operas: *Hugh the Drover* and *The Pilgrim's Progress.* Other works: *A London Symphony* and *Fantasia on Greensleeves.*
My advice to all who want to attend a lecture on music is "Don't; go to a concert instead!"

1905 **Jane Sherwood Ace:** U.S. radio actress. Starred with her writer husband Goodman Ace in the urbane domestic comedy "Easy Aces" as the slightly addled wife of long-suffering Goodman (1930-45). She was famous for her malapropisms.
Time wounds all heels.

1932 **Dick Gregory:** American stand-up comedian and political activist. Noted for his fasts in behalf of civil rights. Books: *From the Back of the Bus* and *Up from Nigger.*
Education means to bring out wisdom. Indoctrination means to push in knowledge.

1935 **Luciano Pavarotti:** Italian opera tenor. Today's best-selling classical vocalist. Has won three Grammys and one Emmy. Noted for his two concerts with Jose Carreras and Placido Domingo. Made the forgettable movie, *Yes, Giorgio.*
I must enjoy myself when I sing....If everything is lovingly done, everything will be all right.

1935 **William Raspberry:** American journalist. Syndicated columnist for the *Washington Post.* Writes on minority issues.
We must teach our young girls to honor and respect the temple of their bodies. We must make our boys understand the difference between making a baby and being a father.

October 13

1853 **Lillie Langtry:** British actress. First society woman to go on the stage. Famed for her beauty. Mistress of Edward VII. Her autobiography, *The Days I Knew.* Toured the United States. Langtry, Texas, is named for her.
Anyone who limits his vision to his memories of yesterday is already dead.

1885 **Harry Hershfield:** American cartoonist and humorist. Created comic strip "Abie the Agent." Panelist on the long running radio program "Can You Top This?"
New York is a city where everyone mutinies but no one deserts.

1902 **Anna Bontemps:** American writer. Author of *God Sends Sunday, Pogo and Fifina* (with Langston Hughes), *Story of the Negro* and *Hold Fast to Dreams.*
You don't want to stand on a corner and be told to get off it when you got nowhere to go. And we want somewhere else to go.

1909 **Herblock:** Pen name of Herbert L. Block. U.S. cartoonist and author. Became editorial cartoonist with the *Washington Post* in 1946. Books: *Herblock's Here and Now, Herblock's Special for Today* and *Straight Herblock.*
If it's good, they'll stop making it.

1925 **Lenny Bruce:** American entertainer and comedian. Constantly arrested for saying things in clubs and concerts that are considered tame today on prime-time television. His life was the subject of a biopic starring Dustin Hoffman.
Every day people are straying away from the church and going back to God.

1925 **Margaret Thatcher:** British politician. Britain's only woman prime minister in 800 years of parliamentary history. Served 1979–90 when she resigned.
In politics if you want anything said, ask a man. If you want anything done, ask a woman.

1970 **Nancy Kerrigan:** U.S. figure skating star. Attacked by a man with a tire iron, apparently by those who didn't wish her to be competition for skater Tonya Harding. Kerrigan captured the silver medal in 1992 Winter Olympics.
My confidence isn't bruised. Just my knee.

October 14

1644 **William Penn:** English Quaker who founded Pennsylvania and laid out the city street plan of Philadelphia. Champion of religious toleration. Wrote: *The Great Case of Liberty of Conscience.*
True silence is the rest of the mind; it is to the spirit what sleep is to the body, nourishment and refreshment.

1890 **Dwight D. Eisenhower:** "Ike." Thirty-fourth U.S. president. Held rank of five-star general in the U.S. Army; supreme allied commander in Europe. Led the invasion that defeated Germany. President of Columbia (1948–50). As U.S. president, ended Korean War. Sent troops to Little Rock, Arkansas, to force compliance with desegregation order.

An intellectual is a man who takes more words than necessary to tell more than he knows.

1894   e.e. [Edward Estlin] cummings: American poet and painter. Wrote his name and poetry always in lower case and unorthodox typography. Used a highly experimental approach to style and diction. Verses: "Portraits," "Poem, or Beauty Hurts Mr. Vinal" and "One Times One."

for life's not a paragraph / and death i think is no parenthesis.

1894   Lillian Gish: U.S. actress whose career spanned 75 years in films. "The First Lady of the Silent Screen." Deceptively frail, she possessed a vibrant spirit that the camera always caught. Silent films: *Broken Blossoms, Way Down East, Orphans of the Storm.* Appeared in several Broadway plays in the thirties. Talkies: *Duel in the Sun* and *The Night of the Hunter.*

What you get is a living; what you give is a life.

1906   Hannah Arendt: German-born U.S. political scientist. Author of *The Origins of Totalitarianism, The Human Condition* and *Men in Dark Times.* First female full professor at Princeton. Also professor at University of Chicago and the New School for Social Research.

To expect truth to come from thinking signifies that we mistake the need to know with the urge to know.

1910   John Wooden: American basketball coach. His UCLA teams won ten national titles (1964–65, 1967–73, 1975). Only member of Basketball Hall of Fame inducted as both player and coach.

Do not let what you cannot do interfere with what you can do.

1932   Bernie S. Siegel: American surgeon and self-help therapist. Author of *How to Live Between Office Visits* and *Love, Medicine and Miracles.*

Doctors are busy playing God when so few of us have the qualifications, and besides, the job is taken.

October 15

70 B.C.   Virgil: Roman poet. Most famous work is the unfinished epic poem, *The Aeneid,* about the founding of Rome. By the 3rd century his poems, considered classics even in his own time, ranked as sacred books.

Death tickles my ear, "Live," he says, "I am coming."

1830   Helen Hunt Jackson: American author. Throughout most of her career signed her works as "Saxe Holm" and "H.H." Had a deep sympathy for American Indians. Works: *A Century of Dishonor* and *Ramona.*

Words are less needful to sorrow than to joy.

1844   Friedrich Nietzsche: German philosopher, classical scholar and poet. Most famous for his theory of the "superman" which he developed in *Thus Spake Zarathustra.* Other works: *Beyond Good and Evil, The Birth of Tragedy* and *Ecce Homo.*

Man is a rope stretched between the animal and the Superman—a rope over an abyss.

1881   P.G. [Pelham Grenville] Wodehouse: English writer and humorist. His whimsical novels featured the Honorable Bertie Wooster and Jeeves his valet. Books: *Leave It to Psmith, Jeeves* and *French Leave.*

So always look for the silver lining / And try to find the sunny side of life.

1908   John Kenneth Galbraith: Candian-born U.S. economist, educator, government official and author. Harvard professor. Ambassador to India, Chairman of the Americans for Democratic Action. Author of *American Capitalism: The Concept of Countervailing Power, The Affluent Society* and *The New Industrial State.*

Politics is not the art of the possible. It consists in choosing between the disastrous and the unpalatable.

1920 **Mario Puzo:** American novelist. Author of *The Godfather*. Won Oscars for the screenplays of *The Godfather I* and *The Godfather II*.
A lawyer with his briefcase can steal more than a hundred men with guns.

1924 **Lee A. Iacocca:** U.S. business executive. Son of Italian immigrant parents. Advanced from engineer to president of Ford Motor Co. When fired by Henry Ford, II, took over bankrupted Chrysler Corporation in 1979. Wrote best-selling *Iaccoca*.
People want economy and they will pay any price to get it.

October 16

1758 **Noah Webster:** U.S. teacher and publisher. Wrote best-selling grammar and spelling books. His *American Dictionary of the English Language*, published in 1828, took 25 years to write.
Language, as well as the facility of speech, was the immediate gift of God.

1854 **Oscar Wilde:** Irish-born poet, novelist and playwright. Advocated "Art for Art's Sake." Eccentric dresser with many idiosyncrasies. Accused of homosexual practices, tried, convicted and imprisoned. Works: *The Picture of Dorian Gray, Lady Windermere's Fan, The Importance of Being Earnest* and *The Ballad of Reading Gaol*.
We are all in the gutter, but some of us are looking at the stars.

1886 **David Ben-Gurion:** Polish-born Israeli statesman. First prime minister of Israel (1948–52 and 1954–63). Called the "Father of the Nation." Chaired the World Zionist Organization during the struggle to create the nation of Israel.
In Israel in order to be a realist you must believe in miracles.

1888 **Eugene G. O'Neill:** American playwright. Winner of four Pulitzer prizes. First U.S. playwright awarded a Nobel Prize for literature. Plays: *The Emperor Jones, Anna Christie, Ah, Wilderness* and *Long Day's Journey Into Night.*

The tragedy of man is perhaps the only significant thing about him.

1898 **William O. Douglas:** U.S. jurist. Liberal associate justice of the Supreme Court. His tenure of 36 years was the longest of anyone who served on the court. Advocated a strong interpretation of the Bill of Rights. Author of *A Living Bill of Rights* and *Of Men and Mountains.*
The right to be let alone is indeed the beginning of all freedom.

1927 **Günter Grass:** German novelist and playwright. Literary spokesman for Germans who grew up during the Nazi dictatorship. Author of *The Tin Drum, Cat and Mouse* and *Dog Years.*
The job of a citizen is to keep his mouth open.

1931 **Charles W. Colson:** U.S. presidential advisor to Richard Nixon. A Watergate conspirator who served 18 months in prison for obstructing justice. Became a born-again Christian.
The first 20 stories written about a public figure set the tone for the next 2,000 and it is almost impossible to reverse it.

October 17

1864 **Elinor Glyn:** English novelist. Her best-selling romantic novels, considered daring and naughty at the time, were turned into film vehicles for Clara Bow. Author of *Three Weeks* and *It.*
There are three things a woman ought to look—straight as a dart, supple as a snake, and proud as a tiger lily.

1909 **Cozy Cole:** American jazz drummer. Lead drummer for Cab Calloway and Louis Armstrong bands. Biggest hit: *Topsy II.*
The more you study, the more you find out you don't know, but the more you study, the closer you come.

1915 **Arthur Miller:** American playwright and author. Pulitzer Prize for his best play *Death of a Salesman*. Others: *The Crucible, A View from the Bridge* and *After* *the Fall.* Wrote the screenplay for *The Misfits,* starring Marilyn Monroe to whom he had been married.

An era can be said to end when its brave illusions are exhausted.

1917   **Alfred Khan:** U.S. government official. Chairman of the Council on Wage and Price Stability in the Carter administration.

If you can't explain what you're doing in simple English, you are probably doing something wrong.

1918   **Rita Hayworth:** Beautiful red-headed actress and dancer. Films: *Only Angels Have Wings, Blood and Sand, Gilda, Pal Joey* and *Separate Tables.* Among her five husbands were Orson Welles and Aly Khan. Died of Alzheimer's disease.

Men fall in love with Gilda and wake up with me.

1930   **Jimmy Breslin:** U.S. author and Pulitzer-winning columnist for several New York newspapers. Author of *Can't Anybody Around Here Play This Game?, Table Money* and *The Gang That Couldn't Shoot Straight.*

Nobody ever said you have to torture life to produce history.

1938   **Evel Knievel:** U.S. daredevil motorcycle stunt man. Attempted to sky-cycle jump Snake River Canyon, Idaho. Has broken hundreds of bones attempting his dangerous stunts.

Promoters are just guys with two pieces of bread looking for a piece of cheese.

October 18

1547   **Justus Lipsius:** Belgian humanist, classical scholar and political theorist. Established himself as the leading editor of Latin prose texts. Produced editions of Tacitus and Seneca.

He who does not desire or fear the uncertain day or capricious fate, is equal to the gods above and loftier than mortals.

1785   **Thomas Love Peacock:** English writer, poet and satirical novelist. Novels include: *Headlong Hall, Nightmare Abbey*

and *Crotchet Castle.* Caricatured contemporary figures as thinly disguised eccentrics involved in often ridiculous conversation.

It is well, it works well, let well alone.

1859   **Henri Bergson:** French-born philosopher. The basic premise of his intellectual system is a faith in direct intuition as a means of obtaining knowledge. Nobel Prize for literature (1927). Wrote *Time and Free Will, Laughter* and *The Creative Mind.*

Think like a man of action, act like a man of thought.

1904   **A.J. [Abbott Joseph] Liebling:** American journalist and author. On the staff of *The New Yorker* (1935–69). Books: *Back Where I Came From, The Wayward Pressman* and *Chicago: The Second City.*

People everywhere confuse / What they read in newspapers with news.

1919   **Pierre Trudeau:** Canadian politician. Colorful two-time liberal Canadian prime minister (1969–79 and 1980–84).

Canada is a country whose main exports are hockey players and cold fronts. Our main imports are baseball players and acid rain.

1925   **Melina Mercouri:** Greek actress. Greece's minister of culture before her death. Wife of American director Jules Dassin who directed her in her best known film *Never on Sunday.*

I thought it was death I was afraid of, but now I know my worst fear is that I should no longer be loved.

1956   **Martina Navratilova:** Czechoslovakinan-born tennis star. Holds the record for career singles championships in professional tennis, 158 tournament titles. Number one player in the world 7 times. Has 9 Wimbledon singles titles, 18 Grand Slam singles titles and 37 Grand Slam doubles titles.

I hope when I stop, people will think that somehow I mattered.

October 19

1784   **Leigh Hunt:** English journalist, essayist, poet and political radical.

Imprisoned for attacking the future George V in his one-man journal *Examiner*. Author of the poems "Abou Ben Adhem" and "Jenny Kissed Me."

Say I'm weary, say I'm sad, / Say that health and wealth have missed me. / Say I'm growing old, but add / Jenny kissed me.

1833   **Adam Linsday Gordon:** Australian poet. First to write in the Australian idiom. Author of: "Wormwood and Nightshade," "The Wayside House" and "The Rose of Yesterday."

Life is mostly froth and bubble; / Two things stand like stone; / Kindness in another's trouble, / Courage in your own.

1889   **Fannie Hurst:** American novelist, playwright, Zionist and women's rights activist. Author of best-selling novels: *Humoresque, Back Street, Imitation of Life*, each of which was made into successful women's movies.

I would rather regret what I have done rather than what I have not.

1895   **Lewis Mumford:** American social critic. Wrote on architecture and the city. Professor of humanities, Stanford and of city and regional planning at University of Pennsylvania. Author of: *Sticks and Stones, The City in History* and *The Urban Project*.

Traditionalists are pessimists about the future and optimists about the past.

1922   **Jack Anderson:** American investigative newspaper columnist. Began as a staff member for Drew Pearson. Took over Pearson's syndicated column "Washington Merry-Go-Round" when Pearson died in 1969. Author of *The Case Against Congress*.

The incestuous relationship between government and big business thrives in the dark.

1931   **John Le Carré:** Pseudonym of David John Moore Cornwell. English author of best-selling spy stories. Novels include: *The Spy Who Came in from the Cold, The Little Drummer Girl* and *The Night Manager*.

A committee is an animal with four back legs.

1938   **Renata Adler:** Italian-born American writer, film critic and philosopher. Author of: *Speedboat, A Year in the Dark* and *Reckless Disregard*.

People have been modeling their lives after films for years, but the medium is somehow unsuited to moral lessons, cautionary tales, or polemics of any kind.

October 20

1632   **Sir Christopher Wren:** English architect. He is buried under the choir of his most famous construction, St. Paul's Cathedral. A tablet on the spot bears the inscription "Si monumentum requiris, circumspice" (If thou seekest a monument, look around).

Variety of uniformities makes complete beauty.

1785   **Pauline Bonaparte:** Napoleon's favorite sister. A classical beauty of her time. Noted for her fetish for bathing, moral laxity and innumerable scandalous affairs. Asked how she could pose nude for a marble statue of her by Antonio Canova, she replied:

It was not cold. There was a fire in the studio.

1859   **John Dewey:** American educator, philosopher and author. Adherent of pragmatism. Helped inaugurate the theories and practice of progressive education. Author of: *Democracy and Education, The Theory of Inquiry* and *Problems of Man*.

Anyone who has begun to think places some portion of the world in jeopardy.

1884   **Béla Lugosi:** Hungarian-born actor. Most famous in the U.S. for portraying Dracula in 1930. Appeared in many other horror films including: *Island of Lost Souls, The Black Cat* and *The Body Snatcher*.

...The popularity of horror pictures is understandable. The screen is the ideal medium for the presentation of gruesome tales....

1900   **Wayne Morse:** American politician and lawyer. Elected to the Senate as a Republican from Oregon, he refused to support Eisenhower for the presidency and declared himself an independent. Later became a Democrat. Opposed the Vietnam War from the onset.

I will not wear another man's collar.

1917   **Bobby Locke:** South African professional golfer who offers the expert and duffer alike the excellent advice.

Drive for show. But putt for dough.

1925   **Art Buchwald:** U.S. syndicated columnist. One of the nation's best known satirists. Author of *How Much Is That in Dollars?, I Chose Capital Punishment* and *I Think I Don't Remember.*

Every time you think television has hit its lowest ebb, a new ... program comes along to make you wonder where you thought the ebb was.

October 21

1772   **Samuel Taylor Coleridge:** English poet, essayist and critic. An important spokesman for English Romanticism. Author of: *Lyrical Ballads* (with Wordsworth), "Christabel," "Kubla Khan" and "The Rime of the Ancient Mariner."

In Xanadu did Kubla Khan / A stately pleasure dome decree.

1790   **Alphonse Marie de Lamartine:** French poet, writer and statesman. First truly romantic poet in French literature. Headed the short-lived provisional government after Revolution of 1848. Overthrown by Napoleon III. Author of *Méditations poétiques* and *Histoire des Girondins.*

Man is a fallen god who remembers the heavens.

1833   **Alfred Nobel:** Swedish industrialist, inventor and philanthropist. Discovered and perfected dynamite. Left the bulk of his estate to establish Nobel prizes for peace, literature, physics, chemistry and medicine. Reportedly, there was no mathematics prize because he feared it would go to enemy G.M. Mitlag-Leffler.

Great accumulations of property should go back to the community and common purposes.

1901   **Joseph Sill Clark:** American politician. A silk-stocking Republican-turned-Democrat. First Democrat to be elected (1951) mayor of Philadelphia since 1884. Elected U.S. senator from Pennsylvania (1956).

A leader should not get too far in front of the troops or he will be shot in the ass.

1917   **[John B.] Dizzy Gillespie:** U.S. jazz trumpeter, bandleader, composer and arranger. Known for bullfrog-cheek playing style. Accidentally bent his horn in 1953, and continued to play it that way, claiming he could hear it better. A leader of the Bebop movement. Compositions: "Night in Tunisia," "Groovin' High" and "Blue 'n' Boogie."

Be as you are and hope that it's right.

1929   **Urusla Le Guin:** U.S. science fiction writer and literary critic. Author of *Left Hand of Darkness, Malafreno* and *The Lathe of Heaven.*

Great self-destruction follows upon unfounded fear.

1956   **Carrie Fisher:** U.S. actress, author and script doctor. Daughter of Eddie Fisher and Debbie Reynolds. Films include the *Star Wars* trilogy. Wrote the autobiographical *Postcards from the Edge,* movie version filmed with Meryl Streep.

Females get hired along procreative lines. After 40, we're kind of cooked.

October 22

1811   **Franz Liszt:** Hungarian pianist and composer. Creator of the modern form of the symphonic poem. Innovating genius of modern piano technique. Compositions: "Fantasy," "Reminiscence," "Les Préludes" and 20 "Hungarian Rhapsodies."

What is our life but a succession of preludes to that unknown song whose first solemn note is sounded by death?

1887   **John Reed:** American journalist, poet and revolutionary. An eyewitness to the Russian Revolution of 1917. Wrote the account *Ten Days That Shook the World.* Became a close associate of Lenin. Only American buried in Red Square, Moscow.

Who that has known thee but shall burn / In exile 'till he come again / To do the bitter will, O stern / Moon of the tide of men!

1919   **Doris Lessing:** English novelist and short-story writer. Her *The Golden Notebook*, an experimental novel about a woman writer's struggle to discover the meaning of "self," has become a classic of feminist literature. Also wrote *The Grass Is Singing* and the series *The Children of Violence.*

In university they don't tell you that the greater part of the law is learning to tolerate fools.

1920   **Timothy Leary:** American psychologist who experimented with psychedelic drugs in the sixties. Forced to leave his position at Harvard, he became a guru to the generation.

Turn on. Tune in. Drop out.

1925   **Robert Rauschenberg:** American avant-garde artist, known for his collages and "combines," which incorporate a variety of junk splashed with paint. Sometimes categorized as a pop artist, his works include *Gloria* and *Summer Rental.*

Thinking is our greatest sport.

1930   **Dory Previn:** American composer and singer. Nominated for an Oscar for the film *The Sterile Cuckoo.* Several of her songs were inspired by the breakup of her marriage to Andre Previn, who left her for Mia Farrow.

If I can say something honest about my feelings and thoughts and problems as a minority of one, then won't it be meaningful for all the other individual minorities of one?

1943   **Catherine Deneuve:** Beautiful French actress. Has her own line of perfume. Oscar nominated for *Indochine.* Other films: *The Umbrellas of Cherbourg, Repulsion, Belle de Jour* and *The Last Metro.*

Men are good but women are magic.

October 23

1733   **Francis Jeffrey:** Literary critic and Scottish judge. Editor of *The Edinburgh Review.* Prolific and biased writer of strictures on Wordsworth, Keats and Byron.

Opinions founded on prejudice are always sustained with the greatest violence.

1844   **Sarah Bernhardt:** French actress, revered stage tragedienne. Illegitimate daughter of a Dutch prostitute. Told by her mother that she would die at an early age, she kept a coffin with her at all times, in which she slept and made love.

Life engenders life. Energy creates energy. It is by spreading oneself that one becomes rich.

1869   **John W. Heisman:** American football coach at nine colleges from 1892 to 1927, winning 185 games. Director of athletics, Downtown Athletic Club, New York City (1928–36). Trophy for Best College Player of Year is named for him.

When in doubt, punt, anyway, anywhere.

1885   **Lauren Harris:** Canadian artist, known for his simplified paintings of Canadian landscapes.

A picture can become for us a highway between a particular thing and a universal feeling.

1925   **Johnny Carson:** American television personality. Longtime host of the "Tonight Show." Emmy winner (1976, 1977, 1978 and 1979). Was a writer for television's "The Red Skelton Show" (1953–54). Frequent host of the Academy Awards show.

The difference between divorce and legal separation is that a legal separation gives a husband time to hide his money.

1940   **Pele:** Legendary Brazilian soccer player. Led Brazil to three World Cup titles (1958, 1962 and 1970). Scored 1,281 goals in 22 years.

I was born for soccer, just as Beethoven was born for music.

1942   **Michael Crichton:** American author of best-selling novels: *The Great Train Robbery, The Terminal Man, Rising Sun, Jurassic Park* and *Disclosure,* all of which have been turned into successful films.

If true computer music were ever written, it would only be listened to by other computers.

October 24

1788   Sarah Josepha Hale: American poet and magazine editor, the first woman to hold such a position. Editor of *Juvenile Miscellany* (1826–28); *Ladies Magazine* (1828-37). Best known poem is "Mary Had a Little Lamb."

The whole process of homemaking, house-keeping and cooking, which ever has been woman's special province, should be looked on as an art and a profession.

1830   Belva Ann Bennett Lockwood: American lawyer, women's rights activist, suffragist, pacifist and politician.

I do not believe in sex distinction in literature, law, politics, or trade—or that modesty and virtue are more becoming to women than to men, but wish we had more of it everywhere.

1882   Dame Sybil Thorndike: English actress who enjoyed success from 1904 on British and U.S. stages and in films from 1921. Best know for her lead role in *Saint Joan*.

I was brought up in a clergyman's household so I am a first-class liar.

1890   Mainbocher: American fashion designer born Main Rousseau Bocher. Noted for his elegant and expensive evening gowns. Editor of French *Vogue* (1923–29). Also designed uniforms for WAVES, the Girl Scouts, Red Cross and SPARS.

To be well turned out, a woman should turn her thoughts in.

1904   Moss Hart: American playwright and screenwriter. Wrote *You Can't Take It with You* and *The Man Who Came to Dinner* with George S. Kaufman. Tony winner for *My Fair Lady* (1959).

I suspect the theater is the refuge of many unhappy children.

1914   Jackie Coogan: U.S. actor who made his screen debut at 18 months. Charlie Chaplin's costar at six in *The Kid*, winning the hearts of audiences as a bright-eyed ragamuffin. Had a prolific television career, appearing in some 1400 shows. Best remembered as Uncle Fester in *The Addams Family*.

Hollywood is a lonely place to get knifed in.

1923   Denise Levertov: English-born America poet and essayist. Author of *The Double Image, The Jacob's Ladder* and collection of essays *Poet in the World*.

Life after life after life goes by / without poetry, / without seemliness, / without love.

October 25

1811   Evariste Galois: French mathematician whose genius was cruelly disregarded in his life of less than 21 years. He died in a politically motivated duel, spending the last night of his life dashing off his scientific last will and testament, which has kept generations of mathematicians busy since.

Genius is condemned by a malicious social organization to an eternal denial of justice in favor of fawning mediocrity.

1881   Pablo Picasso: Spanish artist. Founder of Cubism. Most influential painter of the 20th century. Contributed to art in the areas of painting, drawing, graphics, sculpture and theatrical design. Best known paintings: *Seated Nude, Three Musicians, Mandolin and Guitar* and *Guernica*.

We all know that art is not truth. Art is a lie that makes us realize truth.

1888   Richard E. Byrd: U.S. admiral, aviator and explorer. Made first flight over the North Pole (1926) and the South Pole (1928). Conducted five Antarctic exploration expeditions.

A man doesn't begin to attain wisdom until he recognizes that he no longer is indispensable.

1902   Henry Steele Commager: American historian. Prolific writer on a wide range of subjects. Author of *The American Mind, The Great Constitution, Crusaders for Freedom* and editor of the fifty-volume *Rise of the American Nation* series.

If our democracy is to flourish, it must have criticism; if our government is to function, it must have dissent.

1914   John Berryman: American poet. Regarded, along with Robert Lowell, as one of the "confessional poets." Author of *Poems, The Dispossessed* and *77 Dream Songs*.

We must travel in the direction of our fear.

1941   Anne Tyler: American author. Chronicler of modern American family. Author of *Morgan's Passing, Dinner at the Homesick Restaurant* and *The Accidental Tourist.*

It is very difficult to live among people you love and hold back from offering them advice.

1942   Helen Reddy: Australian-born singer and songwriter. Made her stage debut at four. Had her own television series in the early sixties. Biggest hits: "I Am Woman," "Delta Dawn" and "Angie Baby."

Women temper men. We have a good influence on them.

October 26

1759   Georges Jacques Danton: French revolutionary leader. Dominated the Commission of Public Safety after the overthrow of the monarchy. Became critical of the revolutionary for its excesses and was guillotined for treason.

In revolutions authority remains with the greatest scoundrels.

1800   Helmuth Karl, Count Von Moltke: Prussian field marshal. Headed general staff (1858–88). Reorganized Prussian Army which was victorious in the Austro-Prussian and Franco-Prussian wars, leading to German unification.

No plan survives contact with the enemy.

1846   Tennessee Celeste Claflin: American writer, editor and women's rights worker. First woman stockbroker in the United States. Cofounder of *Woodhull and Claflin's Weekly.*

The revolt against any oppression usually goes to an opposite extreme for a time; and that is right and necessary.

1886   Vincent Starrett: Canadian-born critic, editor, bibliophile and novelist. Book columnist with the *Sunday Chicago Tribune.* Books: *The Private Life of Sherlock*

Holmes and *Best Loved Books of the Twentieth Century.*

When we are collecting books, we are collecting happiness.

1911   Mahalia Jackson: American gospel and blues singer. Began recording in 1935 after being given a contract by Decca after an agent heard her singing at a funeral. Hit songs: "Move On Up a Little Higher," "Prayer Changes Things" and "We Shall Overcome."

Blues are the songs of despair, but gospel songs are the songs of hope.

1919   Mohammed Riza Pahlevi: Shah of Iran (1941–79). Pursued a course of rapid industrialization that led to unrest and his eventual overthrow. Tolerated no political opposition. Caused thousands to be arrested in the seventies.

It is no honor to be king in a country where almost everyone is desperately poor.

1948   Hillary Rodham Clinton: Wife of 42nd president of the U.S. Bill Clinton. Perhaps the most powerful first lady of all time for which she is greatly admired and greatly vilified.

Being a Cubs fan prepares you for life—and Washington.

October 27

1466   Desiderius Erasmus: Dutch humanist. First editor of the Greek version of the New Testament. Edited Greek and Latin classics. Defended reason, tolerance and faith. Opposed the notion of predestination. Author of *Praise of Folly* and *The Education of a Christian Prince.*

When I get a little money, I buy books; and if any is left, I buy food and clothes.

1858   Theodore Roosevelt: Twenty-sixth president of the United States (1901-9). As vice president became president when William McKinley was assassinated. Former colonel with the Rough Riders in Cuba during the Spanish-American War. Aggressively broke up trusts and regulated business. Acquired the Panama Canal Zone. Leading conservationist. Awarded the Nobel

Peace Prize in 1906. Lost presidential election at the head of his Progressive or "Bull Moose" Party in 1912.

Speak softly and carry a big stick.

1889 Enid Bagnold: English playwright and novelist. Author of successful novels: *Serena Blandish* and *National Velvet.* Plays: *The Chalk Garden* and *A Matter of Gravity.*

There may be no wonder in money, but, dear God, there is money in wonder.

1914 Dylan Thomas: Welsh poet, short-story writer and playwright. Created an individualistic poetic style, noted for lyrical power, puns, intricate meanings and vivid metaphors. Works: *Portrait of the Artist as a Young Dog, Deaths and Entrances, A Child's Christmas in Wales* and *Under Milk Wood.*

Do not go gentle into that good night, / Old age should burn and rave at close of day; / Rage, rage against the dying of the light.

1926 H.R. Haldeman: U.S. politician. Nixon's White House chief of staff. For his part in the Watergate cover-up he served 18 months in prison for perjury, conspiracy and obstruction of justice.

Once the toothpaste's out of the tube, it's going to be very hard to get it back in again.

1932 Sylvia Plath: American author and poet. Often termed a "confessional poet." Best known for her posthumously published volume of poetry, *Ariel,* written shortly before her suicide and her novel *The Bell Jar.*

Dying, / Is an art, like everything else, / I do it exceptionally well.

1950 Fran Lebowitz: American humorist, essayist and writer. Author of: *Social Studies, Metropolitan Life* and *Observer.*

There is no such thing as inner peace. There is only nervousness and death.

October 28

1907 Edith Head: American motion picture costume designer. Won eight Academy Awards. Nominated for many more Oscars. Some of her most notable designs are found in: *The Heiress, All About Eve, Roman Holiday* and *Sabrina.*

Good clothes are not good luck. They are the result of a pretty thoroughgoing knowledge of the people you are dressing.

1910 Francis Bacon: English artist. Painted expressionist portraits, distorted by terror. Works: *Studies After Velaquez* and *Portrait of Pope Innocent X.* Wrote and illustrated *The Good American Witch.* Did caricatures of notables and alley cats.

Existence, in a way, is so banal, that you might as well make a kind of grandeur of it, rather than be hurried into oblivion.

1914 Jonas Salk: U.S. virologist. Developed the first poliomyelitis vaccine, using dead viruses (1952–55). Founding director of the Salk Institute (1975).

I feel the greatest reward for doing is the opportunity to do more.

1926 Bowie Kuhn: American sports executive. Commissioner of Baseball (1969–84).

Baseball is beautiful ... the supreme performing art. It combines in perfect harmony the magnificent features of ballet, drama, art and ingenuity.

1929 Joan Plowright: English stage and film actress. Wife of Lord Laurence Olivier with whom she starred in *The Entertainer.* Other films: *Equus, Avalon* and *Enchanted April.* Speaking of Olivier:

There is something animal-like about him—like the King of the Jungle.

1955 William H. Gates: American corporation executive. Chairman and CEO of Microsoft Corporation, the world's largest software film. Part inventor, part entrepreneur, part-time salesman and full-time genius.

The ball bearing shouldn't be asking the driver about the grease.

1967 Julia Roberts: Lovely movie star and former model. Sister of actor Eric Roberts. Oscar nominated for *Steel Magnolias.* Other films: *Pretty Woman* and *I Love Trouble.*

You can be true to the character all you want but you've got to go home with yourself.

October 29

1740 James Boswell: Scottish biographer and diarist. Best known for his masterpiece, *The Life of Samuel Johnson, LL.D.* Also revealed to be one of the world's greatest diarists when his journal was published in the 20th century.
A page of my journal is like a cake of portable soap. A little may be diffused into a considerable portion.

1882 Jean Giraudoux: French dramatist, novelist, essayist and diplomat. Spent 30 years in the French diplomatic corps. Author of: *Tiger at the Gates, Ondine* and *The Madwoman of Chaillot.*
Little by little, the pimps have taken over the world. They don't do anything, don't make anything—they just stand there and take their cut.

1891 Fanny Brice: American actress and comedienne with the Ziegfeld Follies, Broadway, films and radio. Her biggest singing hit was "My Man." Portrayed by Barbra Streisand on Broadway and two films. Very popular as radio's "Baby Snooks."
Men always fall for frigid women because they put on the best show.

1897 Joseph G. Goebbels: German Nazi propaganda minister. He and his wife poisoned their five children and then committed suicide at Hitler's Berlin bunker towards the end of World War II.
War is the most simple affirmation of life. Suppress war and it would be like trying to suppress the processes of nature.

1910 A.J. [Alfred Jules] Ayer: British philosopher, professor and author. Books: *Language, Truth and Logic, The Problem of Knowledge* and *The Central Question of Philosophy.*
No morality can be founded on authority, even if the authority were divine.

1921 Bill Mauldin: American cartoonist and author. During WWII, created GIs "Willie" and "Joe." Pulitzer Prize winner for political cartoons (1945 and 1959). Books: *Up Front, Bill Mauldin's Army* and *I've Decided I Want My Seat Back.*
Humor is really laughing off a hurt. Grinning at misery.

1971 Winona Ryder: American actress who gave some remarkably mature performances as a teenager and has developed into a beautiful talented young woman. Films: *Beetlejuice, Heathers, Bram Stoker's Dracula* and Oscar nominated performances in *The Age of Innocence* and *Little Women.*
For my generation I know that no one knows who he is.

October 30

1735 John Adams: Second U.S. president (1797–1801). Lawyer, diplomat. Helped draft the Declaration of Independence. Helped draft the Treaty of Paris, ending the Revolutionary War. Washington's vice president. Father of John Quincy Adams, 6th U.S. president.
Fear is the foundation of most governments.

1751 Richard B. Sheridan: Irish-born English dramatist, orator and statesman. Wrote satirical comedies of manners. Works: *The Rivals, The School for Scandal* and *The Critic.*
There is not a passion so strongly rooted in the human heart as envy.

1840 William G. Sumner: American educator, sociologist and economist. Advocated free trade with sound currency. Opposed socialism. Biographer of Andrew Jackson, Alexander Hamilton and Robert Morris.
The Forgotten Man works and votes— generally he prays—but his chief business in life is to pay.

1877 Irma S. Rombauer: American author of cookbooks. Wrote the all-time best-selling *The Joy of Cooking,* first published in 1931.
Nothing stimulates the practiced cook's imagination like an egg.

1882 **William F. Halsey, Jr.:** "Bull." U.S. admiral. Commander of the Third Fleet which played a major role in the defeat of the Japanese in WWII. The Japanese surrender was signed aboard his flagship, the U.S.S. *Missouri* (1945).
Hit hard, hit fast, hit often.

1885 **Ezra Pound:** American poet, editor and critic. Chief promoter of Imagism, a poetic movement stressing free phrase rather than forced metric. Arrested for his pro–Fascist radio broadcasts from Italy during WWII. Declared mentally unstable, he was never tried for treason. Author of "Mauberley," "Cantos" and "The Spirit of Romance."
Literature is news that stays news.

1886 **Zoë Akins:** U.S. playwright, poet, novelist and screenwriter. Author of *Daddy's Gone a-Hunting, The Greeks Had a Word for It* and her dramatization of Edith Wharton's *The Old Maid*, which won a Pulitzer Prize (1935).
It is much more exquisite to be blown from the tree as a flower than to be shaken down as a shriveled and bitter fruit.

October 31

1795 **John Keats:** English poet. Probably the most talented of the English romantic poets. Died of consumption at age 25 after recovering from a suicide attempt. Author of: "Endymion," "Hyperion," Ode on a Grecian Urn" and "Ode to a Nightingale."
A thing of beauty is a joy forever; / Its loveliness increases; / It will never pass into nothingness.

1860 **Juliette Gordon Low:** American social reformer. Founded the Girl Scouts of America in Atlanta, Georgia, in 1912.
To put yourself in another's place requires real imagination, but by so doing each Girl Scout will be able to live among others happily.

1863 **William G. McAdoo:** U.S. government official and lawyer. U.S. secretary of the treasury (1913–18). Floated $18 billion in loans to finance America's WWI efforts. Founder and chairman of the Federal Reserve Board. Son-in-law of Woodrow Wilson.
It is impossible to defeat an ignorant man in argument.

1887 **Chiang Kai-Shek:** Chinese statesman and soldier. Established himself as head of state (1928–49). Fought Communists as well as the Japanese during WWII. Defeated by the Reds, resumed presidency exile on Taiwan (1949–75).
The aim we and our allies have set before us in the present war is freedom and security for humanity and its civilization.

1900 **Ethel Waters:** American actress and singer. First to sing W.C. Handy's "St. Louis Blues." Nominated for an Academy Award for *Pinky*. Other films: *Cabin in the Sky, The Member of the Wedding* and *The Sound and the Fury.* Speaking of black singers:
We are all gifted. That is our inheritance.

1930 **Michael Collins:** American astronaut. Manned the command module of *Apollo II* while Neil Armstrong and Buzz Aldrin walked on the moon.
I think a future flight should include a poet, a priest and a philosopher ... we might get a much better idea of what we saw.

1937 **Dan Rather:** American broadcast journalist. Anchorman of "The CBS Evening News" (1977–); coeditor, "60 Minutes" (1975–81). Winner of five Emmys.
News is a business, but it is also a public trust.

November 1

636 **Nicholas Boileau-Despréaux:** French poet and critic. Official royal historian. Most influential exponent of classical standards for poetry. Books: *Poetic Art* and the semi-comic *Lutrin.*
A painful burden is having nothing to do.

1871 **Stephen Crane:** American novelist, short-story writer and poet. Often called the first American author. Author of: *Maggie: A Girl of the Streets*, *The Red Badge of Courage*, *The Black Riders* and *War Is Kind*.

A man said to the universe / "Sir, I exist!" / "However," replied the universe, / "The fact has not created in me / A sense of obligation."

1880   **Sholem Asch:** Polish-born American novelist and dramatist, he wrote chiefly in Yiddish. Best known for biblical novels *The Nazarene*, *The Apostle, Mary* and the play *The God of Vengeance*.

The sword conquers for a while, but the spirit conquers for ever.

1880   **Grantland Rice:** Celebrated American sportswriter. Chronicled the Golden Age of Sports in the 1920s. Syndicated columnist (1930–47). Selected All-American football teams for *Collier's* magazine.

For when the One Great Scorer comes to / Mark against your name, / He writes— not that you won or lost / —but how you played the game.

1887   **Isaac Goldberg:** American critic, editor and author. Literary editor of *American Freeman* (1923–32). Wrote: *The Story of Gilbert and Sullivan*, *Tin Pan Alley* and *George Gershwin*.

Diplomacy is to do and say / The nastiest things in the nicest way.

1927   **Marcel Ophuls:** German-born French-U.S. director. Son of Max Ophuls. Films: *The Sorrow and the Pity*, *A Sense of Loss*, *Hotel Terminus: Klaus Barbie—His Life and Times* (Oscar-winning documentary.

Puritanism ... helps us enjoy our misery while we are inflicting it on others.

1935   **Gary Player:** South African professional golfer. Won each of the Masters, U.S. Open, PGA and British Open twice.

Golf asks something of a man. It makes one loathe mediocrity. It seems to say, "If you are going to keep company with me, don't embarrass me."

November 2

1734   **Daniel Boone:** American frontiersman and explorer. Expert hunter and trapper. First to visit Kentucky wilderness. Captured by Shawnee Indians. Adopted by their chief. Escaped to warn Boonesborough of an impending attack. Served in the Virginia legislature. Greatly influenced the extension of the new nation westward.

All you need for happiness is a good gun, a good horse and a good wife.

1755   **Marie Antoinette:** Austrian-born queen-consort of France's Louis XVI. Famed for her beauty. Found guilty of treason, she was executed by the French Revolutionary forces.

There is nothing new except what has been forgotten.

1815   **George Boole:** One of the most original mathematicians England ever produced. Bertrand Russell claimed pure mathematics was discovered by Boole in his work *The Laws of Thought*.

There exist ... certain general principles founded in the very nature of language, by which the use of symbols, which are but the elements of scientific language, is determined. To a certain extent these elements are arbitrary.

1865   **Warren G. Harding:** Twenty-ninth U.S. president. Teacher, newspaperman and Senator from Ohio. Promised a "return to normalcy." His administration was plagued by scandal, notably the Teapot Dome scandal. Died suddenly while on a speaking tour in California.

I have said to the people we mean to have less Government in business as well as more business in Government.

1897   **Richard Russell:** American politician and lawyer. U.S. senator from Georgia. Leader of the Democratic Southern Bloc. Chairman of Senate Armed Forces Committee (1951–69). President pro tem of the Senate (1969–71).

If we have to start over with another Adam and Eve, I want them to be Americans.

1913   **Burt Lancaster:** American gymnast, acrobat and actor. Oscar winner for *Elmer Gantry*. Nominated for *From Here to Eternity*, *Birdman of Alcatraz* and *Atlantic City*. Formed a production company with agent Harold Hecht and producer James Hill.

As long as you are curious, you defeat age.

1942   **Shere D. Hite:** American researcher and writer centered on cultural research in human sexuality. Author of *Sexual Honesty: By Women for Women.*

You cannot decree women to be sexually free when they are not economically free.

November 3

1500   **Benvenuto Cellini:** Italian goldsmith, sculptor and writer. Known for his innovative, picturesque autobiography which greatly influenced the Renaissance.

There are many kinds of conceit, but the chief one is to let people know what a very ancient and gifted family one descends from.

1794   **William Cullen Bryant:** American poet, editor and lawyer. Worked for the *New York Review* and the *New York Evening Post*, becoming editor and part-owner of the latter. A leading abolitionist. Saw John Brown as a martyr to the cause. Poems: "Thanatopsis," "To a Waterfowl" and "The Yellow Violet."

Go forth, under the open sky, and listen / To Nature's teachings.

1831   **Ignatius Donnelly:** American social reformer and author. Known as the "Sage of Nininger." Books: *Atlantis: The Antediluvian World* and *Caesar's Column: A Story of the Twentieth Century.*

The Democratic party is like a mule—without pride of ancestry or hope of posterity.

1879   **Vilhjalmur Stefansson:** Canadian-U.S. explorer and ethnologist. Explored vast areas of Canadian Arctic 1908-12. Discovered new lands in the Arctic archipelago.

False modesty is better than none.

1909   **James Reston:** Scottish-born American journalist, editor and author. Wrote syndicated column "Washington." Books: *Sketches in Sand* and *Prelude to Victory.* Pulitzers for national reporting (1945, 1957).

All politics ... are based on the indifference of the majority.

1918   **Russell Long:** American politician and lawyer. Son of Huey P. Long. U.S. senator from Louisiana (1951–86). Longtime senate finance committee chairman.

A tax loophole is something that benefits the other guy. If it benefits you, it is tax reform.

1952   **Roseanne [Barr Arnold]:** American stand-up comedienne, actress and star of television series "Roseanne." Appeared in movie *She-Devils.* After divorcing Tom Arnold, swore she'd never wear another man's name again.

The world makes you into a bitch, no matter how quietly you go, so you may as well go kicking and screaming.

November 4

1771   **James Montgomery:** British hymnologist, poet and journalist. Best remembered for his hymns and versified psalms. Wrote 23 books of verse.

Beyond this vale of tears / There is a life above, / Unmeasured by the flight of years; / And all that life is love.

1879   **Will Rogers:** American actor, wit and folk hero. Popular entertainer and homespun philosopher. Starred with the Ziegfeld Follies and in films: *A Connecticut Yankee, State Fair, David Harum* and *Judge Priest.* Died in a plane crash with Wiley Post near Point Barrow Alaska.

I don't make jokes—I just watch the government and report the facts.

1906   **Bob Considine:** American journalist and author. Wrote syndicated column "On the Line" for 40 years, starting in 1937. Began as a sportswriter. Books: *Innocents at Home, Man Against Fire* and *The Babe Ruth Story.*

I believe in opening mail once a month whether it needs it or not.

1912   **Pauline Trigere:** French-born American high fashion designer. Had a feeling for classic American look.

Everyone talks to me. That takes time. Where is time? ...for me the end of the day is too soon.

1916 Walter Cronkite: American newspaperman, wire correspondent and broadcast journalist. CBS news anchor from 1962 to 1981, the longest running anchor of all time.
And that's the way it is … and most of the time we hope it isn't.

1918 Art Carney: American actor. Best known for his role as New York City sewer worker Ed Norton on television's "The Honeymooners" costarring with Jackie Gleason. Won an Oscar for *Harry and Tonto.*
I never think of myself as a comedian. I do acting jobs in comedy situations.

1946 Robert Mapplethorpe: Controversial American photographer whose homoerotic pictures shocked and offended many in and out of the art world. Died of AIDS.
You create your own world. The one I want to live in is very precise, very controlled.

November 5

1850 Ella Wheeler Wilcox: American poet. Wrote nearly 40 volumes of sentimental poetry. Books of Verse: *Drops of Water, Shells, Maurine* and *Poems of Passion.* Her best known poem, "Solitude" contains the line:
Laugh, and the world laughs with you; / Weep, and you weep alone.

1855 Eugene V. Debs: American socialist leader and labor organizer. First president of the American Railway Union. Socialist Party presidential candidate five times between 1900 and 1920. Author of: *Walls and Bars.*
While there is a loser class I am in it; while there is a criminal element I am of it; while there is a soul in prison, I am not free.

1857 Ida Tarbell: American journalist, writer and editor. Associate editor of the *American Magazine.* A Muckraker. Books: *The History of the Standard Oil Company, The Ways of Women* and *In the Footsteps of Lincoln.*
A mind which really lays hold of a subject is not easily detached from it.

1885 Will Durant: American lecturer and writer. Author of *The Story of Philosophy,* the ten volume *The Story of Civilization,* the last four written in conjunction with his wife Ariel, and *The Lessons of History.*
Civilization begins with order, grows with liberty, and dies with chaos.

1892 J.B.S. [John Burdon Sanderson] Haldane: English-Indian geneticist. Conducted basic studies of sex-linkage in chromosomes and of mutation rate. Author of *Science and Ethics* and *Biochemistry of Genetics.*
This is my prediction for the future: whatever hasn't happened will happen and no one will be safe from it.

1913 Vivien Leigh: Indian-born English stage and screen actress. Once married to Laurence Olivier. Academy Awards for *Gone with the Wind* and *A Streetcar Named Desire.* Others: *Waterloo Bridge, The Roman Spring of Mrs. Stone* and *Ship of Fools.*
Most of us have compromised with life. Those who fight for what they want will always thrill us.

1942 Paul Simon: American vocalist, composer and guitarist. Teamed with Art Garfunkel on hits: "The Sounds of Silence," "Mrs. Robinson" and "Bridge Over Troubled Water." Went solo in 1971. Hits: "Kodachrome," "Loves Me Like a Rock" and "50 Ways to Leave Your Lover."
Like a bridge over troubled water / I will lay me down.

November 6

1558 Thomas Kyd: English dramatist and scrivener. Author of the most popular drama of his day, *The Spanish Tragedy.* Credited with a share in several plays. May have written an earlier version of *Hamlet.*
Evil news fly faster still than good.

1854 John Philip Souza: "The March King." American bandmaster and composers of marches. Among his 140 marches are: "Stars and Stripes Forever," "El Capitan," "Semper Fidelis" and "The Washington Post." Led U.S. Marine Band (1880–92).

Jazz will endure just as long as people hear it through their feet instead of their brains.

1861   **James Naismith:** Canadian physical education instructor who in 1891 invented the game of basketball at the YMCA Training School (now Springfield College) in Springfield, Massachusetts.

The appeal of basketball is that it is an easy game to play, but difficult to master.

1870   **Lord Herbert Samuel:** English statesman, philosopher, social legislator, administrator and Liberal Party leader. Home secretary (1916, 1931–32). Philosophical works include *Practical Ethics* and *Belief in Action.*

It takes two to make a marriage a success and only one a failure.

1892   **Harold Ross:** American editor. Coeditor of *Stars and Stripes* (1917–19); editor of *The American Legion Weekly* (1919–24); *Judge* (1925) and the *New Yorker* (1925–51).

The **New** *Yorker will be the magazine which is not edited for the old lady in Dubuque.*

1921   **James Jones:** American novelist. Author of best-selling *From Here to Eternity* (National Book Award), *Some Came Running* and *The Thin Red Line.*

Manhood is the ability to outlast despair.

1931   **Mike Nichols:** German-born American actor and director. Teamed with Elaine May in a sophisticated Broadway revue. Oscar winner for directing *The Graduate.* Others: *Who's Afraid of Virginia Woolf? Carnal Knowledge, Silkwood* and *Working Girl.* Married to television newscaster Diane Sawyer.

Nothing trains you for life.

November 7

1867   **Madame Marie Curie:** Polish chemist and physicist. Codiscovered radium with her husband Pierre. Determined that uranium was the source of radioactivity in uranium compounds. Coined word radioactive. Received Nobel prizes in 1911 and 1913. First woman member of French Academy of Medicine.

One never notices what has been done; one can only see what remains to be done....

1900   **Heinrich Himmler:** German Nazi official. Second most powerful man in the Third Reich. Head of the SS; commander of all police forces. Established the first concentration camp at Dachau. Organized extermination camps in Eastern Europe.

We Germans, who are the only people in the world who have a decent attitude toward animals, will also assume a decent attitude towards these human animals.

1903   **Konrad Z. Lorenz:** Austro-German ethologist. Major pioneer in the study of animal behavior. Proposed that all animal behavior is explicable in terms of adaptive evolution. Nobel Prize (1973).

I believe I've found the missing link between animal and civilized man. It is us.

1913   **Albert Camus:** Algerian-born French philosopher, novelist, dramatist and journalist. A close associate of Jean-Paul Sartre and his circle. An intellectual leader of the French Resistance in WWII. Author of: *The Stranger, Myth of Sisyphus, Caligula* and *Le Malentendu.* Nobel Prize (1957).

The absurd is the essential concept and the first truth.

1918   **Billy Graham:** American evangelist. One of the first to utilize television in his crusades. Established the series "Hour of Decision" in 1951.

The Christian life is not a way "out" but a way "through" life.

1926   **Joan Sutherland:** Australian opera singer. One of the world's leading coloratura sopranos in the 1960s and 1970s. Grammy winner for Best Classical Vocalist (1981). Retired in 1990.

If I weren't reasonably placid, I don't think I could cope with this sort of life. To be a diva, you've got to be absolutely like a horse.

1943   **Joni Mitchell:** Canadian-born singer, songwriter, guitarist and pianist. Wrote the hit songs: "Both Sides Now" and "Woodstock." Her biggest recorded hit: "Help Me."

Sorrow is so easy to express and yet so hard to tell.

November 8

1732 John Dickinson: American patriot and lawyer. Called the "Penman of the Revolution." Drafted declaration of rights and grievances of the Stamp Act Congress (1765); but voted against the Declaration of Independence.

Then join hand in hand, brave Americans all! By uniting we stand, by dividing we fall.

1879 Leon Trotsky: Russian Communist leader. After the Bolsheviks seized power in 1917, Trotsky and Lenin emerged as the two top men in the new government. Trotsky became commissar for foreign affairs. When Lenin died, Stalin openly attacked Trotsky who was exiled. He was murdered in Mexico City in 1940.

Old age is the most unexpected of all things that happen to a man.

1883 Arnold Bax: English composer and author. Master of music for George VI and Elizabeth II. Composed the march played at her coronation.

One should try everything once, except incest and folk dancing.

1897 Dorothy Day: American journalist and reformer. Developed program of social reconstruction, which she called the green revolution, establishing settlement houses for the urban poor. Founded *The Catholic World,* a pacifist radical monthly that agitated against nuclear weapons.

Christ is being martyred today in Vietnam, in Santo Domingo and in all places where men are taking to the sword in this world crisis.

1900 Margaret Mitchell: American author who wrote but one novel, *Gone with the Wind,* which was turned into one of the most successful movies ever made. Died in a car accident (1949).

Death and taxes and childbirth! There's never any convenient time for any of them.

1909 Katharine Hepburn: Four-time Oscar winning American actress with eight additional nominations. Among her best films: *A Bill of Divorcement, Alice Adams,*
Bringing Up Baby, The Philadelphia Story, Woman of the Year, Adam's Rib, The African Queen, Long Day's Journey Into Night, The Lion in Winter and *On Golden Pond.* Maintained a longtime affair and friendship with Spencer Tracy.

Without discipline, there's no life at all.

1931 Morley Safer: Canadian-born American broadcast journalist. Member of CBS' television newsmagazine "60 Minutes" reporting team.

Arrogance and snobbishness live in adjoining rooms and use a common currency.

November 9

1832 Émile Gaboriau: French novelist. Founder of the roman policies. Described as the Edgar Allan Poe of France. Detective novels: *L'Affaire Lerouge* and *Monsieur Lecoq.*

Revenge is a luscious fruit which you must leave to ripen.

1869 Marie Dressler: Canadian-born actress in stock, light opera, legitimate stage and films. A Broadway and Vaudeville headliner. Oscar for *Min and Bill.* Hollywood's number-one box-office attraction for four years. Films: *Anna Christie, Tugboat Annie* and *Dinner at Eight.*

I was born serious and I have earned my bread making other people laugh.

1879 John Haynes Holmes: American Unitarian clergyman and author. Editor *Unity* (1921–46). Books: *Religion for Today, The Second Christmas* and *My Gandhi.*

Priests are no more necessary to religion than politicians to patriotism.

1886 Ed Wynn: American actor and comedian. Often billed as "The Perfect Fool." Vaudeville headliner. Appeared in Ziegfeld Follies. Was radio and television's Texaco fire chief. Won the first Emmy as best actor in a series. Oscar nominated for *The Diary of Anne Frank.* Father of actor Keenan Wynn.

A comedian is not a man who says funny things. A comedian is one who says things funny.

1928 **Anne Sexton:** American poet. Wrote "confessional verse." Pulitzer Prize for *Live or Die* (1967). Also wrote: *All My Pretty Ones, The Awful Rowing Toward God* and *The Poet's Story.*
A woman is her mother.

1934 **Carl Sagan:** American astronomer and writer. Pulitzer Prize winner nonfiction (1978). Author of *The Dragons of Eden, Broca's Brain* and *Shadows of Forgotten Ancestors.*
Somewhere, something incredible is waiting to be known.

1935 **Bob Gibson:** U.S. baseball righthanded pitcher with St. Louis Cardinals. Won 20 games or more per season five times. Received two National League Cy Young Awards (1968 and 1970). MVP (1968). Led Cards to two World Series victories (1964 and 67). Had 251 career wins. Hall of Famer. Had more than 3,000 career strike-outs.
Why do I have to be an example for your kid? You be an example for your own kid.

November 10

1483 **Martin Luther:** Augustinian friar. German founder of Protestantism. Believed the Bible to be the sole authority of the church. Called for reformation of the Catholic Church, denying the supremacy of the Pope. Tried for heresy and excommunicated. Lutheran religion named for him.
Superstition, idolatry, and hypocrisy have ample wages, but truth goes a-begging.

1697 **William Hogarth:** English painter and engraver. Best known for series of morality paintings: *The Harlot's Progress, The Rake's Progress* and *Marriage à la Mode.*
All the world is competent to judge my pictures except those who are of my profession.

1728 **Oliver Goldsmith:** Irish-born English poet, playwright and novelist. Noted for his comic verbal faux pas, although this may have been intentional. Author of: *The Citizen of the World, The*

Vicar of Wakefield and *She Stoops to Conquer.*
The true use of speech is not so much to express our wants as to conceal them.

1879 **Vachel Lindsay:** American poet. Attempted to convert America to a love of poetry. His works include: "General William Booth Enters Heaven," "The Congo" and "The Santa Fe Trail."
Never, never, never be a cynic, even a gentle one. Never help out a sneer, even at the devil.

1893 **John P. Marquand:** American novelist. Wrote a popular series about the keen-witted Japanese detective Mr. Moto. Novels: *The Late George Apley* and *Wickford Point.*
I know a fellow who's as broke as the Ten Commandments.

1925 **Richard Burton:** Welsh actor. Nominated eight times for an Oscar, but came up empty handed each time. Nearly as well-known for his two marriages to Elizabeth Taylor as his fine performances in *My Cousin Rachel, Becket, The Night of the Iguana* and *Who's Afraid of Virginia Woolf?*
An actor is something less than a man, while an actress is something more than a woman.

1946 **David Stockman:** American government official. Outspoken and controversial director, Office of Management and Budget (1981–85). Author of: *Triumph in Politics.*
None of us really understands what's going on with all these numbers.

November 11

1741 **Johann Kaspar Lavater:** Swiss writer, patriot, Protestant pastor and founder of physiognomics which he attempted to elevate into a science. Wrote *Essays on Physiognomy* with the assistance of Goethe.
If you wish to appear agreeable in society, you must consent to be taught many things which you already know.

1744 **Abigail Smith Adams:** American first lady. Wife of second president, John Adams. Mother of John Quincy Adams. Author of letters: *New Letters of Abigail Adams* and *The Adams-Jefferson Letters.*

We have too many high sounding words, and too few actions that correspond with them.

1821 **Fyodor Dostoyevsky:** Russian novelist. One of the most influential writers of modern literature. Supreme master of the realistic novel. Wrote *The House of the Dead, The Possessed, The Raw Youth* and *The Brothers Karamazov.*

The second half of a man's life is made of nothing but the habits he has acquired during the first half.

1833 **Aleksandr Borodin:** Russian composer and chemist. Made use of Russian folk themes in his music. Best known works are *In the Steppes of Central Asia, Symphony No. 2* and *Prince Igor.*

Respectable people do not write music or make love as a career.

1885 **George S. Patton, Jr.:** American general in WWII. Nicknamed "Old Blood and Guts." Member of the 1912 Olympic team, competing in the modern pentathlon. Commanded U.S. Army II Corps in North Africa (1942–43). Led 7th Army assault on Sicily (1943) and 3rd Army invasion of occupied Europe (1944).

Take calculated risks. That is quite different from being rash.

1915 **William Proxmire:** American politician. U.S. senator from Wisconsin for more that a quarter of a century. Best known for his Golden Fleece awards, received for exposing waste in government.

You have to adjust your running style when you're running on ice.

1922 **Kurt Vonnegut, Jr.:** American author and journalist. Writes satirical stories of American culture and mores. Works: *Player Piano, Slaughterhouse Five* and *Breakfast of Champions.*

Laughing or crying is what a human being does when there's nothing else he can do.

November 12

1815 **Elizabeth Cady Stanton:** American reformer and women's rights activist. Leader of the woman-suffrage movement. Editor of *Revolution,* a militant feminist publication (1868–70). President of National Woman Suffrage Association (1868-70). Author of *Eighty Years and More.*

Womanhood is the great fact in her life. Wifehood and Motherhood are but accidental relations.

1840 **Auguste Rodin:** French sculptor. Bequeathed most of his work to the French government. Best known for: *Age of Bronze, The Gates of Hell, The Kiss* and *The Thinker.*

I invent nothing. I rediscover.

1866 **Sun Yat-Sen:** Chinese revolutionary leader. Worked to overthrow the Ch'ing Dynasty. While in exile organized the Revolutionary Alliance. Formed Nationalist Party (1912). Elected head of state (1921). Attempted to conquer and unite China.

In the construction of a country it is not the practical workers but the idealists and planners that are difficult to find.

1889 **Dewitt Wallace:** American publisher. Founded the *Reader's Digest* in 1922 with his wife Lila Bell Wallace.

The dead carry with them to the graves in their clutched hands only that which they have given away.

1918 **Jo Stafford:** American singer. Joined the vocal group the Pied Pipers, which as a quartet sang with Tommy Dorsey's band. She went solo in 1944. Regular on radio, often with her husband Paul Weston's band. Hits: "Shrimp Boats," "You Belong to Me," "Jambalaya" and "Make Love to Me."

I find a slim gal is more popular. Why should I need weight—I don't want to sing Wagner.

1929 **Grace Kelly:** Beautiful blonde actress and Monaco princess. Oscars for *Mogambo* and *The Country Girl.* Others: *High Noon, Dial M for Murder, Rear Window* and *To Catch a Thief.*

The freedom of the press works in such a way that there is not much freedom from it.

1961 Nadia Comaneci: Romanian gymnast. In the 1976 Olympics, she earned seven perfect scores and three individual gold medals. Won two additional gold medals in 1980.

I know how to smile, I know how to laugh, I know how to play. But I know how to do these things only after I have finished my mission.

November 13

354 Saint Augustine: Born in what is now Algeria. Church Father and philosopher. By means of his sermons and pastoral letters he exerted a tremendous influence on Christian beliefs. A champion of orthodoxy. Fused the New Testament with Greek philosophy. Wrote: *The City of God* and *Confessions.*

Seek not to understand that you may believe, but believe that you may understand.

1785 Lady Caroline Lamb: English novelist. Wife of Viscount Melbourne, prime minister to Queen Victoria. She is best known for her affair with Lord Byron, whom she caricatured in *Glenarvon,* after he tired of her.

Women, like toys, are sought after and trifled with, and then thrown by with every varying caprice.

1831 James Clerk Maxwell: Scottish mathematician and physicist. Worked out the mathematics that expressed and united electricity and magnetism.

All the mathematical sciences are founded on relations between physical laws and laws of numbers, so that the aim of exact science is to reduce the problems of nature to the determination of quantities by operations with numbers.

1833 Edwin Booth: American actor. One of the greatest 19th century stage actors. Known for his Hamlet. Brother of John Wilkes Booth.

An actor is a sculptor who carves in snow.

1850 Robert Louis Stevenson: Scottish novelist, poet and essayist. Author of the very popular novels *Treasure Island, The Strange Case of Dr. Jekyll and Mr. Hyde* and *Kidnapped.* Also known for *A Child's Garden of Verses.*

I regard you with an indifference closely bordering on aversion.

1856 Louis D. Brandeis: American jurist and Zionist leader. Appointed to the Supreme Court by Woodrow Wilson in 1912. Known as the people's attorney. Brandeis University is named for him. Books: *Other People's Money, Business, a Profession* and *The Curse of Bigness.*

We can have democracy in this country or we can have great wealth concentrated in the hands of a few, but we can't have both.

1866 Abraham Flexner: American educator, educational pioneer, administrator of philanthropies and author. With Carnegie Foundation for Advancement of Teaching (1908). Director, Institute of Advanced Study, Princeton, N.J. (1930–39). Books: *The American College, A Modern College* and *Funds and Foundations.*

Probably no nation is rich enough to pay for both war and education.

November 14

1840 Claude Monet: French painter. A founder of Impressionism. His painting of Le Havre, entitled *Impression, Sunrise* (1872), gave the name to the movement. Considered to be one of the all-time great landscape painters.

Nobody can count themselves an artist unless they can carry a picture in their head before they paint it.

1889 Jawaharal Nehru: Indian statesman. First prime minister of independent India (1947–64). Associated with Mohandas Gandhi and the Indian National Party, becoming its president in 1929. Tried to pursue a policy of non-alignment as prime minister.

The only alternative to coexistence is co-destruction.

1900 Aaron Copland: Exceptionally gifted American composer. Among his most popular works were those based on folk motifs such as the American ballets *Billy the Kid, Rodeo* and *Appalachian Spring*. Other works: *Lincoln's Portrait* and *Fanfare for the Common Man.*

Music that is born complex is not inherently better or worse than music that is born simple.

1904 Marya Mannes: American writer, journalist and critic. Author of: *More in Anger, But Will It Sell?* and *Out of My Time.*

The real demon is success—the anxieties engendered by this quest are relentless, degrading, corroding. What is worse, there is no end to this escalation of desire....

1906 Louise Brooks: American actress and writer. A pretty, shapely brunette with a boyish-bob hair style, memorable in films: *A Girl in Every Port, Pandora's Box* and *Diary of a Lost Girl.* Author of the series of essays *Lulu in Hollywood.*

I never gave away anything without wishing I had kept it; nor kept anything without wishing I had given it away.

1908 Joseph McCarthy: American politician. Republican Senator from Wisconsin (1947–57). Famous for his highly publicized investigations of alleged communists in the U.S. government. Because of his witch hunt, many people were blacklisted and unable to find work. Censured by the Senate for contempt and abuse.

McCarthyism is Americanism with its sleeves rolled.

1948 Charles: Prince of Wales. First in line to succeed his mother, Elizabeth II, as monarch of Great Britain. An accomplished polo player. The failure of his marriage to Princess Diane has been played out in the world's newspapers and magazines.

Falling madly in love with someone is not necessarily the starting point to getting married.

November 15

1708 William Pitt the Elder: Earl of Chatham. "The Great Commoner." English statesman. Secretary of state (1756–61 and 1766–68). Led England during the Seven Years' War (1756–63), winning vast territory for England, including Canada.

Where law ends, tyranny begins.

1881 Franklin P. Adams: "F.P.A." American sportswriter, columnist and humorist. His column "The Conning Tower," appeared in New York newspapers (1913–41). Remembered for his verse: "Tinker and Evers and Chance." Wrote "The Melancholy Lute."

Middle age occurs when you are too young to take up golf and too old to rush up to the net.

1882 Felix Frankfurter: American jurist. Harvard Law professor (1914–39). Helped found American Civil Liberties Union (1920). Appointed to the Supreme Court in 1930 by FDR. A liberal who advocated judicial restraint.

A clean desk represents an empty mind.

1887 Marianne Craig Moore: American poet. Acting editor of *Dial* (1925–29). Verse is marked by wit and irony, deep moral concern and deep feelings. Pulitzer Prize winner (1951). Works: *What Are Years, Nevertheless* and *Collected Poems.*

Impatience is the mark of independence, / Not of bondage.

1887 Georgia O'Keefe: American painter. Found her unique style in New Mexico where she painted desert scenes, sometimes with the blanched skull of a longhorn in the foreground. Wife of photographer Alfred Stieglitz.

I decided that if I could paint that flower in a huge scale, you could not ignore its beauty.

1891 W. Averell Harriman: U.S. statesman, diplomat and banker. U.S. ambassador to U.S.S.R. (1943–46). Governor of New York (1955–58). As undersecretary of state negotiated limited nuclear test ban treaty and conducted Paris peace negotiations with North Vietnam (1968–69).

Conferences at the top level are always courteous. Name calling is left to the foreign ministers.

1897 Aneurin Bevan: British Labor Party leader. As Minister of Health (1945–51) developed Britain's socialized medicine system. Opposed German rearmament after WWI and Britain's reliance on the U.S. in foreign affairs.

Damn it all, you can't have the crown of thorns and the thirty pieces of silver.

November 16

1811   John Bright: British statesman and orator. Prototype of Victorian radicalism. Populist reformer. Fought for parliamentary reform. Founded the Anti–Corn Law League (1839).

Force is not a remedy.

1827   Charles Eliot Norton: American educator, editor, critic and translator. Cofounder of *The Nation* (1865). Coeditor of the *North American Review* (1864-68). Author of *History of Ancient Art.* Translator of Dante's *The Divine Comedy.*

No great work of imagination has ever been based on illicit passion.

1873   W.C. Handy: American composer and bandleader. Known as the "Father of the Blues." First to write down and publish blues songs including his famous "St. Louis Blues."

The blues is where we came from and what we experience. The blues came from nothingness, from want, from desire.

1889   George S. Kaufman: American playwright and screenwriter. Plays: *The Butter and Egg Man, The Royal Family* and *Dinner at Eight* with Edna Ferber, *Of Thee I Sing* with Morris Ryskind and Ira Gershwin, *You Can't Take It with You,* with Moss Hart, and *The Man Who Came to Dinner.*

Satire is what closes Saturday night.

1899   Mary Margaret McBride: American radio commentator. Hosted a series of daytime talk shows (1934–54). Dispensed homespun and advice. Interviewed the famous people of the day.

Terrible things happen to young girls in New York City....

1905   Eddie Condon: American guitarist, banjoist, jazz promoter and bandleader.

Worked in the Dixieland world. Promoted concerts at New York's town hall. Opened a jazz club in Greenwich Village (1958–67).

For a bad hangover take the juice of two quarts of whiskey.

1935   Elizabeth Drew: American journalist and author. Writes on the Washington political scene. Regular on PBS television's "Thirty Minutes with..."

Too often travel, instead of broadening the mind, merely lengthens the conversation.

November 17

1815   Eliza Woodson Burhans Farnham: American philanthropist and author. Wrote: *Life in Prairie Land, Woman and Her Era* and *The Ideal Attained.*

The ultimate aim of the human mind, in all its efforts, is to become acquainted with Truth.

1887   Bernard Law Montgomery: First Viscount of Alamein. British Army field marshal. Defeated Germany's Erwin Rommel at El Alamein (1942). Commanded Allied landings in Normandy (1944). Led Allied forces through Europe into Germany (1944–45).

I would never go into politics. I think that war is a very rough and dirty game, but politics—by gum!

1916   Shelby Foote: American writer, historian and novelist. As the foremost living authority on the Civil War, he served as the principal guide through the highly successful Civil War series produced for public television by documentary filmmaker Ken Burns.

Longevity conquers scandal every time.

1938   Lorne Michaels: Canadian producer and writer. Producer of television's "Saturday Night Live." Winner of four Emmys.

The pressure to give them less is as great in television because the traffic will bear almost anything.

1942   Martin Scorsese: American director, screenwriter, producer and actor.

Most consistently innovative director working during the past 20 years. Films: *Mean Streets, Taxi Driver, Raging Bull, Goodfellas, Cape Fear* and *The Age of Innocence.*

There's a part of me that loves a kind of Japanese minimalism—I need an unlimited room to think in.

1944 **Danny De Vito:** U.S. actor and director. Memorable for his role of Louie DePalma on television's "Taxi." Won Emmy (1981). Films: *Romancing the Stone, Ruthless People, Batman Returns* and *Hoffa.* Appeared in and directed *Throw Momma from the Train* and *The War of the Roses.* As Louie:

There she was—dejected, desperate and stoned. Everything I could hope for in a woman.

1944 **Tom Seaver:** American Hall of Fame baseball right-handed pitcher with the Mets, Reds and White Sox. Won three Cy Young Awards (1969, 1973 and 1975). Had 311 wins and 3,640 strikeouts in 20 seasons.

There are only two places in this league, first place and no place.

November 18

1647 **Pierre Bayle:** French philosopher. Famous for his encyclopedic dictionary. Held that many long-standing beliefs, including much Christian tradition, were as questionable as the notion that comets presaged catastrophes.

No nations are more warlike than those which profess Christianity.

1836 **W.S. [William Schwenck] Gilbert:** English lyricist collaborated with composer Arthur Sullivan to write a series of light operas, including: *H.M.S. Pinafore, The Pirates of Penzance* and *The Mikado.*

Humor is a drug which it's the fashion to abuse.

1836 **Cesare L. Lombroso:** Italian alienist, criminologist and professor of psychiatry. Interests centered on the relation between mental and physical disorder. Wrote: *Crime, It's Causes and Remedies.*

Genius is one of the many forms of insanity.

1860 **Ignace Jan Paderewski:** Celebrated Polish pianist and composer. A great Polish patriot. Served as Poland's representative to Washington. Named prime minister in 1919. Delegate to the League of Nations. As an artist, a faithful follower of the Romantic school. Compositions: "Minuet in G," "Fantaisie polonaise" and the opera *Manru.*

Before I was a genius I was a drudge.

1870 **Dorothy Dix:** Pseudonym of Elizabeth M. Gilman. U.S. journalist and writer. Wrote syndicated advice to the lovelorn column beginning in 1896.

Women have changed in their relationship to men, but man stands pat just where Adam did when it comes to dealing with women.

1882 **Jacques Maritan:** French Catholic philosopher and man of letters. Came to U.S. after the fall of France in 1940. Wrote sharp attacks on Luther, Descartes, Rousseau and Pascal.

Americans seem sometimes to believe that if you are a thinker, you must be a fawning bore, because thinking is so damn serious.

1939 **Margaret E. Atwood:** Canadian author and poet. Wrote best-selling novel *The Handmaid's Tale.* Also wrote: *Cat's Eye* and *Bluebeard's Egg.* Most widely read writer in Canada.

A divorce is like an amputation; you survive, but there's less of you.

November 19

1600 **Charles I:** King of England and Ireland (1625–49). A firm believer in the Divine Right of Kings, his need for money to fight foreign wars put him into conflict with parliament and led to the English Civil Wars. Charged with high treason, he was beheaded.

Never make a defence or apology before you are accused.

1899 **Alan Tate:** American poet and critic. One of the founders of the seminal literary magazine, *The Fugitive.* Edited *Hound and Horn* (1931–34) and *The Sewanee*

Review (1944–46). Poems, "Ode to the Confederate Dead," "The Mediterranean" and "The Oath."

Man is a creature that in the long run has got to believe in order to know, and to know in order to do.

1917　Indira Gandhi: Indian political leader. Prime minister (1967–77, 1978–84). Daughter of Jawaharlal Nehru. Worked for economic planning and social reform. Assassinated by two Sikh security guards.

You cannot shake hands with a clenched fist.

1921　Roy Campanella: U.S. Hall of Fame baseball catcher with the Brooklyn Dodgers. Led the team to five pennants and their first World Series title (1955). Three-time MVP (1951, 1953, 1955). Paralyzed in a car accident in 1958.

You gotta be a man to play baseball for a living, but you gotta have a lot of little boy in you, too.

1926　Jeane Jordan Kirkpatrick: American diplomat, political scientist and educator. U.S. permanent representative to the United Nations (1981–95).

Words can destroy. What we call each other ultimately becomes what we think of each other, and it matters.

1938　Ted Turner: American entrepreneur, yachtsman, owner of the Atlanta Braves baseball team and founder of CNN. Named *Time*'s "Man of the Year" (1991). Married to actress Jane Fonda.

Life is like a B-grade movie. You don't want to leave in the middle of it, but you don't want to see it again.

1942　Calvin Klein: American fashion designer. Designer of elegant, modern classics. Produces the perfumes "Eternity" and "Obsession."

I think there's something incredibly sexy about a woman wearing her boyfriend's T-shirt and underwear.

November 20

1858　Selma Ottiliana Louisa Lagerlof: Swedish novelist. Wrote *Gosta Berling* saga

and *Wonderful Adventures of Nils*. First woman to win Nobel Prize for literature (1909).

He who is sorrowful can force himself to smile, but he who is glad cannot weep.

1871　Arthur Guiterman: Austrian-born American writer and poet. Wrote historical and legendary ballads and many lyrics. Writer of humorous verse. Author of: *Ballads of Old New York, I Sing the Pioneer* and *Lyric Laughter*.

Amoebas at the start / Were not complex; / They tore themselves apart / And started Sex.

1884　Norman Thomas: American socialist leader, reformer, editor and minister. Helped found ACLU (1920). Socialist candidate for U.S. presidency (1928, 1932, 1936, 1940, 1944 and 1948). Wrote *America's Way Out—A Program for Democracy.*

While I'd rather be right than president, at any time I am ready for both.

1889　Edwin P. Hubble: American astronomer. Discovered that the universe appears to be expanding. In 1924 proved that there are other galaxies far from our own. The space telescope deployed from the space shuttle *Discovery* (1990) is named for him.

Equipped with his five senses, man explores the universe around him and calls the adventure Science.

1908　Alistair Cooke: English–U.S. journalist. Best known as the urbane host of "Omnibus" (1952–60) and PBS's "Masterpiece Theater" (1971–1992). Writer and narrator of television's "America: A Personal History of the United States (1972-73).

Cocktail music is accepted as audible wallpaper.

1917　Robert C. Byrd: American politician and lawyer. Considered one of the most powerful political leaders in the sixties and seventies. Senator from West Virginia (1958–). Senate majority leader (1977–94).

West Virginians have always had five friends: God Almighty, Sears Roebuck, Montgomery Ward, Carter's Little Liver Pills and Robert C. Byrd.

1925   **Robert F. Kennedy:** American politician. U.S. senator from New York (1965–68). Served as his brother John F. Kennedy's attorney general (1961–64). Aggressive fighter for civil rights. He was assassinated in California while campaigning for the Democratic presidential nomination (1968).
Those who dare to fail miserably can achieve greatly.

November 21

1694   **Voltaire:** Pen name of François Marie Arouet. French satirist, philosopher, historian, dramatist and poet. Known for his enmity to organized religion, fanaticism, intolerance and superstition. Worked for political reform. Crusaded against persecution. Wrote first modern historical treatises with a critical method. Writings: *Le Siècle de Louis XIV, Zadig, Candide* and *La Henriade.*
I disapprove of what you say, but I will defend to the death your right to say it.

1729   **Josiah Bartlett:** American Revolutionary patriot. Signer of the Declaration of Independence. First governor of New Hampshire (1792–94).
Custom governs the world; it is the tyrant of our feelings and our manners and rules the world with the hand of a despot.

1886   **Harold Nicolson:** Persian-born English diplomat, biographer and historian. British foreign service (1909–29). Member of Parliament (1933–45). Wrote *The Congress of Vienna.*
The great secret of successful marriage is to treat all disasters as incidents and none of the incidents as disasters.

1888   **Adolph Arthur "Harpo" Marx:** American comedian and actor. Appeared in vaudeville, on Broadway and in movies with his brothers. An inventive pantomimist, he never spoke a line. He had a cherubic face and wore a kinky red wig. His most familiar prop was an old-fashioned taxi horn which he sounded happily as his means of communicating or punctuating his visual puns.
I can talk but I hate to interrupt Groucho.

1907   **Jim Bishop:** American author and editor. Best known for books dealing with the events of a fateful day in history: *The Day Lincoln Was Shot, The Day Christ Died* and *The Day Kennedy Was Shot.*
The future is an opaque mirror. Anyone who tries to look into it sees nothing but the dim outlines of an old worried face.

1920   **Stan Musial:** "The Man." Hall of Fame baseball outfielder and first baseman with St. Louis Cardinals. Seven-time national league batting leader, three-time MVP (1943, 1946, 1948). Had 3,630 career hits and a lifetime batting average of .331.
The first principle of contract negotiations is don't remind them of what you did in the past. Tell them what you're going to do in the future.

1929   **Marilyn French:** American writer and scholar. Author of *The Women's Room* and *Bleeding Heart.*
She died for truth, and she died of it. Some truths are mortal illnesses.

November 22

1819   **George Eliot:** Pen name of Mary Ann Evans. English novelist. Maintained an affair with married George Henry Lewes from 1854 till his death in 1878. Her fiction provides insights into the internal reasons for the choices her characters made in their struggle to understand life. Novels: *Adam Bede, The Mill on the Floss, Silas Marner* and *Middlemarch.*
An ass may bray a good while before he shakes the stars down.

1857   **George R. Gissing:** British novelist, critic and essayist. His novels *The Nether World* and *New Grub Street* are characterized by realism and psychological acuteness. Also wrote *The Private Papers of Henry Ryecroft.*
Time is money—says the vulgarest saw known to any age or people. Turn it round about, and you get a precious truth—Money is time.

1868   **John Nance Garner:** American politician and lawyer. Congressman from

Texas (1903–33). FDR's vice president (1933–41).

A vice president is a spare tire on the automobile of government.

1869 André Gide: French novelist, editor and essayist. Published more than 80 works in what was essentially a religious search. Wrote *The Fruits of the Earth, The Immoralist, Strait Is the Gate* and *The Counterfeiters.*

One doesn't discover new lands without consenting to lose sight of the shore for a very long time.

1890 Charles de Gaulle: French general and statesman. Leader of the French government-in-exile during WWII. President of the Fifth Republic (1958–69). Formed a foreign policy independent of both the U.S. and the U.S.S.R.

Since a politician never believes what he says, he is always astonished when others do.

1918 Clairborne Pell: American politician and business executive. Democratic senator from Rhode Island. Author of: *Megalopolis Unbound* and *Power and Policy.*

People who leave Washington D.C. do so by the way of the box—ballot or coffin.

1943 Billie Jean King: U.S. tennis player and women's rights pioneer. Six-time Wimbledon singles champ. Four-time U.S. champ. First woman to win $100,000 in one year (1971). Defeated aging Bobby Riggs in a "Battle of the Sexes" match (1973).

A champion is afraid of losing. Everyone else is afraid of winning.

November 23

1221 Alfonso X: "The Wise." King of Castile and Leon (1252–84). Patron of learning and literature. Reign was inept because of his pursuit of the title of German king and Holy Roman emperor.

Had I been present at the creation, I would have given some useful hints for the better ordering of the universe.

1760 François-Noël Babeuf: "Gracchus." French journalist and political agitator. Attempted to overthrow the monarchy and set up a Communist republic of equals.

The end justifies the means. To reach a certain goal, one must vanquish everything that stands in the way.

1878 Ernest J. King: American admiral. Commander-in-chief of U.S. fleet (1941–45) and chief of Naval Operations (1942–45). First to hold both positions at the same time. Principal architect of America's victory at sea during WWII.

When the going gets tough, they always send for the sons of bitches.

1887 Boris Karloff: English-born stage and screen actor. Most famous as the monster in Frankenstein. Typecast in horror movies such as *The Old Dark House, The Mummy, The Black Cat* and *The Body Snatcher.* Starred in Broadway production of *Arsenic and Old Lace.*

The monster was the best friend I ever had.

1897 Willie "The Lion" Smith: Born William Bertholoff. U.S. musician and ragtime-stride pianist. Made many jazz recordings. Won his title "the Lion" for bravery in WWI. Compositions: "Echo of Spring," "Ripplin' Waters" and "Keep Your Temper."

Loud people are like a bad drink of whiskey—either you fight them or join them. Either way it's a bad idea.

1904 John Bailey: Powerful American politician, lawyer and power broker. Longtime Democratic Party chairman.

Politics is not a good location or vocation for anyone lazy, thin-skinned or lacking a sense of humor.

1930 William E. Brock: American politician and government official. U.S. secretary of labor under Reagan.

It's an insane tragedy that 700,000 people get a diploma each year and can't read the damned diploma.

November 24

1583 Philip Massinger: English dramatist. Best-known play is the satiric comedy

A New Way to Pay Old Debts. Other plays: *The Duke of Milan, The Maid of Honor* and *The Two Noble Kinsmen.*

Death hath a thousand doors to let out life; / I shall find one.

1632   Baruch Spinoza: Dutch philosopher. Earned his living as a grinder of lens. Major figure in 17th century rationalism. Most eminent expounder of the doctrine of pantheism. Works: *A Treatise on Religious and Political Philosophy* and *Ethics.*

God is the absolutely first cause.

1713   Laurence Sterne: English novelist and clergyman. Best known for *Tristram Shandy* and *A Sentimental Journey.* Considered both an accomplished scoundrel and a sentimental humorist.

Trust that man in nothing who has not a conscience in everything.

1864   Henri de Toulousse-Lautrec: French artist. Known for his post–Impressionist depictions of Parisian night life. Physically misshapen by an accident that resulted in his legs not growing, he probed the emotions of dancers, actresses, singers and prostitutes of Montmartre.

I paint things as they are. I don't comment. I record.

1888   Dale Carnegie: American writer and public speaking teacher. Best known as the author of *How to Win Friends and Influence People.* Also wrote *How to Stop Worrying and Start Living.*

First ask yourself: What is the worst that can happen? Then prepare to accept it. Then proceed to improve on the worst.

1912   Garson Kanin: U.S. director, screenwriter and playwright. Wrote and directed Broadway hit *Born Yesterday.* Wrote hilarious screenplays with his wife Ruth Gordon. Directed: *Bachelor Mother* and *My Favorite Wife.* Books: *Tracy and Hepburn* and *Moviola.*

Amateurs hope. Professionals work.

1925   William F. Buckley Jr.: American editor, columnist, writer and television commentator. Founder and editor of the conservative *National Review* (1966–). Ran unsuccessfully for mayor of New York City (1966). Host of PBS's television'a "Firing Line." Author of *God and Man at Yale* and *Atlantic High.*

Idealism is fine, but as it approaches reality, the cost becomes prohibitive.

November 25

1562   Lope de Vega: Spanish playwright and poet. Creator of the Spanish version of commedia dell'arte. Considered second only to Cervantes among Spanish writers. The world's most prolific playwright. Named "Prodigy of Nature." Works: *Peribanez, El Mejor Alcalde, El Rey* and *La Dorotea.*

No viper has worse venom or keener fangs than a woman enraged because she has been scorned by a man.

1835   Andrew Carnegie: Scottish-born American business tycoon. Financier and philanthropist. Benefactor of more than 2500 libraries, as well as Carnegie Hall. Gave away $300 million in his career. Founder of U.S. Steel.

The man who dies rich, dies disgraced.

1846   Carry Nation: American prohibitionist and social reformer. Deeply involved in the temperance movement. In 1890s began a hatchet-swinging mission of destroying rum joints. Jailed and fined for disturbing the peace, she was not intimidated:

You have put me in here a cub, but I will come out roaring like a lion, and I will make all hell howl!

1881   John XXIII: Angelo Giuseppe Roncalli, Roman Catholic pope (1958–63). Convened Vatican II (1962), to effect reforms in the Church. Worked to promote unity of all Christians.

The family is the first essential cell of human society.

1893   Joseph Wood Krutch: American author, critic, editor and naturalist. Professor of English at Columbia University (1937–52). Books: *Our Changing Morals, Henry David Thoreau, Human Nature and the Human Condition* and *More Lives Than*

One. Drama critic and associate editor, *The Nation* (1924–32).
Logic is the art of going wrong with confidence.

1914   Joe DiMaggio: U.S. Hall of Fame baseball outfielder with the New York Yankees, leading them to 10 World Series titles in 13 years. Lifetime batting average of .325. Most remarkable accomplishment is hitting safely in 56 straight games in 1941. Once married to Marilyn Monroe.
When baseball is no longer fun, it's no longer a game. And so I've played my last game of ball.

1938   Lenny Wilkins: U.S. basketball player and coach. Holds the record for most career victories as coach with Seattle, Portland, Cleveland and Atlanta.
Winning makes everyone a star.

November 26

1731   William Cowper: English poet and hymn writer. Forerunner of the Romanticism movement. Works: *Olney Hymns* and *The Task.*
God moves in a mysterious way / His wonders to perform / He plants his footstep in the sea / And rides upon the storm.

1894   Norbert Weiner: American mathematician and scientist. "Father of Automation." Coined term "cybernetics." Professor at MIT for 41 years. Principally concerned with logic and the similarity of computers and animal nervous systems. Books: *Cybernetics, The Human Use of Human Beings* and *I Am a Mathematician.*
Progress imposes not only new possibilities for the future but new restrictions.

1895   William "Bill W." Griffith Wilson: Cofounder of Alcoholics Anonymous with Robert H. Smith. His wife Lois B. Wilson founded Al-Anon for spouses of alcoholics.
Suddenly the room lit up with a great white light.... It seemed to me, in the mind's eye that I was on a mountain and that a wind not of air but of spirit was blowing. And then it burst upon me that I was a free man.

1912   Eugène Ionesco: Romanian-French dramatist of the Theatre of the Absurd. His grim grotesque farces are basically comic. Works: *The Bald Soprano, The Killer* and *Rhinoceros.*
You can only predict things after they have happened.

1912   Eric Sevareid: American broadcast journalist. CBS correspondent (1939-77). Commentator on CBS News (1964-77). Author of *Not So Wild a Dream* and *This Is Eric Sevareid.*
The chief cause of problems is solutions.

1922   Charles M. Schulz: American cartoonist. Creator of "Peanuts," starring Charlie Brown, Lucy and Snoopy. Emmy winner (1966).
I have a new philosophy. I'm only going to dread one day at a time.

1938   Tina Turner: Born Anna Mae Bullock. Rhythm and blues–rock vocalist and actress. Part of a successful team with guitarist husband Ike Turner whose biggest hit is "Proud Mary." As a solo star had hits, "What's Love Got to Do with It?" "We Don't Need Another Hero" and "Typical Male." Films: *Tommy* and *Mad Max Beyond Thunderdome.*
Physical strength in a woman—that's what I am.

November 27

1874   Charles A. Beard: Among America's most distinguished historians, often writing in conjunction with his historian wife Mary Ritter Beard. Books: *History of the United States, Rise of American Civilization* and *President Roosevelt and the Coming of the War* (1941).
When it is dark enough you can see the stars.

1874   Chaim Weizmann: Zionist leader and biochemist. Participated in the negotiations leading to the Balfour Declaration (1917). President of World Zionist Organization (1920–29, 1935–46). First president of Israel (1949–52).
Einstein explained his theory to me every day, and ... I was fully convinced that he understood it.

1877   **Katharine Anthony:** American biographer of Catherine the Great, Elizabeth I, Louise May Alcott, Dolley Madison and Susan B. Anthony.

Persons who are born too soon, or born too late, seldom achieve the eminence of those who are born at the right time.

1909   **James Agee:** American novelist, film critic and screenwriter. Awarded a Pulitzer Prize for his masterwork *A Death in the Family.* Other works: *Agee on Film* and *Let Us Now Praise Famous Men.*

The English instinctively admire any man who has no talent and is modest about it.

1912   **David Merrick:** American theatrical producer. Noted for his unorthodox publicity stunts, especially feuding with the critics. Productions: *Fanny, The Matchmaker, Gypsy, Becket, Oliver!, Hello, Dolly!* and *42nd Street.*

It's not enough that I should succeed—others should fail.

1927   **William Simon:** American government official and financier. Partner in Salomon Bros. (1964–72). Administrator Federal Energy Office (1973–74). U.S. secretary of the treasury (1974–77). President of Olin Foundation.

We have a love-hate relationship with inflation. We hate inflation, but we love everything that causes it.

1937   **Gail H. Sheehy:** American writer and social critic. Author of *Passages: Predictable Crises of Adult Life, Speed Is of the Essence, Hustling: Prostitution in Our Wide Open Society, Spirit of Survival* and *The Silent Passage: Menopause.*

It is a silly question to ask a prostitute why she does it.... They are the highest paid "professional" women in America.

November 28

1628   **John Bunyan:** English lay preacher and writer. Minister of the nonconformist church of Bedford. Most celebrated work is *Pilgrim's Progress.* Also wrote: *Grace Abounding to the Chief of Sinners* and *The Holy City, or the New Jerusalem.*

He that is down need fear no fall.

1757   **William Blake:** English poet, engraver, printer and mystic. Known for his mysticism and complex symbolism. Had visions which helped him create his own mythology. Works: "Songs of Innocence," "The Book of Thel" and "The Marriage of Heaven and Hell."

No bird soars too high, if he soars with his own wings.

1881   **Stefan Zweig:** Austrian biographer, poet, essayist and dramatist. Wrote numerous essays and biographies of major literary and historical characters. Books: *Balzac, Dickens* and *Dostoyevsky.* Only novel: *Beware of Pity.*

History has no time to be just.... She keeps her eyes fixed on the victorious, and leaves the vanquished in the shadows.

1894   **Brooks Atkinson:** American journalist and critic. Book reviewer, editor and theater critic for the *New York Times.* The most influential critic in America. Called "the autocrat of the aisle seat." Could kill a new show single-handedly with a bad review. Served as foreign correspondent, winning a Pulitzer in 1947.

Every man with an idea has at least two or three followers.

1904   **Nancy Mitford:** English novelist, biographer and editor. Noted for witty novels about upper-class British life and biographies of Voltaire and Madame de Pompadour. Her *Noblesse Oblige* was a diverting treatise on everyday speech that give the tip-off whether one is "U" (upper class) or "non-U."

To fall in love you have to be in the state of mind for it to take, like a disease.

1908   **Claude Lévi-Strauss:** French anthropologist. Founder of structural anthropology. Author of: *The Elementary Structure of Kinship, Structural Anthropology* and *From Honey to Ashes.*

The world began without man, and it will complete itself without him.

1918   **Madeleine L'Engle:** American author and editor. Pen names: "Warren Spencer" and "Charles Grant." Books: *The Small Rain, Ilsa, And Both Were Young* and *The Young Unicorns.*

The great thing about getting older is that you don't lose all the other ages you've been.

November 29

1627   John Ray: English naturalist. Famed for his systems of natural selection. His plant classification greatly influenced the development of systematic botany and is the basis of all modern zoology. Also a collector of proverbs.

If wishes were horses beggars might ride.

1799   Amos Bronson Alcott: American philosopher, teacher and reformer. Leader of the New England Transcendentalist group. Directed the Concord School of Philosophy (1879–88). Father of Louisa May Alcott.

Debate is masculine; conversation is feminine.

1832   Louisa May Alcott: American novelist. Her most famous novel, *Little Women,* sold millions of copies. Also wrote *Little Men, Eight Cousins* and *Jo's Boys.*

Resolved to take Fate by the throat and shake a living out of her.

1898   C.S. [Clive Staples] Lewis: English novelist, literary scholar and essayist on Christian theology and moral problems. He also wrote science fiction. Works: *The Allegory of Love, Out of the Silent Planet, The Lion, the Witch, and the Wardrobe* and *The Screwtape Letters.*

The task of the modern educator is not to cut down jungles but to irrigate deserts.

1902   Inez Robb: American syndicated Scripps Howard columnist, noted for her interviews with the world's famous and covering all newsworthy events. Admits to a gift for infuriating people.

I have all the instincts of a tramp—but a nice one.

1908   Adam Clayton Powell, Jr.: American congressman and clergyman. Prominent black leader. Minister at Abyssinian Baptist Church of New York City (1937-71). Founder and editor of *The People's Voice.* U.S. representative (1945–67 and 1969–70). Expelled from the House for alleged improper acts.

We have produced a world of contented bodies and discontented minds.

1926   Hugh Leonard: Pseudonym of John Keyes Byrne. Irish dramatist. 1978 Tony winner for his play, *Da.*

The problem with Ireland is that it's a country full of genius, but with absolutely no talent.

November 30

1667   Jonathan Swift: Irish-born English satirist, political writer and clergyman. Dean of St. Patrick's Cathedral in Dublin. Works: *The Tale of a Tub, The Battle of the Books, Journal to Stella* and his masterpiece *Gulliver's Travels.*

Satire is a sort of glass, wherein beholders do generally discover everybody's face but their own.

1835   Mark Twain: Pen name of Samuel Langhorne Clemens. American humorist, novelist, short-story writer and lecturer. He took his pen name from the riverboat pilot slang for "two fathoms deep." A number of ill-considered investments drove him into bankruptcy and he spent the latter portion of his life lecturing to raise money. His greatly American works include: *The Adventures of Tom Sawyer, Life on the Mississippi, The Adventures of Huckleberry Finn* and *A Connecticut Yankee in King Arthur's Court.*

The source of humor is not joy but sorrow.

1874   Winston Churchill: English statesman and author. Prime minister, (1939–45 and 1951–55). Provided sterling leadership of the British people during WWII. A powerful orator. Awarded Nobel Prize in Literature for *The Second World War,* a six volume history. Only man to be named an honorary citizen of the United States.

In war: Resolution. In Defeat: Defiance. In Victory: Magnanimity. In Peace: Good Will.

1907   Jacques Barzun: French-born American writer and educator. Dean of faculties and provost at Columbia University.

Works: *Race, a Study in Modern Superstition, The Teacher in America* and *The American University.*
The test of the use of man's education is that he finds pleasure in the exercise of his mind.

1924   Shirley Chisholm: American politician and nursery school teacher. First African-American woman elected to Congress. Democratic U.S. representative from New York (1969–83). Author of: *Good Fight.*
Of my two "handicaps," being female put many more obstacles in my path than being black.

1929   Joan Ganz Cooney: American producer. President of Children's Television Workshop (1970–). Her shows include "Sesame Street" and "Electric Company."
There is a young and impressionable mind out there that is very hungry for information.... It has latched onto an electronic tube as its main source of nourishment.

1936   Abbie Hoffman: American political activist. Rose to prominence as one of the Chicago Seven, tried on charges of conspiring to disrupt the 1968 Democratic Political Convention. He started the loosely organized Yippie movement (1968). Books: *Revolution for the Hell of It* and *Steal This Book.*
Action is the only reality; not only reality but morality as well.

December 1

1863   Oliver Herford: American humorist, poet and illustrator. Author of: *The Bashful Earthquake, and Other Fables and Verses, Cupid's Fair Weather Book* and *The Deb's Dictionary.*
My sense of sight is very keen / My sense of hearing weak / One time I saw a mountain pass, / But could not hear its peak.

1886   Rex Todhunter Stout: U.S. detective story writer. Before turning to writing, he invented a banking system adopted widely in the United States. His most famous creation is the fat private eye Nero Wolfe who appeared in mysteries such as: *A Question of Proof* and *Malice in Wonderland.*

There are two kinds of statistics, the kind you look up and the kind you make up.

1910   Alicia Markova: English-born prima ballerina. Danced with Ballets Russes (1924). Formed the Markova-Dolin Company with Anton Dolin in 1935. Director of Metropolitan Opera Ballet (1963–69).
...To hear in the applause that unmistakable note which ... comes from the heart.... Such a pleasure does not vanish with the fall of the curtain, but becomes part of one's own life.

1913   Mary Martin: American singer and actress. One of the major talents of the Broadway stage. Star of *Leave It to Me, One Touch of Venus, South Pacific* and *The Sound of Music.* Perhaps best remembered for her stage and television appearances as *Peter Pan.*
I had my first love affair at five. I fell in love with my audience.

1935   Woody Allen: American actor, director, screenwriter, playwright, jazz clarinetist. One of the most inventive filmmakers. Oscar winner as director and co-writer of *Annie Hall.* Nominated as actor in the film. Other films: *Play It Again Sam, Manhattan, Hannah and Her Sisters, Crimes and Misdemeanors, Manhattan Murder Mystery* and *Bullets Over Broadway.*
I don't want to achieve immortality through my work ... I want to achieve it through not dying.

1940   Richard Pryor: American comedian and actor. Raised in his grandmother's house of prostitution where his mother worked. Nearly died in 1980, free-basing cocaine. Some of his best movies costar Gene Wilder: *Silver Streak, Stir Crazy* and *See No Evil, Hear No Evil.*
Everyone carries around his own monsters.

1945   Bette Midler: American actress and singer. Known for her bawdy, campy performances in concert and films. Won Grammys for the title number of her film *The Rose* and "Wind Beneath My Wings" from *Beaches.*
After thirty a body has a mind of its own.

December 2

1883 **Nikos Kazantzakis:** Crete-born Greek writer and lawyer. Best known as the author of *Zorba the Greek* and his epic autobiographical narrative poem, "The Odyssey, a Modern Sequel."
Beauty ... is merciless. You do not look at it; it looks at you and does not forgive.

1899 **Sir John Barbirolli:** English-born conductor and cellist of Franco-Italian origin. Played in several leading string quartets (1920–24). Succeeded Toscanini as conductor of the New York Philharmonic, 1937. Permanent conductor of the Halle Orchestra in Manchester (1943–58).
At a rehearsal I let the orchestra play as they like, at the concert I make them play as I like.

1910 **Russell Lynes:** American editor and author. Managing editor of *Harper's*. Books: *Snobs, Guests, Tastemakers* and *Confessions of a Dilettante*.
The only gracious way to accept an insult is to ignore it; if you can't ignore it, top it; if you can't top it, laugh at it; if you can't laugh at it; it's probably deserved.

1925 **Alexander M. Haig, Jr.:** U.S. Army general and statesman. Served in Korea and Vietnam. Became White House chief of staff during last days of Nixon presidency. Supreme NATO commander. Secretary of state (1981–82).
That's not a lie, it's a terminological inexactitude.

1925 **Julie Harris:** Sensitive U.S. actress. Became a Broadway star in *A Member of the Wedding*. Repeated the role in Oscar-nominated screen debut. Also memorable in films *East of Eden* and *Requiem for a Heavyweight*. Won several Tonys and Emmys for her stage and television appearances.
God comes to us in theater in the way we communicate with each other.... It's a way of expressing our humanity.

1931 **Edwin Meese, III:** American government official. Chief of staff to Ronald Reagan when he was governor of California. Meese was the 75th attorney general of the United States.

An expert is somebody who is more than 50 miles from home, has no responsibility for implementing the advice he gives, and shows slides.

1973 **Monica Seles:** Yugoslav tennis player. Ranked number one in the world in 1991 and 1992 after winning the Australian, French and U.S. Opens each year. Youngest to win a Grand Slam title, winning French Open at 16. Stabbed in the back by a male assailant (1993) during a match in Germany.
I don't want to be remembered just as someone who grunted and giggled. I also don't want to be "the one with the knife in the back."

December 3

1807 **Gamaliel Bailey:** American editor. Founder of the anti-slavery journal, *The Cincinnati Philanthropist* (1836) and *The National Era*, Washington (1847), in which Harriet Beecher Stowe's *Uncle Tom's Cabin* first appeared.
The first and worst of all frauds is to cheat oneself.

1826 **George B. McClellan:** U.S. Union general in the American Civil War. Fought in the Mexican War. Appointed by Lincoln to reorganize the Union army. His failure to follow up on his advantage when he forced General Lee to retreat at Antietam caused him to be recalled. Opposed Lincoln for the presidency in 1864.
All quiet along the Potomac.

1857 **Joseph Conrad:** Originally named Jozef Konrad Korzeniowski. Polish born novelist. Joined the British merchant marine and sailed to many parts of the world. Novels: *The Nigger of the Narcissus, Lord Jim, Nostromo* and *Heart of Darkness*.
The terrorist and the politician both come from the same basket.

1895 **Anna Freud:** Austrian-born psychoanalyst. Daughter of Sigmund Freud. Chaired the Vienna Psychoanalytic Society. Emigrated to London in 1938. Organized a residential war nursery for homeless children. A founder of child psychoanalysis.

Creative minds always have been known to survive any kind of bad training.

1922 **Henry Anatole Grunwald:** Austrian-born U.S. editor and author. Joined *Time* magazine as an editor (1945). Books: *Salinger: A Critical and Personal Portrait, Churchill: The Life Triumphant* and *The Age of Elegance.*

Home is one's birthplace, ratified by memory.

1923 **Maria Callas:** Operatic soprano born in New York City of Greek parents. Sang with great authority in all the most exacting soprano roles. Her vocal and dramatic versatility allowed her to sing 43 roles in over 500 performances in every major international opera house.

When my enemies stop kissing, I shall know I'm slipping.

1930 **Jean-Luc Godard:** French director and screenwriter. Emphasized film as an essay, and cinema as a political and social instrument. Films: *Breathless, A Woman Is a Woman, Weekend, Passion* and *Hail Mary! Photography is truth. And cinema is truth twenty-four times a second.*

December 4

1584 **John Cotton:** English-born Puritan clergyman. A tutor at Cambridge before emigrating to Boston. Became head of Congregationalism in the United States. Author of: *The Way of the Church of Christ in New England.*

He who at fifty is a fool, / Is far too stubborn grown for school.

1795 **Thomas Carlyle:** Scottish-born Englishman of letters. Remembered for explosive attack on sham, hypocrisy and excessive materialism. Distrusted democracy and the mob. Best-known works are *Sartor Resartus,* three volumes on the French Revolution and a work on Frederick the Great.

Rest is for the dead.

1835 **Samuel Butler:** English writer, painter and musician. Emigrated to New Zealand. Became attracted to Darwin's theory of evolution. Returned to England

where he wrote his satiric masterpiece, *Erewhon.* Also wrote: *Evolution, Old and New* and *The Way of All Flesh.*

Life is one long process of getting tired.

1865 **Edith Cavell:** English nurse. Matron of the Berkendael Medical Institute, Brussels. Tended friend and foe alike during WWI. Executed by the Germans for helping Belgian and Allied fugitives escape capture.

Standing as I do in view of God and eternity, I realize that patriotism is not enough. I must have no hatred or bitterness toward anyone.

1875 **Rainier Maria Rilke:** German poet. Considered the most significant figure in 20th century German poetry. His three-part poem cycle *The Book of Hours,* written after visiting Russia, is an almost mystical conception of the relationship among God, men and nature. Other works: "The Duino Elegies," "The Sonnets to Orpheus" and *The Notebooks of Malte Laurids Brigge.*

I hold this to be the highest task for a bond between two people: that each protects the solitude of the other.

1892 **Francisco Franco:** Spanish general and dictator (193–75). Because of his close relations with Italian and German Fascists, he took command of the Nationalist forces in the Spanish Civil War. Presided over an authoritarian regime that lasted until his death. Arranged for the monarchy to return upon his death.

Our regime is based on bayonets and blood, not on hypocritical elections.

1921 **Deanna Durbin:** Canadian-born actress and singer who single-handedly saved Universal Studios from bankruptcy with films such as: *Three Smart Girls, 100 Men and a Girl* and *Mad About Music.*

I'm not bitter with Hollywood, but I was never happy making pictures, and so on. And I mean it.

December 5

1782 **Martin Van Buren:** U.S. politician. Eighth president of the United

States. First president born an American citizen. Last sitting vice president before George Bush to be elected president. His four years in office were darkened by financial panic. Forced a measure for a treasury independent of private banks.

The second sober thought of the people is seldom wrong.

1830 **Christina Georgina Rossetti:** English poet. Daughter of poet and painter Gabriel Rossetti. She wrote mainly religious poetry. Also known for her ballads. Best-known single works: "A Birthday," "When I Am Dead" and "Up-Hill."

Better by far you should forget and smile / Than you should remember and be sad.

1839 **George Armstrong Custer:** U.S. soldier with a brilliant career as a cavalry officer in the Civil War. Served in the campaigns against the Indian tribes of the Great Plains. He and his entire command were wiped out by combined Sioux-Cheyenne forces at the Little Bighorn.

If I were an Indian ... I would greatly prefer to cast my lot among those of my people who adhered to the free open plains, rather than submit to the confined limits of a reservation....

1897 **Nunnally Johnson:** U.S. screenwriter, producer and director. Wrote short stories for numerous magazines. Became one of the screen's most prolific and respected writers. Scripts: *The Grapes of Wrath, Roxie Hart, The Keys of the Kingdom* and *My Cousin Rachel.*

Women who have been sewn into their clothes should never drink to excess.

1901 **Walt Disney:** American animator who created an empire with cartoon character Mickey Mouse in 1928. His films won many Oscars over the years. The best of the Disney Studio during his life: *Snow White and the Seven Dwarfs, Pinocchio, Bambi* and *Peter Pan.*

All you've got to do is own up to your ignorance honestly, and you'll find people who are eager to fill your head with information.

1901 **Werner Karl Heisenberg:** German physicist. Awarded 1932 Nobel Prize for the creation of quantum mechanics. Best known for formulating the Uncertainty Principle.

An expert is someone who knows some of the worst mistakes that can be made in his subject and how to avoid them.

1934 **Joan Didion:** American writer. Associate feature editor of *Vogue magazine* (1956–63). Married to writer John Gregory Dunne. Books: *Run River, A Book of Common Prayer, Democracy* and cowrote screenplay for *A Star Is Born* (1976).

Self-respect ... is a question of recognizing that anything worth having has its price.

December 6

1823 **Max Muller:** Anglo-German orientalist and comparative philologist. Works stimulated widespread interest in the study of linguistics, mythology and religion.

Language is the Rubicon that divides man from beast.

1849 **Lord Charles John Darling:** English judge with unusual insight into human nature. Wrote: *Crime and Insanity, Murder and Its Punishment* and *Musings on Murder.*

A timid question will always receive a confident answer.

1886 **Joyce Kilmer:** American poet killed in France during WWI. Best known poem is "Trees." Also wrote "Summer of Love," "The Circus" and "Main Street." Editor: *Dreams and Images: An Anthology of Catholic Poets.*

Poems are made by fools like me / But only God can make a tree.

1887 **Lynn Fontanne:** English-born stage actress, usually teamed with her husband Alfred Lunt. They were brilliant in Noel Coward plays. Broadway's Lunt-Fontanne Theatre, opened in 1958, was named for them. In 1964 they were awarded the U.S. Medal of Freedom.

I am picturesque in a gauche and angular way.

1896 **Ira Gershwin:** American lyricist and author. Pulitzer Prize winner who collaborated with his brother George and many other composers. Among his best songs, "I Got Rhythm," "The Man I Love" and "They Can't Take That Away from Me."
A song without lyrics is like H_2 without O!

1898 **Karl Gunnar Myrdal:** Swedish economist, politician and international public servant. Wrote a classic study of race relations in the United States, *An American Dilemma*. Executive secretary of the U.N. Economic Commission for Europe (1947–57). Also wrote: *The Challenge of Affluence*. Nobel Prize for economics (1974).
Education has in America's whole history been the major hope for improving the individual and society.

1920 **Dave Brubeck:** American pianist, composer and bandleader. Most noted for the Dave Brubeck Quartet, formed in 1951. Composed ballets, a mass and pieces for jazz groups and orchestras.
Jazz is about the only form of art existing today in which there is freedom of the individual without the loss of group contact.

December 7

1542 **Mary, Queen Of Scots:** Became queen upon the death of James V when she was a week old. Married the Dauphin of France, but widowed at 18. Returned to Scotland, a Catholic, she was forced to abdicate in favor of her son by Protestant nobles. Became a prisoner of Elizabeth I. Executed for plotting against the English queen.
Time than fortune should be held more precious / For fortune is as false as she is specious.

1873 **Willa Cather:** American novelist, poet and journalist. Had a high regard for the industry and courage of pioneers and a deep hatred for the modern world. A 1922 Pulitzer Prize winner. Novels: *Death Comes for the Archbishop, My Ántonia, The Song of the Lark* and *O Pioneers!*

The dead might as well speak to the living as the old to the young.

1885 **Zehariah Chafee, Jr.:** American lawyer and Harvard law professor. Recognized as a leading thinker on the subject of civil liberties. Books: *Freedom of Speech, The Inquiring Mind* and *The Blessings of Liberty*.
What is constitutional may still be unwise.

1888 **Heywood C. Broun:** American journalist and novelist. Wrote a liberal-oriented column for several New York City newspapers. Helped found the Newspaper Guild, which annually presents reporting awards in his name.
The tragedy of life is not that man loses but that he almost wins.

1888 **Joyce Cary:** Anglo-Irish novelist. Author of humorous English social history featuring eccentric characters. Best known is the likable scoundrel and painter Gully Jimson in *The Horse's Mouth*. Also wrote: *Mister Johnson* and *Herself Surprised*.
The only good government ... is a bad one in a hell of a fight.

1928 **Noam Chomsky:** American linguist and political activist. Introduced a new theory of language in his *Syntactic Structures*. Opposition to the Vietnam War involved him in the sixties radical movement. Wrote: *American Power and the New Mandarins*.
As soon as questions of will or decisions or reason or choice of action arise, human science is at a loss.

1956 **Larry Bird:** American basketball player. All-American at Indiana State. All-pro with Boston Celtics until his retirement at end of 1992 season. One of three players to win the NBA MVP award three years in a row. Scored more than 20,000 points. Led team to three championships.
What do you need to be a winner? All you've got.

December 8

65 B.C. **Quintus "Horace" Horatius Flaccus:** Latin poet and satirist. Son of a

freed slave. A civil servant. Wrote verses to escape poverty. Became the unrivaled lyric poet of his times. Greatest work: the three books of *Odes*.

Seize the day, and put as little trust as you can in tomorrow.

1626 Christina: Queen of Sweden (1632–54). Daughter and successor of Gustaf II. Educated as a prince. She negotiated the Peace of Westphalia, ending the Thirty Years' War. A patron of the art. Abdicated in 1654 and lived in Rome for the rest of her life.

It is necessary to try to surpass one's self always; this occupation ought to last as long as life.

1865 Jean Sibelius: Finnish composer. A passionate nationalist who wrote a series of symphonic poems based on Finnish fables. Best known for his composition, a tone poem, *Finlandia*.

Pay no attention to what the critics say; no statue has ever been put up to a critic.

1868 George Norman Douglas: English novelist and travel writer. Lived for many years on the island of Capri and in Italy. *Siren Land* is a lively description of Sorrento and Capri. Others: *Fountains in the Sand* and *Old Calabria*.

To find a friend one must close one eye. To keep him—two.

1889 Hervey Allen: American author and editor. Wrote *Israfel, The Life and Times of Edgar Allan Poe, Anthony Adverse* and the series of novels, *The Disinherited*.

Every new generation is a fresh invasion of savages.

1894 James Thurber: American writer and cartoonist. Appointed managing editor of the *New Yorker* (1927). His popular drawings and cartoons were featured in the magazine. Wrote books of humorous essays accompanied by his doodles and *The Secret Life of Walter Mitty*.

Let us not look back in anger or forward in fear, but around in awareness.

1966 Sinead O'Connor: Irish singer and songwriter. Biggest hit: "Nothing Compares 2 U." Combines pop, jazz and Celtic sounds in her songs. Famous for a clean-shaven head and uninhibited observations.

Just because I'm a woman who speaks my mind about things and doesn't behave like some stupid blonde bimbo doesn't mean that I'm aggressive.

December 9

1608 John Milton: English poet and prose writer. One of the best known and most respected of all English literary figures. His early works include: "L'Allegro," "Il Penseroso" and "Lycidas." During the Civil War, he emerged as a champion of the revolution with in a series of pamphlets. Becoming blind in 1652, he wrote his masterpiece, *Paradise Lost*, finishing in 1663.

The first and wisest of them all professed / To know this only, that he nothing knew.

1886 Clarence Birdseye: American businessman and inventor. Developed a process for freezing food in small packages suitable for retailing. President of Birdseye Foods. Credited with over 300 patents.

Go around asking a lot of damn fool questions and taking chances. Only through curiosity can we discover opportunities, and only by gambling can we take advantage of them.

1895 Dolores Ibarruri: "La Pasionaria." Spanish politician and orator. Member of the Central Committee of the Spanish Communist Party. During the Civil War, became the Republic's most emotional and effective propagandist. After the war took refuge in the U.S.S.R.

Better to die on one's feet than live on one's knees.

1898 Emmett Kelly: American clown with Ringling Brothers and Barnum and Bailey circus as Willy the Hobo, delighting generations.

I don't feel funny when I'm in this hobo character. I'm a misfit, a reject. Maybe it's Willy's attempt at a little dignity in spite of everything that tickles folks.

1902 Lucius Beebe: American journalist and social arbiter. Wrote a syndicated column, "This New York" (1934–44). Chronicler in a glorious style of New York's social and gastronomic doings. A devotee of American trains, published the *Terminal Enterprise*. Books: *People on Parade* and *The 20th Century Limited*.

What is subversive today, will almost certainly be patriotic tomorrow.

1906   Grace Brewster Murray Hopper: American mathematician, naval officer and computer pioneer. A rear admiral, she was the oldest active military officer (1943–86). Coinventer of computer language COBOL.

If you do something once, people will call it an accident. If you do it twice, they call it a coincidence. But do it a third time and you've just proven a natural law.

1912   Thomas "Tip" O'Neill: U.S. politician. Democratic representative from Massachusetts (1953–87). Savvy Speaker of the House (1977–87). In 1968 supported Eugene McCarthy's antiwar candidacy and in 1973 as majority leader voted to cut off funding of the air war in Vietnam.

Never kick a man when he is up.

December 10

1602   John Bradshaw: English jurist. Presided as president in 1649 at the trial of King Charles I. Made permanent president of the Council of State and chancellor of the Duchy of Lancaster. Eventually became estranged from Oliver Cromwell.

Rebellion to tyrants is obedience to God.

1824   George MacDonald: Scottish novelist and poet. Best known as a writer of Christian allegories and fairy tales. Works: *Within and Without, Lilith* and *The Princess and the Goblin*.

The love of our neighbor is the only door out of the dungeon of self.

1830   Emily Dickinson: "The Belle of Amherst." American poet. At the age of 23 withdrew from all social contact, living a secluded life, secretly writing over 1,000 poems, most of which were published after her death. Works are intensely personal and spiritual.

I died for Beauty—but was scarce / Adjusted to the Tomb / When One who died for Truth, was lain / In an adjoining Room.

1883   Alfred Kreymborg: American author, poet and editor. Poetry: *Blood of Things, Manhattan Men* and *No More War and Other Poems*. Editor with others of *The American Caravan* and *Lyric America: An Anthropology of American Poetry* (1630–1930).

The sky / is that beautiful old parchment / in which the sun and the moon / keep their diary.

1911   Chester "Chet" Huntley: American broadcast journalist. Teamed with David Brinkley to anchor *NBC Nightly News* (1956–70). Author of: *The Generous Years*.

Journalists were never intended to be the cheerleaders of a society, the conductors of applause, the sycophants. Tragically, that is their assigned role in authoritarian societies, but not here—not yet!

1913   Morton Gould: American composer, conductor and pianist. Orchestra leader on radio's "Chrysler Hour." Composed ballet *Fall River Legend*.

Whatever newness there may be in my music is an ... integration and crystallization of influences in our native musical scene. It is a distillation of the heavy and the light—not necessarily one or the other.

1914   Dorothy Lamour: U.S. actress. Beautiful brunette famed for making the sarong popular in films including: *The Jungle Princess, The Hurricane* and the "Road" movies with Bing Crosby and Bob Hope.

My hips are big, my feet aren't pretty, and my shoulder bones stick out. I'd be glad if I never had to put on a sarong again.

December 11

1803   Hector Berlioz: French composer and conductor. His musical works are conceived as musical embodiments of literary ideas. Compositions: *Symphonie fantastique, Grande messe des morts, Roméo et Juliette* and *La Damnation de Faust*.

Produced seven books including *Treatise on Modern Instrumentation and Orchestration.*

Time is a great teacher, but unfortunately it kills all its pupils.

1849   Ellen Key: Swedish feminist, writer, essayist and educationalist. Her writings, including *The Century of the Child,* advanced her liberal ideas on the feminist movement, child welfare, love, sex and marriage.

Love has been in perpetual strife with monogamy.

1882   Max Born: German-born physicist. Taught at Göttingen, Cambridge and Edinburgh. Shared 1954 Nobel Prize for physics with Walter Rothe for statistical studies on wave functions in the field of quantum physics.

I am now convinced that theoretical physics is actually philosophy.

1882   Fiorella H. La Guardia: "The Little Flower." American politician. Mayor of New York City (1933–45); congressman (1917–21, 1923–33). Famed for reading the comics to the kiddies on radio during a newspaper strike.

Statistics are like alienists — they will testify for either side.

1918   Alexsandr Solzhenitsyn: Russian writer. His writings and criticism of the Stalin regime led to his expulsion from the Soviet Writer's Union and eventual arrest and exile. Has returned home since the fall of the U.S.S.R. Nobel Prize winner (1974). Books: *One Day in the Life of Ivan Denisovich, Cancer Ward, The First Circle* and *The Gulag Archipelago.*

In Russia when you answer questions, you may come to an unfortunate conclusion.

1939   Tom Hayden: American political activist. Cofounder of Students for Democratic Society (1961). Member of "The Chicago 7," tried for attempting to disrupt 1968 Democratic Convention. Liberal California Assemblyman. Once married to Jane Fonda.

A silent majority and government by the people are incompatible.

1950   Christina Onassis: Greek shipping heiress. Daughter of Aristotle Onassis. One of the world's richest women. Died at age 38.

Sometimes when you have everything, you can't tell what matters.

December 12

1745   John Jay: American public official, diplomat and first Chief justice of the Supreme Court (1789–95). Negotiated the Treaty of Paris with Great Britain (1781), ending the Revolutionary War.

The mass of men are neither wise nor good.

1805   William Lloyd Garrison: American abolitionist. Foremost anti-slavery voice in the United States. Published the paper *The Liberator* which argued the case for abolition. Founded the American Anti-Slavery Society.

The success of any great moral enterprise does not depend upon numbers.

1821   Gustave Flaubert: French novelist. One of the great literary artists of the 19th century. Believed in perfection of form and the absolute value of art. Works: *Madame Bovary, Salammbô, L'Éducation sentimentale* and *A Simple Heart.*

What is beautiful is moral, that is all there is to it.

1864   Arthur Brisbane: American journalist and editor. Managing editor, *New York World* (1890–97); editor, *New York Evening Journal* (1897–1921). Later editor, *New York Daily Mirror.* Wrote columns "Today" and "This Week."

Principles were created for compromises.

1897   Lillian Smith: American author. Her popular novel *Strange Fruit* was banned in Boston in 1944. Also wrote: *Killers of the Dream, The Journey, Now Is the Time* and *One Hour.*

Faith and doubt are both needed — not as antagonists but working side by side — to take us around the unknown curves.

1915   Frank Sinatra: U.S. singer and actor. Sang with Harry James and Tommy

Dorsey bands. Became the idol of bobby-soxers. Billed as "The Voice." Film roles before his Oscar for *From Here to Eternity* included: *Anchors Aweigh* and *On the Town*. Later Oscar nominated for *The Man with the Golden Arm*. Songs: "You'll Never Know," "Oh! What It Seemed to Be" and "All the Way."

Hell hath no fury like a hustler with a literary agent.

1929 John Osborne: English playwright, producer and screenwriter. First of England's "angry young men." Oscar winner for *Tom Jones* screenplay. Plays: *Look Back in Anger*, *The Entertainer* and *Luther*.

Asking a working writer what he thinks about critics is like asking a lamp post what it thinks about dogs.

December 13

1585 William Drummond: Scottish poet and laird of Hawthornden. Many of his poems were written for Mary Cunningham, who died on the eve of their wedding. His chief collection, *Poems*, appeared in 1616. He also wrote royalist pamphlets.

He who will not reason, is a bigot; he who cannot is a fool; and he who does not is a slave.

1797 Heinrich Heine: German lyric poet, satirist and journalist. His poetry has been employed in more than 3,000 musical works, including those of Schubert, Schumann, Mendelssohn and Liszt. Works: *Trip to the Harz Mountains*, *Book of Songs*, and *Germany, a Winter Tale*.

Experience is a good school, but the fees are high.

1818 Mary Todd Lincoln: American first lady. Wife of Abraham Lincoln, the 16th president of the United States. After her husband's death she was ruled insane in 1875.

The change from this gloomy earth, to be forever reunited with my idolized husband and my darling Willie would be happiness indeed.

1856 Abbott Lawrence Lowell: American educator and political scientist. Authority on European government. President Harvard University (1909–33). Author of: *The Government of England*, *Public Opinion in War and Peace* and *What a University President Has Learned*.

Universities are full of knowledge; the freshmen bring a little in and the seniors take none away, and knowledge accumulates.

1903 Carlos Montoya: Popular Spanish flamenco guitarist. Traveled throughout the world giving concerts of gypsy melodies. Never having learned to read music, he had help improvising a number of attractive pieces, including *Suite flamenca* for guitar and orchestra.

Only the gypsy can play with his heart.

1911 Kenneth Patchen: American poet and author. Noted for surrealistic poems. Works: *Before the Brave*, *First Will and Testament*, *Memoirs of a Shy Pornographer* and *Hurrah for Anything*.

Oh lonesome's a bad place / To get crowded into.

1920 George P. Schultz: American government official and statesman. Served as U.S. secretary of state during the Reagan presidency. Served as U.S. secretary of the treasury in the Nixon years.

An economist's "lag" may be a politician's catastrophe.

December 14

1533 Henry IV: The first Bourbon King of France (1589–1610). Brought up a Calvinist, he led the Huguenot army at the battle of Jarnac. Survived the massacre of St. Bartholmew's day by proclaiming himself a Catholic. Escaped and renounced his conversion. Became king after the murder of Henry III when he once again became a Catholic, explaining:

Paris is well worth a Mass.

1896 James H. Doolittle: American air force officer. Commanded 16 B-25 bombers which raided Tokyo in 1942, as a message that the United States had not been bombed into submission and helplessness by the Japanese attack at Pearl

Harbor. Commanded the 12th Army Air Force in North Africa and 15th AAF in Italy.

One trouble with Americans is that we're fixers rather than preventors.

1897 **Margaret Chase Smith:** American politician and columnist. Republican U.S. representative from Maine (1940–49) and U.S. senator (1948–72), serving longer than any other woman. Sought Republican presidential nomination (1964).

When people keep telling you that you can't do a thing, you kind of like to try it.

1911 **John "Spike" Jones:** American musician and bandleader. Noted for the use of strange instruments featured in hit novelty songs such as: "Der Fuhrer's Face," "Cocktails for Two," "Chloe" and "All I Want for Christmas (Is My Two Front Teeth)."

When the audience knows you know better, it's satire, but when they think you can't do any better, it's corn.

1919 **Shirley Jackson:** U.S. short-story writer, playwright, novelist and screenwriter. Noted for her tales dealing with the supernatural. Author of: "The Lottery," "The Witchcraft of Salem Village" and "The Haunting of Hill House."

…February, when the days of winter seem endless and no amount of wistful recollecting can bring back any air of summer.

1935 **Lee Remick:** American actress who combined respectability with sensuality. Oscar nominated for *Days of Wine and Roses.* Other films: *A Face in the Crowd, Anatomy of a Murder, The Omen* and *The Long, Hot Summer.*

Breasts and bottoms look boringly alike.

1946 **Patty Duke:** U.S. actress who began her career at seven. Zoomed to stardom before 13 as young Helen Keller in Broadway's *The Miracle Worker.* Repeated the role in the film, winning an Oscar. Star of television's "The Patty Duke Show" (1963–66). President of the Screen Actors Guild (1985–88).

One of the things I've discovered in general about raising kids is that they really don't give a damn if you walked five miles to school.

December 15

37 A.D. **Nero Claudius Caesar:** Emperor of Rome (54–68). Owed his name and position to his mother Agrippina who engineered his adoption by Emperor Claudius, her fourth husband. He was more interested in sex, singing and chariot races than governing. Blamed for the great fire of Rome which he tried to blame on Christians. He committed suicide, commenting:

What an artist dies with me!

1888 **Maxwell Anderson:** American verse playwright. Had his major success from the twenties to the early forties with plays: *Elizabeth the Queen* and *Mary of Scotland.* Wrote the screenplay for *All Quiet on the Western Front.* Pulitzer Prize for the play *Both Your Houses* (1933).

Democracy is government by amateurs.

1892 **J. Paul Getty:** American oilman and art collector. The world's richest man. Left $15 million by his father, he used it to gain control of more than 100 companies. Despite being worth more than a billion dollars, he was noted for his miserliness.

I buy what people are selling.

1904 **Betty Smith:** American novelist and playwright. Best known novel: *A Tree Grows in Brooklyn.* Also wrote: *Tomorrow Will Be Better* and *Joy in the Morning.*

I can never give a "yes" or a "no." I don't believe everything in life can be settled by a monosyllable.

1913 **Muriel Rukeyser:** American poet, biographer, translator and activist. Writes on social and political issues. Translator of the work of Octavio Paz. Books: *Theory of Flight, The Soul and Body of John Brown* and *The Speed of Darkness.*

Women in drudgery knew / they must be one of four: / whores, artists, saints and wives.

1922 **Philip Rieff:** American sociologist and author. Professor of sociology, University of Pennsylvania (1961–77). Books: *Freud: The Mind of the Moralist* and

The Triumph of the Therapeutic: Uses of Faith After Freud.

We are forced to participate in the game of life before we can possibly learn how to use the options in the rules governing them.

1931 Edna O'Brien: Irish novelist and short-story writer. Practiced pharmacy before becoming a writer. Writes of the position of women in society. Books: *The Country Girls, Girls in Their Married Bliss* and *August Is a Wicked Month.*

The vote, I thought means nothing to women. We should be armed.

December 16

1584 John Selden: English lawyer, historian and antiquary. Entered parliament in 1623. Helped draft the Petition of Rights for which he was imprisoned until 1634. Entered the Long Parliament in 1640. Best known book, *Table Talk,* published after his death.

Pleasure is nothing else but the intermission of pain.

1770 Ludwig van Beethoven: German composer of unsurpassed genius. Wrote symphonies, chamber music, concertos and piano sonatas. By his early thirties he was going deaf. Despite this incurable illness which markedly affected his personality, he continued to compose the most spectacular music. Works: *Pathétique, The Moonlight Sonata, Eroica, Fidelio,* and *9th Symphony (Ode to Joy).*

Music is a higher revelation than philosophy.

1775 Jane Austen: English novelist. Had a talent for evaluating ordinary human behavior. Of her six novels, four were published anonymously during her lifetime; the others after her death. Works: *Persuasion, Sense and Sensibility* and *Pride and Prejudice.*

In nine cases out of ten, a woman had better show more affection than she feels.

1863 George Santayana: Spanish-born American skeptical philosopher, poet and novelist. Professor of philosophy, Harvard

(1889–1912). Resided chiefly in Europe thereafter. Works: *The Sense of Beauty, The Life of Reason, Realms of Being* and *The Last Puritan.*

There is no cure for birth and death save to enjoy the interval.

1899 Noël Coward: English playwright, actor, composer and director. A master of English prose. Noted for versatility, wit and sophistication. Wrote much about the spoiled, snobbish British rich. Works: *Private Lives, Design for Living* and *Blithe Spirit.*

Your motivation is your pay packet on Friday. Now get on with it.

1901 Margaret Mead: American anthropologist. Noted for her work on childhood and adolescence, the cultural conditioning of sexual behavior and cultural change. Carried out a number of field studies in the Pacific. Wrote both academic and popular books, including, *Coming of Age in Samoa* and *Culture and Commitment.*

Women want mediocre men, and men are working to be as mediocre as possible.

1917 Arthur C. Clarke: English science-fiction writer. Worked in scientific research before becoming a writer. His themes are exploration and the place humans have in the universe. Books: *Prelude to Space, Rendezvous with Rama* and *2001: A Space Odyssey.*

The only way to define the limits of the possible is by going beyond them into the impossible.

December 17

1616 Roger L'Estrange: English journalist, pamphleteer and translator. Active in the king's cause during the Restoration. Savagely attacked John Milton in "No Blinde Guides."

It is with our passions as it is with fire and water—they are good servants, but bad masters.

1778 Humphrey Davy: English chemist. Discovered the anesthetic effect of laughing gas. Fame rests chiefly on the discovery that chemical compounds can be decomposed into their elements using electricity. Discovered potassium, sodium, barium, strontium, calcium and magnesium.

The most important of my discoveries have been suggested to me by my failures.

1807   **John Greenleaf Whittier:** American poet and social reformer. Popular poet of rural New England. A crusading abolitionist. Founder of the Liberal Party. Wrote: "Snow-Bound," "Barbara Fretchie," "The Barefoot Boy" and "At Sundown."

For all the sad words of tongue and pen, / The saddest are these, "It might have been."

1874   **William MacKenzie King:** Canadian statesman. Leader of the Liberal Party (1919–21). Prime minister (1921–26, 1926–30 and 1935–48). Agreed to help the United States build up defense production during WWII. Signed the Washington Declaration on Nuclear Power (1945).

The promises of yesterday are the taxes of today.

1894   **Arthur Fiedler:** American conductor who originated and conducted the Esplanade concerts in Boston (1929–79). Conducted the Boston Symphony Pops concerts (1930–79).

It's nice to eat a good hunk of beef but you want a light dessert, too.

1908   **Williard Frank Libby:** American chemist. Nobel Prize winner (1960) for his part in the invention of the carbon-14 method of dating ancient findings. Member of the U.S. Atomic Bomb Commission (1954–59).

Death from exposure doesn't come immediately. It doesn't even hurt. You get a lethal dose before you know it.

1929   **William L. Safire:** American journalist and author. Pulitzer Prize winning (1978) writer for *New York Times* since 1973. Noted for articles on word usage.

Is sloppiness of speech caused by ignorance or apathy? I don't know and I don't care.

December 18

1802   **George Dennison Prentice:** American humorist, poet and journalist. Author of "To an Absent Wife" and "Flight of Years."

Though men give you their advice gratis, you will often be cheated if you take it.

1859   **Francis J. Thompson:** English poet and essayist. Best known for the poem "The Hound of Heaven," which describes the divine pursuit of the human soul.

I fled Him, down the nights and down the days; / I fled Him, down the arches of the years; / I fled Him, down the labyrinthine ways / Of my own mind; and in the midst of tears / I hid from Him, and under running laughter.

1870   **Hector Hugh Munro:** Pseudonym Saki. Burma-born English novelist and short-story writer. Worked as a correspondent for several newspapers. Best known for humorous and satiric stories of the supernatural and macabre. Works: *Reginald, The Unbearable Bassington* and *Beasts and Superbeasts.*

A little inaccuracy sometimes saves tons of explanation.

1879   **Paul Klee:** Swiss artist. Became a member of the "Blaue Reiter" Munich group. Taught at the Bauhaus (1920–32). Early works were bright watercolors, but after 1919 he worked in oil. Surrealist painter influenced by primitive African sculptures. Paintings: *Twittering Machine* and *The Mocker Mocked.*

Art is a lie that makes us realize the truth.

1886   **Ty [Tyrus Raymond] Cobb:** U.S. baseball outfielder, mostly with the Detroit Tigers. First man elected to Baseball's Hall of Fame. A fierce competitor, mostly hated by other players. Hit .400 three times. Lifetime BA, .367, the highest ever. Had 4,191 career hits, the most until Pete Rose broke his record.

Every great hitter works on the theory that the pitcher is more afraid of him than he is of the pitcher.

1913   **Willie Brandt:** German statesman. Mayor of Berlin (1957–66). Chancellor of West Germany (1969–74). Nobel Peace Prize winner (1971).

It is better to be the only democrat in Germany where democracy is unknown than one of many in Norway, where everybody understands it.

1947   Steven Spielberg: U.S. film producer, director and screenwriter. His films have been among the most popular and most successful in box-office history. But it wasn't until *Schindler's List* that he received the recognition of his peers with an Oscar. Other films: *Close Encounters of the Third Kind, Raiders of the Lost Ark, E.T.,* the *Extra Terrestrial, The Color Purple, Empire of the Sun* and *Jurassic Park.*

I dream for a living.

December 19

1820   Mary Ashton Rice Livermore: American health reformer, hospital administrator, suffragist, abolitionist and writer. Editor: *American Women* with Francis E. Willard. Founder, *The Agitator* (1869).

...Books have been written by men physicians ... one would suppose in reading them that women possess but one class of physical organs, and that these are always diseased.

1865   Minnie Maddern Fiske: Celebrated U.S. stage actress. Acclaimed for her Ibsen heroines. Married to theatrical manager Harrison Grey Fiske.

The essence of acting is the conveyance of truth through the medium of an actor's mind and person. The science of acting deals with perfecting that medium. The great actors are the luminous ones. They are the great conductors of the stage.

1888   Fritz Reiner: Budapest-born conductor. Arrived in the United States in 1922 to lead the Cincinnati Symphony Orchestra. Joined the Pittsburgh Symphony Orchestra (1938). Spent several seasons with the Metropolitan Opera in NYC. Found his greatest acclaim as conductor of the Chicago Symphony Orchestra (1953–62).

Watch out for emergencies. They are your big chance!

1906   Leonid I. Brezhnev: Soviet leader. General secretary of the Communist Party (1964–82). President of the Supreme Soviet (1977–82). He was the first Soviet leader to hold both positions simultaneously. Signed the SALT I treaty with President Nixon (1972).

God will not forgive us if we fail.

1910   Jean Genet: French writer. Spent many years of his youth in reformatories and prisons. Began to write in 1942 while serving a life sentence for theft. His novel *Our Lady of the Flowers* caused a sensation. Turned to writing plays, *The Maids* and *The Screens.* Granted a pardon in 1948.

Violence is a calm that disturbs you.

1915   Edith Piaf: French singer. Internationally famous cabaret star. Began as a street singer in Paris in 1930. Known for emotional and powerful voice and delivery. Songs: "Milord," "La Vie en rose" and "Non, je ne regrette rein."

I have always made a distinction between my friends and my confidants. I enjoy the conversation of the former, from the latter I hide nothing.

1944   Richard Leakey: Nairobi-born palaeoanthropologist. Son of Mary and Louis Leakey. From an early age worked in the field with his parents. Discovered crania of *Australopithecus boisei, Homo habilis* and *Homo erectus.* Director of the Wildlife and Conservation Management Service, Kenya.

We have to face the fact that one day humanity will disappear. There is no escaping that fact. The question is when?

December 20

1579   John Fletcher: English playwright. Best known for collaboration with Francis Beaumont on such works as: *A King and No King* and *The Maid's Tragedy.* Believed to have collaborated with Shakespeare on *Henry VIII.*

Speak boldly, and speak truly, shame the devil.

1780   John Wilson Croker: English politician and essayist. Said to be the first to use the term "Tory" to refer to one who belongs to the Conservative Party.

A game which a sharper once played with a dupe, entitled, "Heads I win, tails you lose."

1881   Branch Rickey: American baseball executive. Instituted the farm system in 1919. As president of the Brooklyn Dodgers

made Jackie Robinson the first black to play in the modern major leagues in 1947.
Baseball is a game of inches.

1895   Susanne K. Langer: American philosopher and educator. Taught at Radcliffe (1927–42). Published important works in aesthetics. Works: *Philosophy in a New Key, Problems of Art* and *An Essay on Human Feeling.*
If we should have new knowledge, we must get a world of new questions.

1902   Sidney Hook: American philosopher and author. Professor of philosophy, New York University (1939-69). Books: *The Metaphysics of Pragmatism, Common Sense and the Fifth Amendment* and *The Place of Religion in a Free Society.*
In contrast to totalitarianism, democracy can face and live with the truth about itself.

1902   Max Lerner: Russian-born American educator, editor and writer. Professor political science, Williams College (1938-43). Joined Brandeis University (1949). Books: *Ideas Are Weapons, The Unfinished Country* and *Beyond the Power Principle.*
When you choose the lesser of two evils, always remember that it is still an evil.

1911   Hortense Calisher: American novelist and short-story writer. Tells stories of the upper-middle class New Yorkers. Novels: *The New Yorkers, Queenie* and *The Bobby-Soxer.*
Every art is a church without communicants, presided over by a parish of the respectable. An artist is born kneeling; he fights to stand. A critic by nature of the judgment seat, is born sitting.

December 21

1804   Benjamin Disraeli: 1st Earl of Beaconsfield. British statesman and novelist. Leader of the conservatives in the House of Commons after Robert Peel and his followers left the party. Prime minister (1868 and 1874–80). Instituted reforms in housing, public health and factory regulations. Novels: *Vivien Grey* and *Sybil.*
There are three kinds of lies: lies, damned lies and statistics.

1879   Joseph Stalin: The leading Bolshevik followed Lenin into power. Became Soviet dictator with appointment as general secretary of the Communist Party, solidifying his power by killing more than 10 million. Signed a nonaggression pact with Hitler in 1939. After Germany invaded the U.S.S.R., joined the Allies. After the war was able to seize control of much of Eastern and Central Europe.
A single death is a tragedy, a million deaths is a statistic.

1892   Walter Hagan: U.S. pro golfer. Won two U.S. Opens, four British Opens, five PGA championships and five Western championships. six-time Ryder Cup captain. Retired with 40 PGA victories.
Give me a man with big hands, big feet and no brains, and I will make a golfer out of him.

1905   Anthony Powell: English novelist and journalist. Wrote a 12-volume series of novels, *A Dance to the Music of Time,* covering 50 years of British upper-middle class life. Also wrote: *At Lady Molly's, Temporary Kings* and *The Fisher King.*
Growing old is like being increasingly penalized for a crime you haven't committed.

1926   Joe Paterno: American football coach. Led Penn State to two national titles (1982 and 1986). Many believe he deserved another when his team went undefeated in 1994. Four-time coach of the year. Has more than 260 career victories.
Publicity is like poison: it doesn't hurt unless you swallow it.

1935   Phil Donahue: American television host of "Donahue" (1967–96). Emmy winner (1977 and 1979). Married to actress Marlo Thomas.
Suicide is a permanent solution to a temporary problem.

1959   Florence Griffith Joyner: American Olympic runner. Won three gold medals in 1988 Olympics for 100m, 200m and 4×100m relay. Heads President's Council on Physical Fitness and Sports.
A muscle is like a car. If you want it to run well early in the morning, you have to warm it up.

December 22

1639   **Jean Racine:** French dramatic poet. Began to write plays in 1664. Regarded as the master of tragic pathos. Verse tragedies: *Andromaque, Britannicus, Iphigénie, Phèdre* and *Bérénice.*

Crime like virtue has its degrees; and timid innocence was never known to blossom suddenly into extreme license.

1858   **Giacomo Puccini:** Italian operatic composer. An organist and choir-master who wrote his first compositions for the church. Operas: *La Bohème, Tosca, Madama Butterfly* and *Turandot,* unfinished at his death.

Art is a kind of illness.

1869   **Edwin Arlington Robinson:** American poet. Most of his poetry was set in a fictional New England village, Tilbury Town. Three-time Pulitzer Prize winner. Collections of poetry: *The Children of the Night, Collected Poems, The Man Who Died Twice* and *Tristram.*

Life is the game that must be played.

1883   **Edgar Varèse:** French composer who settled in New York City after WWI. Founded the New Symphony Orchestra (1919). Organized the first International Composers' Guild (1921). Works: *Metal, Ionisation* and *Hyperprism.*

Everybody is born with genius, but most only keep it a few minutes.

1912   **Claudia "Lady Bird" Johnson:** American first lady. Wife of Lyndon Baines Johnson, 36th U.S. president. With an inheritance when she was a little girl, she built a great communication center in Austin, Texas.

A politician ought to be born a foundling and remain a bachelor.

1945   **Diane Sawyer:** U.S. television journalist. National Junior Miss (1962). Press aide for President Nixon. Joined "CBS Morning News" (1981), coanchoring with Charles Kuralt. First woman to cohost "60 Minutes." Anchors ABC's "Prime Time."

People assume you can't be shy and be on television. They're wrong.

1951   **Jan Stephenson:** Australian golfer. LPGA Rookie of the Year (1974). Upset some of the ladies when she posed for a calendar of beautiful female golfers.

I may not be the prettiest girl in the world, but I'd like to see Bo Derek rate a "10" after playing 18 holes in 100 degrees heat.

December 23

1790   **Jean François Champollion:** French founder of Egyptology. Used the Rosetta Stone to decipher Egyptian hieroglyphics. Placed study of early Egyptian culture and history on a firm foundation. On his deathbed he gave instructions to the printer of revised proofs of his Egyptian grammar.

Be careful of this—it is my carte de visite to posterity.

1805   **Joseph Smith:** U.S. founder of the Mormons. Received his "call" and was ordained a priest by the angel Moroni. The tenets of the new sect were found in hidden gospels written by a prophet named Mormon. Despite ridicule for its teachings and the practice of polygamy, the Church of Latter Day Saints gained converts. Smith was imprisoned in Carthage, Illinois, and killed by a mob that broke into the jail.

Man is that he might have joy.

1812   **Samuel Smiles:** Scottish author. Best known for his didactic work *Self Help.* Also wrote *Character, Thrift, Duty* and *Gospel of Work.*

Politeness goes far, yet costs nothing.

1860   **Harriet Monroe:** American poet and critic. Founded the highly respected magazine, *Poetry,* in 1912. Published the work of Vachel Lindsay, T.S. Eliot, Ezra Pound and Robert Frost. Author of the "Columbian Ode," for the Chicago World's Columbian Exposition in 1892, celebrating the 400th anniversary of the discovery of America.

...Poetry, "The Cinderella of the Arts."

1881   **Juan Ramón Jiménez:** Spanish lyric poet. Abandoned law studies to write poetry. Left Spain in 1936 because of the Spanish Civil War, settling in Florida. Nobel Prize for literature (1956). Poetry: *Platero and I* and *Spiritual Sonnets*.

Literature is a state of culture, poetry of grace, before and after culture.

1902   **Norman MacLean:** American author and educator. Wrote *Critics and Criticism: Ancient and Modern*. Contributed articles and stories to many magazines. Best known for writing *A River Runs Through It*.

In our family, there was no clear line between religion and fly fishing.

1935   **Paul Hornung:** U.S. football halfback and kicker. Only player to win Heisman Trophy while playing on a losing team, Notre Dame (2-8) in 1956. Three-time NFL scoring leader with Green Bay Packers. His 176 points in 1960 is the all-time record. Voted MVP 1961. Suspended 1963 for betting on his team.

Never get married in the morning, 'cause you never know who you'll meet that night.

December 24

1745   **Benjamin Rush:** American patriot, humanitarian, medical pioneer and author. Signer of the Declaration of Independence. Wrote: *Sermons to Gentlemen upon Temperance and Exercise* and *Essays, Literary, Moral and Philosophical*.

Scandal dies sooner by itself, than we could kill it.

1754   **George Crabbe:** English poet, trained as a surgeon. An ordained minister. His career in writing poetry was interrupted by a 20-years period during which he produced nothing. Works: "The Village," "The Parish Register" and "The Borough."

Habit with him was all the test of truth; / "it must be right: I've done it from my youth."

1822   **Matthew Arnold:** English poet and critic. Crusader for classicism, critical traditionalism and the notion that literature should ennoble man. Made his mark with *Poems: A New Edition* which contained "The Scholar Gipsy." Other poems: "Dover Beach" and "Thyrsis."

The pursuit of perfection, then, is the pursuit of sweetness and light.

1838   **John Morley:** Viscount of Blackburn. English Liberal statesman. Made a notable contribution to literature in writing the official biography of W.E. Gladstone.

You have not converted a man, because you have silenced him.

1905   **Howard Hughes, Jr.:** Reclusive billionaire U.S. businessman, film producer, director and aviator. Basis of fortune was inheriting father's machine tool company. Founded his own aircraft company and designed airplanes. Set several world air speed records. Made movies *Hell's Angels*, *Scarface* and *The Outlaw*.

There are two good reasons why men go to see her [Jane Russell]. They are enough.

1907   **I.F. [Isidor Feinstein] Stone:** U.S. radical journalist. Joined the liberal reformist *New York Post* (1933–38), *New York Nation* (1938–46). Hostile to the Cold War. Opposed U.S. involvement in Vietnam. Founded *I.F. Stone's Weekly* (1951).

The difference between burlesque and newspapers is that the former never pretended to be performing a public service by exposure.

1930   **Robert Joffrey:** American dance, choreographer and teacher. Built the Joffrey Ballet into one of the nation's top companies. His ballets in the sixties combined rock music and multimedia techniques. Also revived contemporary classics.

Ballet does not belong in the rarified realm of an esoteric art, but ... is a living, evolving form which is part of "theater" in its most comprehensive sense.

December 25

1642   **Sir Isaac Newton:** English mathematician, scientist. Recognized as one of the greatest minds in history. Master of the Mint where he proved to be an able administrator. Member of Parliament. Developed calculus independently of Leibniz. Enunciated laws of motion and law of gravitation. Despite signs of a persecution complex and conflicts with other great scientists, he wrote:

If I see further than other men it is because I stand on the shoulders of giants.

1821 **Clara Barton:** U.S. schoolteacher and founder of the American Red Cross. During the Civil War she helped obtain supplies and comforts for the wounded. Worked for the International Red Cross in the Franco-Prussian War. Became first president of the U.S. branch of the Red Cross (1881–1904).

I may be compelled to face danger, but never fear it.

1870 **Rosa Luxemburg:** Revolutionary born in Russian Poland. Became a German citizen. With Karl Liebknecht formed the Spartacus League, which later became the German Communist Party. Known as "Red Rosa," Marxist leader was arrested and murdered during the Spartacus revolt in Berlin.

Be prepared for the day when Socialism will ask not only for your vote but for your life itself.

1886 **Franz Rosenzweig:** Jewish theologian. Reacted against German Idealism. Expounded an existential approach, emphasizing experiences and interests of the individual. In 1913, reaffirmed his Jewish faith, devoting the rest of his life to the study and practice of Judaism.

The sufferer alone is permitted to praise God in his works. But all men suffer.

1892 **Rebecca West:** Pseudonym of Cicily Isabel Andrews. English critic and novelist. Took her pen name from the character she played on the stage in a production of Ibsen's *Rosmersholm*. Best known for *The Meaning of Treason* and *A Train of Power*. Novels: *The Judge* and *The Birds Fall Down*.

But humanity is never more sphinxlike than when it is expressing itself.

1918 **Anwar Sadat:** Egyptian statesman and president (1970–81). Member of the coup that deposed King Farouk. As president, he also assumed the position of prime minister (1973–74), as he sought to settle the conflict with Israel, signed the Camp David Peace Accord with Menachem Begin (1978). Shared the Nobel Peace Prize with Begin. Assassinated by Muslim extremists (1981).

Peace is much more precious than a piece of land.

1924 **Rod Serling:** U.S. television scriptwriter. Author of over 200 television plays. Won six Emmy awards for "Patterns" (1955). Created, wrote and hosted "The Twilight Zone" (1959–64) and "Night Gallery" (1970–73).

Every writer is a frustrated actor who recites his lines in the hidden auditorium of his skull.

December 26

1716 **Thomas Gray:** English poet. Professor of history and modern language at Cambridge. Wrote "Ode on a Distant Prospect of Eton College" and his masterpiece, "Elegy Written in a Country Churchyard."

The paths of glory lead but to the grave.

1792 **Charles Babbage:** English mathematician and inventor. Attempted to perfect two calculating machines: a difference engine to calculate tables of logarithms and an "analytical engine" to perform computations using punched cards. Although not totally successful, his work laid a foundation for today's modern electronic computers.

Every moment dies a man, / Every moment 11/16 is born.

1820 **Dion Bouicault:** Irish-born U.S. actor and playwright. Plays: *The Octaroon, The Shaughram* and *Belle Lamar*. Wrote the lyrics of song, "The Wearin' of the Green."

Men talk of killing time, while time quietly kills them.

1891 **Henry Miller:** American writer who while living in France for nine years wrote his classics, *Tropic of Cancer* and *Tropic of Capricorn*, both banned in the United States because of the explicit sexual nature of the essentially autobiographical works.

Sex is one of the nine reasons for reincarnation ... the other eight are unimportant.

1893   Mao Zedong (Mao Tse-Tung): Founding father of the People's Republic of China. Served as both Chairman of the Communist Party and President of the Republic (1949–76). In 1958, launched his Great Leap Forward, an unsuccessful attempt to quickly make agrarian China an industrial power. In 1965, launched a cultural revolution. His ideas were popularized by his *The Little Red Book.*
Political power grows out of the barrel of a gun.

1894   Jean Toomer: American author, poet and lecturer. "Harlem Renaissance" writer. Books: *Cane, Essentials* and *Portage Potential.*
People mistake their limitations for high standards.

1954   Susan Butcher: One of only two people to win the world-famous Iditarod sled-dog race at least four times. Holds the record for the fastest completion of the grueling 1,157 mile race from Anchorage to Nome.
My goal was never to be the first woman or the best woman. It was to be the best sled-dog racer.

December 27

1571   Johannes Kepler: German astronomer and mathematician. Called the "father of modern astronomy." Announced his first and second laws of planetary motion in 1609, which formed the groundwork for the discoveries of Newton. Promulgated his third law in *Harmonies of the World* (1619).
Nature uses as little as possible of anything.

1822   Louis Pasteur: French chemist and microbiologist. Established that putrefaction and fermination are caused by microorganisms. He demonstrated that sheep and cows "vaccinated" with the attenuated bacilli of anthrax received protection against the disease. Worked at the Institut Pasteur at Paris for the treatment of rabies.

The greatest disorder of the mind is to let will direct belief.

1896   Louis Bromfield: American novelist and journalist. Moved to France in 1923 where he wrote his Pulitzer Prize–winning novel *Early Autumn* and *A Good Woman.*
As soils are deleted, human health, vitality and intelligence go with them.

1901   Marlene Dietrich: German-born actress with the most sensuous face and figure of the early sound era. Her best films were directed by her discoverer Josef von Sternberg, as a seductively androgynous woman of tawdry glamour. Films: *The Blue Angel, Shanghai Express, The Scarlet Empress, Destry Rides Again* and *Witness for the Prosecution.*
Think twice before burdening a friend with a secret.

1906   Oscar Levant: U.S. pianist, composer and actor. A close friend of George Gershwin, as a pianist becoming one of his foremost interpreters. A hypochondriac and caustic wit. Films: *Rhapsody in Blue* and *An American in Paris.*
Happiness isn't something you experience; it's something you remember.

1915   William H. Masters: U.S. human sexuality expert, who with his wife-to-be Virginia Johnson established the Reproductive Biological Research Foundation (1964), where studies of the psychology and physiology of sexual intercourse were carried out. Published *Human Sexual Response* (1966) and *On Sex and Human Loving* (1971).
Sex is a natural function like breathing or eating.

1943   Cokie Roberts: American broadcast journalist. Spent 17 years analyzing the proceedings of Congress for NPR and ABC.
I think the impulse is to trash the Congress, to ridicule the Congress, to always tear down the institution. I'm sorry. I just love the institution. I want it to be better.

December 28

1822   William Rounseville Alger: American clergyman and author. Wrote

The Poetry of the East, The Friendships of Women and *Life of Edwin Forrest, the American Tragedian.*

We give advice by the bucket, but take it by the grain.

1856 **[Thomas] Woodrow Wilson:** American statesman and educator. Twenty-eighth president of the United States (1912-20). President of Princeton University and governor of New Jersey. After WWI, he personally headed up the U.S. delegation to the peace treaty. Proposed his "14 points" and the establishment of the League of Nations, neither of which could he sell to the Congress. Nobel Prize winner (1919).

The world must be made safe for democracy.

1882 **Sir Arthur Stanley Eddington:** English astronomer. Director of the Cambridge Observatories. Worked mainly on the internal structure of stars. He was able to give the first direct confirmation of Einstein's theory of relativity in 1919 with observations of stars during a total solar eclipse.

There is no approach of science to religion and science has nothing to say about religion.

1902 **Mortimer J. Adler:** American philosopher, educator and writer. Taught at the University of Chicago (1930–52). In 1946, helped design the "Great Books" program which popularized great ideas of Western civilization in 54 volumes.

Not to engage in the pursuit of ideas is to live like ants instead of like men.

1903 **John Von Neuman:** Hungarian-born mathematician. In 1933, joined the Institute for Advanced Study, Princeton. Contributions include a new axiomatic foundation for set theory, high-speed calculations, which contributed to the development of computers and the introduction of game theory.

There is grave danger of confusing a technical opinion with a political intuition.

1911 **Sam Levenson:** American comedian and author. Former schoolteacher. Known for gentle satire on everyday life. Hosted television's "Sam Levenson Show."

It is so simple to be wise. Just think of

something stupid to say, then say the opposite.

1954 **Denzel Washington:** American actor. First success with television's "St. Elsewhere." Won an Oscar for the film *Glory.* Nominated for his performance in the title role of *Malcolm X.*

Luck is where opportunity meets preparation.

December 29

1721 **Madame Jeanne Poisson de Pompadour:** French mistress of Louis XV, king of France. For 20 years, this woman of remarkable grace, beauty and wit, swayed state policy and became a patroness of the arts. Largely blamed for the French defeat in the Seven Years' War.

It is a wolf who makes the sheep reflect.

1798 **L.P. [Laurens Perseus] Hickok:** American Presbyterian clergyman, educator, philosopher and author. President of Union College. Wrote *A System of Moral Science: The Logic of Reason.*

Genius is the highest type of reason; talent is the highest type of understanding.

1809 **William E. Gladstone:** British statesman. Prime minister (1868–74, 1880-85, 1886, 1892–94). In 1867 became leader of the Liberal Party. Established a system of national education. His reforms of Parliament went a long way towards universal male suffrage. Worked unsuccessfully for Irish Home Rule.

Liberalism is trust of the people tempered by prudence; Conservatism is distrust of the people tempered by fear.

1876 **Pablo Casals:** Spanish cellist, conductor and composer. Founded the Barcelona Orchestra (1919). Left Spain at the outbreak of the Spanish Civil War. Principal cellist of the Paris Opera.

The cello is like a beautiful woman who has not grown older, but younger with time, more slender, more supple, more graceful.

1907 **Robert Weaver:** U.S. government official and economist. First African-American to serve in the U.S. cabinet. Secretary

of HUD (1966–69). Wrote *Negro Ghetto.* His caution to black students:
...Develop the capacity for individual self-criticism and evaluation ... to meet competition beyond the confines of a segregated world.

1917   Tom [Thomas J.] Bradley: American politician. First African-American mayor of a predominantly white city, Los Angeles (1973–93). Given Spingarn Award (1983).
Attitude was the most important asset we had to break the back of racism.

1936   Mary Tyler Moore: American actress. Most successful in the television series "The Dick Van Dyke Show" and "The Mary Tyler Moore Show." Won many Emmys for her roles. Named "actress of the year"(1974).
Pain nourishes courage. You can't be brave if you've only had wonderful things happen to you.

December 30

1847   John Peter Altgeld: German-born American politician and social reformer. Served in the Union Army during the Civil War. As judge of the Illinois Supreme Court, he is chiefly known for pardoning three anarchists convicted of complicity in the 1886 Haymarket Riots.
The laboring people found the prisons always open to receive them, but the courts of justice were practically closed to them.

1865   Rudyard Kipling: British writer, born in Bombay, India. Worked as a journalist. His satirical verses and short-stories won him a reputation in England. Works: *Soldiers Three, Jungle Books, Kim* and *Just So Stories.*
I kept six honest serving men / they taught me all I know: / Their names are What and Why and When / And How and Where and Who.

1869   Stephen Leacock: English-born Canadian humorist, historian and economist. Head of the economics department McGill University, Montreal. Wrote *The Economic Prosperity of the British Empire.*

Best known for humorous *Literary Lapses, Winsome Winnie* and *Nonsense Novels.*
It is to be observed that "angling" is the name given to fishing by people who can't fish.

1873   Alfred E. Smith: American politician. Joined the New York City Democratic political organization. Rose to be governor of the state (1919–20, 1923–28). First Roman Catholic to make a run for the presidency. Defeated by Herbert Hoover (1928).
Nobody shoots at Santa Claus.

1884   Hideki Tojo: Japanese general and statesman. Prime minister (1941–44). Minister of War (1940–41). Arrested in 1945. Attempted suicide but survived to be tried and convicted of war crimes and hanged.
Japan must go on and develop in ever expanding progress—there is no retreat! ... If Japan's hundred millions merge and go forward, nothing can stop us.... Wars can be fought with ease.

1895   Leslie Poles Hartley: English author. Established a reputation for the macabre with short-stories such as *Night Fears.* Moved on to examinations of psychological relationships. Novels: *The Shrimp and the Anemone, The Boat* and *The Go-Between.*
The past is foreign country; they do things differently there.

1935   Sandy Koufax: Hall of Fame left-handed pitcher with the L.A. Dodgers. Led NL in strikeouts four times, ERA, 5 straight years. Won 3 Cy Young Awards. MVP, 1963. Pitched one perfect game and three other no-hitters. Forced to retire early because of a chronic injury.
Pitching is ... the art of instilling fear.

December 31

1320   John Wycliffe: English philosopher, religious reformer and writer. Attacked the Church hierarchy, priestly power and the doctrine of transubstantiation. Wrote many popular tracts in English as opposed to Latin. Made the first English translation of the Bible.

How should God approve that you rob Peter and give the robbery to Paul, in the name of Christ?

1491   Jacques Cartier: French navigator. Made three voyages of exploration to North America. Surveyed the coast of Canada and the St. Lawrence River. Provided the basis for French claims to the region.

I am rather inclined to believe that this is the land God gave to Cain.

1869   Henri Matisse: French painter. From 1904 he was the leader of the "Fauves" (wild beasts), a name given by a hostile critic. Paintings display a bold use of brilliant colors. Paintings: *Woman with a Hat* and *The Red Studio.*

Derive happiness in oneself from a good day's work, from illuminating the fog that surrounds us.

1880   George Catlett Marshall: American soldier and statesman. Chief of Staff (1939–45). Directed Army through WWII. Became secretary of state in 1947. Originated the "Marshall Aid Plan" for the postwar reconstruction of Europe. Nobel Peace Prize (1953).

If man does find the solution for world peace it will be the most revolutionary reversal of his record we have ever known.

1908   Simon Wiesenthal: Austrian Jewish survivor of Nazi concentration camps. Dedicated his life to tracking down and prosecuting former Nazis who had organized the prosecution of the Jews during WWII. Instrumental in the capture of Adolf Eichmann.

I think I am one of the last witnesses. And a last witness, before he leaves this world, has an obligation to speak out.... My work is a warning for the murderers of tomorrow.

1930   Odetta: American folksinger and musician, born Odetta Holmes Gordon. Known for her mellow style and African motifs. Greatest popularity in fifties and sixties.

Music is medicine that's pleasant to take.

1941   Sarah Miles: English actress. Oscar nominated for *Ryan's Daughter.* Other films: *The Servant, Blow-Up,* and *Lady Caroline Lamb.* Twice married to playwright-director Robert Bolt.

There's a little bit of hooker in every woman. A little bit of hooker and a little bit of God.

Index of People

A

Aaron, Henry   February 5, 1934
Abbott, Berenice   July 17, 1898
Abbott, Charles C.   June 4, 1843
Abbott, George   June 25, 1887
Abdul-Jabbar, Kareem   April 16, 1947
Abel, Niels Henrik   May 5, 1802
Abernathy, Ralph   March 11, 1926
Abrams, Charles   September 20, 1901
Abzug, Bella   July 24, 1920
Ace, Jane Sherwood   October 12, 1905
Achard, Marcel   July 5, 1899
Acheson, Dean   April 11, 1893
Acton, Lord (John E.E. Dalberg)   January 10, 1834
Adams, Abigail Smith   November 11, 1744
Adams, Ansel   February 20, 1902
Adams, Brooks   June 24, 1848
Adams, Charles F.   August 18, 1807
Adams, Franklin P.   November 15, 1881
Adams, Henry   February 16, 1838
Adams, Jane   September 6, 1860
Adams, John   October 30, 1735
Adams, John Quincy   July 11, 1767
Adams, Samuel   September 27, 1722
Adams, Samuel Hopkins   January 26, 1871
Adamson, Joy   January 20, 1910
Addams, Charles   January 7, 1912
Addison, Joseph   May 1, 1672
Ade, George   February 9, 1866
Adenauer, Konrad   January 3, 1876
Adler, Felix   August 13, 1851
Adler, Mortimer J.   December 28, 1902
Adler, Polly   April 16, 1900
Adler, Renata   October 19, 1938
Agassiz, Jean Louis   May 28, 1808

Agee, James   November 27, 1909
Aiken, Conrad   August 5, 1899
Ailey, Alvin   January 5, 1931
Akhmatova, Anna   June 11, 1888
Akins, Zoë   October 30, 1886
Alain   March 3, 1868
Albee, Edward   March 12, 1928
Alberti, Leon Battista   February 14, 1401
Alcott, Amos Bronson   November 29, 1799
Alcott, Louisa May   November 29, 1832
Aldiss, Brian Wilson   August 18, 1925
Alexander, Shana   October 6, 1929
Alfieri, Vittorio   January 16, 1749
Alfonso X   November 23, 1221
Alger, Horatio, Jr.   January 13, 1832
Alger, William Rounseville   December 28, 1822
Algren, Nelson   March 28, 1909
Ali, Muhammad   January 17, 1942
Alinsky, Saul   January 30, 1909
Allen, Ethan   January 21, 1737
Allen, Fred   May 31, 1894
Allen, Gracie   July 26, 1906
Allen, Woody   December 1, 1935
Alsop, Joseph, Jr.   October 11, 1910
Alsop, Stewart   May 17, 1914
Altgeld, John Peter   December 30, 1847
Alvarez, Luis   June 13, 1911
Alvord, Clarence Wadworth   May 21, 1768
Ames, Fisher   April 9, 1758
Amiel, Henri Frédéric   September 27, 1821
Andersen, Hans Christian   April 2, 1805
Anderson, Jack   October 19, 1922

Anderson, Marian   February 17, 1902
Anderson, Maxwell   December 15, 1888
Anderson, Sherwood   September 15, 1876
Angelou, Maya   April 4, 1928
Anouilh, Jean   June 23, 1910
Anthony, Katharine   November 27, 1877
Anthony, Susan B.   February 15, 1820
Aquino, Corazon C.   January 26, 1871
Arafat, Yasir   August 24, 1929
Aragon, Louis   October 3, 1897
Arendt, Hannah   October 14, 1906
Aristide, Jean-Bertrand   July 15, 1953
Armour, Philip D.   May 16, 1832
Armour, Richard   June 22, 1922
Armour, Tommy   September 24, 1895
Armstrong, Louis   July 4, 1900
Armstrong, Neil   August 5, 1930
Armstrong-Jones, Anthony   March 7, 1930
Arnold, Matthew   December 24, 1822
Arnold, Thomas   June 13, 1795
Arzner, Dorothy   January 3, 1900
Asch, Sholem   November 1, 1880
Ash, Mary Kay   May 12, 1915
Ashe, Arthur   July 10, 1943
Asimov, Isaac   January 2, 1920
Asquith, Herbert Henry   September 12, 1852
Astaire, Fred   May 10, 1899
Astor, John Jacob   July 17, 1763
Astor, Nancy   May 19, 1879
Atkinson, Brooks   November 28, 1894
Atlee, Earl Clement   January 3, 1883
Atwood, Margaret E.   November 18, 1939
Auchincloss, Louis S.   September 27, 1917
Auden, W.H.   February 21, 1907
Auerbach, Arnold "Red"   September 20, 1917
Augustine, Saint   November 13, 354
Augustus Caesar   September 23, 63 B.C.
Aurelius, Marcus   April 20, 121
Austen, Jane   December 16, 1775
Axelrod, George   June 9, 1922
Ayer, A.J.   October 29, 1910
Aznavour, Charles   May 22, 1924

B

Babbage, Charles   December 26, 1792
Babbitt, Irving   August 2, 1865

Babeuf, François-Noël   November 23, 1760
Babson, Roger W.   July 6, 1875
Bacall, Lauren   September 16, 1924
Bach, Johann Sebastian   March 21, 1685
Bacon, Francis   January 22, 1561
Bacon, Francis   October 28, 1910
Baez, Joan   January 9, 1941
Bagehot, Walter   February 3, 1826
Bagnold, Enid   October 27, 1889
Bailey, F. Lee   June 10, 1933
Bailey, Gamaliel   December 3, 1807
Bailey, John   November 23, 1904
Bailey, Pearl   March 29, 1918
Baker, Josephine   June 3, 1906
Baker, Russell   August 14, 1925
Bakunin, Mikhail   May 30, 1814
Balanchine, George   January 9, 1904
Baldwin, Faith   October 1, 1893
Baldwin, James   August 2, 1924
Baldwin, Stanley   August 3, 1867
Balfour, Arthur James   July 25, 1848
Ball, Lucille   August 6, 1911
Ballou, Hoseau   April 30, 1771
Balthus   February 29, 1908
Balzac, Honoré de   May 20, 1799
Bancroft, George   October 3, 1800
Bankhead, Tallulah   January 31, 1903
Banks, Ernie   January 31, 1931
Bannister, Roger   March 23, 1929
Bara, Theda   July 20, 1890
Baraka, Inamu   October 7, 1934
Barbirolli, John   December 2, 1899
Bardot, Brigitte   September 28, 1934
Barnard, Christian N.   October 8, 1922
Barnes, Djuna   June 12, 1892
Barnum, P.T.   July 5, 1810
Barr, Stringfellow   January 15, 1897
Barrie, James   May 9, 1860
Barrymore, John   February 15, 1882
Barrymore, Lionel   April 28, 1878
Barth, Karl   May 10, 1886
Bartlett, Josiah   November 21, 1729
Bartók, Béla   March 25, 1881
Barton, Bruce   August 5, 1886
Barton, Clara   December 25, 1821
Baruch, Bernard   August 19, 1870
Baryshnikov, Mikhail   January 27, 1948
Barzun, Jacques   November 30, 1907
Basie, William "Count"   August 21, 1904
Bates, Katherine Lee   August 12, 1859

Bates, Marston   July 23, 1906
Batista y Zaldivar, Fulgenico   January 16, 1901
Baudelaire, Charles Pierre   April 9, 1821
Bax, Arnold   November 8, 1883
Baxter, Frank   May 4, 1896
Bayle, Pierre   November 18, 1647
Beard, Charles A.   November 27, 1874
Beard, James A.   May 5, 1903
Beard, Mary Ritter   August 5, 1876
Beaton, Cecil   January 14, 1904
Beatty, Warren   March 30, 1937
Beaumarchais, Pierre de   January 24, 1732
Beaverbrook, Lord   May 25, 1879
Becker, May Lambeton, August 26, 1875
Beckett, Samuel   April 13, 1906
Beebe, Charles William   July 29, 1877
Beebe, Lucius   December 9, 1902
Beecham, Thomas   April 29, 1879
Beecher, Catherine Esther   September 6, 1800
Beecher, Henry Ward   June 24, 1813
Beecher, Lyman   October 12, 1775
Beerbohm, Max   August 24, 1872
Beethoven, Ludwig van   December 16, 1770
Begin, Menachem   August 16, 1913
Behan, Brendan   February 9, 1923
Belasco, David   July 25, 1853
Bell, Alexander Graham   March 3, 1847
Bellamy, Edward   March 26, 1850
Bellarmine, St. Robert   October 4, 1542
Belli, Melvin   July 29, 1907
Belloc, Hilaire   July 27, 1870
Bellow, Saul   July 10, 1915
Bellows, George Wesley   August 12, 1882
Belmondo, Jean Paul   April 9, 1933
Bemelmans, Ludwig   April 27, 1898
Benchley, Belle   August 28, 1882
Benchley, Robert   September 15, 1889
Benedict, Ruth Fulton   June 5, 1887
Beneš, Edvard   May 28, 1884
Benet, Stephen Vincent   July 22, 1898
Ben-Gurion, David   October 16, 1886
Benny, Jack   February 14, 1894
Bentham, Jeremy   February 15, 1748
Benton, Ezra Taft   August 4, 1899
Berenson, Bernard   June 26, 1865
Berg, Gertrude   October 3, 1899

Berg, Patty   February 13, 1918
Bergman, Ingrid   August 29, 1915
Bergson, Henri   October 18, 1859
Berle, Milton   July 12, 1908
Berlin, Irving   May 11, 1888
Berlin, Isaiah   June 6, 1909
Berlioz, Hector   December 11, 1803
Bernhardt, Sarah   October 23, 1844
Bernie, Ben   May 30, 1891
Bernstein, Leonard   August 25, 1918
Berra, Yogi   May 12, 1925
Berrigan, Daniel J.   May 9, 1921
Berryman, John   October 25, 1914
Bertolucci, Bernardo   March 16, 1940
Betejeman, John   August 28, 1906
Bettelheim, Bruno   August 28, 1903
Bevan, Aneurin, November 15, 1897
Bevin, Ernest   March 9, 1881
Bierce, Ambrose   June 24, 1842
Billings, Josh   April 21, 1818
Bing, Rudolph   January 9, 1902
Bird, Larry   December 7, 1956
Bishop, Jim   November 21, 1907
Bismarck, Otto von   April 1, 1815
Black, Hugo L.   February 27, 1886
Blackstone, Harry, Jr.   June 30, 1934
Blackstone, William   July 10, 1723
Blackwell, Elizabeth   February 3, 1821
Blake, Eubie   February 7, 1883
Blake, Robert   September 18, 1933
Blake, William   November 28, 1757
Blass, Bill   June 22, 1922
Blessington, Marguerite   September 1, 1789
Bloomer, Amelia Jenks   May 27, 1818
Blough, Roger   January 19, 1904
Blume, Judy   February 12, 1938
Boas, Franz   July 9, 1858
Bogart, Humphrey   January 23, 1899
Bohr, Niels   October 7, 1885
Boileau-Despréaux, Nicholas   November 1, 1636
Bolinbroke, Henry St. John Viscount   September 16, 1678
Bolívar, Simón   July 24, 1783
Bombeck, Erma   February 21, 1927
Bonaparte, Joseph   January 7, 1768
Bonaparte, Pauline   October 20, 1785
Bonhoeffer, Dietrich   February 4, 1906
Bontemps, Anna   October 13, 1902
Boole, George   November 2, 1815
Boone, Daniel   November 2, 1734

Booth, Edwin   November 13, 1833
Booth, Shirley   August 30, 1907
Borah, William   June 29, 1865
Borge, Victor   January 3, 1909
Borges, Jorge Luis   August 24, 1899
Borgia, Lucrezia   April 18, 1480
Born, Max   December 11, 1882
Borodin, Alexander   November 11, 1833
Boswell, James   October 29, 1740
Bouicault, Dion   December 26, 1820
Boulanger, Nadia Juliette   September 16, 1887
Bourget, Paul   September 2, 1852
Bourke-White, Margaret   June 14, 1904
Bow, Clara   August 25, 1905
Bowdler, Thomas   July 11, 1754
Bowen, Elizabeth Dorothea Cole   June 7, 1899
Boyd, Malcolm   June 8, 1923
Boyer, Charles   August 28, 1899
Boyle, Robert   January 25, 1627
Bradbury, Ray   August 22, 1920
Bradlee, Benjamin   August 26, 1921
Bradley, Bill   July 28, 1943
Bradley, Frances H.   January 30, 1846
Bradley, Omar   February 12, 1893
Bradley, Pat   March 24, 1951
Bradley, Tom   December 29, 1917
Bradshaw, John   December 10, 1602
Brahms, Johannes   May 7, 1833
Braine, John   April 13, 1922
Brand, Max   May 29, 1892
Brandeis, Louis D.   November 13, 1856
Brandes, Georg   February 4, 1842
Brandt, Willie   December 18, 1913
Braque, Georges   May 13, 1882
Bream, Julian   July 15, 1933
Brecht, Bertolt   February 10, 1898
Brennan, William J., Jr.   April 25, 1906
Breslin, Jimmy   October 17, 1930
Breton, André   February 19, 1896
Brewster, Kingman   June 17, 1919
Brezhnev, Leonid I.   December 19, 1906
Briand, Aristide   March 28, 1862
Brice, Fanny   October 29, 1891
Bridgeman, Percy W.   April 21, 1882
Bridges, Harry   July 28, 1901
Bright, John   November 16, 1811
Brisbane, Arthur   December 12, 1864
Brock, Alice   February, 28, 1941
Brock, William E.   November 23, 1930

Brokaw, Tom   February 6, 1940
Bromfield, Louis   December 27, 1896
Brontë, Charlotte   April 21, 1816
Brontë, Emily   July 30, 1818
Brooke, Rupert   August 3, 1887
Brooks, Gwendolyn   June 7, 1917
Brooks, Louise   November 14, 1906
Brooks, Mel   June 28, 1928
Brooks, Van Wyck   February 16, 1886
Brougham, Henry Peter   September 19, 1778
Broun, Heywood C.   December 7, 1888
Broun, Heywood Hale   March 10, 1918
Brown, Edward "Jerry"   April 7, 1938
Brown, H. Rap   October 4, 1943
Brown, Helen Gurley   February 18, 1922
Brown, John   May 9, 1800
Brown, John Mason   July 3, 1900
Brown, Paul   July 9, 1908
Browning, Elizabeth Barrett   March 6, 1806
Browning, Robert   May 7, 1812
Brownmiller, Susan   February 15, 1935
Brownowski, Jacob   January 18, 1908
Brubeck, Dave   December 6, 1920
Bruce, Lenny   October 13, 1925
Brummell, George Bryan "Beau"   June 7, 1778
Brundage, Avery   September 28, 1887
Bryant, William Cullen   November 3, 1794
Bryce, James   May 10, 1838
Brzezinski, Zbigniew   March 28, 1928
Buber, Martin   February 8, 1878
Buchman, Frank   June 4, 1878
Buchwald, Art   October 20, 1925
Buck, Pearl   June 26, 1892
Buckley, William F., Jr.   November 24, 1925
Budgell, Eustace   August 19, 1686
Buffon, Georges-Louis Leclerc de   September 7, 1707
Bukowski, Charles   August 16, 1920
Bulwer-Lytton, Edward George   May 15, 1803
Bumbry, Grace   January 4, 1937
Bunche, Ralph   August 7, 1904
Bunny, John   September 21, 1863
Buñuel, Luis   February 22, 1900
Bunyan, John   November 28, 1628
Burbank, Luther   March 7, 1849
Burgess, Anthony   February 25, 1917

Burke, Billie   August 7, 1885
Burke, Edmond   January 12, 1729
Burney, Fanny   June 13, 1752
Burns, George   January 20, 1896
Burns, Robert   January 25, 1759
Burroughs, Edgar Rice   September 1, 1875
Burroughs, John   April 3, 1837
Burroughs, William S.   February 5, 1914
Burton, Sir Richard   March 19, 1821
Burton, Richard   November 10, 1925
Burton, Robert   February 8, 1577
Buscaglia, Leo   March 31, 1924
Busch, Wilhelm   April 15, 1832
Bush, Barbara   June 8, 1925
Bush, George   June 12, 1924
Bussy-Rabutin, Comte de Roger   April 13, 1618
Butcher, Susan   December 26, 1954
Butler, Nicholas Murray   April 2, 1862
Butler, Samuel   February 14, 1612
Butler, Samuel   December 4, 1835
Bynner, Witter   August 10, 1881
Byrd, Richard E.   October 25, 1888
Byrd, Robert C.   November 20, 1917
Byrne, David   May 14, 1952
Byrnes, James S.   May 2, 1879
Byron, Lord (George Gordon)   January 22, 1788

C

Cabell, James Branch   April 14, 1879
Cabrini, Francis Xavier   July 15, 1850
Caesar, Gaius Julius   July 12, 100 B.C.
Caesar, Sid   September 8, 1922
Cage, John   September 5, 1912
Cain, James M.   July 1, 1892
Cajal, Santiago Ramon y   May 1, 1852
Caldwell, Taylor   September 7, 1900
Calhoun, John C.   March 18, 1782
Calisher, Hortense   December 20, 1790
Callaghan, James   March 27, 1912
Callas, Maria   December 3, 1923
Calverton, V.F.   June 25, 1900
Calvin, John   July 10, 1509
Camden, William   May 2, 1551
Cameron, Simon   March 8, 1799
Camp, Walter   April 17, 1859
Campanella, Roy   November 19, 1921

Campanella, Tommasso   September 5, 1568
Campbell, Mrs. Patrick   February 9, 1865
Camus, Albert   November 7, 1913
Canby, Vincent   July 27, 1924
Canetti, Elias   July 25, 1905
Canning, George   April 12, 1770
Cannon, Joseph G.   May 7, 1836
Cantinflas   August 12, 1911
Čapek, Karel   January 9, 1890
Capone, Al   January 17, 1899
Capote, Truman   September 30, 1924
Capp, Al   September 28, 1909
Capra, Frank   May 18, 1892
Carleton, William   February 20, 1794
Carmichael, Stokely   June 29, 1941
Carnegie, Andrew   November 25, 1835
Carnegie, Dale   November 24, 1888
Carney, Art   November 4, 1918
Carr, E.H.   June 28, 1892
Carrel, Alexis   June 28, 1873
Carroll, Charles   September 19, 1737
Carroll, Lewis   January 27, 1832
Carson, Johnny   October 23, 1925
Carson, Rachel   May 27, 1907
Carter, Jimmy   October 1, 1924
Cartier, Jacques   December 31, 1491
Cartland, Barbara   July 9, 1901
Caruso, Enrico   February 25, 1873
Cary, Joyce   December 7, 1888
Cary, Phoebe   September 4, 1824
Caryle, Thomas   December 4, 1795
Casals, Pablo   December 29, 1876
Casanova, Giovanni   April 2, 1725
Cassatt, Mary   May 22, 1844
Castro, Fidel   August 13, 1926
Cather, Willa   December 7, 1885
Catherine the Great   April 21, 1729
Catt, Carrie Chapman   January 9, 1859
Catton, Bruce   October 9, 1899
Cauchy, Augustin-Louis   August 21, 1789
Cavell, Edith   December 4, 1865
Cavour, Camillo di   August 10, 1810
Cecil, Robert   September 14, 1864
Cellini, Benvenuto   November 3, 1500
Cervantes, Miguel de   September 29, 1547
Cézanne, Paul   January 19, 1839
Chafee, Zehariah, Jr.   December 7, 1885
Chagall, Marc   July 7, 1887

Chamberlain, Neville   March 18, 1869
Chamberlain, Wilt   August 21, 1936
Champollion, Jean François   December 23, 1790
Chandler, Albert "Happy"   July 14, 1898
Chandler, Raymond   July 23, 1888
Chanel, Gabrielle "Coco"   August 19, 1883
Channing, Carol   January 31, 1923
Chaplin, Charles   April 16, 1889
Chapman, Arthur   June 25, 1873
Charles, Ray   September 23, 1930
Charles I   November 19, 1600
Charles V   February 24, 1500
Charles, Prince of Wales   November 14, 1948
Charlemagne   April 2, 742
Chase, Samuel P.   January 13, 1808
Chase, Stuart   March 8, 1888
Chateaubriand, François René de   September 4, 1768
Chavez, Cesar   March 31, 1927
Chekhov, Anton   January 17, 1860
Cher   May 20, 1946
Chesterton, G.K.   May 29, 1874
Chestnutt, Charles W.   June 20, 1858
Chevalier, Maurice   September 12, 1888
Chiang Kai-shek   October 31, 1887
Chiang Kai-shek, Madame   June 5, 1897
Child, Julia   August 15, 1912
Child, Lydia M.   February 11, 1802
Ching, Cyrus S.   May 21, 1876
Chisholm, Shirley   November 30, 1924
Choate, Joseph H.   January 24, 1832
Choate, Rufus   October 1, 1799
Chomsky, Noam   December 7, 1928
Chopin, Frédéric   February 22, 1810
Chopin, Kate   February 8, 1851
Christie, Agatha   September 15, 1890
Christina   December 8, 1626
Churchill, Caryl   September 3, 1938
Churchill, Charles   February 29, 1731
Churchill, Winston   November 30, 1874
Cicero   January 3, 106 B.C.
Claflin, Tennessee Celeste   October 26, 1846
Clare, John   July 13, 1793
Clark, Jim   March 4, 1936
Clark, Joseph Sill   October 21, 1901
Clark, Kenneth   July 13, 1903
Clarke, Arthur C.   December 16, 1917

Clarke, James Freeman   April 4, 1810
Claudel, Paul   August 6, 1868
Claudius   August 1, 10 B.C.
Clausewitz, Carl von   June 1, 1780
Clay, Henry   April 12, 1771
Cleaver, Eldridge   August 31, 1935
Cleghorn, Sarah N.   February 4, 1876
Clemenceau, Georges   September 28, 1841
Cleveland, Grover   March 18, 1837
Cliburn, Van   July 12, 1934
Clinton, Bill   August 19, 1946
Clinton, Hillary Rodham   October 26, 1948
Clough, Arthur Hugh   January 1, 1819
Cobb, Irvin S.   June 23, 1876
Cobb, Ty   December 18, 1886
Cobbett, William   March 9, 1763
Cockburn, Alison   October 8, 1713
Cocteau, Jean   July 5, 1889
Coffin, William Sloane, Jr.   June 1, 1924
Cohan, George M.   July 3, 1878
Cohen, Morris Raphael   July 25, 1880
Coke, Edward   February 1, 1552
Colbert, Claudette   September 13, 1905
Colbert, Jean Baptiste   August 29, 1619
Cole, Cozy   October 17, 1909
Coleman, Ornette   March 19, 1930
Coleridge, Samuel Taylor   October 21, 1772
Colette   January 28, 1873
Collins, Joan   May 23, 1933
Collins, Marva   August 31, 1936
Collins, Michael   October 31, 1930
Colson, Charles W.   October 16, 1931
Comaneci, Nadia   November 12, 1961
Comenius, Johann Amos   March 28, 1592
Commager, Henry Steele   October 25, 1902
Commoner, Barry   May 28, 1917
Compton, Arthur Holly   September 10, 1892
Comte, Auguste   January 19, 1798
Conan Doyle, Arthur   May 22, 1859
Condon, Eddie   November 16, 1905
Condon, Richard   March 18, 1915
Condorcet, Marie Jean de   September 17, 1743
Conerly, Charlie   September 19, 1921
Congreve, William   January 24, 1670
Connery, Sean   August 25, 1930
Connolly, Cyril   September 10, 1903

Conrad, Joseph   December 3, 1857
Considine, Bob   November 4, 1906
Constable, John   June 11, 1776
Conway, Jill Ker   October 9, 1899
Conyers, John, Jr.   May 16, 1929
Coogan, Jackie   October 24, 1914
Cooke, Alistair   November 20, 1908
Coolidge, Calvin   July 4, 1872
Cooney, Joan Ganz   November 30, 1929
Cooper, James Fenimore   September 15, 1789
Cooper, Peter   February 12, 1791
Copernicus, Nicolaus   February 19, 1473
Copland, Aaron   November 14, 1900
Coratázar, Julio   August 26, 1914
Corbusier, Le   October 6, 1887
Corday, Charlotte   July 27, 1768
Cordobes, El   May 4, 1936
Cotton, John   December 4, 1584
Coty, René   March 20, 1882
Coubertin, Pierre de   January 1, 1863
Coué, Émile   February 26, 1857
Cousins, Norman   June 24, 1912
Cousteau, Jacques   June 11, 1910
Cousy, Bob   August 9, 1928
Cowley, Malcolm   August 24, 1898
Cowper, William   November 26, 1731
Cox, Archibald   May 17, 1912
Crabbe, George   December 24, 1754
Craig, Edward G.   January 16, 1872
Craik, Dinah Mulock   April 20, 1826
Crane, George   April 28, 1901
Crane, Stephen   November 1, 1871
Crawford, Joan   March 23, 1908
Creighton, Mandell   July 5, 1843
Creighton, Michael   October 23, 1942
Crist, Judith   May 22, 1922
Croce, Benedetto   February 25, 1866
Crockett, Davy   August 17, 1786
Croker, John Wilson   December 20, 1780
Cromwell, Oliver   April 25, 1599
Cronin, A.J.   July 19, 1896
Cronkite, Walter   November 4, 1916
Cukor, George   July 7, 1899
Culbertson, Ely   July 22, 1891
Cullen, Countee   May 30, 1903
cummings, e.e.   October 14, 1894
Cuomo, Mario   June 15, 1932
Curie, Marie   November 7, 1867

Curtis, George William   February 24, 1824
Curtiss, Philip   April 19, 1885
Cushing, Richard J.   August 24, 1895
Custer, George Armstrong   December 5, 1839

D

Dalai Lama   July 6, 1935
Daley, Richard J.   May 15, 1902
Dalí, Salvador   May 11, 1904
Damrosch, Walter   January 30, 1862
Dana, Richard Henry, Jr.   August 1, 1815
Daniels, Josephus   May 18, 1862
Dante Alighieri   May 27, 1265
Danton, Georges Jacques   October 26, 1759
Darin, Bobby   May 14, 1936
Darling, Charles John   December 6, 1849
Darrow, Clarence   April 18, 1857
Darwin, Charles   February 12, 1809
Daudet, Alphonse   May 13, 1840
Daugherty, Duffy   September 8, 1915
Davies, Robinson, August 28, 1913
Da Vinci, Leonardo   April 15, 1452
Davis, Adelle   February 25, 1904
Davis, Angela   January 26, 1944
Davis, Bette   April 5, 1908
Davis, Elmer   January 13, 1890
Davis, Jefferson   June 3, 1808
Davis, Miles   May 25, 1926
Davis, Richard Harding   April 18, 1864
Davy, Humphrey   December 17, 1778
Day, Doris   April 3, 1924
Day, Dorothy   November 8, 1897
Day-Lewis, Cecil   April 27, 1904
Dayan, Moyshe   May 20, 1915
Dean, Dizzy   January 16, 1911
Dean, James   February 8, 1931
De Beauvoir, Simone   January 9, 1908
Debs, Eugene V.   November 5, 1855
Debussy, Claude   August 22, 1862
Decatur, Stephen   January 5, 1779
DeFoe, Daniel   April 26, 1661
Degas, Edgar   July 19, 1834
De Gaulle, Charles   November 22, 1890
Deighton, Len   February 18, 1928
Dekker, Thomas   January 8, 1572

De Kooning, William   April 24, 1904
De La Bruyère, Jean   August 16, 1645
Delacroix, Eugène   April 26, 1798
De La Mare, Walter   April 25, 1873
Del Rio, Dolores   August 3, 1905
De Maupassant, Guy   August 5, 1850
DeMille, Agnes   September 18, 1905
DeMille, Cecil B.   August 12, 1881
De Morgan, Augustus   June 21, 1806
Dempsey, Jack   June 24, 1895
Deneuve, Catherine   October 22, 1943
Deng Xiaoping   August 22, 1904
Dershowitz, Alan   September 1, 1938
De Sade, Marquis   June 2, 1740
Descartes, René   March 31, 1596
De Staël (-Holstein), Germaine   April 22, 1766
De Tocqueville, Alexis   July 29, 1805
Deutsch, Helene   October 9, 1884
De Vega, Lope   November 25, 1562
De Vito, Danny   November 17, 1944
Devlin, Bernadette   April 23, 1947
De Voto, Bernard   January 11, 1897
Dewar, James   September 20, 1842
Dewey, John   October 20, 1859
Dewey, Thomas E.   March 24, 1902
Dibdin, Charles   March 4, 1745
Dickens, Charles   February 7, 1812
Dickinson, Angie   September 30, 1931
Dickinson, Emily   December 10, 1830
Dickinson, John   November 8, 1732
Diderot, Denis   October 5, 1713
Didion, Joan   December 5, 1934
Diefenbaker, John G.   September 18, 1895
Dietrich, Marlene   December 27, 1901
DiMaggio, Joe   November 25, 1914
Dinesen, Isak   April 17, 1885
Dinkins, David   July 10, 1927
Dior, Christian   January 21, 1905
Dirksen, Everett   January 4, 1896
Disney, Walt   December 5, 1901
Disraeli, Benjamin   December 21, 1804
D'Israeli, Isaac   May 11, 1766
Dix, Dorothea   April 4, 1802
Dix, Dorothy   November 18, 1870
Dixon, Jeanne   January 5, 1918
Dobie, J. Frank   September 26, 1888
Dobson, Henry A.   January 18, 1840
Doctorow, E.L.   January 6, 1931
Dole, Robert   July 22, 1923
Domingo, Placido   January 21, 1941

Domino, Fats   February 26, 1928
Donahue, Phil   December 21, 1935
Donaldson, Sam   March 11, 1934
Donovan   February 10, 1946
Dooley, Tom   January 17, 1899
Doolittle, James H.   December 14, 1896
Dorr, Julia R.   February 13, 1825
Dos Passos, John   January 14, 1896
Dostoyevsky, Fyodor   November 11, 1821
Douglas, Michael   September 25, 1944
Douglas, Stephen A.   April 23, 1813
Douglas, William O.   October 16, 1898
Douglas-Home, Alec   July 2, 1903
Douglass, Frederick   February 14, 1817
Dowson, Ernest   August 2, 1867
Drabble, Margaret   June 5, 1939
Dreiser, Theodore   August 27, 1871
Dressler, Marie   November 9, 1869
Drew, Elizabeth   November 16, 1935
Drummond, William   December 13, 1585
Dryden, John   August 9, 1631
Du Bois, Guillaume   September 6, 1656
Du Bois, W.E.B.   February 23, 1868
Dubos, René   February 20, 1901
Dubuffet, Jean   July 31, 1901
Duffield, Samuel Willoughby   September 24, 1843
Duhamel, Georges   June 30, 1884
Duke, Patty   December 14, 1946
Dulles, John Foster   February 25, 1888
Dumas, Alexandre (fils)   July 27, 1824
Dumas, Alexandre (père)   July 24, 1902
Du Maurier, Daphne   May 13, 1907
Duncan, Isadora   May 27, 1878
Dunham, Katherine   June 22, 1910
Dunne, Finlay Peter   July 10, 1867
Dunsany, Edward J.M.   July 24, 1878
Durant, Will   November 5, 1885
Durbin, Deanna   December 4, 1921
Durocher, Leo   July 27, 1906
Durrell, Lawrence   February 27, 1912
Duse, Eleanora   October 3, 1858
Dvořák, Antonín   September 8, 1841
Dwight, John Sullivan   May 13, 1813
Dylan, Bob   May 24, 1941

E

Earhart, Amelia   July 24, 1898
Eastman, Max   January 4, 1883

Eben, Abba   February 2, 1915
Eberhart, Mignon Good   July 6, 1899
Ebner-Eschenbach, Marie   September 13, 1830
Eco, Umberto   January 5, 1932
Eddington, Arthur Stanley   December 28, 1882
Eddy, Mary Baker   July 16, 1821
Eden, Anthony   June 12, 1897
Edgeworth, Maria   January 1, 1767
Edison, Thomas Alva   February 11, 1847
Edward VIII   June 23, 1894
Edwards, Edwin W.   August 7, 1927
Edwards, Jonathan   October 5, 1703
Eisenhower, Dwight D.   October 14, 1890
Eldridge, Paul   May 5, 1888
Eliot, George   November 22, 1819
Eliot, T.S.   September 26, 1888
Elizabeth I   September 7, 1533
Elizabeth II   April 21, 1926
Ellerbee, Linda   August 15, 1944
Ellington, Duke   April 29, 1899
Elliott, Ebenezer   March 17, 1781
Ellis, Havelock   February 2, 1882
Ellison, Ralph W.   March 1, 1914
Ellsworth, Henry L.   October 10, 1791
Emerson, Ralph Waldo   May 25, 1803
Engels, Friedrich   September 28, 1820
Ephron, Nora   May 19, 1941
Erasmus, Desiderius   October 27, 1466
Erhard, Ludwig   February 4, 1897
Ericson, Erik   June 15, 1902
Ernst, Max   April 2, 1891
Ernst, Morris L.   August 23, 1889
Erskine, John   October 5, 1879
Erskine, Thomas   January 10, 1750
Ervin, Sam   September 27, 1896
Evans, Bergen   September 19, 1904
Evans, Heloise Cruse   April 151, 1951
Everett, Edward   April 11, 1794
Evers, Medgar   July 2, 1926

F

Fadiman, Clifton   May 15, 1904
Fahrenheit, Gabriel   May 14, 1686
Falana, Lola   September 11, 1946

Falwell, Jerry   August 11, 1933
Farley, James A.   May 30, 1888
Farmer, Fannie   March 23, 1857
Farmer, James   January 12, 1920
Farnham, Eliza Woodson Burhans   November 17, 1815
Faulkner, William   September 25, 1897
Feiffer, Jules   January 26, 1929
Fellini, Federico   January 20, 1920
Ferber, Edna   August 15, 1887
Ferdinand I   March 10, 1503
Ferguson, Adam   June 20, 1723
Fermat, Pierre de   August 17, 1601
Fermi, Enrico   September 29, 1901
Fetchit, Stepin   May 30, 1892
Feuerbach, Ludwig Andreas   July 28, 1804
Fichte, Johann Gottlieb   May 19, 1762
Fiedler, Arthur   December 17, 1894
Field, Eugene   September 2, 1850
Field, Marshall   August 18, 1834
Field, Rachel   September 19, 1894
Fielding, Henry   April 22, 1707
Fields, Joseph   February 21, 1895
Fields, W.C.   January 29, 1880
Fischer, Bobby   March 9, 1943
Fisher, Carrie   October 21, 1956
Fisher, Dorothy Canfield   February 17, 1879
Fisher, Eddie   August 10, 1928
Fiske, Minnie Maddern   December 19, 1865
Fitzgerald, Edward   March 31, 1809
Fitzgerald, Ella   April 25, 1918
Fitzgerald, F. Scott   September 24, 1896
Fitzsimmons, Robert   June 4, 1863
Fitzsimmons, "Sunny Jim"   July 23, 1874
Flagg, James Montgomery   June 18, 1877
Flanagan, Edward J.   July 13, 1886
Flaubert, Gustave   December 12, 1821
Fleming, Alexander   August 6, 1881
Fleming, Ian   May 28, 1908
Fletcher, John   December 20, 1579
Fletcher, Phineas   April 8, 1582
Flexner, Abraham   November 13, 1866
Flynn, Errol   June 20, 1909
Fontanne, Lynn   December 6, 1887
Fontenella, Bernard de   February 11, 1657
Fonteyn, Margot   May 18, 1919

Foote, Shelby   November 17, 1916
Forbes, B.C.   May 14, 1880
Forbes, Malcolm   August 19, 1919
Ford, Betty   April 8, 1918
Ford, Gerald   July 14, 1913
Ford, Harrison   July 13, 1942
Ford, Henry   July 30, 1863
Ford, Henry II   September 4, 1917
Ford, John   April 17, 1586
Foreman, George   January 10, 1949
Forster, E.M.   January 1, 1879
Fosse, Bob   June 23, 1927
Fowler, Henry Watson   March 10, 1858
Foyt, A.J.   January 16, 1935
France, Anatole   April 16, 1844
Franco, Francisco   December 4, 1892
Frank, Anne   June 12, 1929
Frankau, Pamela   January 8, 1908
Frankfurter, Felix   November 15, 1882
Franklin, Benjamin   January 17, 1706
Franklin, John Hope   January 2, 1915
Fraser, Antonia   August 27, 1932
Fraser, John Malcolm   March 21, 1930
Frazier, Joe   January 12, 1944
Frederick the Great   January 24, 1712
Fredericka Louise   April 18, 1917
Freeman, Morgan   June 1, 1937
Freidan, Betty   February 4, 1921
French, Marilyn   November 21, 1929
Freneau, Philip M.   January 2, 1752
Freud, Anna   December 3, 1895
Freud, Sigmund   May 6, 1856
Friedenberg, Edgar Z.   March 18, 1921
Friedman, Milton   July 31, 1912
Frohman, Charles   June 17, 1860
Fromm, Erich   March 23, 1900
Frost, Robert   March 26, 1874
Fry, Elizabeth Gurney   May 21, 1780
Fulbright, J. William   April 9, 1905
Fulghum, Robert   June 4, 1937
Fuller, Margaret   May 23, 1810
Fuller, R. Buckminster   July 12, 1895
Fuller, Thomas   June 19, 1608
Funk, Wilfred   March 20, 1883

G

Gable, Clark   February 1, 1901
Gabor, Zsa Zsa   February 6, 1919
Gaboriau, Émile   November 9, 1832

Gainsborough, Thomas   May 14, 1727
Galbraith, John Kenneth   October 15, 1908
Galilei, Galileo   February 15, 1564
Galois, Evariste   October 25, 1811
Galsworthy, John   August 14, 1867
Galton, Francis   February 16, 1822
Gandhi, Indira   November 19, 1917
Gandhi, Mahatma Mohandes   October 2, 1869
Garbo, Greta   September 18, 1905
Garcia, Jerry   August 1, 1942
Garden, Mary   February 20, 1874
Gardner, Eric Stanley   July 17, 1889
Gardner, John W.   October 8, 1912
Garfield, John   March 4, 1913
Garibaldi, Giuseppe   July 4, 1807
Garland, Judy   June 10, 1922
Garner, John Nance   November 22, 1868
Garrick, David   February 19, 1717
Garrison, William Lloyd   December 12, 1805
Garroway, Dave   July 13, 1913
Garvey, Marcus M.   August 17, 1887
Gaskell, Elizabeth Cleghorn   September 29, 1810
Gates, William H.   October 28, 1955
Gauguin, Paul   June 7, 1848
Gauss, Karl Friedrich   April 30, 1777
Gautier, Théophile   August 31, 1811
Gavin, James M.   March 22, 1907
Gay, John   June 30, 1685
Gehrig, Lou   June 19, 1903
Geisel, Theodor Seuss   March 2, 1904
Genet, Jean   December 19, 1910
George, Chief Dan   June 24, 1899
Gernreich, Rudi   August 8, 1922
Gershwin, George   September 26, 1898
Gershwin, Ira   December 6, 1896
Getty, J. Paul   December 15, 1892
Giamatti, A. Bartlett   April 4, 1938
Gibbon, Edward   April 27, 1737
Gibbons, Euell   September 8, 1911
Gibbons, James   July 23, 1834
Gibran, Kahlil   April 10, 1883
Gibson, Althea   August 25, 1927
Gibson, Bob   November 9, 1935
Gide, André   November 22, 1869
Gielgud, John   April 14, 1904
Gilbert, W.S.   November 18, 1836
Gilbert, William   May 24, 1544

Gillespie, Dizzy   October 21, 1917
Gilman, Charlotte Perkins   July 3, 1860
Gingrich, Newt   June 17, 1943
Ginsberg, Allen   June 3, 1926
Ginsberg, Ruth Bader   March 15, 1933
Giraudoux, Jean   October 29, 1882
Giroud, Françoise   September 21, 1916
Gish, Lillian   October 14, 1894
Gissing, George R.   November 22, 1857
Gladstone, William E.   December 29, 1809
Glaspell, Susan   July 1, 1882
Glass, Carter   January 4, 1858
Gleason, Jackie   February 26, 1916
Glenn, John, Jr.   July 18, 1921
Glinka, Mikhail   June 1, 1804
Gluck, Christoph Willibald   July 2, 1714
Glyn, Elinor   October 17, 1864
Godard, Jean-Luc   December 3, 1930
Goddard, Robert H.   October 5, 1882
Godfrey, Arthur   August 31, 1903
Godwin, Gail   June 18, 1937
Godwin, Mary Wollstonecraft   April 27, 1759
Godwin, William   March 3, 1756
Goebbels, Joseph G.   October 29, 1897
Goering, Hermann   January 12, 1893
Goethals, George W.   June 29, 1858
Goethe, Johann Wolfgang von   August 28, 1749
Goldberg, Arthur J.   August 8, 1908
Goldberg, Isaac   November 1, 1887
Golding, William   September 19, 1911
Goldman, Emma   June 27, 1869
Goldsmith, Oliver   November 10, 1728
Goldwater, Barry   January 1, 1909
Goldwyn, Samuel   August 27, 1882
Gompers, Samuel   January 27, 1850
Goncharov, Ivan   June 18, 1812
Goodall, Jane   March 4, 1934
Goodman, Benny   May 30, 1909
Goolagong, Evonne   July 31, 1951
Gorbachev, Mikhail   March 2, 1931
Gordon, Adam Linsday   October 19, 1833
Gore, Al, Jr.   March 31, 1948
Gosse, Edmund William   September 21, 1849
Gould, Glenn   September 25, 1932
Gould, Morton   December 10, 1913
Gourmont, Remy de   April 4, 1850
Goya y Lucientes, Francisco de   March 30, 1746

Gracian, Balthasar   January 8, 1601
Graham, Billy   November 7, 1918
Graham, Katharine   June 16, 1917
Graham, Martha   May 11, 1894
Grahame, Kenneth   March 8, 1859
Grange, Harold "Red"   June 13, 1903
Grant, Cary   January 18, 1904
Grant, U.S.   April 27, 1822
Grass, Günter   October 16, 1927
Grasso, Ella   May 10, 1919
Graves, Robert   July 26, 1895
Gray, Thomas   December 26, 1716
Graziano, Rocky   June 7, 1922
Greeley, Horace   February 3, 1811
Greenspan, Alan   March 6, 1926
Greer, Germaine   January 29, 1939
Gregory, Dick   October 12, 1932
Gretzky, Wayne   January 26, 1961
Grieg, Edvard   June 15, 1843
Griffith, D.W.   January 22, 1874
Grimm, Jacob   January 4, 1785
Gropius, Walter   May 18, 1883
Grosz, George   July 26, 1893
Grotius, Hugo   April 10, 1583
Grunwald, Henry Anatole   December 3, 1922
Guest, Edgar A.   August 20, 1881
Guevara, Ernesto "Che"   June 14, 1928
Guicciardini, Francesco   March 6, 1483
Guisewitz, Cathy Lee   September 5, 1950
Guiterman, Arthur   November 20, 1871
Gunther, John   August 30, 1901
Guthrie, Janet   March 7, 1938
Guthrie, Woody   July 14, 1912

H

Hagan, Walter   December 21, 1892
Haggard, Merle   April 6, 1937
Haig, Alexander M., Jr.   December 2, 1925
Haile Selassie   July 23, 1891
Haldane, J.B.S.   November 5, 1892
Haldeman, H.R.   October 27, 1926
Hale, Edward Everett   April 3, 1822
Hale, Sarah Josepha   October 24, 1788
Hale, Nathan   June 6, 1755
Haley, Alex   August 11, 1921
Haley, Bill   July 6, 1927
Halliwell, Leslie   February 23, 1929
Halsey, Margaret   February 13, 1910

Halsey, William F., Jr.   October 30, 1882

Hamilton, Alexander   January 11, 1757

Hamilton, William   March 8, 1788

Hamilton, William Rowan   August 4, 1805

Hammarskjöld, Dag   July 29, 1905

Hampton, Lionel   April 12, 1909

Hand, Learned   January 27, 1872

Handel, George Frideric   February 23, 1685

Handy, W.C.   November 16, 1873

Hannegan, Robert E.   June 30, 1903

Hansberry, Lorraine   May 19, 1930

Harburgh, E.Y. "Yip"   April 8, 1898

Harding, Warren G.   November 2, 1865

Hardwick, Elizabeth   July 22, 1916

Hardwicke, Cedric   February 19, 1893

Hardy, G.H.   February 7, 1877

Hardy, Thomas   June 2, 1840

Hare, David   June 5, 1947

Harlow, Jean   March 3, 1911

Harper, Frances Ellen Watkins   September 24, 1825

Harriman, W. Averell   November 15, 1891

Harrington, Michael   February 24, 1928

Harris, Barbara   July 25, 1935

Harris, Julie   December 2, 1925

Harris, Lauren   October 23, 1885

Harris, Sydney J.   September 14, 1917

Harrison, Rex   March 5, 1908

Hart, Moss   October 24, 1904

Harte, Bret   August 25, 1836

Hartley, Leslie Poles   December 30, 1895

Harvey, Paul   September 4, 1918

Harvey, William   April 1, 1578

Havel, Václav   October 5, 1936

Hawking, Stephen   January 8, 1942

Hawks, Howard   May 30, 1898

Hawthorne, Nathaniel   July 4, 1804

Hayden, Tom   December 11, 1939

Hayes, Helen   October 10, 1900

Hayworth, Rita   October 17, 1918

Head, Edith   October 27, 1907

Heatter, Gabriel   September 17, 1890

Heckler, Margaret   June 21, 1931

Hefner, Hugh   April 9, 1926

Hegel, Georg Wilhelm   August 27, 1770

Heifetz, Jascha   February 2, 1901

Heine, Heinrich   December 13, 1797

Heisenberg, Werner Karl   December 5, 1901

Heisman, John W.   October 23, 1869

Heller, Joseph   May 1, 1923

Hellman, Lillian   June 20, 1905

Heloise   May 4, 1919

Helvétius, Claude-Adrien   January 26, 1715

Hemans, Felicia Dorothea   September 25, 1793

Hemingway, Ernest   July 21, 1899

Henie, Sonja   April 8, 1912

Henley, William E.   August 23, 1849

Henri, Robert   June 25, 1865

Henry IV   December 14, 1533

Henry VIII   June 28, 1491

Henry, O.   September 11, 1862

Henry, Patrick   May 29, 1736

Henry, William M.   August 21, 1890

Henson, Jim   September 24, 1936

Henson, Matthew   August 8, 1866

Hentoff, Nat   June 10, 1926

Hepburn, Audrey   May 4, 1929

Hepburn, Katharine   November 8, 1909

Hepworth, Barbara   January 11, 1903

Herbert, George   April 3, 1593

Herblock   October 13, 1909

Herford, Oliver   December 1, 1863

Herrick, Robert   August 24, 1591

Hersey, John   June 17, 1914

Hershfield, Harry   October 13, 1885

Herzl, Theodor   May 2, 1860

Hesburgh, Theodore   May 25, 1917

Hesse, Herman   July 2, 1877

Heyerdahl, Thor   October 6, 1914

Heywood, DuBose   August 31, 1885

Hickok, L.P.   December 29, 1798

Hilbert, David   January 23, 1862

Hill, Benny   January 21, 1925

Hill, Joe   October 7, 1879

Hillary, Edmund   July 20, 1919

Hillman, Sidney   March 23, 1887

Hilton, James   September 9, 1900

Himmler, Heinrich   November 7, 1900

Hindenberg, Paul von   October 2, 1847

Hirohito   April 29, 1901

Hitchcock, Alfred   August 13, 1899

Hitchcock, Tommy   February 11, 1900

Hite, Shere   November 2, 1942

Hitler, Adolf   April 20, 1889

Hobbes, Thomas   April 5, 1588

Ho Chi Minh   May 19, 1890
Hochhuth, Rolf   April 1, 1931
Hockney, David   July 9, 1937
Hoffa, Jimmy   February 14, 1913
Hoffer, Eric   July 25, 1902
Hoffman, Abbie   November 30, 1936
Hoffman, Dustin   August 8, 1937
Hofstader, Richard   August 6, 1916
Hogan, Ben   August 13, 1912
Hogarth, William   November 20, 1697
Holiday, Billie   April 7, 1915
Holland, Josiah Gilbert   July 24, 1819
Holmes, John Haynes   November 9, 1879
Holmes, Marjorie   September 22, 1910
Holmes, Oliver Wendell, Jr.   March 8, 1841
Holmes, Oliver Wendell, Sr.   August 29, 1809
Holt, John Caldwell   April 14, 1923
Holtz, Lou   January 6, 1937
Homer, Winslow   February 24, 1836
Honegger, Arthur   March 10, 1892
Hook, Sidney   December 20, 1902
Hook, Theodore   September 22, 1788
Hooker, Richard   March 12, 1554
Hoover, Herbert C.   August 10, 1874
Hope, Anthony   February 7, 1863
Hope, Bob   May 29, 1903
Hopkins, Gerard Manley   July 28, 1844
Hopkins, Harry L.   August 17, 1890
Hopkins, Mark   February 4, 1802
Hopper, Grace Brewster Murray   December 9, 1906
Hopper, Hedda   June 2, 1890
Horace   December 8, 65 B.C.
Horne, Lena   June 30, 1917
Horney, Karen   September 16, 1885
Hornung, Paul   December 23, 1935
Horowitz, Vladimir   October 1, 1904
Houle, Cyril O.   March 26, 1913
Houston, Sam   March 2, 1793
Houston, Whitney   August 9, 1963
Howe, Edgar Watson   May 3, 1853
Howells, William Dean   March 1, 1837
Hubbard, Elbert   June 19, 1856
Hubbard, Frank McKinney "Kin"   September 1, 1868
Hubble, Edwin P.   November 20, 1889
Hughes, Charles Evans   April 11, 1862
Hughes, Howard, Jr.   December 24, 1905
Hughes, Langston   February 1, 1904

Hugo, Victor   February 26, 1802
Hull, Cordell   October 2, 1876
Hulme, Katharine Cavarly   January 6, 1900
Humboldt, Friedrich von   September 14, 1769
Hume, David   April 26, 1711
Humphrey, George M.   March 8, 1890
Humphrey, Hubert H.   May 27, 1911
Hunt, H.L.   February 17, 1889
Hunt, Leigh   October 19, 1784
Hunter, Alberta   April 1, 1897
Huntley, Chet   December 10, 1911
Huppert, Isabelle   March 16, 1955
Hurst, Fannie   October 19, 1899
Hurston, Zora Neale   January 7, 1901
Hussein, Saddam   April 28, 1937
Huston, John   August 5, 1906
Hutchins, Robert M.   January 17, 1899
Hutchinson, Anne   July 20, 1591
Hutchinson, Frances   August 8, 1694
Hutton, Betty   February 26, 1921
Hutton, James   June 3, 1726
Huxley, Elspeth Josceline Grant   July 23, 1907
Huxley, Julian   June 22, 1887
Huxley, Thomas H.   May 4, 1825

I

Iacocca, Lee A.   October 15, 1924
Ibsen, Henrik   March 20, 1828
Iles, George   June 20, 1852
Ilich, Ivan   September 4, 1926
Iman   July 25, 1956
Inge, William   May 3, 1913
Inge, William R.   June 6, 1860
Ingelow, Jean   March 17, 1820
Ingersoll, Robert G.   August 11, 1833
Ionesco, Eugene   November 26, 1912
Irving, Washington   April 3, 1783
Isabella   April 22, 1451
Isherwood, Christopher   August 26, 1904
Ives, Burl   June 14, 1909

J

Jackson, Helen Hunt   October 15, 1830
Jackson, Janet   May 16, 1966

Jackson, Jesse   October 8, 1941
Jackson, Mahalia   October 26, 1911
Jackson, Michael   August 29, 1958
Jackson, Rachel Robards   June 15, 1767
Jackson, Robert H.   February 13, 1892
Jackson, Shirley   December 14, 1919
Jacob, Max   July 11, 1876
Jagger, Mick   July 26, 1943
James I   June 19, 1566
James, Phyllis Dorothy   August 3, 1920
James, Harry   March 15, 1916
James, Henry   April 15, 1843
James, William   January 11, 1842
Jarrell, Randall   May 6, 1914
Jarry, Alfred   October 8, 1873
Jarvis, Howard   September 22, 1902
Jaspers, Karl Theodor   February 23,
    1883
Jay, John   December 12, 1745
Jeffers, Robinson   January 10, 1887
Jefferson, Joseph   February 20, 1829
Jefferson, Thomas   April 13, 1743
Jeffrey, Francis   October 23, 1733
Jerome, Jerome K.   May 2, 1859
Jerrold, Douglas W.   January 3, 1803
Jewett, Sarah Orne   September 3, 1849
Jiménez, Juan Ramón   December 23,
    1881
Joan of Arc   January 6, 1412
Joel, Billy   May 9, 1949
Joffrey, Robert   December 24, 1930
John XXIII   November 25, 1881
John Paul II   May 18, 1920
Johnson, Betsey   August 10, 1942
Johnson, Chic   March 5, 1891
Johnson, Claudia "Lady Bird"   December
    22, 1912
Johnson, James Weldon   June 17, 1871
Johnson, Lyndon B.   August 27, 1908
Johnson, Nunnally   December 5, 1897
Johnson, Samuel   September 18, 1709
Johnson, Virginia E.   February 11, 1925
Jolson, Al   May 26, 1886
Jones, Bobby   March 17, 1902
Jones, Henry Arthur   September 20,
    1851
Jones, Inigo   July 15, 1573
Jones, James   November 6, 1921
Jones, John Paul   July 6, 1747
Jones, Mother Mary   May 1, 1830
Jones, Spike   December 14, 1911
Jong, Erica   March 26, 1942

Jonson, Ben   June 11, 1572
Joplin, Janis   January 19, 1943
Jordan, Barbara   February 21, 1936
Jordan, Michael   February 17, 1963
Jorgenson, Christine   May 30, 1926
Joseph, Jenny   May 7, 1932
Joséphine   June 24, 1763
Joyce, James   February 2, 1882
Joyner, Florence Griffith   December 21,
    1959
Joyner-Kersee, Jackie   March 3, 1962
Juarez, Benito   March 21, 1806
Juliana   April 30, 1909
Julius III   September 10, 1487
Jung, Carl   July 26, 1875

K

Kael, Pauline   June 19, 1919
Kafka, Franz   July 3, 1883
Kahn, Madeline   September 29, 1942
Kaiser, Henry J.   May 9, 1882
Kallen, Horace Meyer   August 11, 1882
Kanin, Garson   November 24, 1912
Kant, Immanuel   April 22, 1724
Karloff, Boris   November 23, 1887
Kauanda, Kenneth   April 28, 1924
Kaufman, George S.   November 16, 1889
Kaye, Danny   January 18, 1913
Kazan, Elia   September 7, 1909
Kazantzakis, Nikos   December 2, 1883
Keaton, Buster   October 4, 1895
Keats, John   October 31, 1795
Keeler, Willie   March 13, 1872
Keeshan, Bob   June 27, 1927
Keillor, Garrison   August 7, 1942
Keller, Helen   June 27, 1880
Kellogg, J.H.   February 26, 1852
Kelly, Emmett   December 9, 1898
Kelly, Gene   August 23, 1912
Kelly, Grace   November 12, 1929
Kelly, Walt   August 25, 1913
Kemp, Jack   July 13, 1935
Kennan, George   February 26, 1904
Kennedy, John F.   May 29, 1917
Kennedy, Robert F.   November 20,
    1925
Kennedy, Rose   July 22, 1890
Kenton, Stan   February 19, 1912
Kepler, Johannes   December 27, 1571
Kerouac, Jack   March 12, 1922

Kerr, Clark   May 17, 1911
Kerr, Deborah   September 30, 1921
Kerr, Walter   July 8, 1913
Kerrigan, Nancy   October 13, 1970
Kesey, Ken   September 17, 1935
Kettering, Charles Franklin   August 29, 1876
Kevorkian, Jack   May 26, 1928
Key, Ellen   December 11, 1849
Key, Francis Scott   August 1, 1779
Keynes, John Maynard   June 5, 1883
Keyserling, Herman   July 20, 1880
Khan, Alfred   October 17, 1917
Khomeini, Ayatollah   May 17, 1900
Khrushchev, Nikita   April 17, 1894
Kierkegaard, Søren   May 5, 1813
Kilmer, Joyce   December 6, 1886
King, Billie Jean   November 22, 1943
King, Coretta Scott   April 27, 1927
King, Don   August 21, 1931
King, Ernest J.   November 23, 1878
King, Henry   January 10, 1592
King, Martin Luther, Jr.   January 15, 1929
King, Stephen   September 21, 1947
King, William Mackenzie   December 17, 1874
Kingsley, Charles   June 12, 1819
Kinsey, Alfred   June 23, 1894
Kipling, Rudyard   December 30, 1865
Kirk, Lisa   February 25, 1925
Kirkpatrick, Jeane Jordan   November 19, 1926
Kissinger, Henry   May 27, 1923
Klee, Paul   December 18, 1879
Klein, Calvin   November 19, 1942
Kleindienst, Richard G.   August 5, 1923
Knebel, Fletcher   October 1, 1911
Knievel, Evel   October 17, 1917
Knopf, Alfred A.   September 12, 1892
Kock, Charles Paul de   May 21, 1793
Koestler, Arthur   September 5, 1905
Kollwitz, Käthe   July 8, 1867
Kosinski, Jerzy   June 14, 1933
Koufax, Sandy   December 30, 1935
Kovacs, Ernie   January 23, 1919
Kozol, Jonathan   September 5, 1936
Krafft-Ebbing, Richard   August 14, 1840
Krassner, Paul   April 9, 1932

Kraus, Karl   April 28, 1874
Kresege, S.S.   July 31, 1867
Kreymborg, Alfred   December 10, 1883
Kruger, Ivar   March 2, 1880
Krutch, Joseph Wood   November 25, 1893
Kübler-Ross, Elisabeth   July 8, 1926
Kubrick, Stanley   July 26, 1928
Kuhn, Bowie   October 28, 1926
Kuhn, Maggie   August 3, 1905
Kumin, Maxine   June 6, 1925
Kuralt, Charles   September 10, 1934
Kyd, Thomas   November 6, 1558

L

Lafayette, Marquis de   September 6, 1757
Lafollette, Robert M., Sr.   June 14, 1855
LaFontaine, Jean   July 8, 1621
Lagerlof, Selma Ottiliana Louisa   November 20, 1858
Lagrange, J.L.   January 25, 1736
La Guardia, Fiorella H.   December 11, 1882
Lahr, Bert   August 13, 1895
Laing, R.D.   October 7, 1927
Lamarr, Hedy   September 11, 1913
Lamartine, Alphonse Marie de   October 21, 1790
Lamb, Caroline   November 13, 1785
Lamour, Dorothy   December 10, 1914
L'Amour, Louis   March 22, 1908
Lancaster, Burt   November 2, 1913
Lance, Bert   June 3, 1931
Landers, Ann   July 4, 1918
Landon, Alfred M.   September 9, 1887
Landon, Walter Savage   January 30, 1775
Landry, Tom   September 11, 1924
Lane, Mark   February 24, 1927
Langdon, Harry   June 15, 1884
Lange, Jessica   April 20, 1949
Langer, Susanne K.   December 20, 1895
Langtry, Lillie   October 13, 1853
Lansing, Sherry Lee   July 31, 1944
Laplace, Pierre-Simon   March 23, 1749
Lardner, Ring   March 6, 1885
Larkin, Philip   August 9, 1922

Laski, Harold   June 30, 1893

Lasorda, Tommy   September 22, 1927

Lauder, Estee   July 1, 1908

Lauder, Harry   August 4, 1870

Laurel, Stan   June 16, 1890

Laurence, T.E.   August 15, 1888

Laurence, William L.   March 7, 1888

Lavater, Johannes Kaspar   November 11, 1741

Lavoisier, Antoine Laurent   August 26, 1743

Lawrence, D.H.   September 11, 1885

Lawrenson, Helen Brown   October 1, 1907

Lazarus, Emma   July 22, 1849

Leacock, Stephen   December 30, 1869

Leakey, Louis B.   August 7, 1903

Leakey, Mary   February 6, 1913

Leaky, Richard   December 19, 1944

Lean, David   March 29, 1908

Lear, Edward   May 12, 1812

Leary, Timothy   October 22, 1920

Lebowitz, Fran   October 27, 1950

Le Carré, John   October 19, 1931

Ledbetter, Huddie "Leadbelly"   January 20, 1889

Lee, Ann   February 29, 1797

Lee, Harper   April 28, 1926

Lee, Peggy   May 26, 1920

Lee, Richard Henry   January 20, 1732

Lee, Robert E.   January 19, 1807

Lee, Spike   March 20, 1959

Le Guin, Ursula   October 21, 1929

Lehár, Franz   April 30, 1870

Leibniz, Gottfried von   July 1, 1646

Leigh, Vivien   November 5, 1913

Leighton, Claire   April 11, 1900

Lemond, Greg   June 26, 1961

L'Enfant, Pierre Charles   August 2, 1754

L'Engle, Madeleine   November 28, 1918

Lenin, Vladimir I.   April 22, 1870

Lennon, John   October 9, 1940

Leonard, Hugh   November 29, 1926

Leopardi, Giacomo   June 29, 1798

Lerner, Max   December 20, 1902

Lesage, Alain René   May 8, 1668

Lessing, Doris   October 22, 1919

Lessing, Gotthold   January 22, 1729

L'Estrange, Roger   December 17, 1616

Letterman, David   April 12, 1947

Levant, Oscar   December 27, 1906

Levenson, Sam   December 28, 1911

Levertov, Denise   October 24, 1923

Lévi-Strauss, Claude   November 28, 1908

Levitt, William J.   February 11, 1907

Lewes, George Henry   April 18, 1817

Lewis, C.S.   November 29, 1898

Lewis, Jerry   March 16, 1926

Lewis, Jerry Lee   September 29, 1935

Lewis, John L.   February 12, 1880

Lewis, Sinclair   February 7, 1885

Libby, Willard Frank   December 17, 1908

Lie, Trygve   July 16, 1896

Liebling, A.J.   October 18, 1904

Liliuokalani, Lydia Kamekeha   September 2, 1838

Limón, José   January 12, 1908

Lin, Maya   October 5, 1959

Lin Yutang   October 10, 1895

Lincoln, Abraham   February 12, 1809

Lincoln, Mary Todd   December 13, 1818

Lind, Jenny   October 6, 1820

Lindbergh, Anne Morrow   June 22, 1906

Lindbergh, Charles   February 4, 1902

Lindsay, Howard   March 29, 1889

Lindsay, Vachel   November 10, 1879

Linkletter, Art   July 17, 1912

Linnaeus, Carolus von   May 23, 1707

Lipchitz, Jacques   August 22, 1891

Lippmann, Walter   September 23, 1889

Lipsius, Justus   October 18, 1547

Lipton, Thomas   May 10, 1850

Lisle, Claude Joseph Rouget de   May 10, 1760

Liszt, Franz   October 22, 1811

Littler, Gene   July 21, 1930

Livermore, Mary Ashton Rice   December 19, 1826

Livingstone, David   March 19, 1813

Locke, Bobby   October 20, 1917

Locke, John   August 29, 1632

Lockwood, Belva Ann Bennett   October 24, 1830

Logan, Joshua   October 5, 1908

Lombard, Carole   October 6, 1908

Lombardi, Vince   June 11, 1913

Lombroso, Cesare L.   November 18, 1836

Long, Huey P. August 30, 1893
Long, Russell November 3, 1918
Longfellow, Henry Wadsworth February 27, 1807
Loos, Anita April 26, 1893
Loren, Sophia September 20, 1934
Lorenz, Konrad Z. November 7, 1903
Lorimer, George H. October 6, 1868
Louis XIV September 5, 1638
Louis XVI August 23, 1754
Louis, Joe May 13, 1914
Lovecraft, H.P. August 20, 1890
Low, Juliette Gordon October 31, 1860
Lowell, Abbott Lawrence December 13, 1856
Lowell, Amy February 9, 1874
Lowell, James Russell February 22, 1819
Lowry, Malcolm July 28, 1909
Lubitsch, Ernst January 28, 1892
Lucas, George May 14, 1944
Luce, Clare Boothe April 10, 1903
Luce, Henry R. April 3, 1898
Lugosi, Béla October 20, 1884
Lumumba, Patrice July 2, 1925
Luther, Martin November 10, 1483
Luxemburg, Rosa December 25, 1870
Lynd, Robert S. September 26, 1892
Lynes, Russell December 2, 1910
Lynn, Loretta April 14, 1935
Lyon, Mary February 28, 1797

M

McAdoo, William G. October 31, 1863
MacArthur, Charles May 5, 1895
MacArthur, Douglas January 26, 1880
McAuliffe, Christa September 2, 1948
McBride, Mary Margaret November 16, 1899
McCarey, Leo October 3, 1898
McCarthy, Eugene March 29, 1916
McCarthy, Joseph November 14, 1908
McCarthy, Mary June 21, 1912
McClellan, George B. December 3, 1826
McClure, Robert January 28, 1807
McCormick, Anne O'Hara May 16, 1881
McCullers, Carson February 19, 1917
McDaniel, Hattie June 10, 1895

MacDiarmid, Hugh August 11, 1892
McDonald, Country Joe January 1, 1942
MacDonald, George December 10. 1824
MacDonald, James Ramsey October 12, 1866
MacDonald, John D. July 24, 1916
McEnroe, John February 16, 1959
McFadden, Bernarr August 16, 1868
McGee, Gale March 17, 1915
McGinley, Phyllis March 21, 1905
McGovern, George July 19, 1922
McGuffey, William Holmes September 23, 1800
McGuire, Al September 7, 1931
Mach, Ernst February 18, 1838
Machiavelli, Niccolo May 3, 1469
MacInnes, Helen Clark October 9, 1907
McKinley, William January 29, 1843
McKuen, Rod April 29, 1933
MacLaine, Shirley April 24, 1934
McLauren, Norman April 11, 1914
MacLean, Norman December 23, 1902
MacLeish, Archibald May 7, 1892
McLuhan Marshall July 21, 1911
MacMillan, Harold February 10, 1894
McPherson, Aimee Semple October 9, 1907
McRae, Carmen April 8, 1922
Macy, Ann Sullivan April 14, 1866
Madden, John April 10, 1936
Madeleva, Mother Mary May 24, 1887
Madison, Dolley May 20, 1768
Madison, James March 16, 1751
Madonna August 16, 1958
Magnani, Anna March 7, 1909
Mahan, Alfred Thayer September 27, 1840
Mahler, Gustav July 7, 1860
Mailer, Norman January 31, 1923
Maimonides, Moses March 30, 1135
Mainbocher October 24, 1890
Makeba, Miriam March 4, 1932
Malcolm X May 19, 1925
Malthus, Thomas R. February 14, 1766
Manchester, William April 1, 1922
Mandela, Nelson July 18, 1918
Manet, Édouard January 23, 1832
Mann, Anthony June 30, 1906
Mann, Horace May 4, 1796

Mann, Thomas   June 6, 1875
Mannes, Marya   November 14, 1904
Mansfield, Jayne   April 19, 1932
Mansfield, Mike   March 16, 1903
Mao Zedong   December 26, 1893
Mapplethorpe, Robert   November 4, 1946
Marat, Jean-Paul   May 24, 1743
Marceau, Marcel   March 22, 1923
Marcus, Stanley   April 21, 1906
Marcuse, Herbert   July 19, 1898
Marie Antoinette   November 2, 1755
Maritan, Jacques   November 18, 1882
Markham, Edwin   April 23, 1852
Markova, Alina   December 1, 1910
Marlowe, Christopher   February 26, 1564
Marquand, John P.   November 10, 1893
Marquis, Don   July 29, 1878
Marshall, George Catlett   December 31, 1880
Marshall, John   September 24, 1755
Marshall, Thurgood   July 2, 1908
Marti, Jose   January 28, 1851
Martin, Billy   May 16, 1928
Martin, Judith   September 13, 1938
Martin, Mary   December 1, 1913
Martin, Pepper   February 29, 1904
Martin, Steve   August 14, 1945
Martineau, Harriet   June 12, 1802
Marvel, Andrew   March 31, 1621
Marx, Groucho   October 2, 1890
Marx, Harpo   November 21, 1888
Marx, Karl   May 5, 1818
Mary, Queen of Scots   December 7, 1542
Masaryk, Tomáš   March 7, 1850
Masefield, John   June 1, 1878
Mason, Jackie   June 9, 1931
Massey, Vincent   February 20, 1887
Massinger, Philip   November 24, 1583
Masters, Edgar Lee   August 23, 1869
Masters, William H.   December 27, 1915
Mata Hari   August 7, 1876
Mather, Cotton   February 12, 1663
Mather, Increase   June 21, 1639
Mathewson, Christy   August 12, 1880
Matisse, Henri   December 31, 1869
Maugham, W. Somerset   January 25, 1874
Mauldin, Bill   October 29, 1921

Maxwell, James Clerk   November 13, 1831
Mayo, Charles Horace   July 19, 1865
Mayo, William James   June 29, 1861
Mead, Margaret   December 16, 1901
Meany, George   August 16, 1894
Medawar, P.B.   February 28, 1915
Medici, Catherine de   April 13, 1519
Meese, Edwin, 3rd   December 2, 1931
Meir, Golda   May 3, 1898
Melanchton, Philip Schwarzerd   February 16, 1497
Melba, Nellie   May 19, 1859
Mellan, Andrew   March 24, 1855
Melville, Herman   August 1, 1819
Mencken, H.L.   September 12, 1880
Menninger, Karl   July 22, 1893
Menotti, Gian Carlo   July 7, 1911
Mercier, Alfred   June 3, 1816
Mercouri, Melina   October 18, 1925
Merman, Ethel   January 16, 1909
Merrick, David   November 27, 1912
Merrill, Robert   June 4, 1919
Merton, Thomas   January 31, 1915
Mesmer, Franz Anton   May 23, 1734
Metalious, Grace   September 8, 1924
Metternick, Clemens von   May 15, 1773
Meynell, Alice   September 22, 1847
Michaels, Lorne   November 17, 1938
Michelangelo   March 6, 1475
Michelet, Jules   August 21, 1798
Middleton, Thomas   April 18, 1570
Midler, Bette   December 1, 1945
Mies van der Rohe, Ludwig   March 27, 1886
Miles, Sarah   December 31, 1941
Miles, Sylvia   September 9, 1932
Milestone, Lewis   September 30, 1895
Mill, John Stuart   May 20, 1806
Millay, Edna Vincent   February 22, 1892
Miller, Ann   April 12, 1919
Miller, Arthur   October 17, 1915
Miller, Henry   December 26, 1891
Miller, Jonathan   July 21, 1934
Millet, Jean François   October 4, 1814
Millet, Kate   September 14, 1934
Millikan, Robert A.   March 22, 1868
Milne, A.A.   January 18, 1882
Mindszenty, Joseph Cardinal   March 29, 1892
Minnelli, Liza   March 12, 1946

Miro, Joan   April 20, 1893
Mishima, Yukio   January 14, 1925
Mistinguett   April 5, 1873
Mistral, Gabriela   April 7, 1889
Mitchell, Joni   November 7, 1943
Mitchell, Margaret   November 8, 1900
Mitchell, Maria   August 1, 1818
Mitchell, Martha   September 2, 1918
Mitford, Jessica   September 11, 1917
Mitford, Nancy   November 28, 1904
Modigliani, Amadeo   July 12, 1884
Moholy-Nagy, Laszlo   July 20, 1895
Molière   January 15, 1622
Molnár, Ferenc   January 12, 1878
Molthe, Helmuth Karl, Count von
   October 26, 1800
Monet, Claude   November 14, 1840
Monk, Thelonious   October 11, 1917
Monroe, Harriet   December 23, 1860
Monroe, James   April 28, 1758
Monroe, Marilyn   June 1, 1926
Montagu, Ashley   June 28, 1905
Montagu, Lady Mary Wortley   May
   26, 1689
Montaigne, Michel de   February 28,
   1533
Montesquieu, Charles-Louis de Secon-
   dot   January 18, 1689
Montessori, Maria   August 31, 1870
Montgomery, Bernard Law   November
   17, 1887
Montgomery, James   November 4, 1771
Montherlant, Henri de   April 21, 1896
Montoya, Carlos   December 13, 1903
Moody, Helen Willis   October 6, 1905
Moore, Clement   July 15, 1779
Moore, Dudley   April 19, 1935
Moore, George   February 24, 1852
Moore, Henry   July 30, 1898
Moore, Marianne Craig   November 15,
   1897
Moore, Mary Tyler   December 29, 1936
Moore, Terry   January 7, 1929
Moore, Thomas   May 28, 1779
More, Hannah   February 2, 1745
More, Thomas   February 7, 1477
Moreau, Jeanne   January 23, 1928
Morgan, Arthur E.   June 20, 1878
Morgan, John Pierpont   April 7, 1837
Morley, Christopher   May 5, 1890
Morley, John   December 24, 1838
Morley, Robert   May 26, 1908

Morris, Desmond   January 24, 1928
Morris, William   March 24, 1834
Morrison, Toni   February 18, 1931
Morrow, Dwight   January 11, 1873
Morse, Wayne   October 20, 1900
Morton, Ferdinand "Jelly Roll"   Sep-
   tember 20, 1885
Moses, Anna Mary "Grandma"   Sep-
   tember 7, 1860
Motherwell, Robert   January 24, 1915
Motley, John Lothrop   April 15, 1814
Mott, Lucretia Coffin   January 3, 1793
Motta, Dick   September 3, 1931
Moussorgsky, Modest   March 21, 1839
Moyers, Bill   June 5, 1934
Moynihan, Daniel Patrick   March 16,
   1927
Mozart, Wolfgang Amadeus   January
   27, 1756
Muller, Max   December 6, 1898
Mumford, Lewis   October 19, 1895
Munro, Hector Hugh   December 18,
   1870
Munroz Marin, Luis   February 18, 1898
Munsel, Patrice   May 14, 1925
Murdock, Rupert   March 11, 1931
Murrow, Edward R.   April 25, 1980
Musial, Stan   November 21, 1920
Muskie, Edmund   March 28, 1914
Mussolini, Benito   July 29, 1883
Mydral, Karl Gunner   December 6,
   1898

N

Nabokov, Vladimir   April 22, 1899
Nader, Ralph   February 27, 1934
Naipaul, V.S.   August 17, 1932
Naismith, James   November 6, 1861
Nakian, Reuben   August 10, 1897
Namath, Joe   May 31, 1943
Napoléon I (Bonaparte)   August 15,
   1769
Nash, Ogden   August 19, 1902
Nasser, Gamal   January 15, 1918
Nastase, Ilie   July 19, 1946
Nathan, George Jean   February 14, 1882
Nation, Carry   November 25, 1846
Navratilova, Martina   October 18, 1956
Neal, Patricia   January 20, 1926
Nearing, Scott   August 6, 1883

Nehru, Jawaharal November 14, 1889

Nelson, Horatio September 29, 1758

Nelson, Willie April 30, 1933

Nero Claudius Caesar December 15, 37 A.D.

Nettles, Craig August 20, 1944

Nevelson, Louise September 23, 1899

Newman, Edwin January 25, 1919

Newman, John Henry February 21, 1801

Newman, Paul January 26, 1925

Newton, Huey P. February 17, 1942

Newton, Isaac December 25, 1642

Nichols, Dudley April 6, 1895

Nichols, Mike November 6, 1931

Nicklaus, Jack January 21, 1940

Nicolle, Charles Jean Henri September 21, 1866

Nicolson, Harold November 21, 1886

Niebuhr, Reinhold June 21, 1892

Nietzsche, Friedrich October 15, 1844

Nightingale, Florence May 12, 1820

Nijinsky, Vaslav March 12, 1890

Nimitz, Chester W. February 24, 1885

Nin, Anaïs February 21, 1903

Nixon, Patricia March 16, 1912

Nixon, Richard N. January 9, 1913

Nizer, Louis February 6, 1902

Nkrumah, Kwame September 21, 1909

Nobel, Alfred October 21, 1833

Norman, Jessye September 15, 1945

Norris, Frank March 5, 1870

Norris, Kathleen July 16, 1880

Norton, Caroline March 22, 1808

Norton, Charles Eliot November 16, 1827

Noyes, John Humphrey September 3, 1811

Nureyev, Rudolph March 17, 1938

Nyerere, Julius K. March 21, 1922

O

Oates, Joyce Carol June 16, 1938

O'Brien, Edna December 15, 1931

O'Casey, Sean March 30, 1880

O'Connor, Flannery March 25, 1925

O'Connor, Sandra Day March 26, 1930

Odets, Clifford July 18, 1906

Odetta December 31, 1930

O'Keefe, Georgia November 15, 1887

Oliphant, Margaret April 4, 1828

Olivier, Laurence May 22, 1907

Onassis, Aristotle January 15, 1906

Onassis, Christina December 11, 1950

Onassis, Jacqueline Bouvier Kennedy July 28, 1929

O'Neill, Eugene G. October 16, 1888

O'Neill, Thomas "Tip" December 9, 1912

Ophuls, Marcel November 1, 1927

Oppenheimer, J. Robert April 22, 1904

Orwell, George June 25, 1903

Osborne, John December 12, 1929

Oscar II January 21, 1829

Ortega y Gasset, José May 19, 1883

Ostrovsky, Aleksandr April 12, 1823

O'Sullivan, Maureen May 17, 1911

O'Toole, Peter August 2, 1933

Otway, Thomas March 3, 1652

Overbury, Thomas June 18, 1581

Ovid March 20, 43 B.C.

Owens, Jesse September 12, 1913

Oxenstierna, Axel June 16, 1583

Ozawa, Seiji September 1, 1935

P

Pacino, Al April 25, 1940

Packard, Vance May 22, 1914

Paderewski, Ignace Jan November 18, 1860

Pagnol, Marcel February 28, 1895

Pahlevi, Mohammed Riza October 26, 1919

Paige, Leroy "Satchel" July 7, 1906

Paine, Thomas January 29, 1737

Paley, Barbara "Babe" July 5, 1915

Palmer, Arnold September 10, 1929

Pankhurst, Emmeline July 14, 1858

Pankhurst, Sylvia May 5, 1882

Parker, Charlie "Bird" August 29, 1920

Parker, Dorothy August 22, 1893

Parker, Theodore August 24, 1810

Parkhurst, Charles H. April 17, 1842

Parnell, Charles S. June 27, 1846

Parton, Sara Pyson July 9, 1811

Pascal, Blaise June 19, 1623

Pascal, Gabriel June 4, 1894

Pasolini, Pier Paolo March 5, 1922

Pasternak, Boris February 17, 1864

Pasteur, Louis December 22, 1822

Patchen, Kenneth December 13, 1911

Pater, Walter August 4, 1839

Paterno, Joe   December 21, 1926
Paterson, Andrew B. "Banjo"   February 17, 1864
Patmore, Coventry   July 23, 1823
Paton, Alan   January 11, 1903
Patterson, Floyd   January 4, 1935
Patton, George S., Jr.   November 11, 1885
Paul III   February 29, 1468
Paul VI   September 26, 1875
Paul, Les   June 9, 1916
Pauling, Linus   February 28, 1901
Pavarotti, Luciano   October 12, 1935
Pavese, Cesare   September 9, 1908
Pavlov, Ivan   September 14, 1849
Payne, John Howard   June 9, 1791
Paz, Octavio   March 31, 1914
Peabody, George Foster   July 27, 1852
Peabody, Josephine Preston   May 3, 1874
Peacock, Thomas Love   October 18, 1785
Peale, Norman Vincent   May 31, 1898
Peale, Rembrandt   February 22, 1778
Pearson, Lester   April 23, 1897
Peel, Robert   February 5, 1788
Pegler, Westbrook   August 2, 1894
Peguy, Charles P.   January 7, 1873
Pei, I.M.   April 26, 1917
Pele   October 23, 1940
Pell, Clairborne   November 22, 1918
Penn, William   October 14, 1644
Penney, James Cash   September 16, 1875
Pepper, Claude   September 8, 1900
Pepys, Samuel   February 23, 1633
Perkins, Frances   April 10, 1882
Perlman, S.J.   February 1, 1904
Perón, Eva "Evita"   May 7, 1919
Perón, Juan   October 8, 1895
Perot, H. Ross   June 27, 1930
Pershing, John J.   September 13, 1860
Pestalozzi, Johann H.   January 12, 1746
Pétain, Henri   April 24, 1856
Peter I, "The Great"   June 9, 1672
Petrarch, Francesco   July 20, 1304
Phelps, W. Lyon   January 2, 1865
Philip, Prince   June 10, 1921
Piaf, Edith   December 19, 1915
Piaget, Jean   August 9, 1896
Picasso, Pablo   October 25, 1881
Pickford, Mary   April 8, 1894

Pinero, Arthur Wing   March 24, 1855
Pinter, Harold   October 10, 1930
Piper, William T.   January 8, 1881
Pirandello, Luigi   June 28, 1867
Pitkin, Walter B.   February 6, 1878
Pitt, William, The Elder   November 15, 1708
Pitt, William, The Younger   May 28, 1759
Pius IX   May 13, 1792
Pius XI   May 31, 1857
Pius XIII   March 2, 1876
Planck, Max   April 23, 1858
Plath, Sylvia   October 27, 1932
Player, Gary   November 1, 1935
Plowright, Joan   October 28, 1929
Poe, Edgar Allan   January 19, 1809
Poincaré, Henri   April 29, 1854
Poitier, Sidney   February 20, 1924
Polanski, Roman   August 18, 1933
Pollock, Channing   March 4, 1880
Pollock, Jackson   January 28, 1912
Pompadour, Jeanne Poisson de   December 29, 1721
Pompidou, Georges   July 5, 1911
Pons, Lily   April 12, 1904
Pope, Alexander   May 21, 1688
Porter, Cole   June 9, 1892
Porter, Katharine Anne   May 15, 1894
Porter, Sylvia Field   June 18, 1913
Potter, Beatrix   July 28, 1866
Potter, Henry Codman   June 25, 1834
Pound, Ezra   October 30, 1885
Powell, Adam Clayton, Jr.   November 29, 1908
Powell, Anthony   December 21, 1905
Powell, Colin L.   April 5, 1937
Powell, Enoch   June 16, 1912
Prentice, George Dennison   December 18, 1802
Presley, Elvis   January 8, 1935
Previn, Andre   April 6, 1929
Previn, Dory   October 22, 1930
Price, Leontyne   February 10, 1927
Price, Roger   March 6, 1920
Priesand, Sally   June 27, 1946
Priestley, J.B.   September 13, 1894
Priestley, Joseph   March 13, 1733
Prior, Matthew   July 21, 1664
Proxmire, William   November 11, 1915
Pryor, Richard   December 1, 1940
Puccini, Giacomo   December 22, 1858

Pulitzer, Joseph   April 10, 1847
Pushkin, Alexander   June 6, 1799
Putnam, Israel   January 7, 1718
Puzo, Mario   October 15, 1920
Pyle, Ernie   August 3, 1900
Pym, Barbara Mary Crampton   June 2, 1913

Q

Quant, Mary   February 11, 1934
Quarles, Francis   May 8, 1592
Quinault, Philippe   June 3, 1635
Quinn, Jane Bryant   February 5, 1939

R

Rabe, David   March 10, 1940
Racine, Jean   December 22, 1639
Radcliffe, Ann   July 9, 1764
Radford, Arthur   February 27, 1896
Radhakrishnan, Savrepalli   September 5, 1888
Raft, George   September 26, 1895
Rahman, Sheikh Mujibur   March 17, 1920
Rainey, Ma   April 26, 1886
Rand, Ayn   February 2, 1905
Rand, Sally   January 2, 1903
Randolph, A. Philip   April 15, 1889
Randolph, Edmund Jennings   August 10, 1753
Rankin, Jeannette   July 11, 1880
Raspberry, William   October 12, 1935
Rather, Dan   October 31, 1937
Rattigan, Terrence   June 10, 1911
Rauschenberg, Robert   October 22, 1925
Ravel, Maurice   March 7, 1875
Ray, Dixie Lee   September 3, 1914
Ray, John   November 29, 1627
Ray, Man   August 27, 1890
Ray, Nicholas   August 7, 1911
Ray, Satyajit   May 2, 1903
Rayburn, Sam   January 6, 1882
Reade, Charles   June 8, 1814
Reagan, Nancy Davis   July 6, 1921
Reagan, Ronald   February 6, 1911
Reasoner, Harry   April 17, 1923
Reddy, Helen   October 25, 1942

Redgrave, Vanessa   January 30, 1937
Reed, John   October 22, 1887
Reed, Myrtle   September 27, 1874
Reik, Theodor   May 12, 1888
Reiner, Fritz   December 19, 1888
Remarque, Erich Maria   June 22, 1898
Remick, Lee   December 14, 1935
Renan, Joseph Ernest   February 28, 1823
Renault, Mary   September 4, 1905
Renoir, Jean   September 15, 1894
Renoir, Pierre Auguste   February 25, 1841
Repplier, Agnes   April 1, 1858
Reston, James   November 3, 1909
Reuther, Walter   September 1, 1907
Revson, Charles   October 11, 1906
Reynolds, Joshua   July 16, 1723
Ricardo, David   April 19, 1772
Rice, Alice Hegan   January 11, 1870
Rice, Grantland   November 1, 1880
Richardson, Samuel   July 31, 1689
Richelieu, Duc Armand Jean du Plessis   September 9, 1585
Richter, Johann Paul Friedrick   March 20, 1763
Rickey, Branch   December 20, 1881
Rickover, Hyman   January 27, 1900
Ride, Sally   May 26, 1951
Ridgeway, Matthew   March 3, 1895
Riefenstahl, Leni   August 22, 1902
Rieff, Philip   December 15, 1922
Rigg, Diana   July 20, 1938
Riley, James Whitcomb   October 7, 1849
Rilke, Rainier Maria   December 4, 1875
Rimsky-Korsakov, Nikolai   March 18, 1844
Rinehart, Mary Roberts   August 12, 1876
Rivarol, Comte de Antoine   June 26, 1753
Robb, Inez   November 29, 1902
Robbe-Grillet, Alain   August 18, 1922
Roberts, Cokie   December 27, 1943
Roberts, Julia   October 28, 1967
Robeson, Paul   April 9, 1898
Robespierre, Maximilien   May 6, 1758
Robinson, Bill   May 25, 1878
Robinson, Edwin Arlington   December 22, 1869
Robinson, Harriet J.H.   February 8, 1825
Robinson, Jackie   January 31, 1919

Robinson, Smokey   February 19, 1940
Rochefoucauld, François de la   September 15, 1613
Rock, John   March 24, 1890
Rockefeller, Barbara "Bobo"   September 6, 1917
Rockefeller, John D., Jr.   January 29, 1874
Rockefeller, John D., Sr.   July 8, 1839
Rockne, Knute   March 4, 1888
Rockwell, Norman   February 3, 1894
Roddenberry, Gene   August 19, 1921
Rodin, Auguste   November 12, 1840
Rogers, Will   November 4, 1879
Rohmer, Sax   February 15, 1883
Rolland, Romain   January 29, 1866
Rombauer, Irma S.   October 30, 1877
Romney, George W.   July 8, 1907
Romulo, Carlos P.   April 14, 1899
Rooney, Andy   January 14, 1919
Roosevelt, Eleanor   October 11, 1884
Roosevelt, Franklin D.   January 30, 1882
Roosevelt, Theodore   October 27, 1858
Rose, Billy   September 6, 1899
Roseanne   November 3, 1952
Rosenberg, Ethel   September 28, 1915
Rosenzweig, Franz   December 25, 1886
Ross, Harold   November 6, 1892
Rossellini, Roberto   May 8, 1906
Rossetti, Christina Georgina   December 5, 1830
Rossetti, Dante Gabriel   May 14, 1828
Rossini, Gioacchino   February 29, 1792
Rossner, Judith   March 1, 1935
Rostand, Edmond   April 1, 1868
Rosten, Leo   April 11, 1908
Rostenkowski, Daniel   January 2, 1928
Roth, Phillip   March 19, 1933
Rothschild, Meyer   February 23, 1743
Rousseau, Jean-Jacques   June 28, 1712
Rowan, Carl T., Jr.   August 11, 1925
Royko, Mike   September 19, 1932
Rubin, Jerry   July 14, 1931
Rubin, Theodore Isaac   April 11, 1923
Rubinstein, Artur   January 28, 1887
Rudolph, Wilma   June 23, 1940
Rukeyser, Muriel   December 15, 1913
Runyon, Damon   October 4, 1884
Rupp, Adolph   September 2, 1901
Rush, Benjamin   December 24, 1745
Rusk, Dean   February 9, 1909
Ruskin, John   February 8, 1819

Russell, Bertrand   May 18, 1872
Russell, John   August 18, 1792
Russell, Ken   July 3, 1927
Russell, Mark   August 23, 1932
Russell, Richard   November 2, 1897
Russell, Rosalind   June 4, 1908
Ruth, Babe   February 6, 1895
Rutherford, Ernest   August 30, 1871
Ryan, Abram Joseph   February 5, 1888
Ryder, Winona   October 29, 1971

S

Saarinen, Eero   August 20, 1910
Sackville-West, Victoria   March 9, 1892
Sadat, Anwar   December 25, 1918
Safer, Morley   November 8, 1931
Safire, William L.   December 17, 1929
Sagan, Carl   November 9, 1934
Sagan, Françoise   June 21, 1935
Sahl, Mort   May 11, 1927
St. Exupery, Antoine de   June 29, 1900
Saint-Gaudens, Augustus   March 1, 1848
St. Johns, Adele Rogers   May 20, 1894
St. Laurent, Yves   August 1, 1936
Sainte-Marie, Buffy   February 20, 1941
Sakharov, Andrei   May 21, 1921
Salinger, J.D.   January 1, 1919
Salk, Jonas   October 28, 1914
Samuel, Herbert   November 6, 1870
Samuelson, Joan Benoit   May 16, 1957
Samuelson, Paul A.   May 15, 1915
Sand, George   July 1, 1804
Sandburg, Carl   January 6, 1878
Sanders, Colonel Harland   September 9, 1890
Sanger, Margaret   September 14, 1883
Santayana, George   December 16, 1863
Sarandon, Susan   October 4, 1946
Sarnoff, Robert W.   July 2, 1918
Saroyan, William   August 31, 1908
Sartre, Jean-Paul   June 21, 1905
Sawyer, Diane   December 22, 1945
Say, Jean Baptiste   January 5, 1767
Sayers, Dorothy   June 13, 1893
Schiaparelli, Elsa   September 10, 1896
Schiff, Dorothy   March 11, 1903
Schilling, Friedrick von   January 27, 1775
Schlafly, Phyllis   August 15, 1924
Schlegel, Friedrich von   March 10, 1772

Schmidt, Mike   September 27, 1949
Schopenhauer, Arthur   February 22, 1788
Schorr, Daniel   August 13, 1916
Schreiner, Olive   March 24, 1855
Schroeder, Patricia   July 30, 1940
Schubert, Franz   January 31, 1797
Schulberg, Budd   March 27, 1914
Schuller, Robert H.   September 16, 1926
Schultz, George P.   December 13, 1920
Schulz, Charles M.   November 26, 1922
Schumann, Clara Wieck   September 13, 1819
Schumann, Robert   June 8, 1810
Schurz, Carl   March 2, 1829
Schwab, Charles M.   February 18, 1862
Schwarzenegger, Arnold   July 30, 1947
Schwarzkopf, H. Norman   August 22, 1934
Schweitzer, Albert   January 16, 1875
Scorsese, Martin   November 17, 1942
Scott, Hazel   June 1, 1920
Scott, Walter   August 15, 1771
Scribner, Charles, Jr.   February 21, 1821
Seaver, Tom   November 17, 1944
Sedley, Charles   March 5, 1639
Seeger, Pete   May 3, 1919
Segovia, Andrés   February 18, 1894
Segur, Sophie Rostopchine   July 19, 1799
Selden, John   December 16, 1584
Seles, Monica   December 2, 1973
Selfridge, R. George   January 11, 1864
Selznick, David O.   May 10, 1902
Sendak, Maurice   June 10, 1928
Serling, Rod   December 25, 1924
Service, Robert   January 16, 1874
Seton, Elizabeth Ann   August 28, 1774
Sevareid, Eric   November 26, 1912
Sevigne, Marie de   February 5, 1626
Seward, William H.   May 16, 1801
Sewell, Anna   March 30, 1820
Sexton, Anne   November 9, 1928
Shaffer, Peter   May 15, 1926
Shakespeare, William   April 23, 1584
Shaw, George Bernard   July 26, 1856
Shaw, Robert Gould   October 1, 1837
Shedd, John Graves   July 20, 1850
Sheehy, Gail   November 27, 1937
Sheen, Fulton J.   May 8, 1895
Shelley, Mary Wollstonecraft   August 30, 1797
Shelley, Percy Bysshe   August 4, 1792

Sheridan, Philip   March 6, 1831
Sheridan, Richard B.   October 30, 1751
Sherman, Roger   April 19, 1721
Sherman, William Tecumseh   February 8, 1820
Sherwood, Robert   April 4, 1896
Shirer, William L.   February 23, 1904
Shore, Dinah   March 1, 1880
Shostakovich, Dmitri   September 25, 1906
Sibelius, Jean   December 8, 1865
Sickert, Walter   May 31, 1860
Siddons, Sarah   July 5, 1755
Sidey, Hugh   September 3, 1927
Sidney, Margaret   June 22, 1844
Siegel, Bernie S.   October 14, 1932
Sieyes, Emmanuel Joseph   May 3, 1748
Sikorsky, Igor   May 25, 1889
Sills, Beverly   May 25, 1929
Silvers, Phil   May 11, 1911
Sim, Alistair   October 9, 1900
Simenon, Georges   February 13, 1903
Simmel, George   March 1, 1858
Simon, Carly   June 25, 1945
Simon, Claude   October 10, 1913
Simon, Neil   July 4, 1927
Simon, Paul   November 5, 1942
Simon, William   November 27, 1927
Sinatra, Frank   December 12, 1915
Sinclair, Upton   September 20, 1878
Singer, Isaac Bashevis   July 14, 1904
Sitwell, Edith   September 7, 1887
Skelton, Red   July 18, 1913
Skinner, B.F.   March 20, 1904
Skinner, Cornelia Otis   May 30, 1901
Slaney, Mary Decker   August 4, 1958
Sloan, Alfred P., Jr.   May 23, 1875
Smiles, Samuel   December 23, 1812
Smith, Adam   June 5, 1723
Smith, Alfred E.   December 30, 1873
Smith, Betty   December 15, 1904
Smith, Edgar   May 23, 1854
Smith, Ian   April 8, 1919
Smith, Joseph   December 23, 1805
Smith, Lillian   December 12, 1897
Smith, Margaret Chase   December 14, 1897
Smith, Sidney   February 13, 1877
Smith, Stevie   September 20, 1902
Smith, Walter "Red"   September 25, 1905
Smith, Willie "The Lion"   November 23, 1897

Smollett, Tobias   March 19, 1721
Smuts, Jan C.   May 24, 1870
Snow, Carmel White   August 21, 1887
Solzhenitysyn, Alexsandr   December 11, 1918
Sondheim, Stephen   March 22, 1930
Sontag, Susan   January 28, 1933
Southern, Terry   May 1, 1926
Southey, Robert   August 12, 1774
Souza, John Philip   November 6, 1854
Soyinka, Wole   July 13, 1934
Spark, Muriel   February 1, 1918
Spencer, Herbert   April 27, 1820
Spengler, Oswald   May 29, 1880
Spielberg, Steven   December 18, 1947
Spillane, Mickey   March 9, 1918
Spingarn, Joel E.   May 17, 1875
Spinoza, Baruch   November 24, 1632
Spock, Benjamin   May 2, 1903
Springsteen, Bruce   September 23, 1949
Spyri, Johanna   June 12, 1827
Stack, Robert   January 13, 1919
Stafford, Jean   July 1, 1915
Stafford, Jo   November 12, 1918
Stagg, Amos Alonzo   August 16, 1862
Stalin, Joseph   December 21, 1879
Stanford, A. Leland   March 9, 1824
Stanhope, Philip Dormer   September 22, 1694
Stanislavsky, Konstantin   January 17, 1863
Stanton, Elizabeth Cady   November 12, 1815
Stanwyck, Barbara   July 16, 1907
Starr, Ringo   July 7, 1940
Starrett, Vincent   October 26, 1886
Stead, Christina E.   July 17, 1902
Stedman, E.C.   October 8, 1833
Steel, Danielle   August 14, 1947
Steele, Richard   March 12, 1672
Stefansson, Vilhjalmar   November 3, 1879
Steffens, Lincoln   April 6, 1866
Steichen, Edward   March 27, 1879
Stein, Gertrude   February 3, 1874
Steinbeck, John   February 27, 1902
Steinberg, Saul   June 15, 1914
Steinem, Gloria   March 25, 1934
Steinmetz, Charles P.   April 9, 1865
Stendahl   January 23, 1783
Stengel, Casey   July 30, 1889
Stephenson, Jan   December 22, 1951

Stern, Howard   June 16, 1954
Stern, Isaac   July 21, 1920
Sterne, Laurence   November 24, 1713
Stevens, John Paul   April 20, 1920
Stevens, Wallace   October 2, 1879
Stevenson, Adlai E., Jr.   February 5, 1900
Stevenson, Robert Louis   November 13, 1850
Stewart, James   May 20, 1908
Stewart, Mary Florence   September 17, 1916
Stewart, Potter   January 23, 1915
Stewart, Rod   January 10, 1945
Still, William Grant   May 11, 1895
Sting (Gordon Sumner)   October 2, 1951
Stockman, David   November 10, 1946
Stokowski, Leopold   April 18, 1882
Stone, Harlan Fiske   October 11, 1872
Stone, I.F.   December 24, 1907
Stone, Lucy   August 13, 1818
Stone, Sharon   March 10, 1958
Stoppard, Tom   July 3, 1937
Story, Joseph   September 18, 1779
Stout, Rex Todhunter   December 1, 1866
Stowe, Harriet Beecher   June 14, 1811
Strachey, Lytton   March 1, 1880
Stravinsky, Igor   June 17, 1882
Streisand, Barbra   April 24, 1942
Strindberg, August   January 22, 1849
Styron, William   June 11, 1925
Suckling, John   February 10, 1609
Sullivan, Louis H.   September 3, 1856
Sulzberger, Arthur Hays   September 12, 1891
Summerfield, Arthur E.   March 17, 1899
Summerskill, Edith Clara   April 19, 1901
Sumner, William G.   October 30, 1840
Sun Yat-Sen   November 12, 1866
Surtees, Robert Smith   May 17, 1805
Susann, Jacqueline   August 20, 1921
Sutherland, George   March 25, 1862
Sutherland, Joan   November 7, 1926
Swanson, Gloria   March 27, 1899
Swift, Jonathan   November 30, 1667
Swinburne, Algernon   April 5, 1837
Swope, Herbert B.   January 5, 1882
Synge, John Millington   April 16, 1871
Szasz, Thomas   April 15, 1920
Szell, George   June 7, 1897
Szent-Gyorgyi   September 16, 1893

T

Taft, Robert A.　September 8, 1889
Tagore, Rabindranath　May 6, 1861
Taine, Hippolyte A.　April 21, 1828
Tallyrand-Perigord, Charles de　February 2, 1754
Talmadge, Constance　April 19, 1902
Talmadge, Herman　August 9, 1913
Tandy, Jessica　June 7, 1909
Tarbell, Ida　November 5, 1857
Tarkington, Booth　July 29, 1869
Tarkington, Fran　February 3, 1940
Tasso, Torquasto　March 11, 1544
Tate, Alan　November 19, 1899
Tati, Jacques　October 9, 1908
Taylor, Elizabeth　February 27, 1932
Taylor, Frederick　March 20, 1856
Taylor, Jane　September 26, 1783
Teale, Edwin Way　June 2, 1899
Teasdale, Sara　August 8, 1884
Teilhard de Chardin, Pierre　May 1, 1881
Teller, Edward　January 15, 1908
Tennyson, Alfred Lord　August 6, 1809
Teresa, Mother　August 27, 1910
Teresa of Avila　March 28, 1515
Thackeray, William Makepeace　July 18, 1811
Thant, U　January 22, 1909
Tharp, Twyla　July 1, 1941
Thatcher, Margaret　October 13, 1925
Thayer, Ernest L.　August 14, 1863
Thomas, Dylan　October 27, 1914
Thomas, Gwyn　July 6, 1913
Thomas, Isiah　April 30, 1961
Thomas, Lowell　April 6, 1892
Thomas, Martha Carey [Calamity Jane]　January 2, 1857
Thomas, Norman　November 20, 1884
Thompson, D'Arcy　May 2, 1860
Thompson, Dorothy　July 9, 1894
Thompson, Francis J.　December 18, 1859
Thompson, James　September 11, 1700
Thompson, William (Lord Kelvin)　June 26, 1824
Thoreau, Henry David　July 12, 1817
Thorndike, Sybil　October 24, 1882
Thorpe, Jim　May 28, 1888
Tillich, Paul　August 20, 1886
Tito　May 7, 1892

Toffler, Alvin　October 4, 1928
Tojo, Hideki　December 30, 1884
Toklas, Alice B.　April 30, 1877
Tolkien, J.R.R.　January 3, 1892
Tolstoy, Count Leo　September 9, 1828
Tomlin, Lily　September 1, 1939
Toomer, Jean　December 26, 1894
Toulousse-Lautrec, Henri de　November 24, 1864
Toynbee, Arnold　April 14, 1889
Train, Arthur　September 6, 1875
Traver, Robert　June 29, 1903
Trevelyan, George M.　February 16, 1876
Trevino, Elizabeth Barton de　September 2, 1904
Trevor, Claire　March 8, 1909
Trevor-Roper, H.R.　January 15, 1914
Trigere, Pauline　November 4, 1912
Trilling, Lionel　July 4, 1905
Trollope, Anthony　April 24, 1815
Trotsky, Leon　November 8, 1879
Trowbridge, John Townsend　September 18, 1827
Trudeau, Pierre　October 18, 1919
Truman, Harry S　May 18, 1884
Trump, Donald　June 14, 1946
Tuchman, Barbara　January 30, 1912
Tucker, Lorenzo　June 27, 1900
Tucker, Sophia　January 13, 1884
Tunnell, Emlen　March 29, 1925
Tupper, Martin Farquhar　July 17, 1810
Turner, Ted　November 19, 1938
Turner, Tina　November 26, 1938
Tutu, Desmond　October 7, 1931
Twain, Mark　November 30, 1835
Tweed, William Marcy　April 3, 1823
Twining, Nathan　October 11, 1897
Tyler, Anne　October 25, 1941
Tyler, John　March 29, 1790
Tynall, John　August 2, 1820
Tynan, Kenneth　April 2, 1927

U

Udall, Morris　June 15, 1922
Uhnak, Dorothy　April 24, 1930
Unruh, Jesse　September 30, 1922
Unser, Al　May 29, 1939
Updike, John　March 18, 1932
Ustinov, Peter　April 16, 1921

V

Valentino, Rudolph   May 6, 1895
Valois, Ninette de   June 6, 1898
Van Brocklin, Norm   March 15, 1926
Van Buren, Abigail   July 4, 1918
Van Buren, Martin   December 5, 1782
Vandenberg, Arthur H.   March 22, 1884
Vanderbilt, Amy   July 22, 1908
Vanderbilt, Cornelius   May 27, 1794
Van Doren, Carl   September 10, 1885
Van Doren, Mark   June 13, 1894
Van Gogh, Vincent   March 30, 1853
Van Horne, Harriet   May 17, 1920
Van Loon, Hendrik   January 14, 1882
Vanzetti, Bartolomeo   July 11, 1888
Vardon, Harry   May 9, 1870
Varèse, Edgar   December 22, 1883
Vaughan, Sarah   March 27, 1924
Vaughan Williams, Ralph   October 12, 1872
Veblen, Thorstein B.   July 30, 1857
Veeck, Bill   February 9, 1914
Verdi, Giuseppi   October 10, 1813
Verdon, Gwen   January 13, 1925
Vereen, Ben   October 10, 1946
Verlaine, Paul   March 30, 1884
Vico, Giovanna Battista   June 23, 1668
Victoria I   May 24, 1819
Vidal, Gore   October 3, 1925
Vigny, Alfred de   March 27, 1797
Villa-Lobos, Heitor   March 5, 1887
Vinson, Frederick M.   January 22, 1890
Virgil   October 15, 70 B.C.
Voltaire   November 21, 1694
Von Braun, Wernher   March 23, 1912
Vonnegut, Kurt, Jr.   November 11, 1922
Von Neuman, John   December 28, 1903
Von Stroheim, Erich   September 22, 1885
Vos Savant, Marilyn   August 11, 1946
Voznesensky, Andrei   May 12, 1933

W

Wagner, Richard   May 22, 1813
Wainwright, Jonathan   August 23, 1883
Wakoski, Diane   August 3, 1937
Wałesa, Lech   September 29, 1943
Walker, Alice   February 9, 1944

Walker, James J.   June 19, 1881
Walker, Margaret   July 7, 1915
Wallace, DeWitt   November 12, 1889
Wallace, George C.   August 25, 1919
Wallace, Lew   April 10, 1827
Wallenberg, Raoul   August 4, 1912
Waller, Edmund   March 9, 1606
Waller, Fats   May 21, 1904
Wallis, Hal B.   September 14, 1899
Walpole, Horace   September 24, 1717
Walpole, Robert   August 26, 1676
Walter, Bruno   September 15, 1876
Walters, Barbara   September 25, 1931
Walton, Izaak   August 9, 1593
Wanamaker, John   July 11, 1838
Ward, Artemus   April 26, 1834
Ward, Barbara Mary   May 23, 1914
Warhol, Andy   August 6, 1927
Waring, Fred   June 9, 1900
Warner, Charles Dudley   September 12, 1829
Warner, Glenn "Pop"   April 5, 1871
Warren, Earl   March 19, 1891
Warren, Robert Penn   April 24, 1905
Washington, Booker T.   April 5, 1856
Washington, Denzel   December 28, 1954
Washington, George   February 22, 1732
Washington, Martha   June 2, 1730
Waters, Ethel   October 31, 1900
Watson, James D.   April 6, 1928
Watson, Thomas J.   February 17, 1874
Watson, Thomas J., Jr.   January 8, 1914
Watts, Andre   June 20, 1946
Watts, Isaac   July 17, 1674
Waugh, Alec   July 8, 1898
Wayne, John   May 26, 1907
Weaver, Robert   December 29, 1907
Webb, Mary   March 25, 1881
Webster, Daniel   January 18, 1782
Webster, Noah   October 16, 1758
Weil, Simone   February 3, 1909
Weiner, Norbert   November 26, 1894
Weissmuller, Johnny   June 2, 1904
Weizmann, Chaim   November 27, 1874
Welles, Orson   May 6, 1915
Wellesley, Arthur   May 1, 1769
Wellman, William   February 29, 1896
Wells, Carolyn   June 18, 1869
Wells, H.G.   September 21, 1866
Wells, Ida Bell   July 16, 1862
Welty, Eudora   April 13, 1909

Wertmuller, Lina   August 14, 1928
Wesley, John   June 17, 1703
West, Mae   August 17, 1892
West, Rebecca   December 25, 1892
Wharton, Edith   January 24, 1862
Whatley, Richard   February 1, 1787
Whipple, William   January 14, 1730
Whistler, James Abbott McNeil   July 10, 1834
White, Byron R. "Whizzer"   June 8, 1917
White, E.B.   July 11, 1899
White, Theodore H.   May 6, 1915
White, William Allen   February 10, 1868
Whitehead, Alfred North   February 15, 1861
Whiteman, Paul   March 28, 1891
Whitman, Walt   May 31, 1819
Whitney, John Hay   August 17, 1904
Whittier, John Greenleaf   December 17, 1807
Wicker, Tom   June 18, 1926
Wiesel, Elie   September 30, 1928
Wiesenthal, Simon   December 31, 1908
Wiggin, Kate Douglas   September 28, 1856
Wilbur, Ray L.   April 13, 1875
Wilcox, Ella Wheeler   November 5, 1850
Wilde, Oscar   October 16, 1854
Wilder, Billy   June 22, 1906
Wilder, Laura Ingalls   February 7, 1863
Wilder, Thornton   April 17, 1897
Wilkins, Lenny   November 25, 1938
Wilkins, Roy   August 30, 1901
Wilkinson, Charles W. "Bud"   April 23, 1916
Will, George F.   May 4, 1941
William I   April 25, 1533
Williams, Edward Bennett   May 31, 1920
Williams, Hank, Sr.   September 17, 1923
Williams, Robin   July 21, 1952
Williams, Ted   August 30, 1918
Williams, Tennessee   March 26, 1911
Williams, William Carlos   September 17, 1883
Willis, Nathaniel   January 20, 1806
Willson, Meredith   May 18, 1902
Wilson, Charles Eugene   July 18, 1890
Wilson, Colin   June 26, 1931
Wilson, Edmund   May 8, 1895
Wilson, Harold   March 11, 1916
Wilson, Sloan   May 8, 1920

Wilson, William Griffith   November 26, 1895
Wilson, Woodrow   December 28, 1856
Winchell, Walter   April 7, 1897
Winfrey, Oprah   January 29, 1954
Winters, Shelley   August 18, 1922
Winter, William   July 15, 1836
Wise, Isaac Mayer   March 29, 1819
Wister, Owen   July 14, 1860
Wodehouse, P.G.   October 15, 1881
Wolfe, Thomas C.   October 3, 1900
Wolfe, Tom   March 2, 1931
Wonder, Stevie   May 13, 1950
Wooden, John   October 14, 1910
Woodhull, Victoria Claflin   September 23, 1838
Woodruff, Julia Louise   April 29, 1833
Woodworth, Samuel   January 13, 1785
Woolcott, Alexander   January 19, 1887
Woolf, Virginia   January 25, 1882
Wordsworth, William   April 7, 1770
Wotton, Henry   March 30, 1568
Wren, Christopher   October 20, 1632
Wright, Frank Lloyd   June 8, 1869
Wright, Richard   September 4, 1908
Wright, Wilbur   April 16, 1867
Wrigley, William, Jr.   September 30, 1861
Wycliffe, John   December 31, 1320
Wyeth, Andrew   July 12, 1917
Wyman, Jane   January 4, 1914
Wynn, Early   January 6, 1920
Wynn, Ed   November 9, 1886

X

Xavier, St. Francis   April 7, 1506

Y

Yeager, Chuck   February 13, 1923
Yeats, William Butler   June 13, 1865
Yeltsin, Boris   February 1, 1931
Yertushenko, Yevegny   July 18, 1933
Young, Andrew   March 12, 1932
Young, Brigham   June 1, 1801
Young, Coleman   May 24, 1918
Young, Edward   July 3, 1683
Young, Whitney, Jr.   July 31, 1921
Yourcenar, Marguerite   June 8, 1903

Z

Zaharias, Babe Didrikson June 26, 1912

Zangwill, Israel January 21, 1864

Zapata, Emiliano August 8, 1883

Zola, Émile April 2, 1840

Zuckerman, Pinchas July 16, 1948

Zukor, Adolph January 7, 1873

Zweig, Stefan November 28, 1881